Navionics

/ NAV

Ship Finder

cruisersnet.net

Coopilot

Lock channel 13

ActiveCaptain
and
Face Book site

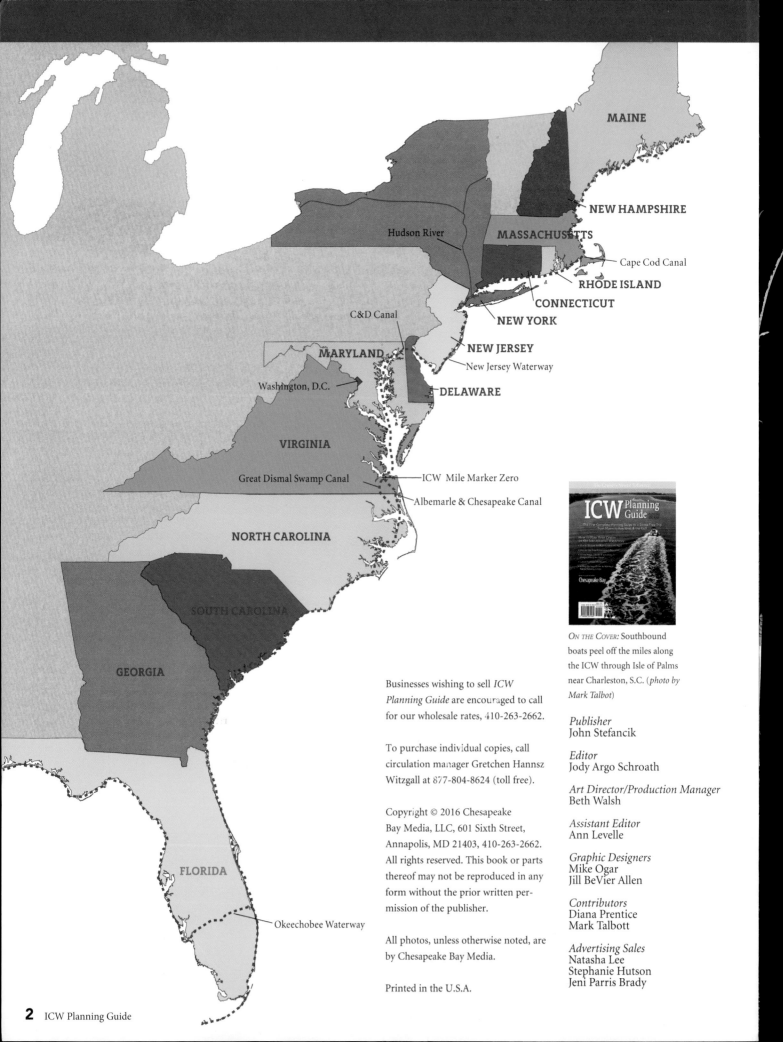

MAINE

NEW HAMPSHIRE

MASSACHUSETTS

Hudson River

Cape Cod Canal

RHODE ISLAND

CONNECTICUT

C&D Canal

NEW YORK

MARYLAND

NEW JERSEY

New Jersey Waterway

Washington, D.C.

DELAWARE

VIRGINIA

Great Dismal Swamp Canal

ICW Mile Marker Zero

Albemarle & Chesapeake Canal

NORTH CAROLINA

SOUTH CAROLINA

GEORGIA

FLORIDA

Okeechobee Waterway

On the Cover: Southbound boats peel off the miles along the ICW through Isle of Palms near Charleston, S.C. (*photo by Mark Talbot*)

Publisher
John Stefancik

Editor
Jody Argo Schroath

Art Director/Production Manager
Beth Walsh

Assistant Editor
Ann Levelle

Graphic Designers
Mike Ogar
Jill BeVier Allen

Contributors
Diana Prentice
Mark Talbott

Advertising Sales
Natasha Lee
Stephanie Hutson
Jeni Parris Brady

Table of Contents

ICW Planning Guide
Planning Your Cruise from Maine to Florida

Why You Need This Book

Sure, you could grab a few charts and set off down the Atlantic Coast and into the Intracoastal Waterway and arrive in Miami . . . eventually. Henry Plummer and his son did it in 1912. But along the way, they ran into a world of trouble. In fact, their whole crazy ordeal made such a great story that the book, *The Boy, Me and the Cat*, is still in print. But the Plummers had no choice. They had no cruise guides to help them along way, no iPad apps, no Active Captain.

Still, you say, everything is so well marked these days, why not just pack up and go? Because you won't know that if you turn up **Jeremy** Creek (SM 430.0), you'll find McClellanville, S.C., one of the prettiest little towns you'll ever meet, with a particularly fine restaurant in an old sundry store and a fresh seafood market just a short walk away. You won't know that if you turn up Kilkenny Creek (SM 613.7) in Georgia, you'll find a fish camp and fine anchorage (watch the current) as well as a restaurant that serves terrific fresh ghost shrimp and grits. Or that if you stop a dozen miles before Kilkenny and go up Delegal Creek, you'll find a jewel of a marina tucked into Skidaway Island. (How lovely? See page 62.) This is an ideal place to stage a rising-tide passage through nearby Hell Gate shoals.

Hidey holes, great restaurants, fresh seafood right off the dock, perfect marinas and ideal anchorages. This is the kind of information that makes a good cruise great.

Which brings us neatly to why you need this book. We tell you how to get the best of all the information out there. We've tried out all the cruise guides and tell you about some of the best. We've tried out dozens of apps for navigation, weather, tides and safety and we give you the best. We tell you how to use crowd-sourced information to get the latest hazards, shoals and bridge changes. We explain government charts and publications and how to use them to help plan your cruise. We give you dozens of good books (including *The Boy, Me and the Cat*) to make your trip even more enjoyable.

Then, after we've explained how to plan each day's cruise, we give you reference information to make that plan work. We give you all the bridges from the C&D Canal to the Florida Keys and then up the Gulf ICW, with a photo, chart and schedule for each. You won't find that anywhere else. We also give you nearly every marina along the most common cruising routes from Maine to Florida.

Finally, we give you maps and more maps. Maps to find the marine weather radio broadcasts for you need as you travel. And maps for locating bridges, towns and major inlets along the way.

—Jody Argo Schroath
Editor, *ICW Planning Guide*
Skipper, *SV/Moment of Zen*

You Are Here

So Are We

NOT EVERY TOWING SERVICE HAS A FLEET STANDING BY TO BACK UP THEIR PROMISES.
We do. TowBoatU.S. has over 600 red boats from coast to coast, so you're never far from help when you need it. Our Captains are licensed professionals that will get you and your boat underway and where you need to go in no time.

CALL OR GO ONLINE NOW TO JOIN FOR JUST $149 ALL YEAR.

TowBoatU.S.®   1-800-395-2628   BoatUS.com/towing

What's It All About? Explaining the ICW

The Inside Route

The Intracoastal Waterway (ICW) is an intricate web of bays, sounds, rivers, creeks and canals that allows commercial and recreational traffic to navigate safe inside waters. While the route runs approximately from Boston, Massachusetts, to Brownsville, Texas, it is not, in truth entirely connected. Instead, it is composed of both long stretches of inshore passages and sizeable stretches of less protected near-shore waters.

If we begin in Boston, the route passes through the Cape Cod Canal and then runs down Long Island Sound, into the East River at New York City and then south along the New Jersey shore. Shallow-draft vessels that have less than 35-feet of vertical clearance can go inside at Massaquan Inlet and stay inside nearly to Cape May at the mouth of Delaware Bay. But most passage-making vessels must stay offshore to Cape May.

The ICW then turns north up Delaware Bay, runs west through the Chesapeake & Delaware Canal and then turns south down the Chesapeake Bay as far as Norfolk.

There the most famous and heavily traveled section of the ICW begins at Mile 0 and continues entirely inside for more than a thousand miles to Miami. At Miami, the main branch of the ICW runs behind (to the west) the Keys to Key West. The second, deeper but less protected branch, known as Hawk Channel, runs just to the east of the Keys, also as far as Key West.

After Key West, boaters must stay offshore up the Gulf Coast of Florida, past the Florida Capes and Ten Thousand Islands, as far as Fort Myers. Here the Okeechobee Waterway, which connects Stuart (on the East Coast) with Fort Myers, joins the Gulf ICW. From there the route stays behind the long string of barrier islands that begin with Sanibel and end 150 miles later at Anclote Key near Tarpon Springs.

Boats must stay offshore from north of Anclote, around the Big Bend to St. Marks on Florida's panhandle. From there the route stays inside all the way around the Gulf Coast to its end in Brownsville.

How Not to Get Lost

The ICW is not a ramrod straight canal that you enter in Norfolk and exit in Miami Instead the route jumps from sound to river to canal to stream to land cut, etc., to form a complex route that will get you where you want to go. In particularly complex sections such as Georgia, the ICW heads off in all directions of the compass as it works its way south.

So how do you know where to go? Two ways.

ICW's Identifying Markers

While there are no road signs to point out the route's twists and turns, there are signs of a type on all of the ICW's aids to navigation. Each marker carries a small yellow triangle or small yellow square indicating, first, that this marker is part of the ICW system, and, second, whether the marker should be considered as a red (triangle) or green (square) marker on that system.

This can get a little complicated in spots, so close attention is required. First let's look at how to keep the right color on the right side of your boat. By far the majority of markers along the ICW will follow this rule: "Red Right Returning to Texas." This means that you keep red markers on your right (starboard) all the way south as far as Key West, and then keep keeping them on your right all the way up and around the Gulf Coast as far as Brownsville, Texas, where the ICW ends. Easy.

Now let's get to the complication. While most of the route is marked by ICW markers alone, there are a number of sections that are used by vessels not following the ICW. For example, the Cape Fear River is a major route for commercial and recreational vessels that have nothing to do with ICW. The Cape Fear River also runs north from Cape Fear Inlet to Wilmington, N.C. That means that red will be on the right for northbound traffic. But the ICW enters the Cape Fear River on the north and follows it south nearly to its mouth before jogging west at Southport. So here ICW travelers will want to keep the river's green markers on their right. To indicate this, the Cape Fear River's green markers all have a small ICW yellow triangle on them to show that these should be treated as red markers for ICW travelers. Is that clear?

The catch with this method is that the little ICW triangles and squares are just that . . . little. This makes them often hard to see until it's too late. They also get hidden by osprey nests and worn away by weather. It's not a brilliant system.

The Famous Magenta Line

There is a better way, and it's called the magenta line.

As far as anyone can tell, the magenta line first appeared on charts in 1912, long before the ICW was complete. In the 1930s, when the route was largely completed as far as we have it today, the line was meant to indicate the best route south. Since then it has remained on all ICW-area charts, though no one has taken responsibility for keeping it up, and so it became increasingly inaccurate as channels shifted. After years of complaints, NOAA decided to begin removing the line whenever it updated a chart. But this left travelers with no way to follow the complex route. More complaints followed. So now NOAA is rethinking the line. You will find it on most charts and navigation apps.

The important thing to remember about the magenta line is that it shows where the route goes, not the deepest water . . . and not always which side to take the markers. Think of it as bread crumbs.

All of which brings up the No. 1 rule of navigating the ICW: Always follow the markers you see in the water, not the markers you see on your chart, or on your chartplotter, or even on your navigation app.

Below, a typical ICW marker, with the yellow inset to indicate that this marker is to be treated as a red. At right, a chart segment of the ICW in Georgia, with the magenta line marking the route from creek to river to creek. Opposite page, the classic Capt. Gabby *cuts through the calm, north of Altamaha Sound, Georgia.*

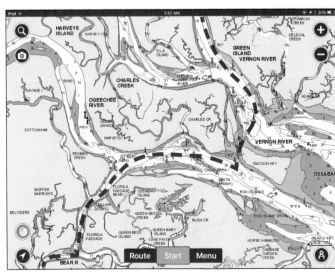

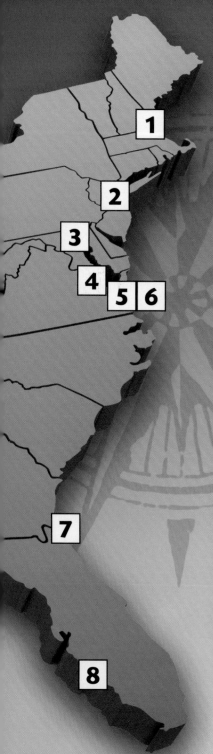

The old tower of the Boca Grande Swing Bridge on Florida's Gulf Coast. The bridge was recently replaced with a new swing bridge.

Resources

Milk, eggs, butter, bread. Let's think of this section of the *ICW Planning Guide* as your cruise-planning supermarket. Just as there are certain staples you know you'll want to keep in your galley, so there are some staples you'll need to plan your cruise—and to take along with you as you go. These are resources that you'll want in order to make your cruise planning easier; resources that will make your cruise more relaxing and enriching. Some of them, like cruise guides and charts, are pretty obvious, while others, like using crowd-sourced information and the federal government's many free publications and websites, are less so.

We've divided this section into six categories of resources: cruise guides, charts, government publications, smartphone and tablet apps, crowd-sourced information and books to take along. Consider this last category the beer on your shopping list, or maybe dessert. It's the category you may need the least, but may enjoy the most.
To continue our shopping metaphor just a little bit longer, let's think of the six segments of Part II as six long aisles in the grocery store, each devoted to a single staple, each stocked top to bottom with a dizzying number of brands and varieties.

Let's consider the cruise guide aisle, for example. There are new guides, old tried-and-true guides, short guides, fat guides, regional guides, anchor guides and marina guides. Whew! Which one do you choose? That's where we come in. We've read them. We've tried them out. We've cruised with them. (Hey, some research is tougher than others!) Finally, we've chosen some of the best, laid them out for you in size and scope and style and told you how to get them. We've even given you our opinion of many of them and pointed out a few of our favorites. And we've done the same thing with charts and the crowded field of apps in all of the main categories you'll need—navigation apps, weather apps, safety apps, and so forth. For crowd sourced and government resources, we've pointed you in the direction of some very useful information you otherwise might overlook. Finally, the beer aisle. Here we've given you a small library's worth of books, some of them written by people over the years about just the cruising you are about to do. Books that have stood the test of time. We also give you books for reference, like *Chapmans*, and books for fun, like bird-watching and fishing.

Once you've been up the down the aisles and picked out what you need, you'll be ready for the next section: Easing the Trip.

Finding the Right Guide

Choosing a guide that will see you through thick and thin, show you the beauty of the route you are taking and explain a bit about its history and geography is a harder task than you might think. You can buy the latest, most recently updated book and yet feel unsatisfied. Perhaps you want more about lovely anchorages and intriguing sidetrips or less about every marina and restaurant along the way. Perhaps it's too wordy. Perhaps it's not wordy enough. Many of us who regularly cruise have tried out a number of guides before settling on the ones that suit us best. When we are cruising the ICW, for example, we regularly travel with several: one straight-forward up-to-date guide that covers the route in well-defined mile-by-mile terms, including trouble spots, anchorages and marinas; and another, perhaps older guide, that delves into the area's history and geography.

There is no comprehensive cruising guide for the entire route from Maine to Florida, but there are several, updated with varying frequency, that cover significant sections of the trip. In addition, there are guides that cover a single state or area that are not updated regularly, yet remain highly readable and useful—with the caveat that specific navigation instructions, channel descriptions, marina listings and depths may likely have changed significantly in the intervening years. Finally, there are a handful of travel books that are wonderful supplements to any cruise.

In the following pages, we've reviewed most of the major cruise guides by geographic area, north to south. We've noted whether they are updated regularly, what you'll find inside and what you won't. Finally, we've indicated their availability. Following the general cruise guides, we've listed guides specific to marinas and anchorages. Finally, we've given you a few of those classic guides we mentioned that will enrich your journey.

Maine to Cape May, N.J. Regional Guides

Northern 2016 Waterway Guide

Maine to Cape May, N.J., including Hudson River
536 pp. Spiral

Description: Updated annually, this comprehensive guide includes chart segments, locator maps for marinas, major ports of call, anchorages, trouble spots, route description, distance charts and bridge tables.

What you get: This is probably the most current and accurate guide for cruising this area. You note it's one of series covering the entire Atlantic Coast.

What you don't get: Detailed information about history, lore and cruises. While this is probably the must-have guide for the new cruiser to this region, the information is succinctly and formally presented. For personality and sprightly writing, we suggest also using the classic Cruise Guide to the New England Coast (see below).

Get it: Widely available at location such as Barnes & Noble, Amazon, West Marine, Waterway Guide website; online nautical booksellers; many ship's chandleries.

New England Coast Maptech Embassy Guides

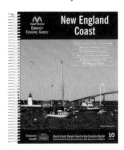

11th Edition:
Maine to Rhode Island
640 pp. Spiral

Description: Updated every two years (in this case, Spring 2015), this guide covers the Atlantic Coast from the Canadian boarder to Rhode Island with chart segments, bridge information, navigation descriptions of major cruising areas, ports of call information, marina and anchorage information.

What you get: This big guide gives you cruising information for a lot of territory, with brief descriptions of the most popular cruising areas.

What you don't get: Because this guide is not updated annually, a few things may be out of date, but most things should remain unchanged. But because Embassy Guides use edition numbers rather than years, it's hard to tell if you have the latest edition. Like the Waterway Guides, Embassy Guides are business-like rather than chatty in tone.

Get it: Not as widely available as Waterway Guides, but generally found at Barnes & Noble, Amazon, West Marine; some ship's stores; Maptech/Embassy Guides website; and online marine publication sellers such as Landfall Navigation.

LI Sound to Cape May Maptech Embassy Guides

15th Edition:
New York Harbor to Block Island,
Hudson and Connecticut rivers,
Long Island's South Shore and the
New Jersey coast
576 pp. Spiral

Description: Like all Maptech Embassy Guides, this one is updated every two years, according to the publisher. This guide includes navigation information, chart segments, marinas and some anchorage information from Long Island Sound south to Cape May.

What you get: Like its companion volumes, the guide gives brief descriptions and some background for the area covered, including a whopping 1,350 marinas as well as GPS waypoints, aerial photos and local navigation tips.

What you don't get: As mentioned earlier, Embassy Guides use edition numbers rather than years, so it's hard to tell when the information was last changed. That means the edition you pick up may or may not be the latest available. (Though to be fair, even guides updated yearly can quickly be out of date.)

Get it: As noted previously, not as widely available as Waterway Guides, but generally found at Barnes & Noble, Amazon, West Marine; some ship's stores; Maptech/Embassy Guides website.

Cruising Guide to the New England Coast

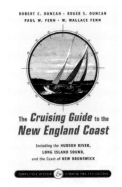

12th edition (2002)
Duncan, Duncan, Fenn, Fenn
Maine to New York, including New
Brunswick, Hudson River and
Long Island Sound
832 pages Hardcover

Description: With wit, humor and generations of experience, this classic New England cruising guide gives a description of nearly every port, anchorage and passage from New Brunswick to Long Island. Black and white photos.

What you get: This book was the first, and, for many years, the most popular guide to the beauties and dangers of the endlessly rich cruising grounds of the New England coast. First published in 1937 and written by Robert Duncan and Fessenden Blanchard, the guide has remained within the family, passing to succeeding generations. As you can tell from the number of years vs. the number of editions, the book has not been updated frequently, and therein lies its greatest drawback and, at the same time, its charm. The descriptions of many of these areas have never been surpassed in a cruise guide for detail and style, but the tone and mention of new technology place it firmly in the past.

What you don't get: We've mentioned some of these failings— the latest updates and lack of technology. To these we must add, color photos, aerial views, chart segments—in short, most of the details we've come to expect from modern cruise guides. For those reasons, we don't recommend this as your only New England cruise guide, but we do recommend it as one of your New England guides. Frankly, we never cruise New England without it.

Get it: Amazon, Barnes & Noble, some of the online nautical booksellers and the Cruising Guide to New England Coast website.

Maine to Cape May, N.J. State Guides

MAINE

Visual Guide to the Maine Coast

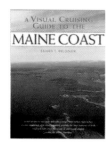

**James Bildner, The Maine coast
256 pp. Spiral**

Description: James Bildner, veteran cruiser and pilot, spent more than 100 hours in his helicopter photographing the remarkably varied cruising grounds of the Maine coast to produce this book.

What you get: Bildner has taken his beautiful and illustrative aerial photographs and superimposed place names and aids to navigation. On the pages opposite the photos, Bildner has given the chart detail for that area plus a brief description. The result is a brand new way of looking at cruising.

What you don't get: This is not, and was never intended to be, a complete cruise guide. It is meant as a highly useful supplement to a cruise guide, such as Taft and Taft's *Cruising Guide to the Maine Coast* (see below), the Duncan/Fenn *Guide to the New England Coast* or even the Waterway or Maptech/Embassy guides.

Where to get it: Amazon, Barnes & Noble, Landfall, some ships stores and bookshops in Maine.

Cruising Guide to the Maine Coast

**5th Edition (2009) Rindlaub, Taft & Taft; Maine Coast, including New Brunswick
465 pp. Hardcover, Softcover**

Description: Veteran Maine cruiser Curtis Rindlaub substantially updated Hank and Jan Taft's classic Maine cruise guide.. This book is considered the Maine cruiser's "bible."

What you get: The Tafts and Rindlaub have assembled a description of every harbor and pretty much every anchorage along the Maine Coast and up into Canada as far as the Saint John's River. There is plenty of history, descriptions, things to do, crucial navigation information and useful symbols for fuel, repairs and restaurants as well as star rankings for hundreds of ports.

What you don't get: Keeping cruise guides up to date is not only a full-time activity, it requires new editions every year or so. That leaves guides published by dedicated enthusiasts, such as this one, open to criticism for being outdated. Yet the best of them—like this one—continue to serve a purpose unmet by larger commercial guides, in their completeness of coverage and in their authority. There are few commercial guides that can meet those high standards.

Where to get it: Landfall Pub., Hamilton Marine, Bluewater Books

NEW JERSEY

Cruising Guide to New Jersey Waters

**2nd Edition (2004)
Donald Launer
The New Jersey waterfront, east, south and west
234 pp. Softcover**

Description: Veteran small-boat cruiser Donald Launer invites you to explore the surprisingly diverse and endlessly fascinating rivers, bays and coastline of New Jersey, which he himself has boated for more than half a century. Launer begins on the Hudson River at the New York line and continues down the coast, including the inshore route, up the Delaware Bay and finally to the end of the navigable Delaware River. Launer includes safe boating tips, explanations of wind and tide cycles and the magnetic compass.

What you get: Reading Launer's New Jersey boating guide is like sitting down with a friend over a couple of beers, as he describes the cruising ground he knows so well. It's a conversation we'd sit in on anytime. Launer clearly knows and loves his subject, and his enthusiasm for it is contagious. A few paragraphs in, we were ready to head for New Jersey waters.

What you don't get: Since this edition was written soon after strict new security measures were put in place following 9/11, it includes some regulations that have since been relaxed. It would be wise to check with relevant government sites for the latest rules. Launer does not pretend to give the cruiser a mile-by-mile description, but rather a useful overview of pitfalls, sights, weather and tide patterns.

Where to get it: Landfall Publications, Amazon, Bluewater Books

Chesapeake Bay Regional Guides

Guide to Cruising Chesapeake Bay 2017
From the Editors of Chesapeake Bay Magazine and The ICW Planning Guide

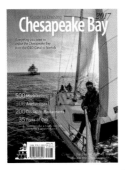

The Chesapeake from the C&D Canal through the Albemarle and Dismal Swamp Canals
368 pp. Spiral

Description: The editors of *Chesapeake Bay Magazine* have combined 50 years of experience cruising the Chesapeake Bay with the latest information on marinas, ports of call, waterfront restaurants and anchorages. Updated annually.

What you get: Details on virtually every river, creek, bay, anchorage and port on the Chesapeake Bay from the C&D Canal to the ICW canals south of Norfolk. Included are maps for 35 favorite ports of call, 300 hundred or so anchorages, roughly 500 marinas and 250 dockside restaurants. There's lots of history and cruising advice as well. Distance charts, locator maps and a tear-out navigator's reference card.

What you don't get: Since this is our guide, we naturally feel it gives you everything you need to cruise this extraordinary estuary in comfort and safety.

Where to get it: *Chesapeake Bay Magazine*'s website (*ChesapeakeBoating.net*), West Marine, Barnes & Noble, Bluewater, Maryland Nautical, Landfall, Paradise Cay

Chesapeake Bay 2016 Waterway Guide

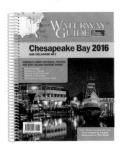

Delaware Bay, Delmarva and the Chesapeake Bay
440 pp. Spiral

Description: Updated annually, the Waterway Guide's Chesapeake Bay edition provides navigation and facilities information for the waters from Cape May, N.J., Delaware Bay, C&D Canal, Chesapeake Bay and the ocean coast of the Delmarva (Delaware-Maryland-Virginia) peninsula.

What you get: Like *Chesapeake Bay Magazine*'s Guide, the Deltaville, Va.-based Waterway Guide's Chesapeake edition is on its home ground here. And it shows. The descriptions and details are up-to-date and full of good information. The Waterway Guide is rich in easy-to-read chart segments and good navigation tips, as well as facilities and anchoring information for cruising this beautiful area.

What you don't get: The principal difference between Chesapeake Bay Magazine's Guide and Waterway's is one of tone. While CBM's Guide often waxes lyrical about its chosen territory, the Waterway's guide (as is true of all its guides) sticks pretty much with straightforward descriptions. It's a matter of personal taste.

Where to get it: West Marine, Barnes & Noble, Bluewater, Maryland Nautical, Landfall, Waterway Guides' website.

A Gunkholer's Guide to Cruising the Chesapeake

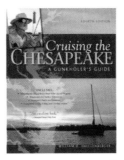

4th Edition (2012)
William H. Shellenberger

Description: The first third of Gunkholer's Guide is devoted to giving an overview of life and industry on the Chesapeake, as well as its vagaries of cruising and navigation for boaters. The remainder follows the Bay from north to south with a bit about each tributary and what it has to offer.

What you get: Unlike many guides that dwell strictly on specific anchorages, the Gunkholer's Guide treats each creek and river as a whole, describing instead the approaches, services that can be found and then anchorages and dockages. Under each heading, Shellenberger rates the creek or river for quality and then provides icons for various services.

What you don't get: The Gunkholer's Guide is neither strictly speaking an anchoring guide nor is it a cruise guide. Instead it settles comfortably somewhere in between the two, which makes it a good source for a quick overview. The book has some area charts with anchorages, mooring areas and launching sites indicated and some street maps of popular ports of call like Annapolis, Rock Hall and Oxford, with their major marinas.

Where to get it: West Marine, Barnes & Noble, Amazon, Landfall, Maryland Nautical

ICW Regional Guides

Chesapeake Bay to Florida

6th Edition
Maptech Embassy
Cruising Guides
Cape May, N.J., to
Fernandina Beach, Fla.
544 pp. Spiral

Description: Chartkit makers Maptech also publish the Embassy Cruise Guides. This one is a bit of a misnomer because it begins in Cape May and ends just across the Florida/Georgia line in Fernandina Beach. Those interested in following Maptech through Florida will need to purchase their Florida cruise guide.

What you get: Embassy Guides follow the usual cruising guide format as it describes the route up Delaware Bay and down the Chesapeake, then along the ICW to north Florida. Included are navigation suggestions, facilities, bridge schedules and shoreside contact numbers. It features a number of good aerial photos and big chart segments.

What you don't get: There are two areas where this and other Embassy guides may run into trouble. First, in covering such a large area, the guide is by necessity less complete in its coverage of some areas. For example, on the Chesapeake, the guide's narrative tends to concentrate more on its well-known ports of call than its waterways.

Second, in publishing only every two years, a bit of its information becomes out of date. As mentioned earlier, that also means that it is difficult to know whether you have the latest edition. Although a fine guide in many ways, it lacks the intimacy of local knowledge found in both the Chesapeake guides we discussed earlier.

Get it: West Marine, Barnes & Noble, Bluewater, Maryland Nautical, Landfall, Maptech website, Paradise Cay

Cruise Guide for the Intracoastal Waterway (ICW)

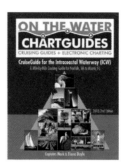

3rd Edition (2016)
Mark and Diana Doyle
A Mile-by-Mile Cruising Guide for
Norfolk, Va., to Miami, Fl.
174 pp. Spiral

Description: The Doyles' brilliant idea is that this is a guide you can keep this book open in your cockpit every mile of the way, whether you are traveling either north to south or returning south to north, because it's just as easy to follow one way or the other. It is meant to be equally useful the first time you do the ICW and the twenty-first.

What you get: The Doyles have distilled an astonishing amount of information into 174 pages, with not a wasted, or poorly written, sentence. Each state is given a brief introduction followed by a fascinating series of vignettes that generally follow the ICW through the state, touching on everything from the turkey vultures to the stars (both celestial and Hollywood). Then after a facility information chart, the guide begins its trip through the state mile by mile, with brief but valuable descriptions of marinas, anchorages, river junctions and bridges as you go. In addition, each page is headed by a Safety Info and a Heads Up! With information like towing, NOAA weather stations for the miles on that page and Coast Guard contact numbers.

What you don't get: There are no charts here, and only a few photos. (You should never use a cruise guide to replace charts, in any case.) Instead the whole affair is organized to give the cruiser the most important information in an easy, clear, useful and entertaining fashion. Have we given ourselves away? In our many trips up and down the ICW ourselves, we have found this the one book (and we have them all) we always have in the cockpit and the one we refer to dozens of times a day. We have followed its advice for anchorages and marinas countless times.

Get it: Here is the bad news. The Doyles announed last year that they are retiring, choosing to withdraw their guides from the market. You may be able to find a few at resellers for the next few years or be lucky enough to inherit one from a friend.

The Intracoastal Waterway, Norfolk, Virginia, to Miami, Florida

**6th Edition (2010)
Jan and Bill Moeller,
revised by John Kettlewell
The Complete Cockpit
Cruising Guide
244 pp. Softcover**

Description: Back in the 1979, well-known cruising couple Jan and Bill Moeller created the first cockpit user-friendly guide to the ICW. Over the decades that followed, legions of cruisers on their way down the Ditch kept a copy of one edition or the other of that guide with them all the way, whether they were ultimately headed for the Keys or the islands. In 2010, John Kettlewell, a highly regarded cruiser himself with more than two dozen trips on the ICW, undertook the task of thoroughly revising and updating the Moellers' guide. This is the result. (Kettlewell and his wife Leslie, have published the very popular ICW Chartbook since 1992.)

What you get: Like the Doyles (even before the Doyles) the Moellers decided that the best way to get people down the ICW was to do it mile by mile. Thousands of cruisers agreed. The book is divided generally by state, though some states because of their length and geography get more than one chapter (Florida gets three). After a short chapter introduction, the guide gets right down to its task with notes on tricky buoy patterns, good anchorages, marinas and, of course, bridges. Unlike the Doyles guide, this one includes a number of chart segments to either the ICW route in confusing spots or the bridges.

What you don't get: Like all cruise guides, the more years that pass by the more outdated the information can get. But like a few of the best guides, utility outlasts age. So it is with this one.

Florida Maptech Embassy Cruising Guides

**6th Edition
Florida's East and Gulf coasts,
the Keys and the Gulf Coast
to Mobile Ala.
560 pp. Spiral**

Description: Another large-coverage volume from Maptech Embassy Guides, this one completes the ICW route south begun with the *Chesapeake Bay to Florida* book.

What you get: The format here follows Maptech Embassy's standard format, with brief descriptions, big chart segments (don't use these to navigate), aerial photos and plenty of destination information. The bridge table is useful (though we've found some errors over the years), as are the facilities listings.

What you don't get: If you want to use Maptech Embassy Guides down the ICW, be sure to buy both volumes. As mentioned earlier, the large area covered by the guide is handy, but forces the editors to limit the number of entries. Also be sure you've got the most recent edition, since the issue dates are not obvious.

Atlantic ICW 2016 Waterway Guides

**Norfolk, Va., to the
Florida border
408 pp. Spiral**

Southern 2016 Waterway Guides

**Florida East Coast, Keys, West
Coast and the Gulf Coast to
Brownsville, Texas
584 pp. Spiral**

Description: The best word to describe Waterway Guide's *Atlantic ICW* and *Southern* volumes is "comprehensive." Between them, they cover all of the Atlantic and Gulf Intracoastal Waterways. So if you want to use this as your primary cruising guide, be sure to get both volumes.

What you get: Like all Waterway Guides, these two are updated annually by a small coterie of cruisers who know the area. You'll find some history, plenty of descriptions of what you're passing by, charts, aerial photographs, bridge information and marina locator charts. There is information on several dozen ports of call and on a few side-trips you might want to make, such as the St. Johns River in Florida.

What you don't get: While you can keep these books open in the cockpit, they're a bit wordy to read as you go. Save that for your nightly planning session or while you're relaxing at anchor or in port.

ICW State Guides

GEORGIA

A Cruising Guide to The Georgia Coast

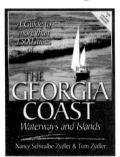

2nd Edition (2004)
Nancy Schwalbe Zydler and
Tom Zydler
1,500 Miles of Georgia Islands and
Waterways
406 pp. Softcover

Description: The Zydlers, lifelong Georgia cruisers, begin by explaining the layout of the Georgia islands and sounds, its wildlife, weather and tides and then spend the rest of the book explaining each area in fine detail.

What you get: The Zydlers open up the puzzling maze of Georgia's wild and remarkable waterways to cruisers who may have passed through only as a series of shallow spots on the Intracoastal Waterway. Their guide includes dozens of small-area charts as well as photos of wildlife and noted sights.

What you don't get: This guide is directed at those who have been persuaded (as we all should be) to stop in Georgia to explore its singular islands and waters. Although the Zydlers do begin with a quick guide to the ICW in Georgia, they spent the remainder of this comprehensive book on all those places that pathway misses. So if you have succumbed to the lure of Georgia cruising, this is the must-have book for you.

Where to get it: Seaworthy Publications, Landfall Publications, Amazon.

FLORIDA

The number of guides for the Florida Gulf Coast, and especially the Keys cannot be numbered on the fingers of both hands. Most, however, are long out of print and sadly out of date. Don't discard them out of hand, however. Most were written by enthusiasts who have years of experience in their chosen area. But don't depend on them for navigation information or as a reliable source of depths for that perfect gunkhole. Here are a few of them. For more, see the Claiborne Young section, which follows.

Cruising Guide to Florida's Big Bend

Rick Rhodes (2003)
Apalachicola, Chattahoochee,
Flint and Suwannee Rivers
357 pp. Softcover

Description: Rick Rhodes loves river cruising, especially the largely ignored rivers of the Florida Gulf Coast between Dunedin and Panama City. Here, region by region and river by river, he follows the coastline north. Black and white photos. Some charts and some nice hand-drawn maps.

What you get: Leaving Dunedin in Pinellas County behind, Rhodes follows the coast with detailed sailing directions, indications of depth, sites to see and places to anchor or tie up for the night. This is territory explored by few cruisers, because of the shallow depths and lack of facilities. Rhodes shows how these impediments can be overcome and the rewards of wildlife and unspoiled waterways that come with the adventure.

What you don't get: This is not an ICW guide, but rather a detailed guide to little traveled, often remote, areas many of which require shallow-draft vessels with low vertical clearance. In other words, blue-water sailing vessels will find that only a little of this area is accessible to them, except by dinghy.

Where to get it: Pelican Press, Landfall Navigation, Bluewater Books, Amazon

Cruising Guide to the Florida Keys

12th Edition (2014)
Frank Papys
With Florida West Coast Supplement
208 pp. Spiral

Description: Frank Papys has been at this a long time, and this is probably the guide to get for cruising the Keys. Each Key gets its day with instructions for navigating and anchoring, aided by large aerial shots. Other chapters include treasure hunting in the Keys, fish, shore-side services and pump-outs and a lot more. Heck, there are even recipes and illustrations on chicken-necking for crabs.

Where to get it: www.cruisingguidetothefloridakeys.com

A Concise Cruising Guide to Florida's Suncoast

4th Edition (2013)
Randy Deering
The Best of Everything from Dunedin to Marco Island

Description: Chart segments, photos and suggestions for the author's favorite restaurants, marinas, anchorages and things to do on this popular section of Florida's Gulf Coast. We mention this particular guide because it is one of the most recent. Even with the recent publication date, however, some of the information is now out of date—and has been for several years. As many a guide writer has discovered, keeping current information in print is a tough job.

A Gunkholer's Cruising Guide to Florida's West Coast

11th Edition (2003)
Tom Lenfestey
From Everglades to Carrabelle
176 pp. Softcover

Description: This is long out of print now, but can be had from used book dealers, as well as through Amazon and Barnes and Noble. We mention it though because it is still full of useful and entertaining information about the Gulf Coast and other subjects, such as Spanish Moss (which is neither Spanish nor moss), warm-weather anchoring and how to make raw conch salad.

The Classics

Claiborne S. Young Guides

What you get: Claiborne Young's well-known cruising guides covering the territory between North Carolina and the Gulf Coast are not currently updated regularly—the Florida Keys guide, not for 15 years—and so are getting increasingly out of date. For that reason, we recommend that you do not use them as your primary information source. But it's not the details that make Young's guides still worth the purchase price. It's the combination of Young's outspoken opinion about places, pro and con (the guide has no ads) and his richly researched histories and local lore that set his guides apart.

What you don't get: We find his format a bit challenging, with straight-forward information sections mixed with sometimes redundant greyed-out navigation pages covering the same area. Maybe it's just us, but we've never caught on. Nevertheless, we recommend settling down with a Young cruising tome (they are very long) over some cold winter nights or while waiting out weather. The future of the guides is uncertain since Young tragically died in a 2014 motorcycle accident. But Salty Southeast Cruisers Network (cruisersnet.net), the website he started, goes on and is updated daily. Many of the current cruise guide authors and editors contribute to it frequently, making it the go-to site for the latest ICW information for legions of cruisers.

Where to get them: Most of Young's guides can be ordered from the publisher, Pelican Publishing Co. (pelicanpub.com). Others may be had from Amazon, Landfall, Bluewater and other online marine bookshops.

Skipper Bob Guides

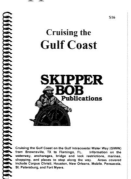

Skipper Bob Guides were among the first published and promptly found a place in the hearts of legions of cruisers. Though they have been only intermittently updated since, they still have a strong following. The guides were recently picked up by Waterway Guides and have been reissued with updates, but they remain essentially the same. Some of them are also available in e-book form.

Marinas Along the Intracoastal Waterway
18th Edition, Skipper Bob
Facilities from the Hudson River to Key West, Fla.
120 pp. Spiral, E-Book

Anchorages Along the Intracoastal Waterway
19th Edition, Skipper Bob
Anchorages, bridges and locks from the Hudson to Key West, including Delaware and Chesapeake bays, Potomac and St. Johns rivers and the Okeechobee Waterway
162 pp. Spiral, E-Book

Cruising the Gulf Coast
11th Edition
Anchorages, bridges, facilities from Brownsville, Texas, to Flamingo, Fla.
101 pp. Spiral, E-Book

Cruising Guide to North Carolina
6th Edition (2007)
All the navigable coastal and inland waters
448 pp. Softcover

Cruising Guide to Eastern Florida
5th Edition (2004)
Fernandina Beach to Miami
560 pp. Softcover

Cruising Guide to Western Florida
7th Edition (2008)
Flamingo to the Big Bend
560 pp. Softcover

Cruising Guide to Coastal South Carolina and Georgia
6th Edition (2005)
All navigable inland and coastal waters
502 pp. Softcover

Cruising Guide to the Northern Gulf Coast
4th Edition (2003)
Appalachicola to Grand Isle, La.
576 pp. Softcover

Cruising the Florida Keys
2nd Edition (2001)
with Morgan Stinemetz
Port of Miami to the Dry Tortugas
600 pp. Softcover

Anchor Guides/Marina Guides

Great Book of Anchorages

Beach House Publications

Description: Veteran cruisers and Chesapeake natives Susan Landry and Charles Baier have added the Chesapeake Bay to their growing list of anchorage books, including the Florida Gulf Coast and the ICW. Both have been writing for boating magazines for many years and both also have been associated with the Waterway Guides.

What you get: With chart segments and to-the-point descriptions, the Great Book of Anchorages takes on the daunting task of describing many of the routes' virtually enumerable anchorages. Each chart shows a suggested approach to the anchorage and each description gives lat/long coordinates, approach and anchor depth, holding, protection and shore access. It's something of a tour de force. Veteran cruisers will enjoy looking to see whether their favorites made the cut.

What you don't get: Like other anchoring guides, these books are not meant to substitute for an all-purpose cruise guide. What we miss in most anchoring guides is an overall map, or even regional map, with the anchorages laid out.

Where to get it: Landfall, Bluewater, Maryland Nautical, Beach House Publications

The Great Book of Anchorages- Chesapeake Bay

The Great Book of Anchorages- The Gulf Coast

The Great Book of Anchorages- Hampton Roads to Florida Keys

On the Water Anchor Guide for the Intracoastal Waterway (ICW)

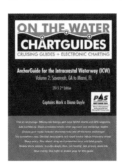

2nd Edition (2015)
Mark and Diana Doyle
Volume 1: Norfolk, Va., to Beaufort, S.C.
134 pp. Spiral
Volume 2: Hilton Head, S.C. to Miami, Fla.
140 pp. Spiral

Description: Charts, soundings, summary and ratings of anchorages, with distances off the ICW, with ratings for protection, scenery and grocery and dog-landing access. Also detailed directions for entering the anchorage. The digital versions offer additional features.

What you get: Most of these anchorages are given in the Doyles cruise guide; these books give all the details. The listings are up-to-date, well-researched and consistently described. This is another excellent Doyle publication.

Where to get it: Like all of the Doyles' publications, this one is no longer in print. A few may remain available from resellers.

Atlantic Cruising Club

What you get: Each marina gets its own page with detailed services, facilities and local access numbers, as well as a description of the setting and notes about the facility. Very complete.

What you don't get: Keeping up-to-date on marinas is a tough job, and there are inevitably errors that creep in. A few marinas that don't take transients are listed here as accepting visiting boaters, and a few marinas have changed ownership or status since this was published.

Where to get it: Atlantic Cruising Club website (*atlanticcruisingclub.com*)

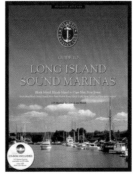

Guide to New England and Canadian Maritime Marinas
7th Edition
(Halifax, Nova Scotia to Warwick, R.I.)

Guide to Long Island Sound Marinas
7th Edition
(Block Island, R.I., to Cape May, N.J.)

Guide to Chesapeake Bay Marinas
7th Edition (Mid-Atlantic/ICWMarinas Hampton, Va., to St. Marys, Ga.)

Guide to Florida's East Coast Marinas
(Fernandina to Key West, Fla.)

Guide to Florida's West Coast Marinas
(Everglades City to Pensacola)

Finding the Right Charts

NOAA Charts

An Overview: Raster versus Electronic Charts

NOAA produces charts of two quite different types: Raster Navigational Charts (RNCs) and Electronic Navigational Charts (ENCs). Here's a brief explanation:

Raster Navigational Charts are the ones that have been used aboard recreational and commercial vessels for more than a century. These are the nation's standard paper charts, the ones on which all others are based, to a greater or lesser degree. Raster Charts come in a wide variety of detail, from small-scale charts, which give a broad view of a large area, such as Cape Sable to Cape Hatteras (Chart No. 13003), to large-scale charts, which give a highly detailed view of a very small area, such as Charleston Harbor (Chart No.11524).

Each of these charts has a catalog number, moving generally from the Texas around and down the Gulf Coast, up the East Coast, then west across the Great Lakes, and finally north to south down the West Coast. It's not always an easy system to decipher if you are not familiar with an area's geography, so you may find it easier to use NOAA's map rather than its numbered catalog to find the chart you need.

Since NOAA has stopped printing its own charts, RNCs have been made available for use on digital devices and can be downloaded free from the NOAA website. (You'll find details on how to do that later.) These RNC files are essentially digital reproductions of existing paper charts, so as you zoom in, you get the same thing only larger—rather like putting on reading glasses. Most of the phone and tablet apps that use NOAAs RNC charts, however, now move seamlessly between small and large scale charts, depending on the level of zoom. We'll talk about these

programs and others that use their own charts in the Chapter 4.

The advantages of using digital RNCs rather than printed charts are that they can be updated frequently and free of cost. And, of course, you don't have the storage issue and you never find yourself without the chart you need. The disadvantages are that it is more difficult to see your course over a long distance, and unless you have a lot of redundancy aboard (such as navigation apps on your smartphone as well as your tablet and your vessel's chartplotter), you can lose your device to a bad battery or the briny deep. Of course, many a boat has lost charts to wind and wave as well.

So a belt and suspenders approach of some variety, whether it's a mix of electronic and print or all electronic, is your best option. We won't weigh in on that argument here, except to say that the government carriage requirement for commercial vessels still includes paper charts—for now.

NOAA's **Electronic Navigational Charts**, on the other hand, are, by their very name and nature, available only in digital form. These have a very different look from the raster charts—more like a cubist's painting of a printed chart—and come embedded with additional information for various features, which can be accessed by clicking (or touching the screen). Clicking on an aid to navigation, for example, can bring up details on its height, structure, light pattern and frequency and any other information specific to that aid. The appearance of ENCs can also be configured in different ways. For example, for low-light or night navigation.

NOAA's Chart No. 1 now includes an explanation of all of the ENC charts' features and is well worth the read in order to get the most out of these charts. (You'll find more on Chart No. 1 on the next page.)

For comparison, here are examples of NOAA chart segments for Cape Lookout, North Carolina. The raster chart is at left and the electronic chart is below.

Getting NOAA Charts

Print on Demand (POD)

A classic trip to a chandlery for a search through its great sideboard's long shallow drawers in search of the latest NOAA charts is becoming a thing of the past, ever since NOAA stopped printing its own charts. But now those charts are available in a number of forms.

First, NOAA certifies a number of companies to print their charts on demand. A few of these are located within large chandleries, such as Fawcett Marine in Annapolis and American Nautical in Miami. Here you can have the charts you need printed while you wait. Most of the others are done by order, either through marine retailers such as West Marine, or directly from the agent by phone or online. You'll find the list of print-on-demand agents at www.nauticalcharts.noaa.gov/ staff/print_agents.html.

PDF Nautical Charts and Chartbooks

Although NOAA has been making .pdf files of its RNC charts available for several years, it has more recently significantly improved the quality of the files, so that now downloaded and printed .pdf charts are clear even at high magnification. These 400 dpi charts can be printed on any printer with a 38-inch format. Or they can be viewed from a computer using a program like Adobe Reader.

NOAA Charting Publications

Here are a few handy websites for getting charts and for finding a few chart-related publications. We'll get to plenty more of those in the following chapter.

U.S. Chart No. 1
www.nauticalcharts.noaa.gov/mcd/chartno1.htm

Chart Catalogs
www.nauticalcharts.noaa.gov/mcd/ccatalogs.htm

Dates of Latest Editions (DOLE)
www.nauticalcharts.noaa.gov/mcd/dole.htm

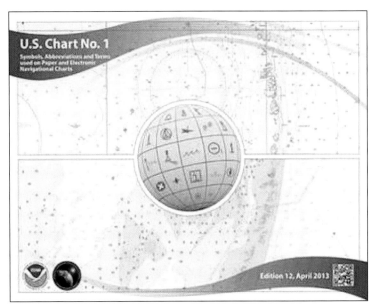

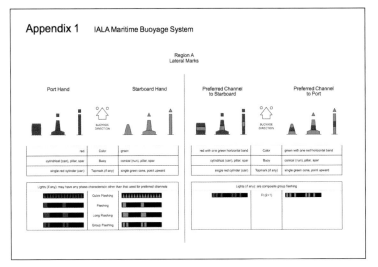

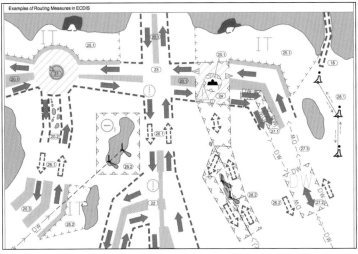

Three pages from U.S. Chart No. 1

ICW Chartbooks

John and Leslie Kettlewell

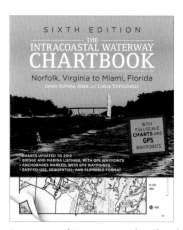

**Intracoastal Waterway
Chartbook
International Marine/
McGraw Hill, 6th Edition
2012**

Get it: Widely available
through online marine book-
stores and some ship's stores.

One of the handiest gizmos
around is an old-fashioned
paper chartbook. And for
a long time the Kettlewell
Intracoastal Waterway Chartbook was the only game in town.
This year, however, cruising gurus Mark and Diana Doyle have
added their own annotated and characteristically precise chartbook to the mix. (We'll talk about that one next.) Chartbooks
allow cruisers to follow the ICW from top to bottom simply by
flipping from one chart to the next. No searching around for the
next applicable chart, no turning the chartbook this way or that
to follow your course.

The Kettlewell chartbook, for years a favorite of ICW cruisers
for its simplicity and ease of use, does one thing and does it well.
It provides a clear view of the ICW route, mile after mile. In the
margins of each chart, you'll find the mile number and a bit of
other information such as bridge schedules. Even if you are also
running a chartplotter and a navigation app on your tablet, you
will find the ICW chartbook a handy way to look ahead, either
for planning your next stop or timing the next bridge. And even
at a fairly stiff $75, the Kettlewell Chartbook is still considerably
cheaper than buying the full-scale chart.

We find two drawbacks to this chartbook, however. One is that
the NOAA charts soon become out of date, so you won't want
to count on it exclusively. (This is where your tablet navigation
apps will shine because those charts can be updated regularly.)
The other drawback is that using the chartbook is like driving
with blinders on. Because it gives you only the ICW, it leaves you
often wondering exactly where you are geographically.
For this reason, we brought along a road map of the East Coast
the first time we made the trip so that we could track our
progress against the names and locations of cities and towns
we knew well.

A related issue, is that if you want to make a sidetrip, up the
Pamlico River to Washington N.C., for example, or to explore
some more of Georgia's remote islands, you'll need to have either
a conventional set of charts for the area, or use your preferred
charting app.

Mark and Diana Doyle

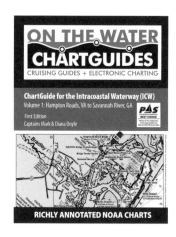

**ICW Chartguides
Volume 1 Hampton Roads,
Va., to Savannah River, Ga.
2016
Volume 2 Savannah River,
Ga., to Cape Florida, Fla.
2016**

Get it: This book, like all the
Doyles' publications, is now
off the market. A few resellers
may still be carrying it and used
copies may begin appearing on
eBay. Otherwise, see if you can
borrow one from a friend.

The original price of $9.95 represented a remarkably small
amount to pay for a full set of charts covering the ICW, even if
it included nothing else. However, the Doyles added a lot more,
including more than 3,000 annotations for marinas, anchorages,
boat ramps, hazards, bridge information and their own sonar
soundings of trouble spots. They even corrected errors made by
NOAA in assembling its own charts, for example relocating a
misplaced boat ramp.

The disadvantages of this kind of chartbook that we mentioned
above apply to this as well. You'll still need to have charts to
make side trips. And the charts will eventually go out of date.
But at this cost, who cares? We're looking forward to taking a set
on our next trip south.

Chart Packages

NV Chartbooks

Nautical Publications GmbH

Get it: Widely available from chandleries and online marine booksellers

German mapmakers NV Charts—who long ago cornered the market on Baltic Sea charts—entered the American chartbook market a few years ago, beginning with New England. Since then, NV has proceeded down the Atlantic Coast and into the islands and Cuba. Now you can get a complete set of their chartbooks for an Atlantic Coast and ICW cruise. They do not yet have charts for the Gulf Coast, however.

NV has taken and modified NOAA charts with a considerable amount of their own work and changed the layout and colors, creating very attractive and clean-looking maps. In addition, the charts include charming sketches of lighthouses and other navigational sights, which make good reference points.

In addition to the individual chartbooks, NV bundles their books into box sets for larger areas. For example, to cover the area from Maine to Florida, you'll need nv-chartbox Maine to Rhode Island, nv-chartbox New England Region 3, nv-chartbox Chesapeake Bay Region 5, nv-chartbox Intracoastal Waterway Region 6 and nv-chartbox Florida Region 8. NV includes a CD for use on the computer and has an app.

The minor criticism we do have of NV charts, and one that we're sure is being corrected with time, is that a few of the placenames are misspelled. And a very few are mislocated. (NOAA charts, we must point out, are not free of this failing either. For example, the Northeast River in the northern Chesapeake changes from one word to two from large-area to small-area charts. This error continues in navigation apps that use NOAA raster charts.)

Maptech and Richardsons' Chartbooks

Get it: Widely available at chandleries such as West Marine and from online booksellers.

Maptech's spiral-bound chartbooks and Richardsons' waterproof chartbooks have long been an economical option for boaters, whether they are cruising long distances along the coast and inland waterways or are staying close to home. The company reconfigures traditional NOAA raster large-area and small-area charts for a particular geographic area—such as Block Island, R.I., to the Canadian border—into a single package. The 22- by 17-inch size makes long-distance planning using traditional navigation tools easy and makes finding the marked route through crowded areas such as harbors easy to see because of their large size.

To cover the area from the Canadian border south, you'll need ChartKit 2 (Block Island to the Canadian Border), ChartKit 3 (NY to Nantucket and to Cape May, N.J.), ChartKit 4 (Chesapeake and Delaware Bays), ChartKit 6 (Norfolk, Va., to Florida and the ICW), ChartKit 7 (Florida East Coast and Keys) and ChartKit 8 (Florida West Coast and Keys). These chartbooks sell for about $90 to $140 each. Like NV charts, all of these come with a CD of the charts for use on your computer.

Richardson Waterproof Charts cover the Florida West Coast and Keys in two books and the New England Coast to Long Island Sound in four books. These generally sell from about $50 to 70.

The downside of all chartbooks like these is that they become out-of-date and so require repurchase every few years. They also tend to be unwieldy on boats without a dedicated nav table. And storing the ones you're not currently using can be a challenge, though there are probably more boaters sleeping with chartbooks tucked under their mattresses than the non-boating public can imagine.

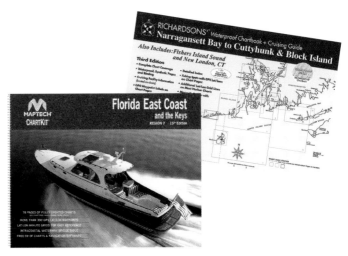

Mining Government Resources

A Government Marine Products Who's Who

Here's a cruiser's glossary of what government agency does what by way of maritime products and publications. Don't worry, there won't be a test! Instead you can use this as a quick reference when you go looking for real-time water levels, light lists or notices to mariners. We'll give you the specifics on all of those in the pages that follow and tell you why you might want to make use of them. But first, let's try to make sense of it all.

All but two of the agencies you'll want to know about fall under the Department of Commerce. One of those two, U.S. Army Corps of Engineers, is part of the Defense Department. The other, the Coast Guard, falls under the Department of Homeland Security.

See, it's easier already.

A beautiful end to a day's cruise ,at Dataw Island Marina near St. Helena Sound, South Carolina.

U.S. Army Corps of Engineers (USACE)

When we think of the U.S. Army Corps of Engineers, we probably think first of dredging, and for the ICW, we think of dredging of the problem areas around inlets. And dredging is certainly one of the USACE's principal responsibilities. But it has many more. One of them—surveying traditionally shoal areas—we'll talk about later in this chapter. Other USACE duties include regulating the use of navigable waters, removing of sunken vessels that threaten navigation, and issuing permits for structures such as docks and for dredging and filling. The USACE also defines and regulates restricted areas. These areas are shown on large-scale charts and the restrictions for each of them described in the Coast Pilot for that area. For our purposes, the Corps is also responsible for the Dismal Swamp, Albemarle & Chesapeake Canal and the Okeechobee Waterway, so that's where you want to look for the latest water levels and lock schedules. We'll give you those below.

U.S. Coast Guard

A comprehensive list of the Coast Guard's responsibilities would be long and interesting, but for our purposes we'll mention only a few that most directly affect coastal and ICW cruisers. First, of course, the Coast Guard is in charge of maintaining law and order in the nation's waters. Then there is its crucial search and rescue function. In addition, the Guard sets and maintains all of the navigational markers, investigates all accidents and is responsible for ice-breaking operations. Last but not least, the Guard publishes the Light List and weekly Local Notices to Mariners.

U.S. Department of Commerce

National Oceanic and Atmospheric Administration (NOAA)

Let's start big. NOAA does research and collects data on oceans, atmosphere, space and the sun. Its agencies produce a wide range of products to make commercial and recreational boaters (among others, of course). These include charts, weather forecasts, and tide and current tables. Here are the agencies that most concern boaters: National Ocean Service, National Weather Service, the National Marine Fisheries Service, the National Environmental Satellite, Data and Information Service and NOAA Research. We're going to limit ourselves here to the National Ocean Service and the National Weather Service.

National Ocean Service (NOS)

The big picture is that NOS is concerned with the health and safety of the nation's coasts and oceans. That's a big picture, indeed. Within the NOS, the agency that has the greatest impact on cruisers is the Office of Coast Survey.

Office of Coast Survey (OCS)

This is the agency responsible for nothing less than producing and updating more than one thousand nautical charts. These are the charts on which all other charts, chart programs and charting apps-from Maptech to Navionics-are based. In their raster and vector forms, these are the charts that the government gives away in digital form for free. We've covered NOAA charts in the previous chapter. The OCS also publishes the Coast Pilots and compiles the Distances Between Ports. We'll tell you more about these and how to get them in the section that follows.

Tides & Currents (CO-OPS)

Not as glamorous as the Office of Coast Survey with all its charts, perhaps, but CO-OPS is a useful agency to know because it collects, predicts and distributes water levels and other meteorological data at hundreds of monitoring stations in the nation's bays and harbors. This is particularly important during storm surges.

Physical Oceanographic Real Time System (PORTS)

Like CO-OPS, PORTS is concerned with gathering and distributing real-time water levels, but in this case at sights in 20 areas along the country's waterways. For our purposes these include Tampa Bay, New York/New Jersey Harbor, Narragansett Bay, Delaware Bay and Chesapeake Bay. The information is directed particularly to commercial shipping but has uses for private vessels as well.

National Weather Service (NWS)

We're going to concern ourselves with just two aspects of this very big and far-reaching agency: the National Data Buoy Center and the Marine Weather Forecasts, including NOAA Weather Radio.

National Data Buoy Center (NDBC)

The NDBC is responsible for the hundreds of meteorological buoys in the nation's waterways and along its coasts. These buoys are capable of sending out real-time information on wind, weather and waves to mariners in a variety of ways, from NDBC web pages to apps developed for smart phones and tablets. You'll find a couple of these apps in the Choosing the Right Apps section, which follows. You'll find a link to the NDBC website below.

Marine Weather Forecasts

Four times each day, the National Weather Service issues forecasts for coastal and offshore waters, inland waterways and the Great Lakes. It also issues marine weather warnings of all varieties, including hurricane warnings, gale warnings, storm warnings, small-craft warnings, flood warnings and dangerous storms and squalls. These warnings and forecasts are disseminated in a variety of ways, most importantly over NOAA Weather Radio, by way of more than 900 transmitters. Forecasts are also posted on NWS marine webpages and through a number of apps and private webpages.

Finding Government Documents Online

Coast Pilot

U.S. Coast Pilots, issued and regularly updated by NOAA's National Oceans Service, is perhaps the most underutilized of all the free government documents available to boaters. At one time, the Coast Pilots were the only cruise guides available for commercial and recreational boaters along the nation's coasts. Now it is almost impossible to walk into a store and purchase a print copy. Happily, Coast Pilots are readily available for free download on NOAA's website. There you can also easily access updates between editions. (Coast Pilot 3, which covers the Atlantic Coast from Sandy Hook, N.J., to Cape Henry, Va., is now in its 48th edition.)

What do you get? Not surprisingly, much of each Coast Pilot book is taken up with piloting information for the coasts and bays, hundreds of creeks, harbors and wharfs. For example, "The Great Wicomico River, on the west side of the Chesapeake Bay 13 miles northward of Windmill Point Light, is entered between Dameron Marsh and Bull Neck, 1.7 miles to the northward. The principal marks for the entrance are Great Wicomico Light and the buildings at Fleeton on Bull Neck." A typical cruise guide will have a great deal more to say on the subject, but the Coast Pilot gives you what you need to know about getting in. There are also tide tables, some color aerial photos and some anchorages, generally for larger vessels. Most importantly, though, the Coast Pilot is where you turn when you want to know about the coast's many restricted areas. Here you'll find details that you won't get in any of the cruise guides. In fact, many of them refer the reader to the Coast Pilot.

Where do you get them? Occasionally you can find print copies for your local area in West Marine or other marine suppliers. You can order print copies of the Coast Pilots from the official NOAA printing agents listed here: *www.nauticalcharts.noaa.gov/staff/print_agents.html* Or you can download Coast Pilots in .pdf form at *www.nauticalcharts.noaa.gov/nsd/cpdownload.htm.*

Above, Eastport, Maine; below, Chatam Roads, and Stage Harbor, Massachusetts.

Coast Pilot 1
Covers the coasts of Maine, New Hampshire, and part of Massachusetts, from Eastport, ME to Provincetown, MA.
www.nauticalcharts.noaa.gov/nsd/coastpilot_w.php?book=1

Coast Pilot 2
Covers the Atlantic coast from Cape Cod, MA to Sandy Hook, NJ, including the coasts of Rhode Island, Connecticut, and New York.
www.nauticalcharts.noaa.gov/nsd/coastpilot_w.php?book=2

Coast Pilot 3
Covers the Atlantic coast from Sandy Hook, NJ to Cape Henry, VA, including Delaware Bay and Chesapeake Bay.
www.nauticalcharts.noaa.gov/nsd/coastpilot_w.php?book=3

Coast Pilot 4
Covers the Atlantic coast from Cape Henry, VA to Key West, FL.
www.nauticalcharts.noaa.gov/nsd/coastpilot_w.php?book4

Coast Pilot 5
Covers Gulf of Mexico from Key West, FL to the Rio Grande, including Puerto Rico and the Virgin Islands.
www.nauticalcharts.noaa.gov/nsd/coastpilot_w.php?book=5

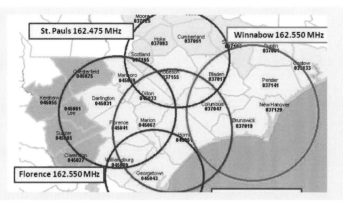

Marine Weather Radio

Finding the right weather station for the area you want on the VHF can be a time-consuming one since you usually have to wait through a multi-day forecast to see whether it's going to give your area. To help you through that, we've put a Marine Weather Radio coverage map with channel numbers at the opening of each chapter of the Reference Section. The maps in the Reference section will show the channel you need.

National Data Buoy Center

The NDBC provides a direct link for real-time information from the National Weather Services meteorological buoys. Information varies from buoy to buoy, but usually includes wind speed and direction, gusts, air and water temperature, and barometric pressure. Some buoys also give wave height and direction.

Here is the zoomable map: *www.ndbc.noaa.gov/*

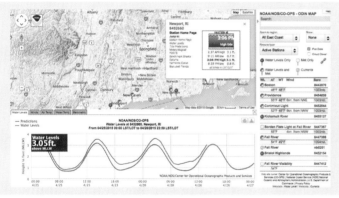

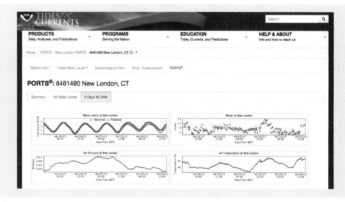

Real-Time and Predicted Water Levels for Selected Bays

The Center for Operational Oceanographic Products provides nowcasts and forecasts for water levels, currents, water temperature, salinity and winds for several major East Coast (for our purposes) areas. The information can be accessed through the websites by locating pins on a map or by searching a particular area. Here are the websites for each area:

Port of New York and New Jersey
tidesandcurrents.noaa.gov/ofs/nyofs/nyofs.html

Delaware Bay and River
tidesandcurrents.noaa.gov/ofs/dbofs/dbofs.html

Chesapeake Bay
tidesandcurrents.noaa.gov/ofs/cbofs/cbofs.html

St. Johns River
tidesandcurrents.noaa.gov/ofs/sjofs/sjofs.html

Real-time tide and current data for ports and harbors

The PORTS system, like CO-OPS, provides useful real-time and predicted data, in this case primarily tides and currents for selected ports. Although this information is aimed primarily at shipping interests, it is useful for cruisers as well.

The PORTS include Charleston Harbor, Chesapeake North and South, Delaware Bay and River, Jacksonville, Narragansett Bay, New Haven, New London and New York/New Jersey Harbor.

Here's the website: *tidesandcurrents.noaa.gov/ports.html*

Army Corps of Engineers Survey Maps

While the USACE has not been able to do as much dredging over tW use it -notably Georgia and South Carolina-they have been busy surveying some of the notoriously shoal areas. So although the latest news for funding in South Carolina looks promising, the Corps survey maps will remain an excellent resource for cruisers.

Unfortunately, the survey charts are not always easy to pry out of the various USACE websites, because each division of the Corps has the autonomy to do a lot of things their own way. The result is that the files are located in different places on each website, and the survey maps look different from division to division when you do get them open. Usually-but not always-a search for "hydrographic surveys" will get the results you need. But perseverance can pay off, and you can add the information you glean by studying the depth shadings (or the tiny little numbers for those that are in black and white) to the advice you've found in Active Captain posts and Salty Southwest Cruisers Network (see the chapter on the Power of Numbers) and your charts, to feel out the best route.

A note of caution on using the USACE maps, however. Since these are areas that are notoriously changeable, the channel may be shifted since the USACE soundings were taken. Check the date.

Here is the way into the survey maps for each district:

New England District
www.nae.usace.army.mil/
Click on Survey in the Navigation box, then choose the state and then the project.

New York District
www.nan.usace.army.mil/Missions/Navigation/ControllingDep-thReports.aspx

Philadelphia District
http://www.nap.usace.army.mil/Missions/CivilWorks/Surveys/Projects.aspx

Baltimore District
www.nab.usace.army.mil/Missions/CivilWorks/NavMaps.aspx

Norfolk District
www.nao.usace.army.mil/
Click on Electronic Survey Distribution System and agree to the disclaimer.

Wilmington District
http://www.saw.usace.army.mil/
Click on Missions, then Navigation, then Hydrographic Surveys.

Charleston District
Hydrographic maps
www.sac.usace.army.mil/Missions/Navigation/Hydrographic-Maps.aspx

Channel conditions
www.sac.usace.army.mil/Missions/Navigation/ChannelConditions.aspx

Savannah District
www.sas.usace.army.mil/About/DivisionsandOffices/Operations-Division/NavigationBranch/WW

Jacksonville District
www.saj.usace.army.mil/Missions/CivilWorks/Navigation/Hydro-Surveys.aspx

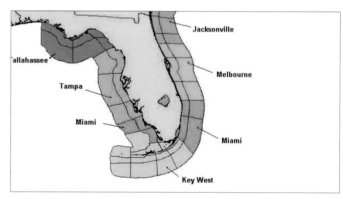

You will find more ways to access this information in the chapter on phone and tablet apps.

Marine Weather Forecasts

Sometimes it's just easier to check the marine weather forecast with your computer, phone or tablet than waiting through the radio forecast. Although there is no government app, the information is readily available by bookmarking each section to your phone or tablet screen. These forecasts are updated four times a day, but you'll still need the radio for the very latest warnings or bulletins.

Here are the websites for the NWS marine weather zones:

Northern: Maine through Charleston, S.C.
www.nws.noaa.gov/om/marine/zone/east/ermzn.htm

Southern: Charleston, S.C. through Florida Gulf
www.nws.noaa.gov/om/marine/zone/south/stheastmz.htm

USACE Locks and Canals

Here are the Army Corps of Engineers websites with links to the latest information on the Atlantic Coast's three canal routes that have locks. Pay special attention to the Dismal Swamp and Okeechobee canal updates because these may change-or even close-in times of low water levels or other issues.

Albemarle & Chesapeake Canal/Dismal Swamp Canal
www.nao.usace.army.mil/Missions/CivilWorks/AIWW.aspx

Okeechobee Waterway
www.saj.usace.army.mil/Missions/CivilWorks/LakeOkeechobee/OkeechobeeWaterway%28OWW%29.aspx

Local Notices to Mariners

This document is published each week by the Coast Guard. You can sign up to receive reminders by email. Yes, it's a chore to scan through the document each week, but it is also true that each week you'll generally find something well worth noting, whether it's shoaling, a new bridge schedule or a missing marker.

Here are the websites:

District 1
www.navcen.uscg.gov/?pageName=lnmDistrict&region=1

District 5
www.navcen.uscg.gov/?pageName=lnmDistrict&region=5

District 7
www.navcen.uscg.gov/?pageName=lnmDistrict&region=7

Light List

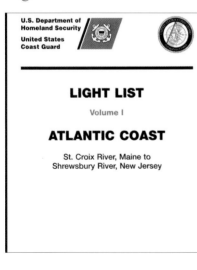

Here is the website for the Light Lists, published by the U.S. Coast Guard. Click on the map to download a .pdf for that area. The page also has a link to the Weekly Light List with changes. The publications include not only a list of lights, but also sound signals, buoys, daybeacons and all the other aids to navigation. The Coast Guard is in the process of removing the bells and whistles from many buoys along navigation channels, so many of the chart notations are now incorrect. This is an especially important publication if you are planning night passages.

www.navcen.uscg.gov/?pageName=lightList

Choosing the Right Apps

It's no news to anyone that smartphones and tablets have revolutionized the way we boat. There are now apps for everything we do on the water, from plotting a course and finding a good anchorage to monitoring the engine systems and performing first aid. If it has to do with a boat, chances are good that's already covered by an app. Search in the app store for Apple, Windows or Android devices and you'll find them by the hundreds.

As might be expected, some of these are terrific, a boon to coastal and intracoastal cruising, while others are close to useless. And price is not the determining factor. In the last five years we've tried dozens and dozens of apps and found only a few that we continue to use with pleasure. Many, we're sorry to say, we've discarded as useless, awkward or incomplete. It's not a good average.

On the following pages, we are going to help you sort through this proliferation of boating apps. We've picked out a few that have worked for us—in fact, we'll tell you our favorites—and we'll point you in the direction of a few alternatives.

It would be foolish to attempt to offer a comprehensive review of all the boating apps available for smartphones and tablets. It would take up an absurd amount of time—on your part and ours—and it would be sorrowfully out of date by the time you got around to reading it. Instead we've created four categories of apps—navigation, weather and tides/currents, safety and stuff left over. We've suggested some things to look for in these categories, and then we've chosen a half-dozen or so of the best and most popular apps in each area. Consider this a starting point.

Screenshots of the Elizabeth River, Norfolk, Va., as displayed by three navigation apps on an iPad. From top, iNavX, Navionics and Garmin.

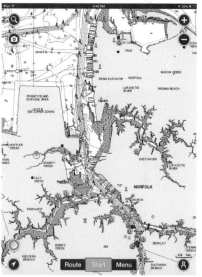

Navigation Apps

In the navigation apps category, you won't go wrong by choosing any of first three navigation apps in our list. You can download and use them with confidence, and they will do a very good job for you. They are, in fact, our favorites—the ones we use regularly. And, as we mentioned earlier, we've tried dozens. But there are plenty of other good ones out there, and other boaters have come to prefer some of them for a variety of reasons. So we've given you some of these too. And just because an app didn't make our list, doesn't mean that it won't be the perfect one for you. We encourage you to try several until you find one you are comfortable with.

Some of these apps use raster charts—almost always NOAA's—while others use vector charts, either NOAA's or, in the case of Navionics and Garmin for example, their own. Some, like iNavX, allow you to toggle between raster and vector charts. ("Raster" charts, as far as apps are concerned, are essentially digital photos of the traditional print charts we all know. "Vector" charts are digital only and usually contain layers of information, which can be switched on and off. For a more involved explanation of "raster" and "vector" see Chapter 2.) If you are more comfortable with one kind of chart over another, you may want to choose that kind of app.

There are other differences too. For example, if you frequently plot your course with waypoints, you'll want an app that allows you to set those up easily. Some apps (like Garmin) will run

Navigation Apps continued...

Active Captain along with the charts. (We'll talk about Active Captain in Chapter 5, Power of the People.) Others offer a wide variety of different features. Navionics, for example, is pioneering crowd-sourced sonar soundings that appear on the charts when selected. Still others will connect with your onboard instruments, even allowing you to control the auto-pilot from your tablet. You'll find a wide variety. You just have to decide which apps offer the features you want.

Or you can do what we do, which is to run several apps simultaneously on our tablet, which we keep mounted at the helm station next to our Garmin chartplotter. This way we can switch back and forth between apps, depending on which information we want at the moment. We use Navionics for the clarity and accuracy of its charts, the Garmin app for Active Captain's bridge information and hazard warnings, and iNavX for its raster charts, which are always a good check. When we're running through the notoriously shoal areas of Georgia and South Carolina, we've recently been substituting the new Nobeltec Time Zero app for the iNavX app because in addition to its raster charts, it also features a sidebar with an easy-to-read tide and current graphic that moves as we move. This makes it extra easy to keep track of where we are in the tide cycle, whether we are negotiating shallow water or coming up to a low bridge.

Other veteran cruisers we know (with larger helm stations than we have) run one program on their tablet, one on their chartplotter and another on their laptop computer, usually Open CPN.

With all this technology, it can get pretty crazy! But that's the thing. The apps, especially in this category, keep getting better. Established programs keep improving and new apps introduce brand new ideas. For example, one app allows you to chart a course and set waypoints by dragging your finger across the screen. Amazing!

On the down side, the current trend in navigation and charting programs is to sell them piecemeal, requiring additional annual payment for most of their "premium" features, like weather and routing. This makes the monetary investment into the full program significantly more substantial. Happily, there are still several fine basic programs that can be downloaded for little or nothing. A number of the more sophisticated apps offer a free trial with the bells and whistles, so you can give it a try before you make a commitment. The whole process, however, makes finding and learning each new program more difficult and time-consuming.

Even with all these extra costs, however, purchasing a navigation program for your tablet remains significantly cheaper than doing the same for your chartplotter. And it is considerably easier to update the charts on your apps than on your chartplotter.

iNavX

Charts: NOAA Raster (free); Navionics Gold as well as a variety of Canadian and European charts can be purchased through X-Traverse.

Selected features: AIS, tides and currents (through Aye Tides), weather (through Theyr.com and GRIB), waypoint and route planning, NMEA connectivity through TCP/IP, integrates external AIS, GPS and vessel instruments; anchor alarm; mirrors MacENC software; Waterway Guides points of interest.

Comments: With all of its features, its years of experience and its commitment to frequent updates, it's little wonder that iNavX is consistently the favorite of tech-savvy cruisers, from Practical Sailor magazine to the gurus at Annapolis School of Seamanship. All of this complexity, however, comes with a fairly steep learning curve. The good news is that iNavX—unlike a number of other programs that want you to figure it out for yourself—comes with a good users manual and willing

support from the company. MacENC was the first navigation program for the Mac OS and was among the first in the app market with iNavX. We've been users from the beginning though we still haven't hit the bottom of its well of goodies.

Our main objection is that while we are underway, the program will automatically shift to the next NOAA chart, but when we want to look ahead to do some planning we have to shift and choose the charts for ourselves. Doable, yes, but considerably more cumbersome than many other programs whose raster charts are stitched together. This is obviously not a problem if you run Navionics electronic charts on iNavX.

Navionics

Charts: Navionics

Selected features: Toggle between government, Navionics and Navionics Sonarcharts; points of interest; tides and currents; community edits; map view options and filters;

route planning module with ETA, distance and fuel consumption; autorouting; tracks; distance; wind forecasts; sync tracks between devices; Raymarine WiFi plotter sync.

Comments: For sheer clarity and accuracy, Navionics charts remain ahead of the pack, just one of the features that has helped make Navionics the most used navigation app in the world. The fact that it offers charts worldwide and across multiple platforms such as iOS and Windows doesn't hurt either. We are not going to argue with the masses here.

Based on our own experience running the NOAA raster charts, Garmin Blue Charts and Navionics simultaneously, we have found that Navionics charts are consistently more accurate, especially areas where the markers are changed frequently because of constantly shifting conditions. In addition, we find Navionics charts the easiest to follow when entering a busy harbor for the first time. As its Sonar Charts become richer and more accurate thanks to crowdsourcing, it becomes a good option for feeling our way through shoal areas.

Other features set Navionics apart as well: easily accessed tide and current data, easy distance and route set up. The charts also maintain their detail when zoomed out, making it possible to quickly shoot a reasonably accurate rhumb line over a fairly long distance (from Cape Charles, Va., to Thomas Point Light, Md., for example, a distance of 96 nautical miles).

The bottom line is that for cruisers along the Atlantic Coast and ICW, Navionics is a excellent option. It does have a few failings, however. It's not very good at giving information about bridges, marinas, anchorages and so forth. While it does have some points of interest, it can't begin to compete with Active Captain's wealth of useful information. But for sheer beauty, accuracy and ease of use, it can't be beat.

Garmin

 Charts: Garmin

Selected features: Transfer routes to a Garmin chartplotter over WiFi; Active Captain; tides and currents; weather; routes and waypoints; distance measure; track.

Comments: Garmin's excellent BlueChart app rounds out our Big Three. It takes its place at the top of the heap with tried and true Garmin charts and ease of use. It also runs Active Captain, a feature that adds immeasurably to its utility with information on bridge schedules, shoaling areas, hazards, marinas with contact information and all the other things that revolutionary program has to offer.

Garmin doesn't have as many bells and whistles as iNavX or even some other newer programs, but it is frequently updated, intuitive, quick and reliable. It also has a good users manual accessible offline. As we mentioned earlier, we always keep it running on our iPad as we cruise and toggle between it and Navionics during the day.

TimeZero

 Charts: NOAA raster

Selected features: Local weather; tides and currents; tracking; plotter; SOG and COG; distance to waypoint; time of arrival; 3-D display; satellite view; range and bearing measure.

Comments: If you can live with raster rather than vector charts, this is a great program for coastal cruising. While it doesn't have NMEA connectivity, it does have a few unique features that we do like. The NavData runs down the left side of the screen with all the navigation data plus a running tide height and current graph that is a plus while running in shallow areas, where timing the tide cycle is crucial.

We particularly like to switch on the satellite plus 3-D view for a good perspective of what's coming up. It's not a perfect program and the $39 price for free NOAA charts is pretty steep. But unlike many apps now it's the only price you pay for all the program's features.

iSail GPS

 Charts: NOAA raster

Selected features: Waypoints and routes; built-in help guide; low price with no extra costs.

Comments: At only $7.99, this is a great simple, straightforward app. You can even create waypoints and routes. Practical Sailor rated this their number one navigation app in the free-and-cheap category. Downloading the charts can be a bit taxing if you want to do a lot a one time, but that's a small price to pay in exchange for the actual cost. The downside, like iNavX, is that while planning your route you have to go to the list and choose the correct chart. But also like iNavX, iSail will automatically load the next downloaded chart as you travel.

NavPlay

 *Charts:* NOAA vector

Selected features: Track export to Google maps; WiFi instruments and AIS through TCP/IP; range and bearing; weather buoys; configured layers; tide and current displays; routes and tracks; and virtual horizon view.

Comments: This is a full-featured, easy to use, navigation program with multi-layered vector charts and tons of options, including views with road maps, satellite and hybrid over the vector charts. Charts are downloaded as you need them, although if you are offline, it would be good to download them first.

Most of the options are available on a bar across the bottom. The eye at the top, however, provides this app's singular feature. It accesses the camera on your device to display the view with an overlay of markers and AIS targets in real time. Click on the marker or target to get more information. This can be a big help in an area of confusing markers or multiple AIS targets.

Apps for Weather

When you start looking at weather apps, you'll notice that they fall into three categories: general weather, radar and wind. There are a lot of wind apps. But even if you don't have a mainsail or a long board to call your own, don't ignore them, because wind kicks up waves, and wind blowing against tide kicks up big waves. So while it's tempting to start the day with a quick glance at the Weather Underground or Weather Channel app and leave it at that—especially if you are on the protected waters of the ICW—don't. The wind for Charleston, S.C.'s downtown may be predicted at 5 to 10 mph, but out in Charleston Bay, it may be piping up to 20 kts, pushing up waves 3 to 4 feet. You might still decide to go, but at least you'll know what you're going to get: a bumpy ride.

Once cruisers reach the narrow confines of the ICW, the importance of the weather does diminish somewhat, especially if there are no big bodies of water, like Charleston Bay or Albemarle Sound, on the day's agenda. Yes, it's still important if it's going to be blowing a gale outside, but it's not as important as it is if you were headed around Cape Ann to Gloucester. Once you're inside the ICW, you can sometimes travel on days that would be miserable—or even dangerous—on the outside. But you still need to know what's coming at you.

One final point: Although an increasing number of navigation apps include weather and radar, it usually comes with a fairly hefty subscription price. We usually find it easier to use our phones to keep up to date on the current weather, including radar. For that, we use MyRadarPro's excellent interface—which now includes winds—to get a better picture faster, even with the pro-version's modest one-time cost. So here are a few radar apps and our suggested daily plan.

1 Go ahead and check in with your favorite general weather app. It will give you a good overall view of the next 3 to 5 days. (We particularly like Weather Underground's app because about half-way down the scroll it offers the option of reading its Scientific Discussion. This begins with a nice synopsis and then launches into a detailed discussion of what's coming over the next few days. Some of it we even understand.)

Wunderground

Selected features: Graphic forecasts for current and favorite locations; settings allow forecast to follow you; rain chances; wind; l0-day, daily and hourly forecasts; radar; daylight and dark graphics; air quality; Scientific Discussion; marine and weather warnings; and blogs. Wunderground's new Storm app that has a marine feature for weather.

Comments: Accuweather, Weather Channel, Weather Bug, Weather Underground cover much the same territory. To a large degree it depends on which interface you find most appealing. As we mentioned above, we are partial to the Scientific Discussion by area meteorologists.

Weather Channel

Selected features: Much the same features as Weather Underground's app, including 10-day forecast; hourly forecast; radar; weather advisories; brief videos on area and national forecasts; and local airport conditions.

Comments: As might be expected, Weather Channel has a nice interface with settings to allow favorites and follow-me options. It features video clips rather than text.

WeatherBug

Comments: This is another good all-round weather app, with pretty much the same information arranged in a slightly different way. It has a particularly good radar and Spark, an app within an app that shows nearby lightning strikes and distance from your location.

AccuWeather

Selected features: Current, hourly and 10-day weather, winds, dew point, pressure, visibility; cloud cover; humidity; cute sun and moon graphics; weather map.

Comments: AccuWeather offers a few more numbers and fewer graphics than either of its competitors, but the idea is essentially the same. We haven't found any way to get a more complete forecast on either this or Weather Channel.

2

Next, check the marine weather forecast for where you are now and where you plan to be during the day's cruise. Then check it for the rest of the week. If bad weather is coming, you'll want to have a secure anchorage or marina lined up well ahead of time.

There are several easy ways you can get the marine forecast:

• Listen to the local WX channel on your VHF radio (check the WX forecast coverage maps and channels at the front of each section of this book for the right station)—this takes the longest time, but has the most current forecast. (Always tune in here if you see storms on the horizon.

• Use your computer, smartphone or tablet to get the NWS marine forecast for your area by way of the Internet. You'll find the overall map with forecast zones here: *www.nws.noaa.gov/om/marine/zone/usamz.htm*. This is the next best way to get the marine forecast. (We have each zone bookmarked on our iPhone screen for quick access.)

• Use a marine forecast app, either a simple one like Boat Weather or a more feature-heavy app like Marine Weather or Outcast.

Weather on the Web

We should mention here that there are also a number of websites that will give you similar weather information. We have about half a dozen bookmarked that we used well before there were apps to help plan our day on the water. These include *www.Sailflow.com*, which we mentioned earlier, *www.passage-weather.com* and our favorite, crownweather.com, where you'll find more weather maps than you ever thought possible.

There are a number of excellent NWS charts, graphs and maps. We've given you the best of these websites in Chapter 3: Mining Government Resources.

And don't overlook local resources. For example, if you happen to find yourself in Southport, N.C., doing the ICW or ready to jump offshore, we encourage you to attend an evening session at Southport Marina with retired meteorologist Hank Pomeranz. Hank puts together an excellent daily briefing on the weather and navigation hazards for that section of the ICW, complete with the latest Army Corps of Engineers soundings maps. Check out his website at *www.carolinayachtcare.com/tides-and-weather/*. You'll find another excellent resource on Channel 72 of your VHF radio at 9 every morning in St. Augustine, Fla.

Boat Weather

Selected features: Marine weather forecast

Comments: This really is a simple app. You want the marine weather forecast. Here it is. It opens to the forecast you've set. To look elsewhere, you open Settings, which gives you a choice of state, then the choice of zone within the state. Our only criticism is that it leaves out the general forecast that opens all NWS forecasts.

Marine Weather

Selected features: Marine weather forecast; buoys data; radar; tides and currents.

Comments: We think of this as our go-to marine forecast app because you only get one feature at a time, and we leave the forecast option checked. But the app also gives buoy data (though not complete for the Chesapeake's smart buoys), tide and current predictions. Everything is based on clicking dots on a map. Nice, quick and simple. We like it because it's easy to click along the coast to get forecasts outside our current location.

3 Once you've gotten a basic idea of the weather with steps 1 and 2, you can then get as sophisticated as you want. For those times when the weather is really important—let's say you are coastwise cruising in Maine, exploring Florida's Ten Thousand Islands, or even headed offshore—there are a number of good apps that give you a whole raft of predictions and current conditions in areas like temperature, winds, frontal movements and precipitation, while also giving you radar, tides/currents and buoy reports. All this lets you put together a good picture of the weather pattern. One (Predict Wind), for a hefty subscription, even plans your route, taking in account of the weather.

PocketGrib

Selected Features: Downloadable files for viewing offline in map or meteogram form. You choose the area to be downloaded to get 8-day predictions in temperature, wind, pressure, waves, cloud cover, humidity and current.
Comments: This is a handy program with lots of raw information from NOAA's Global Forecast System (GFS) and no subscription costs, updated four times a day. This information let's you do your own forecasting.

PredictWind

Selected Features: MarineCast gives you data from the SailFlow website in an app form with current observations, wind graphs, NWS marine forecasts and maps for wind, radar, and tides and currents.

Comments: MarineCast is easy to use and provides graphic and table views of predicted weather in all the standard areas.

MarineCast

Selected features: Information on wind, rain, cloud cover, isobars, sea temperatures, waves in table, graph and map form. With subscriptions, added observations, weather routing and departure planning.
Comments: On a basic level, PredictWind provides the same information as a number of other programs, including MarineCast (above). But with the level of subscription, the level of sophistication increases, up to weather routing and best times to leave. You tell the app where you're going and about when; the app plans your route and suggests the best time to leave.

MyRadarPro

Selected features: High-resolution radar with optional wind flow.
Comments: Radar images vary remarkably from one app to another and this one is probably no more accurate than the rest. But it's sharp, fast and easy to read. We have used many times to watch the progress of squalls coming at us across Chesapeake Bay.

NOAA Radar US

Selected features: Another high-resolution radar app. Not government affiliated, despite the name.
Comments: Essentially the same thing as MyRadarPro and a number of other programs. Quick, simple and colorful.

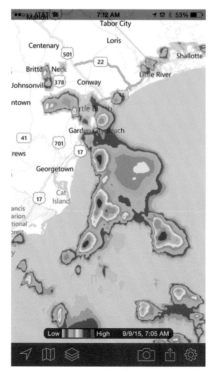

Screenshot of MyRadar running on an iPhone.

Apps for Tides & Currents

Having knowledge of the tides and currents is nearly as important as the weather, depending on where you're cruising. So we have included a few Tides and Currents apps here. Although there are many tides apps—many of which are free—few of them include currents. This is somewhat puzzling since knowing the current speed and direction is sometimes more important than knowing where the tide is. And all of the information comes from the same place—NOAA. Many navigation apps now also feature access—free or for a subscription fee—to predicted tides and currents, as well as real-time buoy information if you have an Internet connection.

AyeTides

Selected features: Tides and currents.
Comments: This long has been, and remains, hands down the best app for finding predicted tides and currents. It has more locations, is easier to search and to use, and gives both a table and graphic representation. It is also easier to look ahead than most other tide apps.

Tides Near Me

Selected features: Tides and currents.
Comments: While this app gives current readings as well, it doesn't differentiate between the two in its listings, which means that finding a current reading is hit or miss. From there it's difficult to get the current speed rather than just the highest flows.

Apps for Buoys

Finally, we've a couple of apps that will give you current buoy information, such as wind speed and direction, and air and water temperature. Some buoys will also provide wave height, direction and timing—terrific information if you can get it. Remember, though, unlike predicted tides and currents apps and navigation apps, buoy and weather apps require an Internet connection, whether it's a separate app or inside a navigation app.

NOAA Buoy and Tide Data

Selected features: Information from NOAA's National Buoy Data Center and predicted tides.
Comments: This is the Aye Tides of buoy apps—reliable, stable, comprehensive and relatively complete, including wave information when available. The search interface is user friendly, with choices for searching nearby, favorites and by name or region. You can also search using the map. The search results list includes the buoy name, distance from your location, and current wind speed (though not the direction). Once you open the one you want, you get whatever data the buoy is monitoring, usually wind speed and direction, pressure, air temperature and dew point. If you want more information, there are links at the bottom of the screen to its National Buoy Data Center webpage, and to local weather and radar.

Smart Buoys

Comments: This free app gives you all the data gathered by the Chesapeake Bay's Smart Buoys. This includes the usual information about the weather and (when it's working) waves, but also the water quality and chemistry. There is even a short history that goes along with each of the buoys, all of which mark important locations throughout the Bay, including First Landing, Stingray Point and Jamestown. Fun, educational and useful for fishermen.

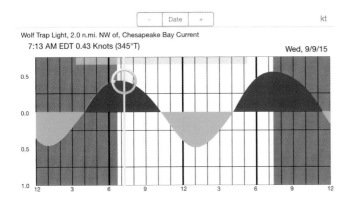
Screenshot of current predictions for Wolf Trap Light, Chesapeake Bay on an iPhone running Aye Tides.

Screenshot of the Smart Buoys app running on an iPad.

Apps for Safety

We come to our third category, Safety. Of course, all of the apps we've already talked about have at least something to do with safety. Safer navigation, better weather awareness and knowledge of the tides and currents all make cruising safer and more relaxing. But here are several apps that are directly related to getting us out of trouble or keeping us out of trouble. We don't use them often—in fact, we hope never to use them—but if something bad happens this is where we'll go for help.

MOB

 Selected features: This app does only one thing and does it well, register's the position of a man overboard. The screen's big red button registers a position when pushed and then helps guide you back to the spot. The position can also be used as a reference when calling in the emergency.

Comments: We keep this running in background on our iPad at the helm, which we also keep plugged in because the GPS uses lot of battery. We also use this app for man overboard practice and suggest you do too.

First Aid

 Selected features: This app is divided into learning, preparation, emergency and quiz sections for a broad range of common health problems from allergy and asthma attacks to broken bones, hypothermia and strokes.

Comments: This is the Red Cross's first aid app, and it is general, not specifically for boating emergencies. But the information is basic, well-organized, brief and to the point. The learning section gives more information, while the emergency section is extremely brief. Within each section, there are also a brief video and a question and answer section.

This is not necessarily the best first aid app; there a number of others. Whichever one you choose, we recommend that you keep at least one on your phone and/or tablet.

Pet First Aid

 Selected features: Modeled on the same line as the Red Cross's general app, this one is also divided into learning, preparation and emergencies for each of its dozen or so categories. There is also a section on establishing what is normal for animals.

Comments: This is a good app to keep right next to your general first aid app on your phone or tablet. You can also toggle between dog and cat issues and treatment. Parrots? Not so much.

BoatU.S.

 Selected features: Button for calling a tow; current latitude and longitude position; basic weather information for your position and a graphic of the tide for the nearest reporting position.

Comments: This app saves scrambling around to get your BoatU.S. member number. Once you've entered it, all you have to do is push the Call a Tow button and the app does the rest.

SeaTow

 Selected features: Button for calling for assistance; some weather and tide information as well as basic weather. GPS position.

Comments: Not surprisingly, the SeaTow app does about the same things as the BoatU.S. app. To get your latitude and longitude, however, you have to go to the menu and select GPS.

TorchPro

 Selected features: Flashlight and emergency signaling app with a variety of settings, including flashlight, on when touched, strobe; the Morse setting sends SOS light signal or send a message in Morse code that you've entered into the text box.

Comments: This is a great app for signaling an emergency across the water, either as an SOS or a message. The strobe is good for attracting attention and the speed can even be changed. It's also a good flashlight. Of course, all of this is good only as long as your battery lasts. To help that you can use the dimmer switch. longitude, however, you have to go to the menu and select GPS.

AIS apps

If your boat does not have an integrated AIS system but you want to see what other boats are out there, possibly along your route, there are three apps that will do a pretty good job of receiving that information. And one of them, Boat Beacon, will also act as an AIS transmitter, so that other AIS boats will know that you're out there as well.

Boat Beacon

Comments: Boat Beacon manages to both receive and send an AIS signal as a phone or tablet app. It will give you the standard AIS vessel information, like speed, draft and destination, but will also give you its bearing, range and closest point of approach, very much like a dedicated AIS system. Some sailing races now use it so that all entrants, as well as all interested parties, can keep track of the fleet.

Marine Traffic & Ship Finder

Comments: These two apps have been around for a few years and both have improved during that time. Sometimes we have better luck with one over the other, but that seems to change the next time we start them up. Both give standard AIS information like ship name, length, draft, speed and destination. This is particularly useful during night passages in or near shipping lanes. But they are by no means infallible. No AIS system is. In addition to all that, Ship Finder now has a nifty augmented reality (AR) feature that uses your camera to show you where the ships are and how far away they are as you scan the horizon. (Or the walls of your office, if you are anywhere near the water.)

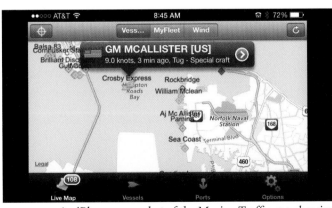

An iPhone screenshot of the Marine Traffic app showing ships in Hampton Roads, Va..

Knot-Tying Apps

How many times have you wished you could remember how to join two lines with an elegant alpine butterfly bend? Or wished you hadn't forgotten how to do a chain splice? The answer to your befuddlement, of course, is to load a knot app on your phone or tablet.

Grog Knots, How to tie Knots, & Knots 3D

Comments: Our favorite knot app is Grog Knots, which has been instructing us all in knot-tying nearly as long as there has been computer animation. Grog and others let you run the animation at varying speeds or pause entirely while you try to catch up. (How to Tie Knots app is particularly good at this.) They will also usually flip the knot so you can see it from both sides.

What Grog adds that we particularly like is an information page for each knot with its uses, history, advantages (or otherwise) and similar knots—almost as good as the venerable Ashley Book of Knots (which does not, as far as we know, make an app).

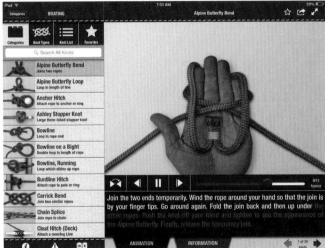

Screenshots of Grog Knots on an iPad

Anchor Alarm Apps

Here are two anchor alarm apps that seem to work fine. There are several more out there that we've yet to try, but which probably work just fine. On quiet nights, we often just drop a pin in a couple of navigation programs on the phone when we have the anchor set. That way we can just check the phone when we wake up during the night. Not perfect, but not bad.

Drag Queen & Anchor Watch

Comments: These are both simple straightforward programs. Drag Queen can be set up to your boat's specifics to make the alarm more accurate. Anchor Watch will even send you an email. Both have a good user's guide.

An App for Fun and Education

Boat Lights

Comments: You can download Chapman's and other weighty boating tomes into your ebook library, but if you get confused when the tug captain tells you he's going to give you a two-whistle pass, here's a charming little app that will let you discover the answer. Open Boat Lights, click on the sounds button and then add two short blasts to the box and hit search, and up comes the answer: "Approaching vessel is altering its course to port." (In other words he's going to pass you his starboard to your starboard.) You can do the same thing with lights by dragging the red, green, yellow and white lights you see displayed by a ship at night and the app will tell you what you're looking at. You can do the same for day-shapes, as well.

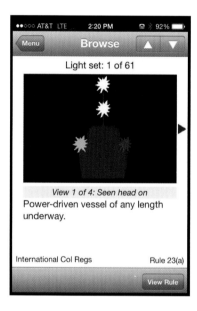

Screenshot of Boat Lights on an iPhone

Want more information on available apps?

We recommend Mark Messerli's i-marineapps.blogspot.com and Ben Ellison's Panbo.com. Their reviews are thorough and fair. They also stay up to date, always a problem in finding out about the latest apps. Most boating magazines have reviewed the available apps at one time or another—*Practical Sailor, Boating, Cruising World, SAIL*, etc.—but most of the articles are now three or four years old, ancient history in the world of digital applications.

The Power of Numbers: Online Sites, Crowd-Sourcing & Cruising Organizations

This planning guide would be incomplete without a mention of the day-to-day online and digital sources that take a lot of the stress out of cruising, especially in areas subject to frequent change, like the ICW's notorious shoals in South Carolina and Georgia. Here are some of the most useful.

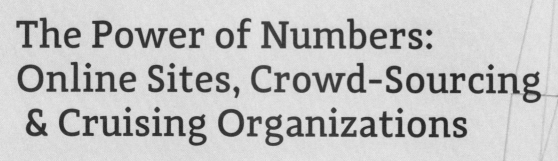

Snowbirds flock north with the spring, here near Spooners Creek, North Carolina.

Active Captain

First and foremost among these must be the phenomenon known as Active Captain. That single—and singular—program has engineered a dramatic change in the way people cruise by making a treasure-trove of up-to-date information available to boaters as they cruise. Its concept is simple: crowd-source information on trouble spots, marinas, bridge schedules and anchorages. Make it free and easy to use. Make it available in a multitude of charting programs. Make it usable without an internet connection.

Active Captain founders Jeff and Karen Siegel continue to add useful features to their site, like electronic boat cards and programs that let you see where your friends are cruising, but the core of their program remains the most important. The program is accessible online at activecaptain.com and requires a simple registration to start using it. It is also available as a free add-on with myriad chart-plotting apps, including Garmin and Coastal Explorer. (You'll find a complete list on their website, *activecaptain.com*.) That way, cruisers can look just ahead to see the latest conditions, including missing markers or hazards in the channel.

The biggest disadvantage of any crowd-sourced information is the reliability of the posts. The Siegels vet the posts generally, but regular users (like us) learn which posters are the most accurate, and so they scroll through the comments to find those names and then follow that advice. It's not a foolproof system, but it gives cruisers immediate access to the experience of those who may have pass through the same difficult area only hours before.

Salty Southeast Cruisers Network

For more closely vetted information, ICW cruisers have long depended on Salty Southeast Cruisers Network, the invention of the late cruising guide writer Claiborne S. Young. The website, *cruisersnet.net*, is full of information about changes on the ICW from Norfolk to the Keys and along the West Coast, contributed by many of the current cruising guide writers and a dozen or so experienced cruisers. The site is free and requires no registration. It does, however, require Internet access. And it covers only the Norfolk to Miami and Gulf Coast sections of the ICW.

Boat U.S.

When it comes to boating, the Boat Owners Association of the United States (BoatU.S.) is big . . . really big. Its 500,000 members make it larger by far than any other club or organization on the water—probably combined. So you can imagine it carries the very big stick when it comes to advocating for boaters, whether it's the level of ethanol in marine gasoline or anchoring rights in south Florida. BoatU.S. also covers a lot of the bases cruisers are looking for: Safety information, shared experience, how-to videos and articles and up-to-date cruising alerts.

If you don't feel like downloading and sifting through the Coast Guard's weekly Notice to Mariners for your district (which, of course we all should, but don't always manage to do), bookmark BoatU.S.'s weekly summary. (It's a little hard to find the page the first time, so on the BoatU.S. website (boatus.com) click on Resources, then Message Boards and scroll down to East Coast Alerts.) It's not as good as reading the Notices for yourself, but it's better than not looking at all.

And, of course, BoatU.S. does towing. Regular membership is inexpensive, only $30, but its rates for towing insurance are one of boating's great bargains and the single price applies to all of your boats.

In fact, buying the best towing insurance you can afford from either BoatU.S. or SeaTow (*www.seatow.com*) is one of the smartest things you can do. In fact, if you haven't done it yet, stop right here and do it now. We guarantee you'll never regret it! Both BoatU.S. and SeaTow have smartphone apps that store your information and make calling for help that much easier.

Cruising Forums

For those cruising farther afield, there are a number of forums with hundreds of members willing to help answer questions and offer advice. Most require registration to use all of the features, like the search engine and comments, but all are free. Two of the oldest and biggest are Sailnet (*sailnet. com*) and Cruisers Forum (*cruisersforum.com*). Each of these offers about a dozen subcategories for cruisers in various regions or discussions on a variety of subjects from cruising with pets to replacing your exhaust manifold. There are also several forums for those primarily interested in fishing, including Hull Truth (*hulltruth.com*) and Tidal Fish (*tidalfish.com*). There are also, of course, Internet sites for nearly every boating interest, from Tartan owners to multihull enthusiasts, and marine electronics (*Panbo.com*) and boating magazine blogs (*Sailfeed.com*). These we will leave for you to discover for yourself.

Cruising with Facebook

In the past year or two, Facebook has taken over a lot of the discussions previously found on Internet forums. Like it or not, Facebook is quick, easy to read and post, and is available without fuss using the Facebook app. With that in mind, here are a few of those most useful to ICW and coastal cruisers along the East Coast. If you have a Facebook account, they are all available, though some require a request to join.

Active Captain: Yes, the Siegels are here too, answering questions and posting comments as they travel.

Seven Seas Cruisers Association: Here you'll find posts from many of the cruising guide writers and speakers, like Mark and Diana Doyle, Wally Moran and Dietmar Petutschnig of Good Anchorages. Though the posts are spread worldwide, there is a lot of good information here. (For more on that group, see below.)

Other sites are specific to the Norfolk to Miami ICW, including Sailing and Cruising: ICW; ICW 2015-16; and Sail Magazine Secrets of the ICW. Though many of these are geared to specific southbound rallies, they offer good information about the route.

And there are plenty of sites, both on the Internet and on Facebook, that are specific to certain interests. For example, both the Livingaboard and the Liveaboards pages offer lots of advice about that lifestyle.

In addition, cruise guide authors Mark and Diana Doyle's On the Water ChartGuides page is a good supplement to their books because they are reliably quick in getting new information up. They also share information and tips from other cruising experts too, such as Active Captain's Jeff and Karen Siegel. Waterway Guide, too, keeps an active website, as does BoatUS.

Cruising Organizations
Tapping into Collective Experience

While you are still in the planning stage, you may want to consider joining one or more of the following organizations, which are chock full of like-minded individuals who are either at the same stage of planning as yourself and so have the same questions, or have been there before you and have at least some of the answers. Many of these groups hold meetings (or "gams") several times a year in several locations so that members can make friends and share information. Many also hold seminars or talks on a variety of cruising-related subjects, such as provisioning and weather-forecasting. They are also a good source for blogs, written by those who have been there before. It's a good way to get acquainted with the cruisers' pace of life.

Here are a few of the most active.

Seven Seas Cruising Association

This is the grandparent of all cruising organizations . . . worldwide. Founded in 1952 by offshore cruisers, Seven Seas Cruising Association (SSCA) was the first to pool information for members who were taking their boats all over the world. At one-time full membership meant showing that you had spent extensive time making long offshore passages. More recently, full membership has been widened to include coastal and short-hop cruisers. In addition to shared knowledge, SSCA provides educational courses, far-flung member stations and surveys on equipment. SSCA also advocates for cruisers' rights on such issues as Florida anchoring limits. There is a forum, but most of the discussion has moved to its Facebook page. Membership fee is $55. (*ssca.org*)

Marine Trawler Owners Association

Despite its name, this popular organization is not limited to trawler owners, but includes some sailboat and sports fishing boat owners as well. The group, now about 2,000 strong, holds several well-attended rendezvous each year and offers training and education, as well as an easy way to meet and make friends with other people who are enjoying the same cruising lifestyle you are—or want to. There is an annual membership fee of $65. (*www.mtoa.net*)

America's Great Loop Cruisers' Association

You see their burgees everywhere as you cruise. Founded in 1992, America's Great Loop Cruiser's Association (AGLCA) was, as its name implies, aimed at those people who were, wanted to, or had completed the Great Loop. The Great Loop is the country's great circle route that comes up the East Coast, through New York waterways to the Great Lakes, then down through Illinois, Tennessee and Mississippi or Alabama waterways to the Gulf of Mexico and around Florida (or through it) to close the circle on the East Coast. Though a significant portion of the route is not included in this Atlantic Coast planning and ICW guide, a substantial portion of it is, so we include it here. The group, like others, shares information and provides the opportunity for meeting friends and learning from the experience of others. Membership is $75 a year. (*greatloop.org*)

Stocking the Library

Nothing but blue sky and turquoise water south of the Florida Capes.

No argument. Cruise guides and charts are indispensable when cruising, whether it's long distance or short haul. But when the rains fall and the winds howl, there is nothing finer than curling up in the warm dry cabin and losing yourself in a good book. Of course, the same goes for a crackling fire and a soft easy chair when winter is doing her worst and the snow drifts are making a moonscape out of your lawn. So with that in mind, we've selected some our favorite reading appropriate to cruising the Atlantic coast and the ICW. We've also indicated when a book is available digitally, since we know you won't have room for absolutely everything.

We begin with Cruising Along. Here we offer up some of our favorite cruising books, some of them written more than a century ago.

Next we move on to the category we've named Extra Credit. Sometimes you want to know more about the areas you are passing through as you cruise the coast. With that in mind, we've given you a few of the best. There are many, many more.

Speaking of more, in the next category, More Than a Few, we've picked out three series, two of which make boats an integral part of the story. The third series is Cynthia Voigt's remarkable and award-winning Tillerman trilogy for young adults.

Category number four, Just for Fun, is devoted to books that give us information and insight into regional food, general birding and fishing while cruising.

In out last category, Get Serious, we've listed a few essential books that should find a place either on your bookshelf or on one of your electronic devices, whether it's a tablet, phone or computer.

Cruising Along

This first group of books is devoted to cruising itself. A few of these—like Anthony Bailey's lovely meditation on New England cruising, the *Coast of Summer*— are specific to a certain area, but many are ripping tales of journeys down the coast and the waterway to the promised land of unquenchable sunlight. And even those devoted to cruises in specific areas—like R.J. Rubadeau's *Bound for Rocque Island*—cast our whole notion of setting out on the water in a new light.

You'll notice that more than a few of these books were written a century or more ago. But as you read books like George and Robert Barrie's 1901 *Cruises on the Bay of the Chesapeake*, you'll be charmed not only by the differences in the way we cruise then and now, but at the timelessness of it all . . . and the timelessness of the landscape. And they make for exciting reading.

There is probably no single book of cruising the Atlantic Coast and ICW better than *The Boy, Me and the Cat*, written by Henry Plummer in 1912. If you only choose one book out of this lot, make it this one. Or all three. Read it while you're cruising or read it before you go or when you've come back. It doesn't matter. And while you're reading it, pull out a chart or—as British small-boat cruiser Dylan Winter suggests in one of his *Keep Turning Left* videos—open Google Earth and follow along.

Although there are other fine cruising books, most are no longer readily available, so we've made a little list in case you run across them someday on the marina giveaway shelf.

One of the cruising books that is still in print, and was written quite recently, is *Narrow Dog to Indian River*. In this book, a couple in their 70s ships their British canal boat (60' X 6') to Norfolk in order to do the ICW. This they proceed to do, in company of their "narrow dog," a whippet named Jim and as colorful a cast of characters as you'll ever hope to meet. All along the way they are convinced that disaster is lurking just around the corner; if they don't wash out to sea, they will be eaten by alligators, bitten by snakes or shot by desperados. This does not prevent them from having a grand time nonetheless.

Although there is less pure "boating" here than many of other books, it is rewarding on two levels. First, because we feel that if these elderly and uncertain foreigners can make the trip, we can too. And second, because it makes us take an awkward but ultimately satisfying look at ourselves. "We'll get fat," says Monica early on, after seeing the jumbo portions served everywhere in restaurants. "No doubt," Terrence replies, "but what can you do? The North American continent is blessed with the riches of nature and covered thinly with maple syrup."

On the other hand, *Honey, Let's Get a Boat* is full of useful information for doing the Great Loop, which of course takes in the bulk of the Atlantic coast and all of the ICW. And there's adventure here too. In fact, this is the book that inspired hundreds—perhaps thousands—of couples to get a boat of their own and do the same thing.

These days, most of the Loopers and snowbirds who write about their trips do it in blogs. You'll find links to a lot of these on sites such as Active Captain and Seven Seas Cruising Association as well as special-interest sites such as Hunter or Kady Krogen owners groups and the Marine Trawlers Association. Some of these blogs include recipes, others technical and maintenance tips; some are long, some short. Whatever your preferences, you're sure to find one that interests you. Or start your own.

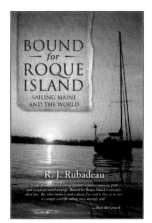

Rubadeau, R.J.

Bound for Roque Island: Sailing Maine and the World
Bascom Hill Publishers 2010

Get it: New and used copies are available through independent booksellers. It is also available for Kindle.

If you read the title and say, "Yes, I love reading about cruising off the coast of Maine," then read no farther. But if you say, "I don't give a fig about Down East cruising," then read on. *Bound for Roque Island* is only the tip of this big iceberg of a book. Beneath the surface, you'll learn more about the gentle art of cruising than you will in a dozen how-to books. And if you learn more about life, too, then consider that a bonus.

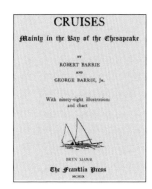

Barrie, George and Robert

Cruises Mainly in the Bay of the Chesapeake
Franklin Press 1909

Get it: There are a few original copies available at $200 or more (depending on edition) from book dealers. Happily the book is out of copyright and has been scanned for reading free online and as an ebook. You'll find the links on the *Chesapeake Bay Magazine* website, *ChesapeakeBoating.net*. Early in the 20th century, brothers Robert and George Barrie brought a succession of boats down from their home in Philadelphia to the Chesapeake Bay to spend a few weeks or month exploring these waters. Their descriptions are a delight, particularly to those who know and love the Bay. The hazards to navigation remain, as do the favorite ports of call, though we no longer need to accost farmers in search of fresh eggs and chickens to keep the larder stocked.

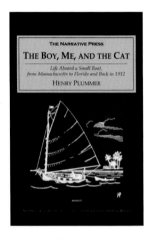

Henry Plummer

The Boy, Me and the Cat

Narrative Press 2003

Get it: Still in print after 100 years and generally available. No electronic edition.

Late in the year 1912, Henry Plummer loaded son Henry Jr. and cat Scotty aboard the 24-foot 6-inch catboat Mascot and, dragging a launch with an inboard motor behind them, left Buzzard's Bay, Mass., for Miami. And therein hangs a tale. What a tale! Thanks in large part to Plummer's idiosyncratic style, it's an adventure that never dims, as evidenced by the fact that unlike most cruising stories it is still in print. Here is Mascot off the coast of North Carolina (they had to go outside periodically since the ICW was now yet entirely connected): "And then came a big comber to which we rose, and crunch-o, the nose of the launch went through our bilge for a 6 in. hole. Up she went again, and bang-o there was another hole. My eye! We would soon be a pepperbox at that rate."

Anthony Bailey

The Coast of Summer

Sheridan House 1999

Get it: Readily available. No electronic edition.

New Yorker writer Bailey and his artist wife take their classic Tartan 27 *Lochinvar* on a slow summer cruise from Stonington, Conn., to Provincetown, Mass. Along the way they meander in and out of harbors, where they anchor, go ashore to explore and then set off for the next stop. Pushed along by Bailey's gentle prose, it's a lovely summer idyll, never dull, but never strident.

Elliott Merrick

Cruising at Last

Lyons Press 2005

Get it: Used and new copies are available. No electronic edition. A book on coastal cruising succeeds or fails on the quality of the writing. And there are few better tellers of that tale than Elliott Merrick. Toward the end of a long and productive career, Merrick and his wife (he in his 60s and she in her 70s) sailed their 20-foot boat from South Carolina to Maine and back three times. This book is the happy compilation of those trips. The prose is impeccable, the delight in the world at sea is unquenchable and the profit to the reader is rich.

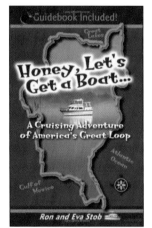

Ron and Eva Stob

Honey, Let's Get a Boat ... A Cruising Adventure of America's Great Loop

Raven Cove Publishing 2010 (revised edition)

Get it: Readily available. No electronic edition. This is the classic book on doing the Great Loop, which includes the ICW and a bit of the Atlantic Coast. Ron and Eva Stob wrote this book after completing the 6,300-mile circle route on their 40-foot trawler. When published in 1999, the book found a wide of audience of dreamers and enthusiasts eager to set off themselves. And many of them did, scheming and planning their own adventure with the help of this book. The Stobs' style is lively, amusing and informative. When they began their trip they had no pretentions as old salts, but they soldiered on ... and had a grand time along the way. *Honey, Let's Get a Boat* continues to serve as part inspiration, part instruction guide for legions of future Loopers.

Sunrise through the palms along the Tampa Bay waterfront in St. Petersburg, Florida.

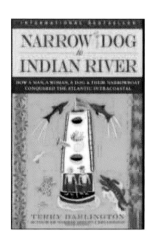

Terry Darlington

Narrow Dog to Indian River

Delta 2009

Get it: Widely available. Kindle edition.

Hot on the heels of a successful trip across the English Channel and into the canals of France to Carcassone with their English narrow boat (60' X 6'), Brits Terry and Monica Darlington turned next to America and the Intracoastal Waterway. They sent their narrow boat by ship and their 6-inch wide whippet (the eponymous Narrow Dog) by plane to Norfolk, Va., and set off down the "ditch," which of course turned out to be far from the straight and narrow passage they were anticipating. Convinced that they would meet their end at any moment from any number of possible threats, from alligators and monitor lizards to crazy banjo-playing locals and wide narrow-boat destroying seas, they proceeded on their way, making friends everywhere and avoiding sweet tea as much as possible.

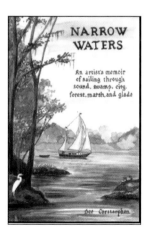

Dee Castarphen

Narrow Waters: An Artist's Memoir of Sailing Through Sound, Swamp, City, Forest, Marsh, and Glade

Pen & Ink Press 1998

Get it: Available in good and very good used condition at reasonable prices. No electronic edition.

Artist and sailor Dee Castarphen of Virginia, has loaded her story of a trip south along the ICW with a treasure trove of drawings and paintings large and small and dozens of lovely hand-drawn charts. Even the text is handmade pen and ink.

Extra Credit

This second category offers a few especially good books about certain areas, usually its history, but sometimes its flora and fauna as well. There are plenty of others, though many of those are hard to find outside their particular geographic area—and even then it can be difficult.

A few of the books on our shortlist—like William Warner's Pullitzer Prize-winning *Beautiful Swimmers*—are classics of their kind and worth reading even if you never make it to the Chesapeake Bay. Others, like the *Log of the Skipper's Wife* (not reviewed here), are unsurpassed in their portrait of a lost time.

Bland Simpson's *Great Dismal* gives a fine portrait of that swamp and its popular route south, while that even the greater swamp, the Everglades, gets its due in two books, Marjorie Stoneman Douglas's groundbreaking *Everglades: River of Grass*, written in 1947, and Michael Grunwald's recent and more accessible *The Swamp*.

But for those few of you that want to make the slog, we highly recommend *The Travels of William Bartram*. Bartram trekked and boated along the coastal waters from North Carolina to North Florida from 1773 to 1777. Along the way, he encountered nearly all of the hazards that so worried the British narrow boat cruisers (see *Narrow Dog to Indian River* in the Cruising Along section) who followed him down the ICW nearly 250 years later. Along the way, Bartram stayed with Native Americans, plantation owners and desperados, all the while he collected plants, made drawings and kept a journal of his trip. The book was wildly popular when it was first published in the 1790s. Now you can read it on your Kindle.

William Bartram

The Travels of William Bartram

Dover Publications 1995

Get It: A new copy of the Dover edition of Bartram's travels is generally available. Available electronically on Nook.

There is nothing else like it in American literature and natural history. This is what academics call source material. From 1773 to 1779 William Bartram traveled—by foot, horse and boat—though the countryside of eastern North Carolina, South Carolina, Georgia and north Florida. Along the way, he collected plants and spent time in the Seminole, Creek, Choctaw and Cherokee villages he came

across along the way. Many of the things he saw will never be seen again, for example, the 45 square miles of forest composed entirely of magnolia and dogwood trees. Here are descriptions of what the land we pass through on today's ICW once looked like. When it was published in 1791, *Bartram's Travels* influenced English poets Wordsworth and Coleridge, and American essayists Emerson and Thoreau.

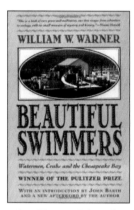

William Warner

Beautiful Swimmers: Watermen, Crabs and the Chesapeake Bay

Back Bay Books, reprint edition 1994

Get it: Readily available.

Warner, a modern-day naturalist, wrote a book of great beauty and scientific precision about the secret life of blue crabs and of the waterman culture that they have engendered. *Beautiful Swimmers* won a Pulitzer Prize for nonfiction the year it was published, 1976. Since then it has stayed in print and firmly entrenched in the hearts of all those who love the Chesapeake and its way of life.

Christopher White

Skipjack: The Story of America's Last Sailing Oystermen

Rowman & Littlefield Publishers 2011

Get it: Widely available. Kindle and Nook, as well.

If William Warner's *Beautiful Swimmers* was a paean to blue crabs and watermen, Christopher White's beautifully written book *Skipjack* is the oyster's reply. White, a science writer and naturalist, signs onto several of the Chesapeake's last oystering skipjacks and uses that platform to try to understand the life of Eastern Shore watermen and the not-quite-lost art of oystering from skipjacks, those beautiful, over-canvased, shallow and quirky icons of the Bay.

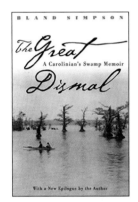

Bland Simpson

The Great Dismal: A Carolinian's Swamp Memoir

Chapel Hill Books 1998

Get it: Available from University of North Carolina press and online sellers such as Amazon. Electronic editions available from UNC, Nook and Kindle.

Bland Simpson, who teaches creative writing at UNC and grew up in North Carolina, combines his own experiences wandering the Dismal Swamp with travel narrative, history, natural history and conversations with people he meets along the way to weave together an enchanting portrait of this mysterious section of the ICW.

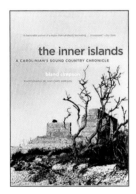

Bland Simpson

The Inner Islands: A Carolinian's Sound Country Chronicle

University of North Carolina Press 2010

Get it: Readily available. Electronically from UNC, Nook and Kindle.

This time Bland Simpson has turned his attention to the islands of North Carolina's sounds. He begins with one that every boater who has followed the Dismal Swamp route has passed, though very few have ever known its name. Machelhe Island sits at the Narrows of Elizabeth City and forms the landing spot for the town's bascule bridge. Its history is much more interesting than that, of course, as Simpson demonstrates in the pages that follow. Each island or island group (like the Currituck) gets a chapter of its own, but in the end you'll learn a great deal more about this fascinating part of the coast than the history of a handful of islands.

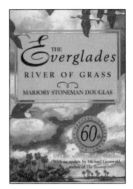

Margory Stoneman Douglas

The Everglades: River of Grass

Pineapple Press, 50th Anniversary Edition 1997

Get it: Available in hardcover and paperback. No electronic edition.

When *The Everglades: River of Grass* was published in 1947 it's effect was immediate. The vast territory south of Lake Okeechobee that up to that point had been considered wasteland, deserving only of draining and developing, was suddenly a place worth conserving. In the years that followed, and up until her death in 1998, Douglas continued to fight to save the swamp. This book, like Rachel Carson's *Silent Spring*, had a remarkable and long-lasting impact.

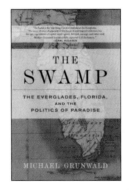

Michael Grunwald

The Swamp: The Everglades, Florida, and the Politics of Paradise

Simon & Schuster, Reprint Edition 2007

Get it: Readily available. Kindle and Nook electronic editions.

In some sense, Grunwald's book is a sequence to Douglas's, but easier to read. Grunwald, a *Washington Post* reporter, has written a well-researched, well-written and engrossing story that links natural history with the social and political history of the Everglades up to current billion-dollar project to restore it.

More Than a Few

Here are two book series, Christine Kling's Seychelle murder mysteries and Robert Macumber's Honor series. We include them simply because—unlike a number of other novels that are set along the coast, notably Nora Roberts Chesapeake series and Randy Wayne Whie's Doc Ford series of Florida novels—these two involve boats and ships as an integral part of the plot.

Because we wanted to include something for children, here too you'll find the Homecoming, Cynthia Voigt's extraordinary trilogy for and about young adults that begins in the Northeast and ends on the Eastern Shore of Maryland. And yes, boating plays an important role.

Christine Kling

Seychelle Series

Tell-Tale Press

Get it: Available in print and on Kindle and Nook.
Kling has written four books in her Seychelle Sullivan series of suspense/murder mysteries. Her protagonist is a tug and salvage captain working out of Fort Lauderdale, Fla.

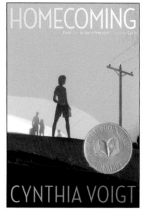

Cynthia Voigt

Tillerman Trilogy: Homecoming, Dicey's Song and Solitary Blue

Atheneum Books for Young Readers, Reprint

Get it: Widely available. Kindle and Nook.
Voigt's Newberry award-winning books tell the story of the Tellerman children, who suddenly find themselves abandoned by their mother and so must find a new home to love and be loved. It is especially the story of the eldest, Dicey, who keeps them going and herself finds a love and appreciation for boats as the children cross the Chesapeake Bay bound for Crisfield, Md.

Robert N. Macumber

Honor Series

Pineapple Press

Get it: Widely available in print. Kindle and Nook in electronic editions.
Historical fiction. Through 11 books, Macumber has taken Peter Wake through the Civil War and into the early 20th century as a member of the U.S. Navy commanding a series of ships in Florida. The books are good reads, both for their history and for their sailing locations.

Just For Fun

Name three hobbies you can pursue cruising. How about cooking, birding and fishing?

There are plenty of cookbooks for cruisers, including John Barber's *One-Pot Wonders, Feasts Afloat* by Jennifer Trainer Thompson and Elizabeth Wheeler, and *The Boat Galley Cookbook* by Carolyn Shearlock—all of which are readily available from the usual sources. But there are few books that involve both cruising and eating. For that reason, we've chosen Ann Vanderhoof's highly entertaining *An Embarrassment of Mangoes*, which involves both cruising and cuisine along the Atlantic Coast and ICW and then the Islands.

On the other hand, the birding books we've chosen—The *Sibley Guide to Birds, Stokes Field Guide to Birds of North America*

and *The Crossley ID Guide: Eastern Birds*—have nothing to do with boats at all. Instead, they are simply three general highly regarded bird books, any of which will certainly enrich your cruising experience by helping you identify at least some of the dozens of species you'll spot while lying at anchor or out cruising.

And then there's fishing. Out of all the world's fishing books, we've selected *The Cruiser's Handbook to Fishing*. Why? Because it's the generally considered the book for this popular pastime, the one specifically aimed at the special conditions encountered by cruisers, whether it's off the deck of your boat, from your dinghy or while reef diving, this is the book that you'll want.

Birdwatching

What better place to watch birds—especially waterfowl, of course—than from your boat. Whether it's underway or at anchor, your boat is the ideal platform for birdwatching. So with that in mind, we've listed a few of the many many available. Since we're not qualified to jump into the debate over the best birding guide, so instead we're offering three—two that are often listed as among the best and a another, new to the market, that has generated a lot of discussion as the most interesting. All three of these books are pretty hefty, which happily doesn't matter when you don't have to lug it any farther than the cockpit, so you may want another, lighter volume for trips afield.

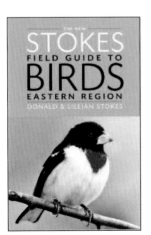

Donald and Lillian Stokes

Stokes Field Guide to Birds of North America

Little, Brown & Co. 2010

Get it: Available widely at booksellers.

Modern bird books generally fall into one of two categories: photographs and drawings. The advantages and disadvantages are fairly apparent. Advocates of photographs argue that these books show birds as they actually look. Advocates of a drawings counter that drawings are better able to show each bird's

identifying characteristics because they can be portrayed in any pose. Donald and Lillian Stokes's *Stokes Field Guide to Birds of North America* is one of the most popular and highly regarded examples of the photo school of bird books. It's well organized, beautifully photographed and full of good information and descriptions. The Stokes also publish a guide to Eastern birds and a beginners guide to birding.

David Allen Sibley

The Sibley Guide to Birds

Knopf 2014 *(Look for Second Printing of the Second Edition, March 2014. The color and print of first printing were badly flawed)*

Get it: Available at most booksellers.

When David Allen Sibley first published *Sibley Guide to Birds* nearly 15 years ago, it quickly became the standard reference book for birding, upending the classic Peterson's Guides with thousands of lively and colorful drawings and expert commentary, all produced by Sibley himself. Even with the advent of numerous guides based on photographs, Sibley's guides remain the favorite of many experts. They are, however, reference books rather than field guides. The second edition, published in 2014, adds hundreds of new drawings and improved taxonomy.

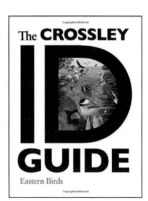

Richard Crossley

The Crossley ID Guide: Eastern Birds

Princeton University Press 2011

Get it: Available at most booksellers. Kindle and Nook.

Now for something almost completely different. In 2011, Richard Crossley came out with the *Crossley ID Guide: Eastern Birds*. While it falls under the photograph category of bird books, it does so in a new way. Crossley has taken many photos of each kind of bird—close up, in the distance, flying, resting, and so forth—and put them together in a montage over a background that represents their natural habitat. The idea is to show the birds as you are likely to see them in the wild.

Whether or not you find it successful, it makes for a very striking book and one that makes you look at birdwatching in a new and exciting way. Many of the criticisms of the book have centered not on the photo montages themselves, but on the text that accompanies them, which some complain is too small to read easily and not always as detailed as one could wish. We haven't tried Crossley yet, but we will. Since we have a hard time making up our minds on anything, both the Sibley and Stokes guides have long been on our cabin bookshelf.

Cruising and Food

Ann Vanderhoof

An Embarrassment of Mangoes

Doubleday Canada 2005; Crown Publishing 2005; Penguin Random House 2004

Get it: Readily available. Kindle and Nook.

Okay, we're going to say it: This book is a delicious read! Canadian Vanderhoof and her husband Steve leave the workday world behind for a two-year trip down the coast and across to the islands getting as far as the Leewards. Along the way, they make a leisurely exploration of the local food and culture. Here you'll find recipes for some iconic dishes, including Chesapeake Bay Crabcakes and Low Country Shrimp and Grits, before they jump off to the islands. And sure, those recipes are good too.

Fishing

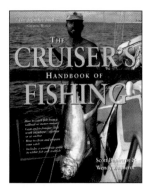

Scott Bannerot

The Cruiser's Handbook of Fishing

International Marine/Ragged Mountain Press 2003)

Get it: Readily available. Kindle. While this book covers the oceans of the world, it is generally considered as the essential guide for cruising boaters who also want to fish as they cruise. Bannerot takes you through everything from choosing the right tackle to rigging and preparing the line as well as how to read the water and currents. Finally he also explains how to prepare what you catch.

Get Serious: A Few Reference Books

We've spent a considerable amount of time and space talking about some of the many excellent books that will make your cruise more memorable. But now we come to the essentials. It's time to get serious.

If you look down the page, you'll notice that the list is short. How come? The advancement of electronic resources for boaters has made print reference books considerably less important that in the past. Take tides and currents, for example. Where once we would have put a publication such as *Eldridge Tide & Piloting Book* near the top of the list, now we only mention it in passing, in the event that you do not have current tide tables in any other form. But since they are so readily and inexpensively available as smartphone and tablet apps (see Chapter 4), it seems now all but unnecessarily. Nevertheless you'll find *Eldridge* below.

So what reference books should you carry aboard? Charts and guide books are of course essential, and we've discussed them elsewhere (Chapters 1 and 2). Light lists and rules to navigation are also important, and these too we've touched on in discussions of government publications such as Coast Pilots and the Light List (Chapter 3) and in the apps section (Chapter 4). We've given you two other publications that many consider essential to a happy trip.

The first is *Chapman Piloting & Seamanship*, which will teach you everything from the rudiments of sailing to which flag to fly for any different occasion. You'll also find good information on heavy weather boating, rules of the road, how to make a storm anchor and the etiquette for opening a bridge. In other words, if it's about boating, chances are very good it'll be found in *Chapman*. But since it's something you might go a long time without consulting, you might be wise to get it in an electronic version.

You could argue that as well for our second big book recommendation, Nigel Calder's *Boatowners Mechanical and Electrical Manual*, often simply referred to at Calder's. If it's on your boat, this book will more than likely tell you how it works and how to maintain and fix it. It too is a heavy book that is now available in electronic form.

One of the most important things you can do is to carry manuals for every system on your boat. You can now get many of these online, so download them and keep them in a designated folder on your computer so you can access them anywhere and any time.

The final category of serious books is for medical emergencies. We gave a couple of suggestions in the chapter on apps, but we also recommend having one or more of these books in print form. If you are in the middle of a storm and someone gets injured, you are not going to want to open up your phone or tablet to look at the diagrams or symptoms. We are not recommending these three to the exclusion of all others, though they are all well reviewed. But we are recommending that you have a good book on first aid aboard and that you have read through to understand its organization. And it goes without saying that you should include a first-aid course in your preparation.

The rest of the serious book portion of your bookshelf is up to you. Consider some books on anchoring, weather forecasting, and engine mechanics as well

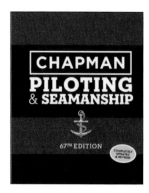

John Eaton

Chapman Piloting & Seamanship

Hearst, 67th Edition 2013

Get it: Available at widely, including from most nautical booksellers. Electronically for Nook and from iTunes. Many West Marine stores and many chandleries.

Pound for pound, the per-page cost of the 6-pound, 920-page "bible" of yachting is without a doubt a good deal. However, it's a lot of book to carry in the limited space generally allotted to books aboard. *Happily, Chapman Piloting & Seamanship,* 67th edition is also available in an electronic version, so that on those rare but important occasions when nothing else will do, you can open it up on your smart phone or tablet. It is available that way from iTunes and from Barnes & Noble (Nook). Interestingly enough, not in Kindle form.

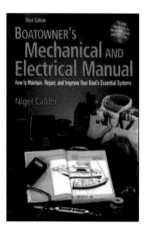

Nigel Calder

Boatowners Mechanical and Electrical Manual

International Marine/Ragged Mountain Press, 4th Edition 2015

Get it: Widely available. Electronic editions for Kindle and Nook.

If Chapman's is the "bible" for general boating, then Calder's *Boatowners Mechanical and Electrical Manual* is the "bible" for general marine systems. And at 960 pages and nearly 5 pounds it is nearly as big. It is also available in electronic form. But if you are going to choose one heavy weight boating book to keep onboard, this is arguably the one. *Practical Sailor* says of it, "If you had to choose a single book to help you assess and maintain your boat gear, this would be it." And if you have diesels, we also recommend Calder's *Marine Diesel Engines*, Hearst 2003.

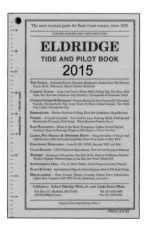

Robert E. White Jr. and Linda White

Eldridge Tide and Pilot Book 2015

Eldridge Tide and Pilot, 2015
(You'll need to buy a new edition each year)

Get it: Marine booksellers and most West Marine stores, as well as other chandleries.

Eldridge has been providing tide tables from Halifax to Key West since 1875. The book includes lights and lighthouses, marine rules, a weather almanac, rules for flying marine flags, illustrations showing currents and charts, and navigation rules. In short, for less than $15 you can have a wealth of information at your fingertips, all in one slim volume. Just don't lose your reading glasses, because there is no large-print edition.

Douglas Justin and Colin Berry

First Aid at Sea

Paradise Cay Publications, 4th Edition 2010
Get it: Widely available

Peter F. Eastman and John M. Levinson

Advanced First Aid Afloat

Cornell Maritime Press, 5th Edition 2009
Get it: Widely available

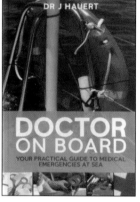

Jurgen Hauert

Doctor on Board

Sheridan House 2010
Get it: Widely available

Here are three good basic first aid books directed at cruising boaters. Since this book is directed at inland and coastal cruisers rather than bluewater cruisers, these will do the job. All come with plenty of clear, simple explanations and good illustrations. Which one you choose is up to you. Although we mentioned a couple of first aid apps for smartphones and tablet in Chapter 4, we also recommend that at least one of these (or similar) print books deserve a place on your bookshelf . . . or better yet, with your first aid kit.

Easing the Trip
Tips, Tricks & Strategies

A northbound trawler slices through the morning stillness on the South Amelia River south of Fernandina Beach.

How to Use the Marine Radio

Most cruisers will already know how to use the boat's VHF marine radio, but here are a few extra tips.

Keep the radio on Channel 16 and keep the volume up high enough to hear it from the helm. On certain stretches of the ICW, cruisers stay in touch by radio, offering alerts to those behind for hazards in the water, offering advice on getting through the shoal areas. Cruisers also use Channel 16 when they want to pass (see *The Art of the Slow Pass*) and when there is a question of which side to take when crossing. Channel 16 is also used sometimes to contact commercial vessels, especially tugs, to confirm their actions.

If there is a lot of commercial traffic in the area, or you have no luck contacting them on Channel 16, switch to Channel 13, the commercial traffic channel. You'll probably have better luck.

Of course, Channel 16 is for contact and emergencies only. So choose a working channel to continue your conversation.

If your radio is down below, keep a handheld up at the helm, so you don't have to dive down to get the radio every time someone calls. You'll also need it to communicate with locks and bridges.

How to Negotiate Bridges

Controlling Heights

Bridges come in two general categories: opening and fixed. The ICW has plenty of both. Your ability to negotiate the ICW at all is determined principally by the height of your mast. The controlling height for fixed bridges on the Norfolk to Key West portion of the ICW is 65 feet, except one in Miami, which is easy to go out and around. So if your mast is taller than that, you'll need to go offshore most of the way. There are in fact a few 64-foot high bridges, but you can generally play the tides to get enough clearance since the measurement is taken at high tide.

The controlling height for the Fort Myers to Anclote section is 55 feet, while the Okeechobee Waterway is limited by the 49-foot-high Mayaca Railroad Lift Bridge. The St. Marks to Brownsville ICW is 50 feet. "Controlling," by the way, means the lowest height—or shallowest depth—on that route.

Fixed Bridges

Passing under fixed bridges is pretty straight forward. Simply look for the small light hanging down from the superstructure. This indicates which span to use—it's usually but not always at the center.

There are two caveats that apply to both fixed and opening bridges. First, be aware that the current can be strong just before, during and after a bridge as the water funnels through the opening. Second, the boat running with the current has priority over a boat running against the current. Those boats should be permitted to come through the bridge first because they have less control than those pushing against the flow. Check the current tables (see Choosing the Right Apps) before you arrive or simply observe the flow of water around navigation markers as you near the bridge.

Near Fort Myers, beachcombers and the Cape Coral Bridge.

Dawn along the Okeechobee Canal at the Hwy 98 fixed bridge, just east of the Mayaca Lock.

Busy Norfolk, with Gilmerton Lift Bridge, Norfolk South 7 Bascule Bridge and the fixed High Rise Bridge beyond.

Opening Bridges

Opening bridges come in several varieties: single bascule (one span that pivots up), double bascule (two sections that open from the middle to pivot up), swing and lift, (which act pretty much the way they sound). Swing and bascule bridges have an unlimited height when opened, while lift bridges are limited by the height of their towers. Swing bridges are usually the slowest opening and generally will not open in winds over 25 or 35 mph.

It is wise to look ahead at the day's bridge schedules so that you don't have to wait around 50 minutes or so for a bridge that opens only once an hour. Or for one that is closed two hours during morning or afternoon rush hour. (The bridge schedules are all given by state in the Reference of this book, along with a photo, chart segment and description.)

But the most important thing to know is that you will need to call each and every opening bridge to request an opening. Call even if you are the fourth boat in line. It avoids confusion or having the bridge close before you get there.

And call on the right channel. In Virginia and Maryland, bridges monitor Channel 13. Elsewhere they monitor Channel 9.

Here's a sample call:

"Gilmerton Bridge, this is the southbound sailing catamaran Moment of Zen out of Annapolis. We'd like to come through on your next opening."

The important elements here are: Give the exact name of the bridge (in some places, half a dozen other bridges will be monitoring the same conversation). Give your direction of travel and a brief description of your vessel type, both so the tender can identify which vessel is calling. Some bridge tenders will want to know the name and hailing port of your vessel, so you can give that right away or wait to be asked. Finally, specify when you want to come through. If the bridge opens on request, make that request. If it opens at a certain time, repeat the time to confirm that you have the right schedule.

How to Transit a Lock

If you are traveling down the ICW to Miami or the islands, you will have only one or two locks to contend with, depending on whether you choose the Dismal Swamp Canal (two locks) or Albemarle & Chesapeake Canal (one lock) route. There are locks too along the Okeechobee Waterway, if you choose to that route. But all of the locks operate pretty much the same from the boater's point of view. The major difference is that on the first set, you provide your own lines, and on the Okeechobee you use theirs. All of these locks use Channel 13.

Let's walk through transiting the first Dismal Swamp Lock.

You switch the radio to Channel 13 and say, "Deep Creek Lock, this is the southbound catamaran *Moment of Zen*. We'd like to lock through on your 11 a.m. opening." (You'll find all the lock schedules in Park Four with the bridges).

The lock tender will reply: "*Moment of Zen*, wait for the green light and then enter the lock. You'll be taking the starboard side. (Sometimes you have your choice of side.) Have your fenders out and a long bow and stern dockline ready."

On the green, you pull into the lock and follow the lock tender's directions. Once you're in, he (his name is Robert, by the way) will reach down with a boat hook and ask you to place the middle of the line on the hook, but hold on to the end not already attached to your cleat. This the lock tender will loop over a bollard at the top of the lock bulkhead.

Then as the water in the lock rises, you'll pull in the line to keep the boat from drifting out into the lock. When the lock is filled, the lock tender will have you pull your line off the bollard and proceed out of the chamber. He will get into his pickup truck and drive down to open the bridge just beyond. (This is the one time you won't have to request an opening.)

Welcome to the Dismal Swamp Canal.

1. Lux *enters the Deep Creek Lock on the Dismal Canal on the green light.*

2. *Locktender reaches down with a boathook to take the line.*

3. Lux's *crew tends the bow and stern lines as the boat rises in the lock.*

4. *At the top of the rise, the locktender gives the order to release the lines.*

Southbound traffic bunches up with boats of all description just beyond the Hobucken Bridge north of Beaufort, North Carolina.

Master the Art of the Slow Pass

The ICW in October and November is a very busy place, with boats of every size, description and speed all headed the same direction: south. For slower boats like sailboats and trawlers, the ICW in high season can also be a very bumpy and uncomfortable place, as bigger, faster boats pass them by, leaving behind a mountainous and potentially dangerous wake.

Enter the art of the slow pass, a particular form of courtesy virtually unknown outside the ICW—more particularly the ICW from Norfolk to about Stuart, where most of the fall waterway traffic that time of year is snowbirds moving south. It's a boon for everyone, but most particularly for boats getting passed.

Here's how it works.

"*Moment of Zen*, this is the sportfish *Gladiator* coming up on your stern. If you slow down, I'll give you a slow pass."

"Thanks, *Gladiator*, I'm pulling back now."

Moment of Zen then throttles back nearly to idle . . . or to the slowest speed that maintains control. This allows *Gladiator* to slow down as well, keeping the wake to a minimum but able to pass in a reasonably short amount of time. *Gladiator* and *Moment of Zen* can then quickly resume their respective speeds. The wake is minimal, *Gladiator* has done a good deed and everyone is happy. That's all there is to it.

The request for a slow pass can also come from *Moment of Zen*, who is keeping a good watch behind as well as in front and sees *Gladiator* coming up quickly.

Read the Land to Find Deep Water

Much of the ICW's network of cuts, creeks and inlets is subject to frequent shoaling. Learn to watch the contour of the land to understand how the current scours out channels and builds up sand. If you don't know the water, try the outside of curves first for the best depths. Conversely, stay away from points of land and the inside of curves. That's where sand gets deposited as the faster water runs the long way around. There are exceptions to this rule, but 90 percent of the time, it works.

Use this method too, when entering and exiting manmade cuts and canals between two larger bodies of water. Square off your turns in both directions, giving the edges of both sides a wide berth. Go all the way out to the next channel before making your turn. Don't cut the corners and you'll save yourself a lot of grief.

An early riser motors into the dawn on Delegal Creek near Hell Gate, Georgia.

Tips Before You Leave

Quarters and $5s

Go to the bank before you leave and get rolls of quarters for feeding the washers and dryers along the way. Cost ranges from free to $2 a load. Get a packet of $5 bills while you're there. That way you'll always have change for tips.

Spares

You'll probably need to change the oil at least once during the trip. Buy the right oil filters and oil before you go, even if you have someone else do it. You won't have to wait for parts. Carry spare fuel filters, belts and impellers as well. Those are the basics. The rest is up to you.

Towing Insurance

The best money you will spend on the whole trip will be comprehensive towing insurance from either Tow Boat US or Sea Tow. And keep the number posted near the radio, or download their free app for immediate response. Join Boat U.S. too. Many marinas offer a modest discount for members.

Dock Lines

Keep plenty of good long docklines. Don't skimp on the quality or the diameter or length. Then keep them handy.

Fenderboard

Put together a fenderboard to use when riding against pilings, especially in high tide and high current tide areas. You'll find instructions for a nifty one using two fenders and a PVC pipe at *ChesapeakeBoating.net* or other versions of fenderboards using wood and fenders online.

Warm Weather Clothes

It's going to be cold before it gets warm. It's not all shorts and flipflops. Bring some warm clothes, and don't forget the watch cap, warm socks and fleece gloves.

Be Prepared!

Get an MMSI number for your radio so when you press that red button, the Coast Guard will know a lot about your boat right away. It's free on the BoatU.S. website.

Discuss what you will do if the engine quits or you lose steering. Do you know where the emergency tiller is located?

Be prepared to drop the anchor at once; that will give you time to decide what to do next.

Fly swatter and bug repellent

You'll use it.

At top, Bindi dresses for the cold weather on a fall trip down the ICW. Above, a trawler and a tug and tow follow the same course.

Putting it all Together

It's time to see how we can put all of the information in this book together to make cruise planning easier. At the beginning of this book, we promised you a lot of information to make the task easier, both before the start of the cruise and then day-to-day along the way. To do that we've reviewed the best cruise guides, apps and charts available. We've shown you how to get a lot of good free government information, from U.S. Army Corps of Engineers soundings to real-time wind and water reports. Then we've given you all the information you'll need on bridges—heights, schedules, charts and photos— from the time you enter the Chesapeake & Delaware Canal to the time you reach Fort Myers at the western end of the Okeechobee Waterway or the Florida Keys, depending on your destination. And we've given you a comprehensive list of the facilities within easy reach of the main Atlantic Coast and ICW route from Maine to Florida.

Finally, we have provided a variety of maps for planning and reference. Distance maps, NOAA weather radio maps and bridge locator maps. We think that pretty much covers everything except what to pack in your suitcase, and we're going to leave that up to you.

By now, you should have a good idea which guides, charts and apps will best suit your purposes. Which brings us to the subject of part three. Putting it all together. To do that we're first going to talk about how to plan a cruise and then we're going to reintroduce the five couples and friends we met in the introduction. The ones with all the questions, probably very much like yours. And we'll see how they are putting all this information together by following each on a day's run.

First, though, let's begin with the basics of cruise planning.

How to plan a cruise

The best advice you'll ever get when planning your cruise is: STAY FLEXIBLE. This applies equally to planning a daily route or a month-long cruise. Never tie yourself a rigid schedule. Never let yourself get put into the position where you MUST go. There, we've said it three different times. We can't say it enough.

There are a lot of factors that can play havoc with your well-laid plans. Mechanical trouble is an obvious one. And so is the simple desire to stay an extra day or two to visit an enchanting spot you've just discovered. Or perhaps you just need a break from the daily pressure of putting another fifty or a hundred miles behind you. Time to do the laundry or a bit of shopping. All of these are good reasons for altering the plan.

But the single biggest factor that will play havoc with your plan is the weather. Although a lot of the ICW section of the trip is in protected waters, there is also a sizable amount of it that entails crossing large bodies of water. In North Carolina,

for example, there are the sounds to be crossed, like Albemarle and Pamlico, as well as some good-sized rivers like the Cape Fear and the Neuse. All of these are very much subject to the wind and waves. Farther down the coast, in South Carolina and Georgia, you'll be following the ICW channel out a few of the sounds so near to the ocean that you'll be able to hear the waves breaking along the shore. These are not crossings to be made in rough weather. So here is the next piece of advice: Look ahead each day to see what rivers and sounds you'll be traveling so you can weigh that against the day's forecast.

In fact, although you will probably want to lay out a rough plan for the entire trip, you will find that it's your daily plan, or even your two- or three-day plan, that is much more important. By all means, look at the route well ahead of time to choose places you particularly want to visit. It's even a good idea to have a few places picked out where you'll have easy access to a grocery store. (You can use both the facility listings and Active Captain to help with this.) And be sure plan far enough ahead to be sure you'll have access to fuel and a pump out. (Same two resources here too.)

A pristine sand beach and a stand of mangroves. This could only be one of the remote Ten Thousand Islands along Florida's Gulf Coast south of Marco Island.

Calculating your daily run

Now let's get down to brass tacks. First, let's look at how to calculate the number of miles a day you'll want to cover. Take your boat's cruising speed, then factor in how many hours a day you want to be on the water. Look at our five "case studies" later in this section, and you'll notice that each of them has different expectations for the trip. Some are in a big hurry, while others want to take their time and savor the cruise. Some want to leave at first light and stop early in the afternoon so they can relax and spend some time exploring each new port—or doing a little fishing at the anchorage. Some want to go from dawn to dusk and then get up and do the same thing the next day and the next until they get to their destination. Pick out the case that best fits your vessel type and cruising preferences and see how they have put together their plans.

No matter what your preferences, however, your plan will also be influenced by more than just the boat speed. Of course, a power cruiser is going to get farther faster most of the time than a heavy displacement bluewater sailboat. Some vessels are going to be more influenced by the current, which can run several knots in a few areas. Then too, some boats are going to be restricted by their draft and their vertical clearance. There are also plenty of shoal areas and opening bridges along the way, and all of these need to be taken into account. If your boat draws more than 5 feet (or as little as 4 feet in a couple of extreme areas), you'll need to plan your trip so that you cross the worst of the shallow areas at mid- to high tide. And if a bridge only opens once an hour, there is no use racing along only to have to spin in slow circles for 45 minutes while you wait for the next opening. All of this means looking ahead, both long term and short term.

So when planning each day's run, consider your boat's speed, the height and number of the bridges, any shoal areas you'll encounter and how many hours you want to be on the water.

If you are leaving from the Northeast, you won't have to consider bridges or shoal areas in your plan until you reach Norfolk and the ICW. And when you reach southern Florida, you may want to consider some hops outside to avoid the staggering number of opening bridges between Palm Beach and Miami. Happily, that part of Florida has some deep wide inlets that make going in and out easy. Assuming that the weather is good, of course.

So by now you've determined your speed and number of hours a day you want to cruise and arrived at a very general sense of how many miles a day you'll be doing. Now you can look up the distances between ports in any number of ways. You can flip to the distance charts at the opening of each section in the Reference section of this book. Or you can download the government's Distances between Ports and use their tables. You can use the distance function on one of your navigation apps to measure between locations. Or you can use a paper chart and a pair of dividers. Once you get down to the ICW with your planning, the simplest way is to look at the mile marker and then add the number of miles you think you'll be cruising each day. Then check our facilities list to find the nearest marina that suits you, or consult the cruise guide you've chosen for the nearby anchorages.

If you are doing your long distance plan, you don't have to go much farther, because frankly after the first few days, you'll probably be so far one way or the other of that point that you'll be looking elsewhere for marinas or anchorages anyway. But even knowing that it's not likely to work out the way you have it planned, the exercise of leap-frogging down the coast in this fashion, you'll get a good general sense of when you'll be where. This will give you the chance to plug in a few extra days every so often for that rest/laundry/shopping/day off/WEATHER we talked about. And to make reservations if you are planning to visit a popular cruising destination like Charleston, S.C., or New Smyrna Beach, Fla.

It all comes down to today ... and maybe tomorrow

Once you get started, though, you'll be shifting the burden of your planning to a day or two at a time. This is the most important planning you'll do, and it's a good idea to begin it the day before, after you've tied up or dropped anchor for the night. That's when you want to take a good look at the next day's route to consider the tides, currents, bridges, shoals and whether you will be crossing any wide bodies of water. And remember that one of the crowd-sourced resources like Active Captain or Cruisersnet.net is the best way to check for the latest information on trouble spots or changes in bridge schedules.

And of course you'll want to take a good look at the weather forecast, not only for the next day, but for a few days beyond that. If small craft warnings are going to be posted in the next day or two, you will need to be sure you'll be traveling in protected waters all that day or you'll need to locate a good protected place to stop while you wait a day or two for the wind and waves to subside. This is also a good time to plan your next fuel stop. This is especially true in a few areas of the ICW, notably in Georgia, where marinas and fuel stops are few and far between.

This is also a good time to pull out those cruise guides or extra credit reading material in Chapter 6 in the Resources section to learn about the area you'll be traveling through in the day to come. This reading may also suggest some places just off your route, where you can stop to visit. A side trip to somewhere like Cumberland Island will greatly enrich your trip.

While you are planning your next day's run, always locate three destinations. First, a short run, in case time, tide and/or weather hold you back. Second, determine the run you would reasonably expect to make. And finally, plan a long run, in case everything is working to push you along farther than you might expect. Now find a set of three good anchorages or suitable marinas, or some mix, near all three of these spots. Just have something definite in mind for all three distances. If you are aiming for a marina, you may want to call them in the morning to be sure you'll have a spot when you arrive. Later, if you see you're not going to make it, be sure to call the marina to cancel. They'll understand and appreciate your courtesy.

Once you are underway, look ahead to see what bridge schedules you'll need to meet and check for upcoming hazards or shoal areas you located the day before. Be sure to jot down anything new or unexpected you come across, so that when you make the trip again you'll have it noted. We generally do this by writing directly in the mile-by-mile guide we keep open in the cockpit and in our daily log book. If it's a specific hazard, we place a mark and a note directly into your charting program. In any case, note the mile marker or nearest aid to navigation (or latitude and longitude) and the stage of the tide. If it's a dangerous unmarked hazard in the channel, contact the Coast Guard by VHF radio so they can broadcast it for others.

Finally, as you go through the day, don't forget to check the latest weather forecast from time to time, both on NOAA weather radio (check our maps in the Reference section for the right station) and general weather sites such as Weather Underground and Weather.com. And if storms are threatening, keep an eye on your radar app.

It's all good

And now you can relax and enjoy the trip. Really. After a few days, everything we've discussed will become routine. As long as you keep looking ahead at the route, the weather and your fuel gauge, you'll be fine. Then you can enjoy what you came for—being out on the water, watching the dolphins play around your boat, while ospreys and herons hunt in the sky and along the shore. Marvel at the marsh grass that seems to stretch into infinity in every direction. Thrill to the mystery of the Waccamaw River. Buy fresh oysters off the dock at McClellanville. Eat ghost shrimp overlooking the Kilkenny River. Be dazzled by the clear blue water of the Keys. Watch for alligators waiting with infinite patience along the shores of the Okeechobee Waterway near Indiantown. It's all there. It's all good. And it's all yours!

A quiet cruise in late fall on Spa Creek off the Severn River in Annapolis, Maryland.

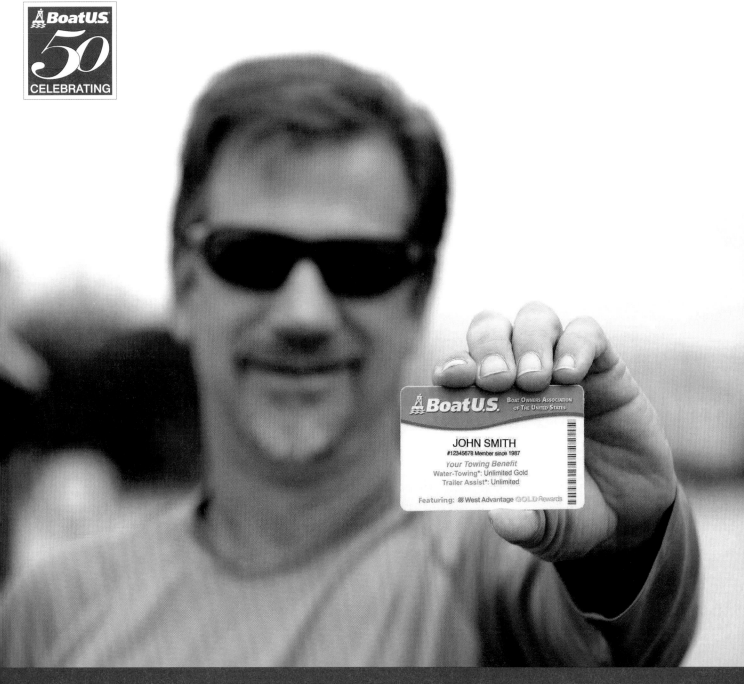

THIS CARD COMES WITH DISCOUNTS

BoatU.S. Membership is your key to discounts at 1,000+ boating and fishing businesses nationwide. Join today to receive a personalized card for savings and 25+ benefits at **BoatUS.com** or by calling **800-395-2628**. Just look for the buoy – it's a sure sign of savings.

BoatU.S. MEMBERS SAVE MONEY ON:

- ▶ Fuel
- ▶ Transient Slips
- ▶ Repairs
- ▶ Storage
- ▶ Fishing Charters
- ▶ and More!

BoatU.S.® MAKES BOATING BETTER – Insurance • Towing • Membership

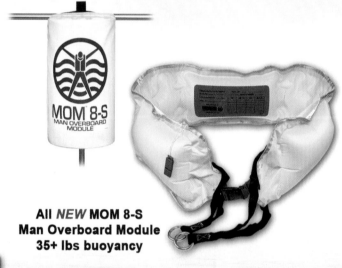

The big and the really big at the Palm Beach Yacht Show.

Reference

We come now to our unique Reference section. Here you will find a lot of the information you'll need to make your coastal cruise a breeze

Here's how it's organized:

First, everything in this section is divided by state, from Maine to Georgia. Florida—with its long coastine, dozens and dozens of bridges and hundreds of facilities—is subdivded into four parts. These are: Florida North; Florida Southeast; Florida Keys; and Florida Southeast Gulf. Also note that the Chesapeake & Delaware Canal is included in Delaware, because that's where it begins, and the Dismal Swamp and Albemarle & Chesapake canals are included in Virginia, because that's where *they* begin.

At the beginning of each state section (or subsection, in the case of Florida), there is an opening page with two mapss. The larger map has the location and ICW mile number, where applicable, of all the bridges in that state, indicating whether they are open-

ing or fixed. This map also includes the state's major cruising destinations with their ICW mile number, as well as the location and mile number of the major inlets along the ICW.

On the smaller map, you'll find the location of all the NOAA weather radio stations and their coverage area, as well as their WX channel number. This will allow you to tune into the station covering the area you need as you travel north or south

Following the map page, you'll find a complete listing for every bridge along the inside cruising route, beginning with the Chesapeake & Delaware Canal and ending on Gulf Coast at Anclote Key near Tarpon Springs. For each bridge, you'll find a photo, a chart segment and information, such as height and opening schedule. You'll also find warning and issues, where applicable.

Following the bridge listings you'll find a comprehensive listing of facilities, marinas and fuel docks for that state, located within an easy cruise of the ICW.

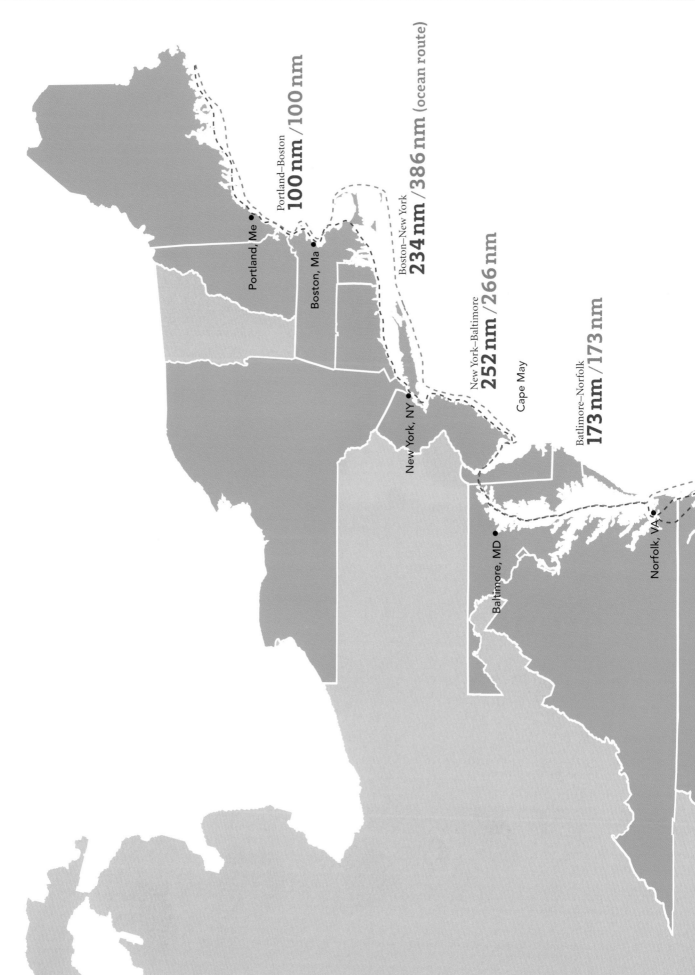

Portland–Boston **100 nm / 100 nm**

Boston–New York **234 nm / 386 nm** (ocean route)

New York–Baltimore **252 nm / 266 nm**

Baltimore–Norfolk **173 nm / 173 nm**

Portland, Me

Boston, Ma

New York, NY

Cape May

Baltimore, MD

Norfolk, VA

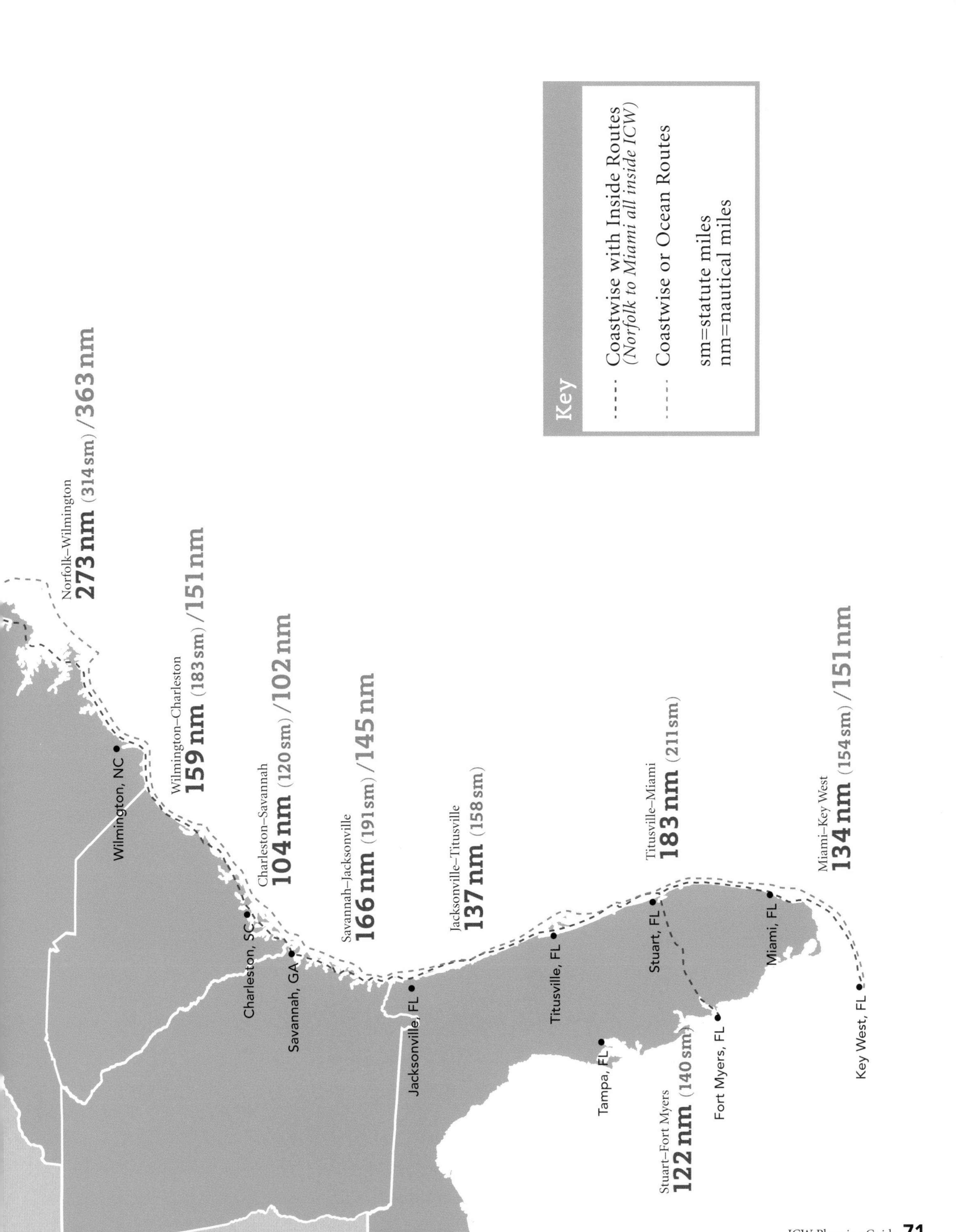

Key

------- Coastwise with Inside Routes
(Norfolk to Miami all inside ICW)

------- Coastwise or Ocean Routes

sm=statute miles
nm=nautical miles

Norfolk–Wilmington
273 nm (314 sm) / **363 nm**

Wilmington–Charleston
159 nm (183 sm) / **151 nm**

Charleston–Savannah
104 nm (120 sm) / **102 nm**

Savannah–Jacksonville
166 nm (191 sm) / **145 nm**

Jacksonville–Titusville
137 nm (158 sm)

Titusville–Miami
183 nm (211 sm)

Miami–Key West
134 nm (154 sm) / **151 nm**

Stuart–Fort Myers
122 nm (140 sm)

Wilmington, NC

Charleston, SC

Savannah, GA

Jacksonville, FL

Titusville, FL

Stuart, FL

Miami, FL

Tampa, FL

Fort Myers, FL

Key West, FL

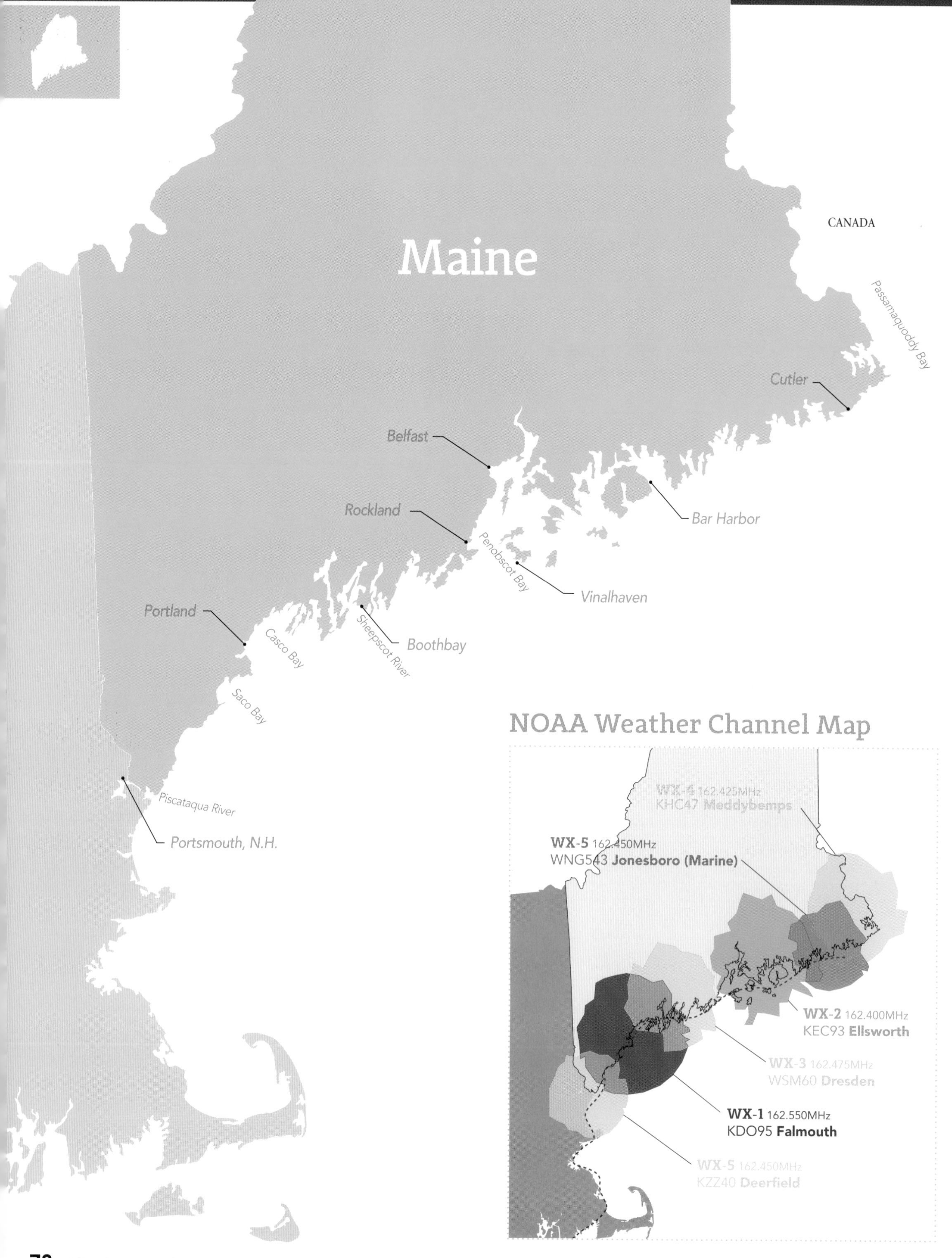

Maine

CANADA

Passamaquoddy Bay

Cutler

Belfast

Bar Harbor

Rockland

Penobscot Bay

Vinalhaven

Portland

Casco Bay

Sheepscot River

Boothbay

Saco Bay

Piscataqua River

Portsmouth, N.H.

NOAA Weather Channel Map

WX-4 162.425MHz
KHC47 **Meddybemps**

WX-5 162.450MHz
WNG543 **Jonesboro (Marine)**

WX-2 162.400MHz
KEC93 **Ellsworth**

WX-3 162.475MHz
WSM60 **Dresden**

WX-1 162.550MHz
KDO95 **Falmouth**

WX-5 162.450MHz
KZZ40 **Deerfield**

Maine

	MLW	Transient Slips/Moorings	Floating docks	Gas	Diesel	Pumpout	Showers	Pool	Laundry	Wi-Fi	Haulout	Repairs	Other
Hinckley Yacht Service Southwest Harbor 207-244-5531 www.hinckleyyachts.com	12'			•	•	•	•		•		•	•	moorings; full-service yard; ship's store
Dysart's Great Harbor Marina Southwest Harbor 207-244-0117 www.dysartsmarina.com	12'	•	•	>	•	•	•		•	•	>	•	Acadia National Park
Morse Cove Marine Penobscot River 207-326-4800 www.morsecovemarine.com	5'					•					•	•	full-service boatyard and brokerage
Winterport Marine & Boatyard Penobscot River 207-223-8885 www.winterportmarine.com	12'	•	•	•	•	•	•		•		•	•	
Lyman Morse at Wayfarer Marine Penobscot Bay 207-236-4378 www.wayfarermarine.com	10'	•		•	•	•			•	•	•	•	moorings; courtesy car, launch services
Knight Marine Service Penobscot Bay 207-594-4068 www.knightmarineservice.com	10'	•	•	•	•	•			•		•	•	full-service boatyard/marina
Gamage Shipyard Damariscotta River 207-644-8181 www.gamageshipyard.com	8'	•	•	•	•						•	•	ship's store, ice, boom truck, heated storage
Ocean Point Marina Damariscotta River 207-633-0773 www.oceanpointmarina.com	20'	•	•	•	•	•			•	•	•	•	
Brown's Wharf Marina Boothbay Harbor 207-633-5440 www.brownswharfinn.com/	20'	•	•	>	>	•	•		•	•	>	>	
Robinhood Marine Center Sheepscot River 207-371-2343 www.robinhoodmarinecenter.com	10'	•	•	•	•	•			•		•	•	Yanmar, Westerbeke, Raymarine; Moorings
Sebasco Harbor Resort Casco Bay 877-389-1161 www.sebasco.com	6.5'	•	•	•	>	•	•	•	•	•			Moorings only
Brewer South Freeport Marine Harraseeket River 207-865-3181 www.byy.com	11'	•	•	•	•	•	•		•	•	•	•	Beautiful customer lounge; Factory-trained technicians.
Spring Point Marina Portland Harbor/Casco Bay 207-767-3254 www.portharbormarine.com	7'	•	•	•	•	•			•	•	•	•	
Portland Yacht Services Casco Bay/Entrance to Portland Hrbr 207-774-1067 www.portlandyacht.com	13'	•		>	>	•	•		•		•	•	moorings
Dolphin Marina and Restaurant Casco Bay/Potts Harbor 207-833-5343 www.dolphinmarinaandrestaurant.com	15'	•	•	•	•	•	•		•		•	•	On-site restaurant, beach
Maine Yacht Center Casco Bay 207-842-9000 www.maineyacht.com	12'	•	•	•	•	•	•		•	•	•	•	
DiMillo's Old Port Marina Fore River/Casco Bay 207-773-7632 www.dimillos.com	25'	•	•	•	•	•	•		•	•		•	In heart of Old Port, restaurants, groceries, attractions nearby
South Port Marine Portland Harbor 207-799-8191 www.southportmarine.com	8'	•	•	•	•	•	•		•	•	•	•	chandlery/store; restaurant on-site
Chicks Marina Kennebunk River 207-967-2782 www.chicksmarina.com	6'	•		•	•	>	•		•		•	>	Moorings
Kittery Point Yacht Yard Piscataqua River 207-439-9582 www.kpyy.net	6'	•	•			•					•	•	Moorings; maintenance, service yard,

New
Hampshire

Portland, Me.

Portsmouth

Piscataqua River

Hampton Harbor Inlet

Rockport, Mass.

NOAA Weather Channel Map

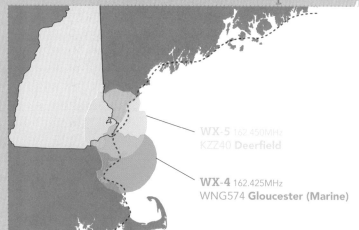

WX-5 162.450MHz
KZZ40 **Deerfield**

WX-4 162.425MHz
WNG574 **Gloucester (Marine)**

New Hampshire

	MLW	Transient Slips/Moorings	Floating docks	Gas	Diesel	Pumpout	Showers	Pool	Laundry	Wi-Fi	Haulout	Repairs	Other
Wentworth By the Sea Marina Little Harbor/New Castle Island 603-433-5050 www.wentworthmarina.com	9'	•	•	•	•	•	•	•	•	•			moorings; courtesy car, launch, tennis, concierge, restaurants
Great Bay Marine Piscataqua River 603-436-5299 www.greatbaymarine.com	6'	•	•	•	•	•		•	•	•	•	Over 40,000 sf of inside storage space; restaurant; boat ramp

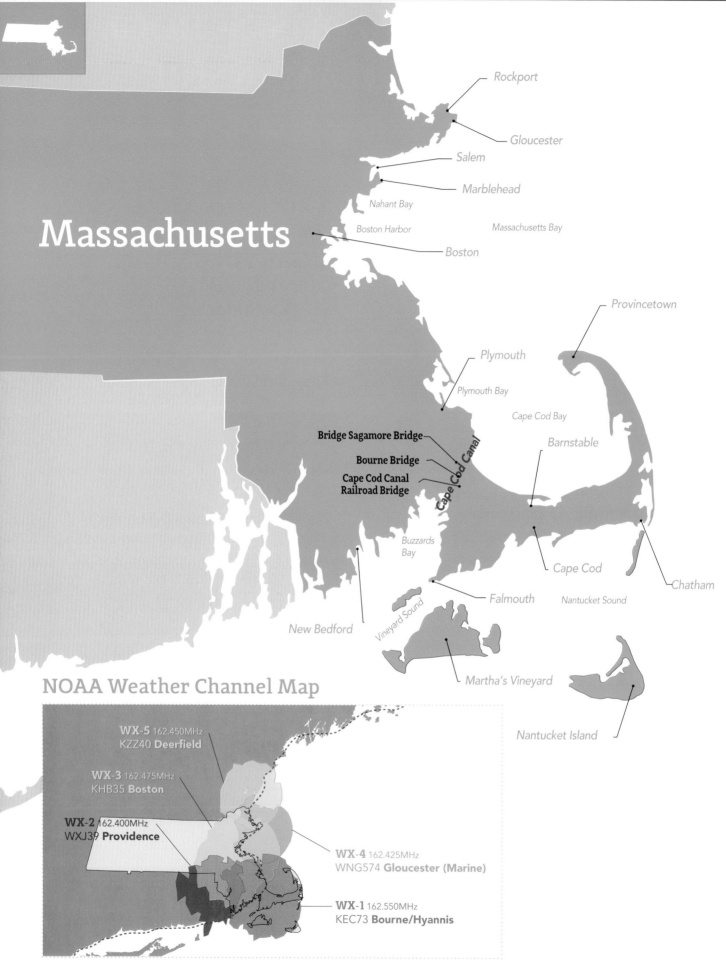

Massachusetts

Rockport

Gloucester

Salem

Marblehead

Nahant Bay

Boston Harbor

Massachusetts Bay

Boston

Provincetown

Plymouth

Plymouth Bay

Cape Cod Bay

Barnstable

Bridge Sagamore Bridge

Bourne Bridge

Cape Cod Canal Railroad Bridge

Cape Cod Canal

Buzzards Bay

Cape Cod

Chatham

Falmouth

Nantucket Sound

New Bedford

Vineyard Sound

Martha's Vineyard

Nantucket Island

NOAA Weather Channel Map

WX-5 162.450MHz
KZZ40 **Deerfield**

WX-3 162.475MHz
KHB35 **Boston**

WX-2 162.400MHz
WXJ39 **Providence**

WX-4 162.425MHz
WNG574 **Gloucester (Marine)**

WX-1 162.550MHz
KEC73 **Bourne/Hyannis**

Massachusetts

Newburyport to Salem

	MLW	Transient Slips/Moorings	Floating docks	Gas	Diesel	Pumpout	Showers	Pool	Laundry	Wi-Fi	Haulout	Repairs	Other
Bridge Marina — Merrimack R./Newburyport — 978-462-2274 — www.bridgemarinama.com	15'			•	•	•				•	➤		marine supplies
Cape Ann's Marina Resort — Annisquam R/Gloucester Harbor — 978-283-2116 — www.capeannmarina.com	8'	•	•	•	•	•	•	•	•	•	•	•	Mile Marker One Restaurant & Bar, waterfront hotel, VHF10
Enos Marine/Pier 7 Marina — Gloucester Harbor/South Channel — 978-281-1935 — www.enosmarine.com	10'	•	➤	➤		•				•	•		
Brown's Yacht Yard — Gloucester Harbor — 978-281-3200 — www.brownsyy.com	10'	•	•	•	•	•	•		➤	•	•	•	Marine store, full-service marina
Liberty Marina — Danvers River — 978-774-5105 — www.libertymarina.net	8'	•	➤	➤		•		•		•	•		
Hawthorne Cove Marina — Salem Harbor — 978-740-9890 — www.byy.com	6'	•	➤	➤	•	•		•		•	•		270 Moorings; BBQ station, easy walk to shops/restaurants
Pickering Wharf Marina — Salem Sound — 978-744-2727 — www.pickeringwharf.com	7'	•	➤	➤		•		•		➤	➤		
Admirals Hill Marina — Boston Harbor/Mystic R. — 617-889-4002 — www.admiralshillmarina.com	6'	•	•	•	•		•	•		•	•	•	easy access to Boston
Boston Harbor Shipyard & Marina — Boston Harbor — 617-561-1400 — www.bhsmarina.com	25'		•	•	•	•		•		•	•	•	Fitness center, lounge, 24-hr security, water-taxi pickup
Constitution Marina — Boston Harbor — 617-241-9640 — www.constitutionmarina.com	20'	•	•	➤	➤	•	•	•	•	•	➤	•	on Boston's Freedom Trail; close to Boston
Spectacle Island Marina — Boston Harbor/Is. Nat'l Park — 508-388-9047 — www.maritime.edu	7'	•	•			•							Snack bar, restrooms
Boston Yacht Haven — Boston Harbor — 617-367-5050 — www.thebostonyachthaven.com	25'	•	•	•	•	•	•		•	•	➤	➤	Close to historic sites, Quincy market, downtown Boston
The Marina at Rowes Wharf — Boston Harbor — 617-748-5013 — www.themarinaatroweswharf.com	25'	•	➤	➤	•	•	•	•	•				Megayacht marina; 3 restaurant/bars; located downtown
Captain's Cove Marina — Boston Harbor/Town River Basin — 617-328-3331 — www.captainscovemarina.com	20'	•	•	➤	➤	•	•		➤	•	➤	➤	well protected, slips up to 80', BBQ, pet-friendly
Bay Pointe Marina — Weymouth Fore R./Town R. — 617-471-1777 — www.bpmarina.com	6'	•	•	•	•	•	•		•		•	•	award-winning restaurant on-site. 50-ton lift, repairs,
Marina Bay on Boston Harbor — Boston Harbor/Dorchester Bay — 617-847-1800 — www.marinabayboston.com	14'	•	•	•	•	•	•		•	•	•	•	
Tern Harbor Marina — Back River — 781-337-1964 — www.ternharbormarina.com	10'	•	➤	➤	•	•				•	•		moorings
Hingham Shipyard Marinas — Back River — 781-749-2222 — www.hinghamshipyardmarinas.com	15'	•	•	•	•	•		•	•	•	•		100 moorings, marina village, restaurants, theater, shopping
Hingham Shipyard Marina/Hewitt's Cove — Hingham Bay — 781-749-6647 — www.hinghamshipyardmarinas.com	15'	•	•	•	•	•		•	•	•	•		secured gates, moorings with launch service
Steamboat Wharf Marina — Hingham Bay — 781-925-0044 — www.steamboatwharfmarina.com	12'	•	•	➤	➤	•	•		➤	•	•	•	numerous restaurants in walking distance, short walk to beach
Green Harbor Marina — Green Harbor — 781-837-1181 — www.greenharbormarina.com	6'	•		•	•	•	•			•	•	•	Restaurant on-site, ship's store, easy walk to shops/provisions
Taylor Marine — Green Harbor — 781-837-9617 — www.taylormarinecorp.com	5'		•	•	•	•	•			•	•	•	
Bayside Marine — Plymouth Bay/Duxbury Bay — 781-934-0561 — www.baysidemarinecorp.com	6'	•	•			➤				•	•	•	

	MLW	Transient Slips/Moorings	Floating docks	Gas	Diesel	Pumpout	Showers	Pool	Laundry	Wi-Fi	Haulout	Repairs	Other
Brewer Plymouth Marine Plymouth Bay 508-746-4500 www.byy.com	9'	•	•	•	•	•	•		•		•	•	On-site restaurant, marine supplies, yacht brokerage
Sandwich Marina Cape Cod Canal/East End 508-833-0808 www.sandwichmarina.com	11'	•		•	•	•	•				•		Boat ramp
Millway Marina Cape Cod Bay/Barnstable Harbor 508-362-4904 www.millwaymarina.com	5'	•		•	➤						•	•	moorings

Cape Cod to Buzzards Bay

	MLW	Transient Slips/Moorings	Floating docks	Gas	Diesel	Pumpout	Showers	Pool	Laundry	Wi-Fi	Haulout	Repairs	Other
Nauset Marine East Pleasant Bay 508-255-3045 www.nausetmarine.com	5'	•		•	•	•	•					•	Full-service; short walk to Village of East Orleans
Allen Harbor Marine Service Nantucket Sound/Harwich Port 800-832-2467 www.allenharbor.com	5'	•		•	•						•	•	
Bass River Marina Bass River 508-394-8341 www.bassrivermarina.com	4'	•	•	•	➤	•	•			•	•	•	Parker, Tidewater boats; Yamaha & Volvo dealers. Ship store
Ship Shops Nantucket Sound/Bass River 508-398-2256 www.shipshops.com	6'	•		•	•					•	•	•	evinrude, mercruiser, suzuki certified techs
East Marine Nantucket Sound 508-540-3611 www.eastmarine.com	6'	•		•	•		•				•	•	
MacDougalls' Cape Cod Marine Vineyard/Nantucket Sounds 508-548-3146 www.macdougalls.com	10'	•	•	•	•	•	•		•	•	•	•	
Falmouth Marine & Yachting Center Vineyard Sound 508-548-4600 www.falmouthmarine.com	8'	•	•	•	•	•			➤		•	•	moorings
Woods Hole Marine Buzzards Bay/Woods Hole 508-540-2402 www.woodsholemarine.com	6'						•						Shops, restaurants nearby
Brewer Fiddlers Cove Marine Buzzards Bay/N. Falmouth 508-564-6327 www.byy.com	6'	•	•	•	•	•	•		•	•	•	•	Marine supplies, Valvtech fuel, lounge, pool table, Cable tv
Quissett Harbor Boatyard Buzzards Bay/Quissett Harbor 508-548-0506	10'	•	•			•			•	•	•	•	Moorings, marine railway, pumpout boat
Kingman Yacht Center Buzzards Bay/Red Brook Harbor 508-563-7136 www.kingmanyachtcenter.com	6.5'	•	•	•	•	•	•		•	•	•	•	beach; on-site restaurant; moorings
Parker's Boat Yard Buzzards Bay/Red Brook Harbor 508-563-9366 www.parkersboatyard.com	6'	•	•	•	•	•			•	•	•	•	130 moorings; Full-service yard, loaner bikes, walking trails
Brewer Onset Bay Marina Buzzards Bay/Onset Bay 508-295-0338 www.onsetbay.com	6'	•	•	•	•	•	•		•	•	•	•	Awlgrip specialist; moorings; groceries, restaurant nearby
Stonebridge Marina Buzzards Bay/Onset Bay/East R. 508-295-8003 www.atlanticboats.net	5'	•	•	•	➤		•	•					moorings, restaurant on site, bait, ice, beach, grills
Monument Beach Marina Buzzards Bay/Phinneys Harbor 508-759-3105 www.townofbourne.com	6'	•	•	•		•	•						public beach, boat ramp
Taylor Point Marina Buzzards Bay/Butler Cove 508-759-2512 www.townofbourne.com	6'		•	•				•					Marine store, boat ramp
Burr Bros. Boats Buzzards Bay/Sippican Harbor 508-748-0541 www.burrbros.com	6'	•		•	•	•					•	•	Moorings; full-service yard
Zecco Marina Buzzards Bay/Wareham R. 508-295-0022 www.zeccomarine.com	6'	•	•	•	•	•			➤	•	•	•	Marine store; Mercury certified
Barden's Boat Yard Buzzards Bay/Sippican Harbor 508-748-0250 www.bardensboatyard.com	6.5'			•	•	•					•	•	
Dick's Marine Buzzards Bay/Wareham R. 508-759-3753 www.zeccomarine.com/dicks.html	4'	•		•	•	•	•			•	•	•	All new docks! Full service marina

	MLW	Transient Slips/Moorings	Floating docks	Gas	Diesel	Pumpout	Showers	Pool	Laundry	Wi-Fi	Haulout	Repairs	Other
Mattapoisett Boatyard Buzzards Bay/Mattapoisett Harbor 508-758-3812 www.mattapoisettboatyard.com	5'	●	●	●	●	●	●			●	●	●	
Earl's Marina Buzzards Bay/Nasketucket Bay 508-993-0008 www.earlsmarina.com	5'	●		●	●	●	●			●	●	●	70 moorings; dinghy dock
Wareham Boatyard and Marina Buzzards Bay/Wewantic River 508-748-1472 www.Wareham-Boatyard-Marina.com	3'	●		●		●	●			➤	●	●	Mercury/Mercruiser certified; moorings; marine supplies
Moby Dick Marina Buzzards Bay/New Bedford Harbor 508-994-1133 www.mobydickmarina.com	6'	●	➤	●	●	●				●	●	●	
Fairhaven Shipyard and Marina Buzzards Bay/New Bedford Harbor 508-999-1600 www.fairhavenshipyard.com	15'	●	●	●	●		●			●	●	●	●	ship's store, restaurants, shops w/in walking distance, beaches
Sea Fuels Marine Services Buzzards Bay/New Bedford Harbor 508-992-2323 www.seafuelsmarine.com	16'			●	●							➤	
Davis and Tripp Buzzards Bay/Apponagansett Bay 508-993-9232 www.DavisTripp.com	7'	●	➤	➤	●						●	●	Dealer for: Yamaha, Yanmar, BRP
South Wharf Yacht Yard Buzzards Bay/Apponagansett Bay 508-990-1011 www.southwharf.com	11'	●	➤	➤	●	●		●	●			●	restaurant on site, deep water access, ice machine

Martha's Vineyard/Nantucket

	MLW	Transient Slips/Moorings	Floating docks	Gas	Diesel	Pumpout	Showers	Pool	Laundry	Wi-Fi	Haulout	Repairs	Other
Hyannis Marina Nantucket Sound/Hyannis Harbor 508-790-4000 www.hyannismarina.com	14'	●		●	●	●	●	●	●	●	●	●	●	
Oyster Harbors Marine Vineyard Sound 508-428-2017 www.oysterharborsmarine.com	6'			●	●	●	●					●	●	Full-service
Crosby Yacht Yard Nantucket Sound 508-428-6900 www.crosbyyacht.com	6'	●		●	●	●	●					●	●	moorings
Madaket Marine Nantucket Sound/Hither Creek 508-228-1163 www.madaketmarine.com	6'			●	●	●						●	●	Marine store, parts dept.
Nantucket Boat Basin Nantucket Sound/Nantucket Isl. 800-626-2628 www.nantucketboatbasin.com	12'	●		●	●	●				●			●	concierge services; restaurants, shops, sites nearby
Edgartown Harbormaster Martha's Vineyard/Edgartown Harbor/ 508-627-4746 www.edgartownharbor.com	18'	●		●	●	●	●				➤	➤		
Vineyard Island Marina Martha's VineyardLagoon Pond 508-693-4174 www.vineyardislandmarina.com	5'	●	●	●	➤	●				➤	●	●	occasional moorings
Vineyard Haven Marina Martha's Vineyard/Vineyard Haven Hbr 508-693-0720 www.vineyardhavenmarina.com	12'	●		●	●	●	●	●	➤	●				moorings; restaurant; West Marine on-site
Tisbury Wharf Co. Marthas Vineyard/Vineyard Haven Hbr 508-693-9300 www.tisburywharf.com	16'	●		●	●	●	●			●	➤	➤		Swimming beaches, restaurants, shops, entertainment nearby
Oak Bluffs Marina Martha's Vineyard/Oak Bluffs Harbor 508-693-4355 www.oakbluffsmarina.com	9'	●		●	●	●	●				●	●		moorings

Constitution Marina—
The Best of Boston Just Off Your Bow

Constitution Marina

28 Constitution Road, Boston, MA 02129
Ph: 617-241-9640 | Fax: 617-242-3013
Email: cm@bosport.com
ConstitutionMarina.com

description of facilities

Located right on the Freedom Trail in Boston's fashionable neighborhood of Charlestown, we are just a five-minute walk to North Station and the Boston Garden, along with all that Boston has to offer.

We are the destination of choice for boaters from around New England and beyond. We regularly host yacht clubs, sportfishing tournaments, sailboat races and flotillas of all descriptions.

It is simple to make reservations for guest dockage. We have room for visiting vessels up to 150-feet for a day, weekend, week or longer.

Our staff would be happy to arrange for reservations at many of the fine restaurants in the area or tickets to a Red Sox game. Ask about our special discounts to area merchants and take advantage of our "courtesy car" to pick up groceries down the street. We can also book you a private charter, or reserve a dockside Bed and Breakfast on one of our unique and reasonably priced B&B boats.

marina approach & docking

Take the main channel into Boston Harbor, with downtown off your port side. Take a left at the Coast Guard station, and head towards the mouth of the Charles River. The marina is on your right, just past the U.S.S. Constitution. Primary entrance to the marina is by the bridge. Hail us on VHF 69.

LAT: 42° 22' 21.2874"N
LON: -71° 3' 26.64"W

at a glance

DOCKAGE RATE: $3.00 to $5.00/ft/day. Call for weekly, monthly, and special event rates

PAYMENT: Credit card/cash

HOURS: 8am – 8pm

TRANSIENT SLIPS/TOTAL SLIPS: 265

VHF/WORKING: 69

MLW/LOA*: 20´+/200´

ELECTRIC: 30/50 amp; single and 3-phase 100 amp

PUMP-OUT: Stationary and mobile

FUEL: Nearby

REPAIR: Yes

RESTAURANT/MILES: On premises and 150 within 1 mile

POOL: Yes

HAUL-OUT: Nearby

HEAD/SHOWER: Yes/Yes

LAUNDRY: Yes

INTERNET ACCESS: High-speed wireless

CABLE: Yes

NEAREST TOWN/MILES: In Boston

SHOPPING: Yes

GOLF/TENNIS: No/Nearby

AIRPORT/MILES: Logan/2

TRANSPORTATION: Yes

YACHT BROKERAGE: Yes

SPECIAL: The most protected docking on Boston Harbor! Located on the Historic Freedom Trail. Concierge service, water taxi available, pool and deck

*MLW = Mean Low Water Depth
 LOA = Longest vessel that can be accommodated

New England's Premier Marina and Waterfront Complex

Marina Bay
on Boston Harbor

333 Victory Road, North Quincy, MA 02171
Ph: 617-847-1800 | Fax: 617-847-1840
Email: marinabay@flagshipmarinas.com
MarinaBayBoston.com

description of facilities

Marina Bay is New England's premier marina and waterfront complex located in Dorchester Bay with easy access from routes 93 and 128. This lively urban community hosts a 685-slip marina and nine restaurants from casual to upscale dining, including indoor and outdoor nightclubs.

Accommodating Yachts up to 150 feet, the yacht basin has a 13 foot MLW entrance and is surrounded by a continuous breakwater while enjoying a panoramic view of Boston's skyline. Ample complimentary parking, pump-out, yard services, boat maintenance and repair by certified marine techs, controlled access to docks, courteous dock staff, laundry and shower facility and a 150 foot fuel dock operating daily April through November, 8:00 a.m. to 5:00 p.m., are added enticements. Summer dockage is offered on a seasonal or a transient basis, while winter storage is offered dry and wet with a liveaboard option.

marina approach & docking

Marina Bay is located in Dorchester Bay. The MLW is 13 feet at the entrance of the yacht basin. We monitor VHF channel 10. From buoy "3" off Castle Island, head into Dorchester Bay. At lighted buoy R "12" take a left into Squantum Channel. Our latitude is 42°18′3.9594′N and longitude is -71°1′37.9554W. ICW north channel buoy. Please honor the channel.

Marina Bay is easily accessible by land from routes 128 and 93. Located in North Quincy on East Squantum Street just off Quincy Shore Drive and Wollaston Blvd. Route 93 N-exit 11. Route 93 S-exit 12; Gallivan Blvd. to Quincy Shore Drive, left on East Squantum St.

LAT: 42° 18′ 3.9594″N
LON: -71° 1′ 37.9554″W

at a glance

DOCKAGE RATE: Call for rates and info

PAYMENT: MC/Visa/Amex

HOURS: Mon-Fri, 9am – 5pm

TRANSIENT SLIPS/TOTAL SLIPS: Yes/700

VHF/WORKING: VHF 10/617-847-1800

MLW/LOA*: 14′/300′

ELECTRIC: Yes

PUMP-OUT: Yes

FUEL: Yes

REPAIR: Master mechanic on-site

RESTAURANT/MILES: Restaurant on-site

POOL: No

HAUL-OUT: Yes

HEAD/SHOWER: Yes/Yes

LAUNDRY: Yes

INTERNET ACCESS: Yes

CABLE: No

SHIP'S STORE: Complete full-service store

NEAREST TOWN/MILES: Boston

SHOPPING: Nearby

GOLF/TENNIS: Both nearby

STORAGE: Yes

AIRPORT/MILES: Nearby

TRANSPORTATION: Available

YACHT BROKERAGE: Yes, Norwood Yacht Sales

*MLW = Mean Low Water Depth
 LOA = Longest vessel that can be accommodated

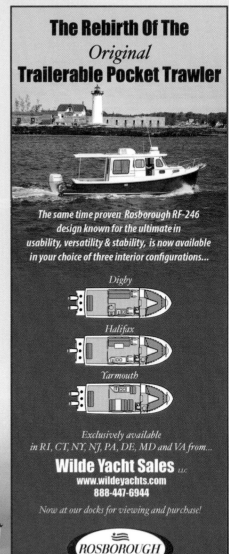

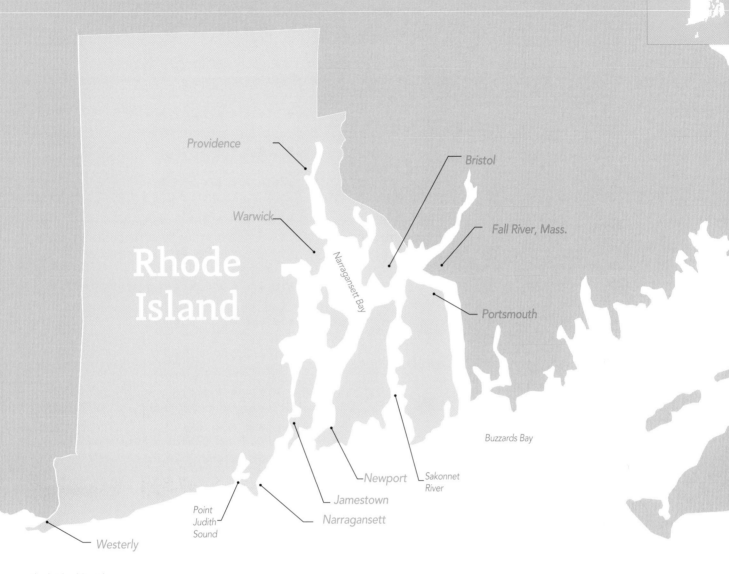

Providence

Bristol

Warwick

Fall River, Mass.

Rhode Island

Narragansett Bay

Portsmouth

Buzzards Bay

Newport

Sakonnet River

Jamestown

Point Judith Sound

Narragansett

Westerly

Rhode Island Sound

Block Island

NOAA Weather Channel Map

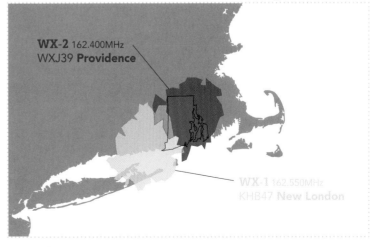

WX-2 162.400MHz
WXJ39 **Providence**

WX-1 162.550MHz
KHB47 New London

Rhode Island

	MLW	Transient Slips/Moorings	Floating docks	Gas	Diesel	Pumpout	Showers	Pool	Laundry	Wi-Fi	Haulout	Repairs	Other
Standish Boatyard Sakonnet R./Tiverton Basin 401-624-4075 www.yachtworld.com/standishboat	10'	●		●	●	●	●				●	●	Marine Store, mechanics avail on weekends
Pirate Cove Marina Sakonnet R./Tiverton Basin 401-683-3030 www.piratecovemarina.net	6'	●		●	●	●	●			●	●	●	moorings, ship's store
Brewer Sakonnet Marina Sakonnet River/Mt. Hope Bay 401-683-3551 www.byy.com/bsm/	8'	●	●	●	●	●	●	●	●		●	●	Picnic area, grills, volleyball, playground
New England Boatworks Narragansett Bay/East Passage 401-683-4000 www.neboatworks.com	14'	●	●	●	●	●	●	●	●		●	●	Full-service yard

Newport Harbor

	MLW	Transient Slips/Moorings	Floating docks	Gas	Diesel	Pumpout	Showers	Pool	Laundry	Wi-Fi	Haulout	Repairs	Other
West Wind Marina Newport Harbor 401-849-4300 www.waiteswharf.com/westwindmarina	12'	●	●	➤	●	●	●		●	●	➤		park, beaches; full-service; restaurants, walk to bars, shops
The Brown & Howard Wharf Marina Newport Harbor 401-846-5100 www.marinaatbrownandhoward.com	14'	●	●	➤	●	●				●			In the heart of town; all amenities nearby; yachts up to 250 ft
Forty 1 North Newport Harbor 401-846-8018 www.41no.com	10'	●	●	➤	➤	●	●		●	●			concierge, dockside dining on your boat, laundry service
Newport Yachting Center Marina Newport Harbor 800-653-3625 www.newportyachtingcenter.com	12'	●	●	●	●	●	●	●	●	●		●	24-hour security, concierge service
Bannister's Wharf Newport Harbor 401-846-4556 www.bannistersnewport.com	16'	●	●	●	●	●	●		➤				restaurants, shopping nearby
Newport Harbor Hotel and Marina Newport Harbor 800-955-2558 www.newporthotel.com	18'	●	●	➤	➤	●	●	●	●	●	➤	➤	
Newport Shipyard/American Shipyard Newport Harbor 401-846-6000 www.newportshipyard.com	25'	●	●	●	●	●	●		●		●	●	ship's store, cafe, fitness center, crew housing
Goat Island Marina Newport Harbor 401-849-5655 www.newportexperience.com	9'	●	●	●	●	●	●		●	●			24-hr security, cable TV, restaurant on-site
Oldport Marine Services Newport Harbor/Sayers Wharf 401-847-9109 www.oldportmarine.com	17'	●		➤	➤	●						●	moorings; marine store, engine servies, harbor tours, water taxi

Narraganseett Bay to Point Judith Pond

	MLW	Transient Slips/Moorings	Floating docks	Gas	Diesel	Pumpout	Showers	Pool	Laundry	Wi-Fi	Haulout	Repairs	Other
Jamestown Boat Yard Narragansett Bay/Jamestown Island 401-423-0600 www.jby.com	8'	●		➤	➤						●	●	moorings
Conanicut Marina Narragansett Bay/East Passage 401-423-7157 www.conanicutmarina.com	20'	●		●	●	●	●		●	●	●	●	in heart of Jamestown Village, services available, 160 moorings
Hinckley Yacht Services Narragansett Bay/East Passage 401-683-7100 www.hinckleyyachts.com	18'	●	●	➤	●	●	●		●		●	●	full-service; concierge services

	MLW	Transient Slips/Moorings	Floating docks	Gas	Diesel	Pumpout	Showers	Pool	Laundry	Wi-Fi	Haulout	Repairs	Other
Stanley's Boat Yard — Providence River — 401-245-5090 — www.stanleysboatyard.com	8'			➤	➤	•	•		➤		•	•	35-ton lift,
Brewer Cove Haven Marina — Providence R./Bullock Cove — 401-246-1600 — www.byy.com/chc/	7.5'	•	•	•	•	•	•	•		•	•	•		Ships store, grills, groceries nearby; next to Haines State Park
Bristol Marine — Bristol Harbor — 401-253-2200 — www.bristolmarine.com	8'	•	➤	➤	•	•						•	full-service yard
Apponaug Harbor Marina — Greenwich Bay — 401-739-5005 — www.apponaugmarina.com	6'	•	•	➤						•	•	•		
Brewer Greenwich Bay — Greenwich Bay/Warwick Cove — 401-884-1810 — www.byy.com	7'	•	•	•	•	•	•	•	•	•	•	•	➤	Protected harbor, full-service yard,
Brewer Cowesett Marina — Greenwich Bay — 401-884-0544 — www.byy.com	7'	•	•	➤	➤	•	•				•	•	•	Full-service, restaurant on-site, ship's store; E. Greenwich close
Norton's Shipyard and Marina — Greenwich Bay — 401-884-8828 — www.nortonsmarina.com	9'	•		➤	➤	•	•		➤	•	•	•	•	100+ moorings; marine store, 35T lift; picnic; walk downtown
Brewer Wickford Cove Marina — Narragansett Bay/Wickford Harbor — 401-884-7014 — www.byy.com	7'	•		•		•	•	•	•	•	•	•		In Historic Wickford Village
Wickford Marina — Mill Cove section of Wickford Harbor — 401-294-8160 — www.wickfordmarina.com	6'	•	•	➤	➤	•	•	•	•					beach, groceries, restaurant, drugstore nearby
Wickford Shipyard — Narragansett Bay Wickford Harbor — 401-294-3361	9'	•	•	•		•	•			•	•	•	•	Marine store
Dutch Harbor Boat Yard — Narragansett Bay, West Passage — 401-423-0630 — www.dutchharborboatyard.com	12'	•		➤	➤	•	•			•	•		•	moorings, launch service, walk to Jamestown Village
Point Judith Marina — Point Judith Pond — 401-789-7189 — www.pjmarina.com	10'	•	•	•	•	•	•	•		•	•	•	•	Beautiful grounds, pets welcome, restaurants nearby
Silver Spring Marine — Point Judith Pond — 401-783-0783 — www.silverspringmarine.com	4'	•	•	➤	➤	➤	•	•		➤	•	•	•	Mercury and Yamaha certified; restaurant, groceries nearby
Stone Cove Marina — Pt. Judith Pond/Salt Pond — 401-783-8990 — www.stonecovemarinaRI.com	6'	•	•	•	➤	•	•			•	•	•		restaurant, supplies nearby
Ram Point Marina — Point Judith Pond/Upper Pond — 401-783-4535 — www.rampointmarina.com	5'	•	•	•	•	•	•			•	•		•	grilling area, SUP/kayak rentals; restaurant nearby
Snug Harbor Marina — Point Judith Pond/gr. #7 — 401-783-7766 — www.snugharbormarina.com	4.5'				•	•							➤	bait & tackle shop; snack bar; live lobsters, marine supplies

Block Island

	MLW	Transient Slips/Moorings	Floating docks	Gas	Diesel	Pumpout	Showers	Pool	Laundry	Wi-Fi	Haulout	Repairs	Other
Payne's Dock — Block Island/Great Salt Pond — 401-466-5572	14'	•		•	•	•	•						➤	restaurant and bar on the docks
Block Island Boat Basin — Block Island/Great Salt Pond — 401-466-2631 — www.blockislandboatbasin.net	9.5'	•	•	➤	➤	•	•			•			•	Car rental; fishing charters; ships store
Champlin's Marina & Resort — Block Island/Great Salt Pond — 401-466-7777 — www.champlinsresort.com	15'	•	•	•	•	•	•	•	•	•	•		•	On-site restaurant; groceries, car rental, marine supplies, hotel
Watch Hill Boat Yard — Pawcatuck R./Colonel Willie Cove — 401-348-8148 — www.watchhillboatyard.com	5.5'		➤	➤	•	•					•	•		customer clubhouse; restaurants nearby; full-service
Frank Hall Boat Yard — Pawtuck R./Avondale — 401-348-8005 — www.frankhallboatyard.com		•				•	•			•	•			18 moorings, dinghy dock

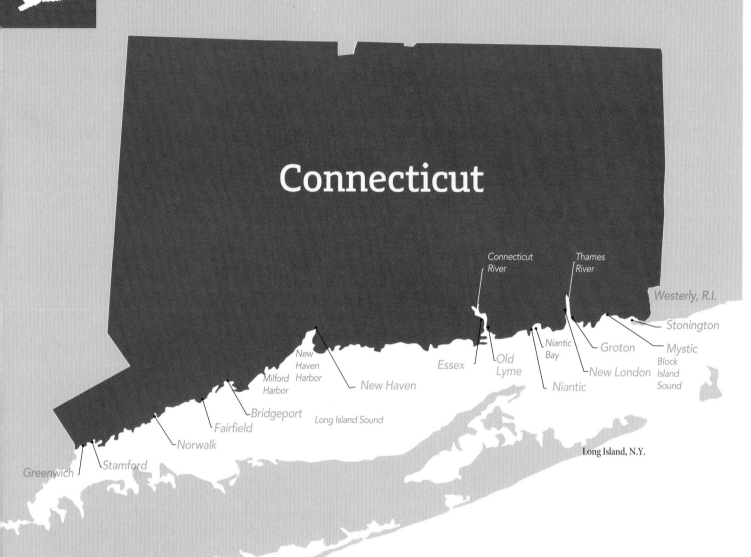

Connecticut

Connecticut River

Thames River

Westerly, R.I.

Stonington

New Haven Harbor

Milford Harbor

New Haven

Essex

Old Lyme

Niantic Bay

Niantic

Groton

New London

Mystic

Block Island Sound

Bridgeport

Long Island Sound

Fairfield

Norwalk

Stamford

Greenwich

Long Island, N.Y.

NOAA Weather Channel Map

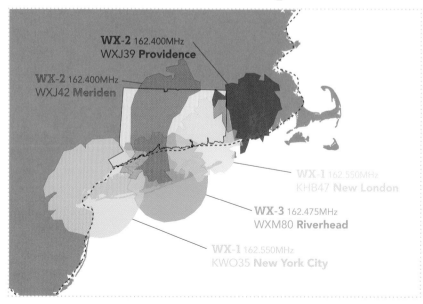

WX-2 162.400MHz
WXJ39 **Providence**

WX-2 162.400MHz
WXJ42 **Meriden**

WX-1 162.550MHz
KHB47 **New London**

WX-3 162.475MHz
WXM80 **Riverhead**

WX-1 162.550MHz
KWO35 **New York City**

Connecticut

	MLW	Transient Slips/Moorings	Floating docks	Gas	Diesel	Pumpout	Showers	Pool	Laundry	Wi-Fi	Haulout	Repairs	Other
Pawcatuck River to Niantic Bay													
Norwest Marine — Pawcatuck River — 860-599-2442 www.norwestmarine.com	6'	•	•	•	➤	•	•		•	•	•	•	Full-service marina; Yamaha Master Technicians
Dodson Boat Yard — Stonington Harbor — 860-535-1507 www.dodsonboatyard.com	9'	•		•	•	•	•		•		•	•	moorings, launch service
Brewer Yacht Yard at Mystic — Mystic River — 860-536-2293 www.byy.com	8'	•	•	•	•	•	•	•	•	•	•	•	15 min. from L.I. Sound, in protected location
Noank Shipyard/Seaport Marine — Mystic River — 860-536-9651 www.noankshipyard.com	8'	•	•	•	•	•	•		•	•	•	•	In downtown Mystic, restaurants, attractions nearby
Mystic Downtown Marina — Mystic River — 860-572-5942 www.mysticdowntownmarina.com	7'	•		➤		➤	•		•	•	•	➤	pet friendly, cable, patio dock, ice
Mystic River Marina — Mystic River/Mason's Island — 860-536-3123 www.mysticrivermarina.com	9'	•	•	•	•	•	•	•	•	•	•	•	Kitchen Little restaurant, ship store, kayaks/SUP loaners
Fort Rachel Marina — Mystic River — 860-536-6647 www.fortrachel.com	8'	•	•	➤	➤	➤	•		•	•		•	Yamaha certified mechanic. Walk to downtown Mystic
Mystic Seaport Museum — Mystic River — 860-572-5391 www.mysticseaport.org	10'	•		➤	➤	•	•		•	•	➤		world class museum, restaurants, shops, sites adjacent
Mason's Island Marina — Mystic River — 860-536-2608 www.masonsislandmarina.net	5'	•		➤	•	•	•			•	•		20 moorings, marine store
Mystic Shipyard — Mystic River — 860-536-6588 www.mysticshipyard.com	12'	•		➤	➤	•	•	•	•	•	•	•	Full service marina, kayaks, SUPs, Walk to downtown Mystic
Noank Village Boatyard — Mystic River — 860-536-1770 www.noankvillageboatyard.com	7'	•	•	➤	➤	•	•		•	•	•	•	grocery, liquor store in walking distance; moorings
Spicer's Marina — West Cove Noank — 860-536-4978 www.spicersmarina.com	7'	•	•	➤		•	•		•	•	•	•	restaurants, tackle shop, marine store, launch service, moorings
Pine Island Marina — Pine Island Bay — 860-445-9729 www.pineislandmarina.com	4'	•	•	➤	➤		•		•	•	•	•	Yamaha factory training service & Parts; moorings
Thames View Marina MM — Thames River/Navy Base — 860-694-3164	12'	•	•	➤	➤	•	•	➤	•	•			
Crocker's Boatyard — Thames River/Shaw Cove — 860-443-6304 www.crockersboatyardinc.com	12'	•	•	•	•	•	•		•	•	•	•	Marine store; full-service marina; dockage to 160'
Thamesport Marina — Thames River — 860-442-1151 www.thamesportmarina.com	12'	•		•	•	•	•		•				restaurants on site, walk to beaches
Gales Ferry Marina — Thames River — 860-464-2146 www.galesferrymarina.com	7'	•	•	•			•				•	•	marine store, sales and service; Suzuki repower specialist
Marina at American Wharf (The) — Thames River — 860-886-6363 www.americanwharf.com	10'	•	•	•	•	•	•	•	•	•	➤	➤	located minutes from Mohegan Sun casino, shuttle to/from
Boats, Inc. — Niantic Bay/Niantic R. — 860-739-6251 www.boatsinc.com	6'	•	•	➤	➤	•	•	•		•		•	Cable TV, picnic facilities
Harbor Hill Marina & Inn — Niantic River — 860-739-0331 www.innharborhill.com	6'	•	•	➤	➤	•	•		➤	•		➤	Walk to Niantic Village
Port Niantic — Niantic River — 860-739-2155 www.portniantic.com	6'		•	➤	➤	•	•	•	➤		•	•	
Three Belles Marina — Niantic River — 860-739-6264 www.threebellesmarina.com	5'	•	•	•	•	•	•	•	➤	•	•	•	Cafe, picnic area, hobie rentals, outfitters store, moorings

Connecticut River to Branford Harbor

	MLW	Transient Slips/Moorings	Floating docks	Gas	Diesel	Pumpout	Showers	Pool	Laundry	Wi-Fi	Haulout	Repairs	Other
Old Lyme Dock Company — Connecticut R./Lyme — 860-434-2267 www.oldlymedock.com	13'	•	•	•	•		•				•	•	ship's store, discount fuel
Old Lyme Marina — Connecticut R./Lyme — 860-434-1272 www.oldlymemarina.com	12'	•		>	>		•				•	•	moorings, launch service
Cove Landing Marine — Connecticut R./Lyme — 860-434-5240 www.covelanding.com	9'	•					•		•		•	•	full-service boatyard, transient moorings, kayak/SUP rentals
Chrisholm Marina — Connecticut R./Chester — 860-526-5147 www.chrisholmmarina.com	6'	•	•	•	>	•	•			•	•	•	across from Gillette's Castle
Petzold's Marine Center — Connecticut R./Portland — 860-342-1196 www.petzolds.com	10'	•		•	>	•		•			•	•	Ship's Store
Portland Boat Works — Connecticut R./Portland — 860-342-1085 www.portlandboatworks.com	8'		•	•	>	•	•				•	•	Full-service yard
Yankee Boat Yard & Marina — Connecticut R./Portland — 860-342-4735 www.yankeeboatyard.com	7'	•	•	•	•	•	•			•	•	•	volvo certified/mercruiser; Yamaha service, Cape Horn dealer
Brewer Deep River Marina — Connecticut River/Marker 35 — 860-526-5560 www.byy.com	6'	•	•	•	•	•	•	•	•	>	•	•	•	moorings
Seaboard Marina — Connecticut River — 860-657-3232 www.seaboardmarina.com	17'	•		•	>	•	•	•			•	•	Full-service gas dock, picnic areas, cable TV, snack bar
Brewer Dauntless Marina — Connecticut R./Essex — 860-767-8267 www.byy.com	8'	•		•	•	•	•	•		•	•	•	
Brewer Dauntless Shipyard — Connecticut R./Essex — 860-767-0001 www.byy.com	8'	•		•	•	•	•	•			•	•	60 moorings
Brewer Essex Island Marina — Connecticut R./Essex — 860-767-2483 www.byy.com	8'	•		•	•	•	•	•			•	>	
Essex Boat Works — Connecticut R./Essex — 860-767-8276 www.essexboatworks.com	10'	•	•	>	>	•				•	•	•	in historic Essex Village. Full-service marina/boatyard
Middle Cove Marina — Connecticut R./Essex — 860-767-0000 www.the-clark-group.com	6'		•	>	>	>	•		>	•		>	Town Park nearby
Island Cove Marina — Connecticut R./Ferry Point — 860-388-0029 www.islandcoveyachtsales.com	7'	•	•		>		•		•	•	•	•	moorings and slips; lounge, gazebo
Oak Leaf Marina — Connecticut R./Ferry Point — 860-388-9817 www.oakleafmarina.com	8'	•	•	>	>	>	•		•	•	•	•	walk to restaurants; Merc & Mercruiser certified
Ragged Rock Marina — Connecticut R./Old Saybrook — 860-388-1049 www.raggedrockmarina.net	5'	•		>	>	•	•		•	•	•	•	
Harbor One Marina — Connecticut R./Old Saybrook — 860-388-9208 www.harboronemarinact.com	8'	•		•	•	•		•	•	•	>	•	Restaurant on-site; Sea Tow base; close to Old Saybrook
Between The Bridges — Connecticut R. btw. rr/Rt 1 bridges — 860-388-1431 www.betweenthebridges.com	6'	•	•	•	•		•	•			•	•	Back Porch Restaurant
Saybrook Point Marina — Connecticut River mouth — 860-395-3080 www.saybrookpointmarina.com	12'	•	•	•	•	•	•	•	•	•	•			pools, free shuttle to town, bikes, marine supplies, restaurant
Brewer Pilots Point Marina — Long Island Sound/Westbrook — 860-399-7906 www.byy.com	8'	•	•	•	•	•	•	•	>	•	•	•	courtesy vans, on-site restaurant
Port Clinton Marina — Long Island Sound — 860-669-4563 www.portclintonmarina.net	4'	•		>	>	•	•		•		•	•	

	MLW	Transient Slips/Moorings	Floating docks	Gas	Diesel	Pumpout	Showers	Pool	Laundry	Wi-Fi	Haulout	Repairs	Other
Cedar Island Marina Long Island Sound/Clinton Harbor 860-669-8681 www.cedarislandmarina.com	8'	●	●	●	●	●	●	●	●	●	●	●	certified Mercruiser, hot tub, fitness center, restaurants, pool
Pier 76 Marina Patchogue River 860-399-7122 www.pier76.com	3.5'	●	●	➤	➤				●			●	Mercury, Mercruiser; kayak rental; Bait & Tackle; Restaurant
Brown's Boat Yard West River/ Guilford Harbor 203-453-6283 www.brownsboatyard-CT.com	5'		●	●	●					●	●	●	full-service boatyard (emergency haul up to 42')
Guilford Boat Yards West River 203-453-5031 www.guilfordboat.com	5'	●	●	➤	➤	➤				●	●	●	mercruiser, mercury ob, certified mechanics, marine supplies
Branford Landing Branford River 203-483-6544 www.branfordlandingmarina.com	8'	●	●	●	●			●			●	●	close to Village of Branford; train station
Brewer Bruce & Johnson's Marina Branford River 203-488-8329 www.byy.com/branford	7'	●		●	●	●	●	●	●		●	●	moorings, swimming pool, picnic area, Dockside Restaurant

New Haven to Cos Cob

	MLW	Transient Slips/Moorings	Floating docks	Gas	Diesel	Pumpout	Showers	Pool	Laundry	Wi-Fi	Haulout	Repairs	Other
Milford Landing Marina Long Island Sound/Milford Harbor 203-874-1610 www.ci.milford.ct.us	8'	●		➤	➤	●	●		●				bars, restaurants, marine supplies within walking distance
Milford Boat Works Long Island Sound/Milford Harbor 203-877-1475 www.facebook.com/Milford-Boat-Works	7'		●	●	●	●			●		●	●	
Spencer's Marina Long Island Sound/Milford Harbor 203-874-4173 www.facebook.com/Spencers-Marina-Inc	8'	●		●	➤						●	●	
Brewer Stratford Marina Housatonic R./Stratford 203-377-4477 www.byy.com	12'	●	●	●	●	●	●	●	●	●	●	●	courtesy transportation, picnic area with grills, fine dining
Boardwalk Marina Housatonic R./Stratford 203-378-9300 www.boardwalkmarinact.com	8'	●	●	➤	➤		●				●	●	Full-service repairs; dockage to 100'
Ryan's Marine Services Bridgeport Harbor 203-579-1319 www.ryansmarineservices.com	14'	●	●	➤	➤	●			●		●	●	near train station, bass pro shop
Cedar Marina Long Island Sound/Black Rock Harbor 203-335-6262 www.cedarmarina.com	7'	●		➤	➤	●	●		●		●		
Captain's Cove Seaport Long Island Sound/Black Rock Harbor 203-335-1433 www.captainscoveseaport.com	17'	●	●	●	●	●			●	●	●	●	Restaurant on-site; fishing charters, special events
Norwalk Cove Marina Long Island Sound/Norwalk Harbor 203-838-2326 www.norwalkcove.com	6'	●	●	●	●	●	●		●	●	●	●	Ship's store and nautical boutique; restaurant, mini golf
Rex Marine Center Norwalk Harbor/1/2 mile N of can 21 203-866-5555 www.rexmarine.com	8'	●	●	➤	➤	➤	●		➤	●	●	●	Walk to downtown Norwalk; south of all bridges
Seaview House Marina Long Island Sound/Westcott Cove 203-219-4693 www.seaviewhousemarina.com	8'		●	●	●	●	●						
Harbor Point Marinas Long Island Sound/Stamford Harbor 203-724-9048 www.harborpt.com	9'	●	●	●	●			●			●	●	restaurants, shops, entertainment
Brewer Yacht Haven Stamford Harbor 203-359-4500 www.byy.com	9'	●	●	●		●			●	●		●	Marine supplies, ice, picnic area
Stamford Landing Marina Stamford Harbor/West Branch 203-965-0065 www.harborpt.com	9'	●	●	➤	➤	●	●		●	➤	➤	➤	restaurants, entertainment, shops
Palmer Point Marina Mianus River/Cos Cob Harbor 203-661-1243 www.palmerpointmarina.com	6'	●	●	●	●	●	●		➤		●	●	Marine store, snacks, farm stand, bait & tackle next door

New England's Finest Yacht Basin

Mystic River Marina
36 Quarry Road, Mystic, CT 06355
Ph: 860-536-3123
MysticRiverMarina.com

description of facilities

Mystic River Marina is located on tranquil Mason's Island on the Mystic River, with beautiful views of Fisher's Island and Long Island Sound. The marina is in a protected area below all bridges. Our full service marina has been family-owned and operated since 1957. Our 155-slip, full-service facility provides boaters with the highest quality services. We are experienced, committed caretakers of vessels for many discriminating boaters from Florida through New England. Dedication to dependable service has been our trademark for over 55 years. We offer seasonal and transient dockage, Shell fuels, a swimming pool, clubhouse, patio, bbq grills, cable tv, free wi-fi, immaculate heads, free pump out, laundry facilities, a playground, and Kitchen Little restaurant. Our ship's store has all the supplies you'll need, including Sperry Top-siders. Our services include diesel and gas engine and generator service, repowers, underwater hardware service, premier fiberglass/paint work, onboard systems repairs, Interlux- and Sealand/Dometic-authorized, Crusader, Westerbeke, and most inbds/IO's/outboards. Many customers enjoy a 10% dockage discount with our year round savings plan. Mystic River Marina offers free daily paddle board and kayak loaners to our transient and annual slip holders. We are also a sales and full service dealer for Honda Marine.

marina approach & docking

Mystic River Marina is located at 36 Quarry Rd., Mystic CT. The marina is a few miles away from the heart of historic Mystic, CT's #1 tourist destination. You can enjoy all the sights of scenic Mystic, and still enjoy a peaceful, private homeport!

HONDA MARINE

LAT: 41° 20' 15.7848"N
LON: -71° 58' 16.8096"W

Easy to Get to and Close to where you want to Be

MYSTIC SHIPYARD

at a glance

DOCKAGE RATE: $3.00/ft, up to 150′

PAYMENT: MC/Visa/Discover

HOURS: Mon-Sat 8am – 5pm, Sun 9am – 5pm, Sat and Sun winter hours by appointment

TRANSIENT SLIPS/TOTAL SLIPS: Call/175

VHF/WORKING: 9/68

MLW/LOA*: 15′/150′

ELECTRIC: 30/50 Amp

PUMP-OUT: Yes

FUEL: No

REPAIR: Certified diesel and refrigeration mechanics, hydraulic techs, fiberglass repair, shipwright services, complete rigging service

RESTAURANT/MILES: In town/1

POOL: Yes

HEAD/SHOWER: Yes/Yes

LAUNDRY: Yes

CABLE: No

NEAREST TOWN/MILES: Mystic/1

SHOPPING: Plenty in historic Mystic

GOLF/TENNIS: Nearby/Nearby

AIRPORT/MILES: Providence/40

TRANSPORTATION: Rental cars, taxi, bikes

YACHT BROKERAGE: Spring Line Yacht Sales

SPECIAL: Certified shipwright for wooden boats, custom canvas, yacht rigging

Mystic Shipyard, LLC
100 Essex Street, Mystic, CT 06355
Ph: 860-536-6588 | Fax: 860-536-7081
MysticShipyard.com

description of facilities

Mystic Shipyard is in one of New England's top cruising destinations. The beautiful Mystic River is a serene, safe setting that has always appealed to mariners. It features plenty of dockage, transient slip space, outside and inside storage for your boat, extensive on-site services, yacht brokerage and sales from one of the nation's most service-oriented yacht dealerships, and has a beautiful riverside pool. The Shipyard has long been known for its high degree of yacht services. Today, the Shipyard continues to improve on that tradition with expanded facilities and a strong commitment to quality.

Cast off, and you are just a few minutes to the Long Island Sound. Close by are perfect places for daysailing with beautiful beaches and swimmable water.

marina approach & docking

Entering the Mystic River, you will pass by scenic Noank with historical churches and the famous Abbott's Lobster. Continue up the river only half a mile, north of Six Penny Island, and you will find the Mystic Shipyard. Mystic Shipyard is conveniently located on the west side of the Mystic River and south of all bridges. As you approach the Mystic Shipyard, you will find four docks, all with available T-heads. The dockmaster monitors VHF channel 9 and 68 for your convenience. Please call upon approach for slip assignment and docking assistance. Slips range in size from 20 to 150 feet with ample depth to 25 feet. Slips include fingerpiers for side boarding.

LAT: 41° 20′ 18.564″N
LON: -71° 58′ 19.8474″W

*MLW = Mean Low Water Depth
LOA = Longest vessel that can be accommodated

New York

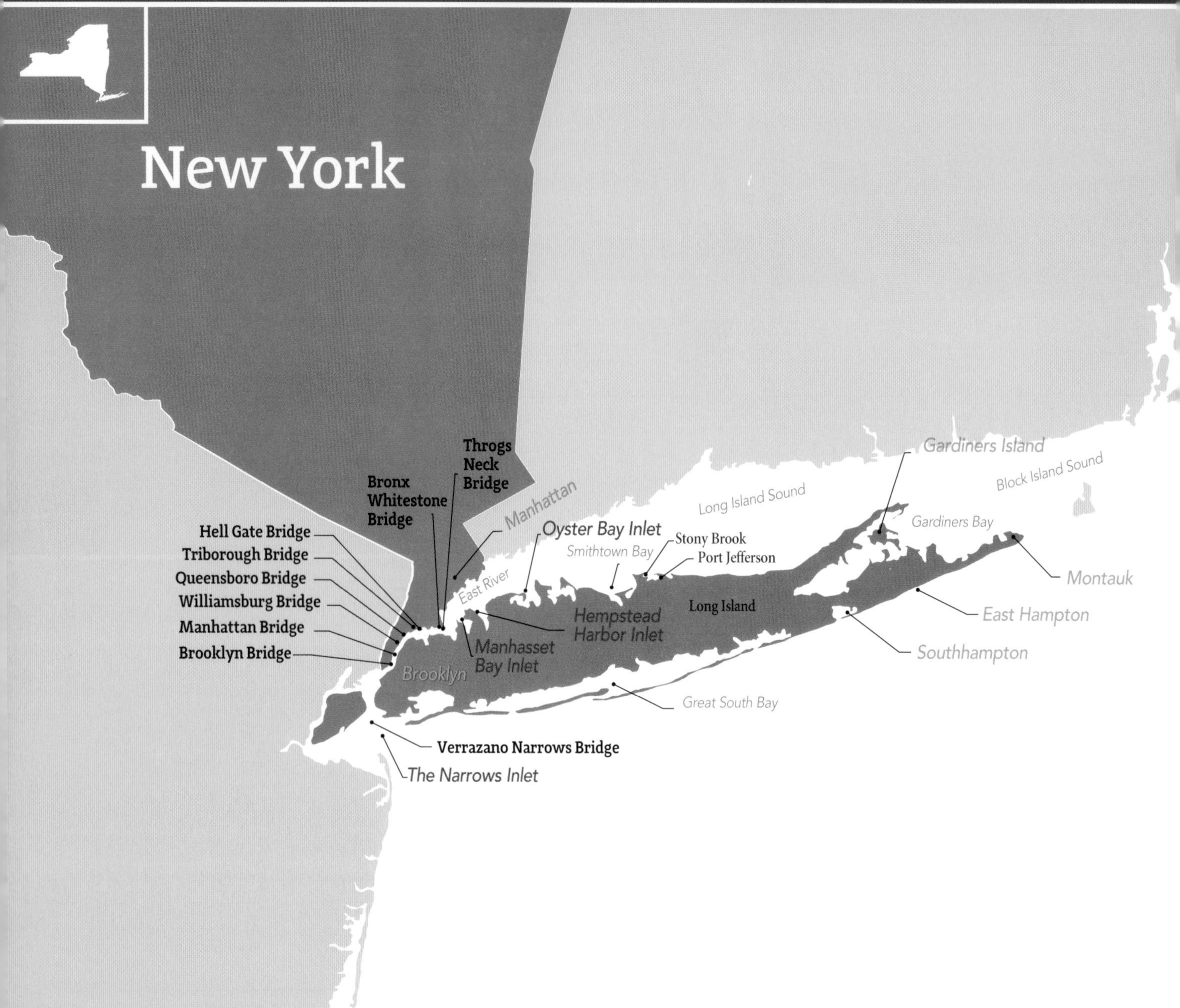

Throgs Neck Bridge

Bronx Whitestone Bridge

Manhattan

Hell Gate Bridge

Triborough Bridge

Queensboro Bridge

Williamsburg Bridge

Manhattan Bridge

Brooklyn Bridge

Oyster Bay Inlet

Stony Brook

Smithtown Bay

Port Jefferson

Long Island Sound

Gardiners Island

Block Island Sound

Gardiners Bay

Montauk

East River

Manhasset Bay Inlet

Hempstead Harbor Inlet

Long Island

East Hampton

Southhampton

Brooklyn

Great South Bay

Verrazano Narrows Bridge

The Narrows Inlet

* Denotes opening bridge

NOAA Weather Channel Map

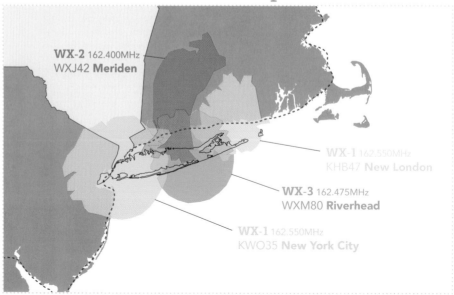

WX-2 162.400MHz
WXJ42 Meriden

WX-1 162.550MHz
KHB47 **New London**

WX-3 162.475MHz
WXM80 **Riverhead**

WX-1 162.550MHz
KWO35 **New York City**

New York

Long Island Sound to Huntington Bay

	MLW	Transient Slips/Moorings	Floating docks	Gas	Diesel	Pumpout	Showers	Pool	Laundry	Wi-Fi	Haulout	Repairs	Other
Montauk Yacht Club and Marina E. Long Island/Montauk Harbor 631-668-3100 www.montaukyachtclub.com	12'	●		➤	➤	●	●		●	●	●			private beach, fitness center, shuttle, waterfront dining
Pirates Cove Marine Fishers Island Sound 631-788-7528	9'		●	➤	➤					●	●	●		
Brewer Stirling Harbor Marina E. Long Island/Gardiners Bay 631-477-9594 www.byy.com	6'	●		●	●	●	●	●	●	●			●	complimentary shuttle, picnic area, fitness center, restaurant
Star Island Yacht Club Block Island Sound/Montauk 631-668-5052 www.starislandyc.com	9'	●		●	●	●	●	●	●	●		●	●	Full service marina, ABYC certified mechanics, 70-ton lift
Brewer Yacht Yard at Greenport E. Long Island/Gardiner Bay 631-477-9594 www.byy.com	8'			●	●	●	●	●	●			●	●	
Brick Cove Marina Southold Bay/Peconic River 631-477-0830 www.brickcove.com	6'	●		➤	➤	●	●	●	●	●		●	●	beach, tennis club
Cutchogue Harbor Marina Cutchogue Harbor/Paconic Bay 631-734-6311 www.newsuffolkshipyard.com	7'	●	●	●	●	●	●		●			●	●	
Strong's Marine E. Long Island/Great Peconic Bay 631-298-4770 www.strongsmarine.com	5'	●	●	●	●	●	●	●	➤	➤		●	●	Yamaha master techs, volvo certified; boat rentals
Lighthouse Marina Flanders Bay/Peconic River 631-722-3400 www.lighthousemarina.com	6'	●	●	●	●	●	●		●			●	●	
Britannia Yachting Center Long Island Sound/Huntington Bay 631-261-5600 www.britanniayachtingcenter.com	5'	●	●	●	●	●	●	●	●	➤		●	●	complete services, Dive Center
Seymour's Boatyard Long Island Sound/Huntington Bay 631-261-6574 www.seymoursboatyard.com	7'			●	●	●						●	●	railway 50T
Wyncote Yacht Club Huntington Bay 631-470-1201 631-470-6282 www.wyncoteclub.com	7'	●		●	●		●						➤	reciprocal yacht club privleges
Willis Marine Center Huntington Bay 631-421-3400 www.willismarine.com	12'	●		●	●	➤	●		➤	●		●	●	moorings; monitor VHF Ch 9; full-service facility
Coneys Marine Huntington Bay 631-421-3366 www.coneys.com	6'	●		➤	➤	●	●		➤	●		●	●	moorings

Long Island Sound Oyster Bay to Manhattan

	MLW	Transient Slips/Moorings	Floating docks	Gas	Diesel	Pumpout	Showers	Pool	Laundry	Wi-Fi	Haulout	Repairs	Other
Bridge Marine Sales & Tackle Oyster Bay 516-628-8686 www.bridgemarinesales.com	7'		●	➤	➤					●		●	●	clam bar; launch service
Oyster Bay Marine Center Oyster Bay 516-624-2400 www.obmc.com	20'	●	●	●	●	●	●		➤	●		●	●	moorings, L.I. Railroad nearby, walk to town, restaurants, beach
Brewer Yacht Yard at Glen Cove Hempstead Bay/Glen Cove Cr. 516-671-5563 www.byy.com	8'	●		●	●	●	●	●	●			●	●	marine supplies, waterside cafe, picnic area, ice
Brewer Capri West & East Marina Manhasset Bay/Port Washington 516-883-7800 www.byy.com	6.5'	●		●	●	●	●	●	●	●		●	●	sailing school, restaurant on site, golf carts
Manhasset Bay Marina Manhasset Bay 516-883-8411 www.manhassetbaymarina.com	6'	●		●	●	●	●		●	●		●	●	waterfront restaurant, ice, ship's store
Toms Point Marina W. Long Island/Manhasset Bay 516-883-6630 www.tomspointmarina.com	3'		➤	➤	●	●			●			●	●	

Atlantic Shore Long Island

Name / Location	MLW	Transient Slips/Moorings	Floating docks	Gas	Diesel	Pumpout	Showers	Pool	Laundry	Wi-Fi	Haulout	Repairs	Other
Brewer Post Road Boat Yard W. Long Island Snd/Mamaroneck Hbr 914-698-0295 www.byy.com	8'	•		•	•		•					•	chandlery on site, ice; groceries, restaurants nearby
South Minneford Yacht Club W. Long Island Sound/East River/Bronx 718-885-3113 www.southminneford.com	5'	•	•	>	>		•		>	•	•	>	secure dock access, 24-hour dockhands, public transit nearby
Surfside 3 Marinemax Manhattan/Chelsea Piers Hudson R.Chelsea Piers/Manhattan 212-336-SURF www.marinemax.com	7.5'	•		>	>								
Hampton Watercraft and Marine E. Long Is/Peconic Bay/Shinnecock Cnl 631-728-8200 www.hamptonwatercraft.com	4.5'	•	•	•		•				•	•	•	Canal Cafe, ship's store, free ice
Jackson's Marina E. Long Is/Peconic Bay/Shinnecock Cnl 631-728-4220 www.jacksonsmarina.com	6'	•	•	•	•	•				•	•	•	
Moriches Boat & Motor Moriches Bay 631-878-0023 www.morichesboatandmotor.com	4'		•									•	Full Service center
Windswept Marina W. Hampton/Moriches Bay 631-878-2100 www.windsweptmarina.net	4'	•		•	>	•	•				•	•	restaurant, ship store, bait, ice
Blue Point Marina Great South Bay/Corey Creek 631-363-2000 www.bluepointmarina.com	5'			•		>					•	•	restaurant on site, town beach nearby, marine supplies
Morgans Swan River Marina Swan River Great South Bay 631-758-3524 www.morgansmarina.com	4'	•	•	•		•	•				•	•	Beach House Restaurant
Oakdale Yacht Marina The Great River/Connetquot River 631-589-1087 www.oakdaleyacht.com	5'	•	•	•	•	•	•	•	•		•	•	tiki bar; washer/dryer, ice, food service
West Sayville Boat Basin Great South Bay/West Sayville 631-589-4141 www.boatbasin.com	4'	•	•	•	•	•	•			•		•	keypad gates, security, 2 beaches, minutes to Fire Island
Seaborn Marina Great South Bay/Bay Shore 631-665-0037	4.5'	•		•	•						•	•	
De Garmo Boatyard Great South Bay/Babylon 631-669-0789	6'	•		•	•	•	•				•	•	
Babylon Marine Great South Bay/Babylon 631-587-0333	6'	•		>	>	•				•	•	•	
Bay Village Marina Great South Bay/Amityville 631-691-4631 www.bayvillagemarina.com	5'	•		>							•	•	
Whaleneck Marina Merrick Bay/Jones Inlet 516-378-8025 http://whaleneckmarina.com/	5'	•	>				•	•			•	•	beach
Jones Inlet Marine Hudson Canal/Jones Inlet 516-379-BOAT www.jonesinletmarine.com	6'	•		>	>	•	•				•	•	
All Island Marine East Rockaway Channel 516-764-3300 www.allisland.com	10'	•	•	•	•	•	•				•	•	
Kings Plaza Marina Mill Basin/Jamaica Bay/Brooklyn 718-253-5434 www.kingsplazamarina.com	25'	•	>	>			•				•	•	marine supplies
Marine Basin Marina Gravesend Bay 718-372-5700 www.marinebasinmarina.net	6'	•	•				•		•			•	
Atlantis Marina & Yacht Club Lower Bay/Great Kills Harbor/Staten Is 718-966-9700 www.atlantismarinasi.com		•	•			•	•				•	•	ship's store, club house, bbq area

A young Norwegian cruiser takes an early morning walk along a pier overlooking Annapolis Harbor.

New Jersey

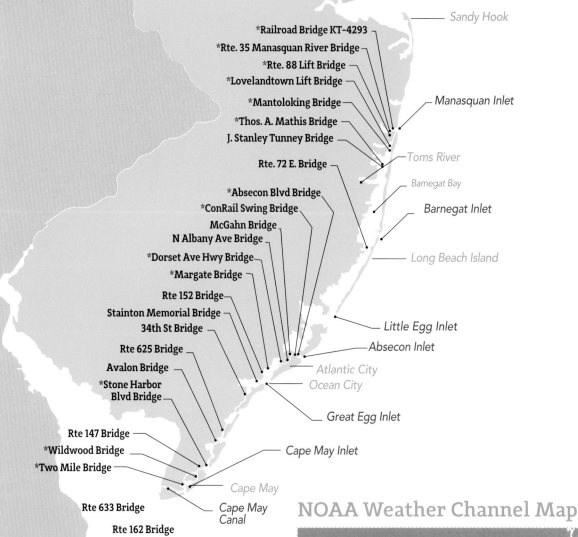

*Railroad Bridge KT-4293
*Rte. 35 Manasquan River Bridge
*Rte. 88 Lift Bridge
*Lovelandtown Lift Bridge
*Mantoloking Bridge
*Thos. A. Mathis Bridge
J. Stanley Tunney Bridge
Rte. 72 E. Bridge

*Absecon Blvd Bridge
*ConRail Swing Bridge
McGahn Bridge
N Albany Ave Bridge
*Dorset Ave Hwy Bridge
*Margate Bridge
Rte 152 Bridge
Stainton Memorial Bridge
34th St Bridge
Rte 625 Bridge
Avalon Bridge
*Stone Harbor Blvd Bridge

Rte 147 Bridge
*Wildwood Bridge
*Two Mile Bridge
Rte 633 Bridge
Rte 162 Bridge

Sandy Hook
Manasquan Inlet
Toms River
Barnegat Bay
Barnegat Inlet
Long Beach Island
Little Egg Inlet
Absecon Inlet
Atlantic City
Ocean City
Great Egg Inlet
Cape May Inlet
Cape May
Cape May Canal

* Denotes opening bridge

NOAA Weather Channel Map

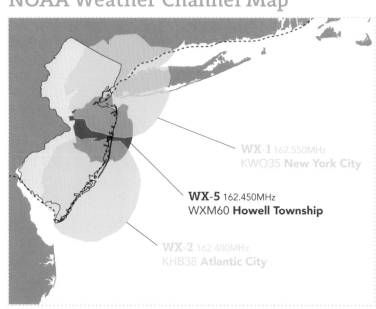

WX-1 162.550MHz KWO35 **New York City**

WX-5 162.450MHz WXM60 **Howell Township**

WX-2 162.400MHz KHB38 **Atlantic City**

New Jersey

Hudson River to Sandy Hook Bay

Marina	MLW	Transient Slips/Moorings	Floating docks	Gas	Diesel	Pumpout	Showers	Pool	Laundry	Wi-Fi	Haulout	Repairs	Other
Lincoln Harbor Yacht Club Hudson River 201-319-5100 www.lincolnharbormarina.com	6'	•		➤	•	•	•		•	•		•	Gateway to NYC; 24-hr security, lounge, slips to 250'
Newport Yacht Club and Marina Hudson River 201-626-5550 www.igy-newport.com	8'	•		•	•	•	•		•		•	•	dockage up to 200', PATH subway to Manhattan on-site
Liberty Landing Marina Lower Hudson River 201-985-8000 www.libertylandingmarina.com	18'	•		•	•	•	•		•		•	•	water taxi to NYC, 24-hour security, propane, marine store
Lockwood Boat Works Raritan Bay/S. Amboy 732-721-1605 www.lockwoodboatworks.com		•	•	•	•	•	•			•	•	•	full-service boatyard, marina, store, new/used boat sales
Atlantic Highlands Municipal Harbor Sandy Hook Bay 732-291-1670 www.ahnj.com	8'	•	•	•	•	•	•		➤	•	➤		NJ Clean Marina, tennis courts, playground, security, moorings
Sandy Hook Bay Marina Sandy Hook Bay 732-872-1511 www.sandyhookbaymarina.com	7'	•	•	➤	➤	•	•	•	•		•		restaurant, ferry to NY, adjacent beach; Mobile marine svc
Baker's Marina on the Bay Sandy Hook Bay 732-872-9300 www.marinaonthebay.biz	9'	•		•	➤	➤	•		➤	•	•	•	restaurant next door, high-speed ferry service to NY, national park

Navesink River to Toms River

Marina	MLW	Transient Slips/Moorings	Floating docks	Gas	Diesel	Pumpout	Showers	Pool	Laundry	Wi-Fi	Haulout	Repairs	Other
Fair Haven Yacht Works Navesink River 732-747-3010 www.fairhavenyachtworks.com	6'	•	•	➤	➤	•	•		➤	•	•	•	moorings; full-service marina
Channel Club Marina Shrewsbury River 732-222-7717 www.thechannelclubmarina.com	6'	•	•	•	•	•	•	•		•	•	•	courtesy shuttle, walk to beach, restaurant/tiki bar
Covesail Marina Shrewsbury River/Buoy #26 RF 732-842-5319	13'	•		➤	➤	•	•		➤	•	•	•	Restaurant on-site; beach
Surfside Marina Shrewsbury River 732-842-0844 www.surfside-marina.net	4.5'	•	•	➤	➤	•	•		•	•	•	•	Cert. Yamaha mechanic, pwc repair, electronics, beach, grills
Garden State Marina Manasquan River 732-892-4222 www.gardenstateyachtsales.com	6'			➤	➤	•	•					•	
Fisherman's Supply Dock Manasquan River/Point Pleasant Beach 732-892-2058	9'			•	•								fuel dock only
Clark's Landing Marina Manasquan River 732-899-5559 www.clarkslandingnj.com	4'	•		•	•	•	•				•	•	sales, service, fishing charters, ship's store
Baywood Marina Barnegat Bay/ICW 19 due west 732-477-3322 www.baywoodmarina.com	4'	•		•		•	•	•	•	•	•	•	Evinrude, Mercury, Yamaha, Honda, Suzuki, Volvo, Wellcraft
Coty Marine Barnegat Bay 732-288-1000 www.cotymarine.com	3'	➤					•			•			
Ocean Beach Marina Barnegat Bay 732-793-7460 www.oceanbeachmarina.com	5'	•		•		•	•		•			•	
Ocean Beach Marine Center Lanoka Harbor 609-242-2200 www.oceanbeachmarina.com	5'	•		•	•	•	•		•		•	•	marine supplies
Dillon's Creek Marina Toms River/Dillon Creek 732-270-8541 www.dillonscreekmarina.net	5.5'	•		➤	➤	•	•	•	•	•	•		
Ocean Gate Yacht Basin Toms River 732-269-2565 www.oceangateyachtbasin.com/	6'	•		•	•	•	•				•	•	ship's store
Shore Point Marina Toms R./Pine Beach 732-244-2106 www.shorepointmarina.com		•	•	•	•	•			•	•	•		ship's store; restaurants, shops minutes away

Barnegat Bay to Cape May

	MLW	Transient Slips/Moorings	Floating docks	Gas	Diesel	Pumpout	Showers	Pool	Laundry	Wi-Fi	Haulout	Repairs	Other
Cedar Creek Sailing Center/Marina Barnegat Bay/Cedar Creek 732-269-1351 www.ccscmarina.com	5.5'	•		➤	➤	•	•		•			•	•	
Silver Cloud Harbor Marina Barnegat Bay/Forked River 609-693-2145 www.forkedrivermarinas.com	6'	•		•	•	•	•	•	•	➤		•	•	Travelift, forklift services
Wilbert's Marina Barnegat Bay/Forked River 609-693-2145 www.forkedrivermarinas.com	6'	•		•	•	•	•	•		➤		•	•	
Silver Cloud Harbor Marina Barnegat Bay/Forked River 609-693-2145 www.forkedrivermarinas.com	7'	•		•	•	•	•	•	•	➤		•	•	
Tide's End Marina Barnegat Bay/Forked River 609-693-9423 www.tidesendmarina.com	6'	•		•	➤	•	•					•	•	
Key Harbor Marina Barnegat Bay/Marker 42 609-693-9355 www.keyharbormarina.com	5.5'	•		•								•	•	
Morrison's Marina Barnegat Bay/Beach Haven 609-492-2150 www.morrisonslbi.com	5'	•	•	•	•	•	•				•	•	•	ship's store on-site; groceries, restaurants nearby
Sheltered Cove Marina Little Egg Harbor/Tuckerton Cove 609-296-9400 www.shelteredcovemarina.com	4'			•	•	•	•						•	
Harbour Cove Marina Great Egg Harbor Bay 609-927-9600 www.harbourcovemarina.com	5'	•	•	•			•	•			•		➤	restaurant on site, storm protected basin
Kammerman's Atlantic City Marina Absecon Inlet/Clam Creek 609-348-8418 www.kammermansmarina.com	8'	•	•	•	•	•	•		•					High-speed fuel pump; close to restaurants, groceries
Senator Frank S. Farley State Marina Absecon Inlet/Clam Creek 1-800-876-4386/609-441-8482 www.goldennugget.com	8'	•	•	•	•	•	•	•	•	•			➤	
Deebold Boatyard Absecan Inlet/Bonita Tideway 609-266-3214	12'	•		•								•	•	
Pier 47 Marina Richardsons Channel 609-729-4774 www.pier47.com	6'	•	•	•	➤	•				•		•	•	Ship's store; certified Volvo and Master yamaha techs
Canyon Club Resort Marina Cape May Harbor 609-884-0199 www.canyonclubmarina.com	8'	•	•	•	•	•	•	•	•	•		•	•	high speed, in-slip fueling; ship's store
Utsch's Marina Cape May Harbor 609-884-2051 www.capemayharbor.com	7'	•		•	•	•	•		•			•	•	
South Jersey Marina Cape May Harbor/Schellengers Creek 609-884-2400 www.sjmarina.com	10'	•	•	•	•	•	•		•				•	ship's store, restaurant on-site
Miss Chris Marina Cape May/Spicer Creek 609-884-3351 www.misschrismarina.com	8'	•		•	•	•								live bait, ice, tackle shop, restaurant, kayak rentals,

Delaware Bay

	MLW	Transient Slips/Moorings	Floating docks	Gas	Diesel	Pumpout	Showers	Pool	Laundry	Wi-Fi	Haulout	Repairs	Other
Bayway Marina Delaware Bay/Bidwell Cr. 609-465-1676	4.5'	•	•	•	•	•	•					•	•	
Hancock Harbor Marina Cohansey R./Greenwich 856-455-2610 www.hancockharbor.com	25'	•	•	•	•			•		•		•		marine supplies, courtesy car
Port Norris Marina Delaware Bay/Maurice R. 856-785-0270		•	•	•				•						ship's store, ice, restaurant adjacent

Sandy Hook Bay Marina

One Willow Street, Highlands, NJ 07732
Ph: 732-872-1511 | Fax: 732-219-1967
Email: info@sandyhookbaymarina.com
SandyHookBayMarina.com

description of facilities

Sandy Hook Bay Marina is located on the shores of Sandy Hook Bay in the historic town of Highlands, NJ. Our premier port of call has been designed to delight boat owners, captains, crew and guests alike with state-of-the-art facilities and concierge style amenities.

If you are looking for a safe haven to enjoy boating in New Jersey then look no further. Our secure, wave protected, deep water access and basin with floating docks and full length finger piers provides the perfect safe harbor for vessels of all sizes. We have 130 slips available with approximately 15 reserved for transients, and full time dock attendants to assist you. Some of our amenities include an onsite restaurant, outdoor Captain's bar, swimming pool, Ship's Store, ice, showers, laundry facilities, fire pits and BBQ area.

marina approach & docking

From the tip of Sandy Hook, steer a course of 180° to Red Buoy #6. Turn up to 120° and look for the entrance to Sandy Hook Bay Marina directly across from Green Buoy #7.

LAT: 40° 24' 32.3532"N
LON: -74° 0' 1.9800"W

at a glance

DOCKAGE RATE: Rates available for Daily, Monthly, Seasonal

PAYMENT: Visa, Master Card, Amex

HOURS: Open Daily in Season

TRANSIENT SLIPS/TOTAL SLIPS: 15/130

VHF/WORKING: 7

MLW/LOA*: 7'/85'

ELECTRIC: 30/50/100 Amp service

PUMP-OUT: Available by appointment

FUEL: within 1 mi

REPAIR: Mechanic available

RESTAURANT/MILES: On-site with outdoor bar and café

POOL: Yes

HEAD/SHOWER: Yes/Yes

LAUNDRY: Yes

INTERNET ACCESS: Yes

CABLE: No

NEAREST TOWN/MILES: 1 mi

SHOPPING: 1 mi

GOLF/TENNIS: Nearby/Nearby

AIRPORT/MILES: Approximately 40 mi

TRANSPORTATION: Bicycles/Taxi

YACHT BROKERAGE: No

SPECIAL: Adjacent Beach, Ferry Service to NYC, Henry Hudson Trail, Across from Sandy Hook Gateway Park

*MLW = Mean Low Water Depth
LOA = Longest vessel that can be accommodated

Delaware & C&D Canal

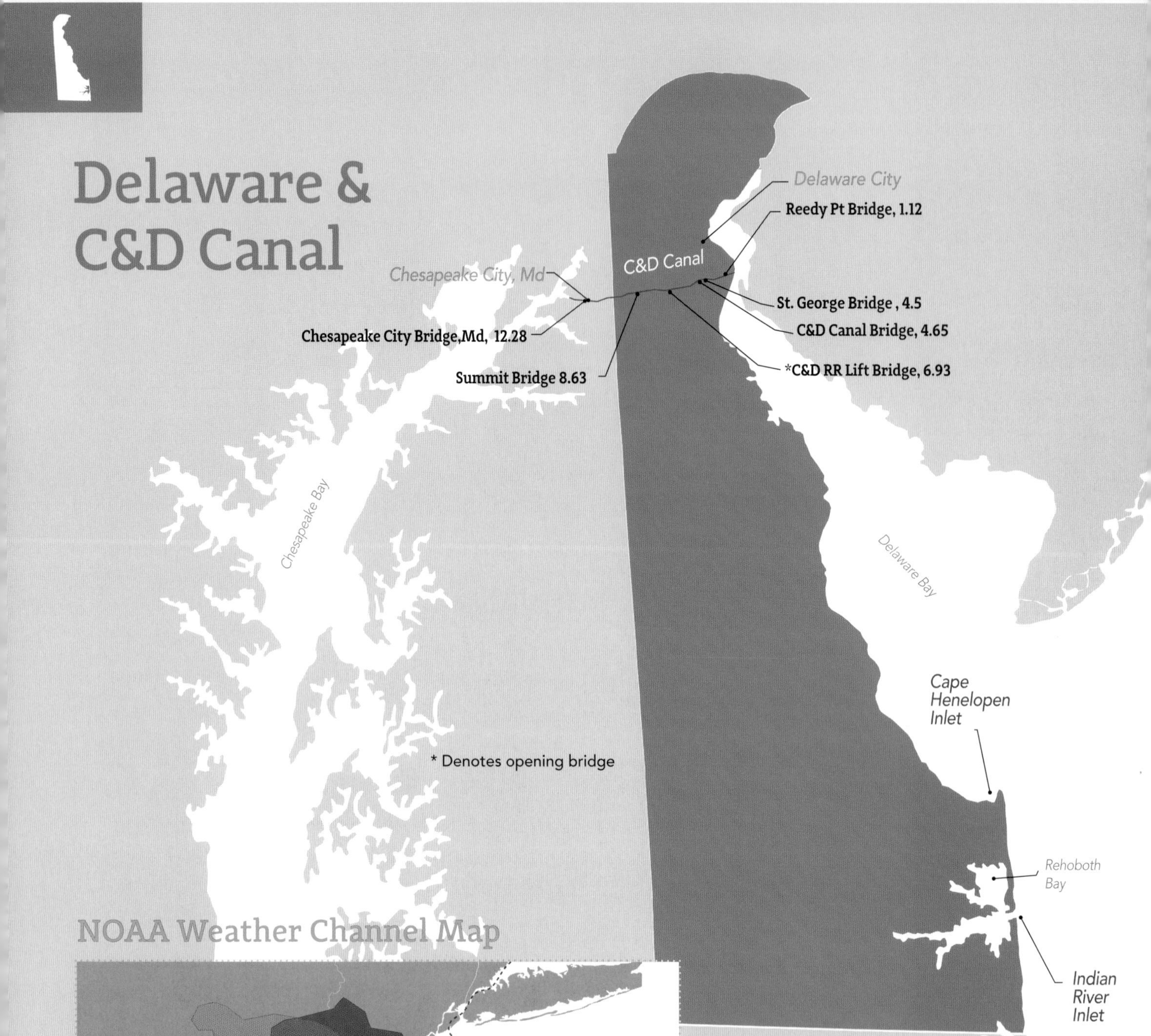

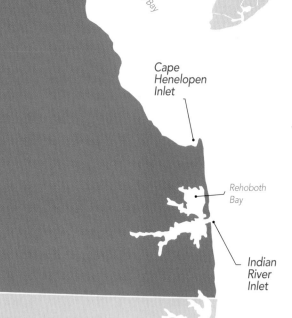

Delaware City
Reedy Pt Bridge, 1.12
C&D Canal
Chesapeake City, Md
St. George Bridge , 4.5
C&D Canal Bridge, 4.65
Chesapeake City Bridge,Md, 12.28
***C&D RR Lift Bridge, 6.93**
Summit Bridge 8.63

Chesapeake Bay

Delaware Bay

* Denotes opening bridge

Cape Henelopen Inlet

Rehoboth Bay

Indian River Inlet

NOAA Weather Channel Map

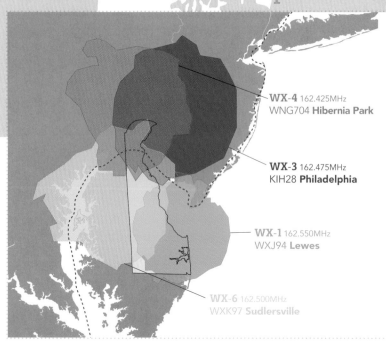

WX-4 162.425MHz
WNG704 **Hibernia Park**

WX-3 162.475MHz
KIH28 **Philadelphia**

WX-1 162.550MHz
WXJ94 **Lewes**

WX-6 162.500MHz
WXK97 **Sudlersville**

(Canal distances in nautical miles from east entrance)

C&D Canal Mile 1.12
39°55.82'N 075°58.25'W

Reedy Point Bridge
Type: Fixed
Height: 136'
Comments: Be conscious of drift caused by strong currents when approaching this and all of the bridges on the canal. Monitor VHF 13 and 16 as you transit the canal.

C&D Canal Mile 4.5
39°55.26'N 075°65.11'W

St. Georges Bridge
Type: Fixed
Height: 137'

C&D Canal Mile 4.65
39°54.98'N 075°65.63'W

C&D Canal Bridge
Type: Fixed
Height: 142'

C&D Canal Mile 6.93
39°54.34'N 075°70.30'W

*C&D RR Lift Bridge
Type: Lift
Closed Height: 45'
Schedule: Open except for trains
Contact: VHF 13 (see *Comments*)
Comments: The only notice that the bridge will be lowered for a train will be given over VHF 13. Also, be cautious in low light or at night because bridge will not necessarily be lighted.

C&D Canal Mile 8.63
39°54.12'N 075°73.81'W

Summit Bridge
Type: Fixed
Height: 131'

C&D Canal Mile 12.28
39°52.92'N 075°81.36'W

Chesapeake City Bridge
Type: Fixed
Height: 140'
Comments: Be conscious of drift caused by strong currents when approaching this and all of the bridges on the canal. Monitor VFH 13 and 16 as you transit the canal.

Delaware

			MLW	Transient Slips/Moorings	Floating docks	Gas	Diesel	Pumpout	Showers	Pool	Laundry	Wi-Fi	Haulout	Repairs	Other
Delaware Bay															
Delaware City Marina Delaware River/C&D Canal	302-834-4172	www.delawarecitymarina.biz	7'	•	•	•	•	•	•		•		•	•	Marine store, gift shop, walking distance to historic town
Summit North Marina C&D Canal	302-836-1800	www.summitnorthmarina.com	7.5'	•	•	•	•	•	•	•	•		•	•	
Delaware Seashore															
Rehoboth Bay Marina Rehoboth Bay	302-226-2012	www.rehobothbaymarina.com	5'	•		•	➤	•	•		•				
Indian River Marina Indian River Inlet/Delaware Seashore SP	302-227-3071	www.destateparks.com	7.5'	•	•	•	•	•	•		•		•	•	Ship store, waterfront restaurant/bar

Maryland

Havre de Grace

Elk River

C&D Canal

Sassafras River

Baltimore

Patapsco River

Rock Hall

Chester River

Chesapeake Bay Bridge

Eastern Bay

St. Michaels

DISTRICT OF COLUMBIA

Annapolis

Choptank River

Oxford

DELAWARE

Patuxent River

Solomons

Tangier Sound

VIRGINIA

Potomac River

Crisfield

Chesapeake Bay

NOAA Weather Channel Map

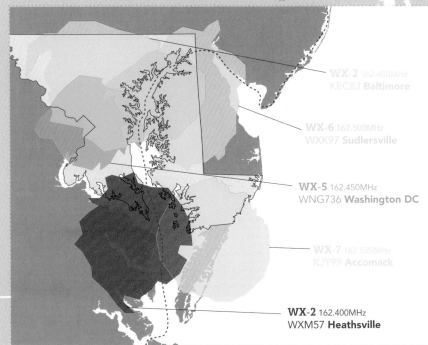

WX-2 162.400MHz
KEC83 **Baltimore**

WX-6 162.500MHz
WXK97 **Sudlersville**

WX-5 162.450MHz
WNG736 **Washington DC**

WX-7 162.525MHz
KJY99 **Accomack**

WX-2 162.400MHz
WXM57 **Heathsville**

38°59.622'N 076°22.911'W

Chesapeake Bay Bridge
Type: Fixed
Height: 186'
Comments: Keep a sharp lookout for shipping traffic moving up and down the Bay. Ships will announce their approach to the bridge on VHF 16.

Maryland

	MLW	Transient Slips/Moorings	Floating docks	Gas	Diesel	Pumpout	Showers	Pool	Laundry	Wi-Fi	Haulout	Repairs	Other
Atlantic Shore													
Ocean City Fisherman's Marina, Inc. Ocean City Inlet 410-213-2478 www.ocfishermansmarina.com	8'	•		•	•		•		•			➤	
Ocean City Fishing Center Ocean City Inlet 800-322-3065 www.ocfishing.com	7'	•		•	•	•	•	•	•		•	➤	Dockside bar and grill, bait, tackle
Sunset Marina Ocean City Inlet 410-213-9600 www.ocsunsetmarina.com	8'	•		•	•	•	•	•	•	•	•	•	fitness center, game room, in-slip fueling
Western Chesapeake Bay/Northeast to Annapolis													
McDaniel Yacht Basin Northeast R./Bouy 14 410-287-8121 www.mcdanielyacht.com	6'	•		•	•	•	•	•	•	•	•	•	Canvas shop, repairs, prop shop, storage, boat sales
Anchor Marina North East River 410-287-6000 www.anchorboat.com	8'	•	•	•	➤	•	•			•	•		Yanmar certified; Nauti Goose restaurant, park next door
Shelter Cove Marina/Jackson Marine Sales Marker #10/North East River 410-287-9400 www.jacksonmarinesales.com	5'	•	•	•	•	•	•		•	•	•	•	MD Clean Marina, Restaurant on site, playground
Charlestown Marina Northeast R./Charlestown 410-287-8125 www.charlestownmarina.com	6'	•		•	➤	•	•		•	•	•	•	park and beach next door, restaurants nearby
Havre de Grace Marine Center at Log Pond Susquehanna River 410-939-2221 www.Hdgmarinecenter.com	6.5'	•	•	➤	➤	•	•			•	•	•	On-site canvas shop, sail loft, full-service marine repair facility
Tidewater Marina Susquehanna River/Havre de Grace 410-939-0951 www.tidewatermarina.com	8'	•		•	•	•	•		➤	•	•	•	Marine store; free shuttle, Wi-Fi, moorings
Porter's Seneca Marina Middle River/Seneca Creek 410-335-6563 www.portersenecamarina.com	6'	•	•	•	➤	•	•	•	➤	•	•		Sheltered; floating piers, mounted electric, gas dock
Bowley's Marina Middle River 410-335-3553 www.bowleysmarina.com	8'	•		•	•	•	•	•	•	•	•		Volleyball, bar/lounge, grills, haul outs, mechanic
Beacon Light Marina Middle River/Seneca Cr. 410-335-6200 www.beaconlightmarina.com	4'	•		•		•	•		➤	•	•	•	New bulkheads, catwalks and electric. Wi-Fi, marine supplies,
Maryland Marina Middle River/Frog Mortar Cr. 410-335-8722 www.marylandmarina.net	6'	•	➤	➤	•	•		•	•	•	•		Service, Wi-Fi, Sunset Cove Cafe, live web cam

Marina	MLW	Transient Slips/Moorings	Floating docks	Gas	Diesel	Pumpout	Showers	Pool	Laundry	Wi-Fi	Haulout	Repairs	Other
Sunset Harbor Marina — Middle River/Norman Creek — 410-687-7290 www.sunsetharbor.com	4'	●	➤			●	●		●	●	●		Picnic area, grills; indoor rack storage to 38'
Young's Boat Yard — Patapsco River/Jones Cr. — 410-477-8607 www.youngsboatyard.com	6'	●	➤	➤	●	●				●			Protected deep water slips. 15-ton open lift
Old Bay Marina — Patapsco River/Jones Cr. — 410-477-1488 www.oldbaymarina.com	6'	●	➤	➤	●	●		➤	●	●	●		30-ton lift, boat prep for overseas shipping
Anchor Bay East Marina — Patapsco River/Bear Cr. — 410-284-1044 www.anchorbayeastmarina.com	9'	●	●	●	●	●		●	●	●		●	Open daily; emergency service always avail.
Baltimore Marine Centers at Lighthouse Point — Baltimore Inner Harbor/Canton — 410-675-8888 www.bmcmarinas.com	12'	●	●	●	●	●	●	●	●	●	●	➤	●	West Marine on-site, Full-service marina, slips to 200 feet
Anchorage Marina — Baltimore Inner Harbor — 410-522-7200 www.anchoragemarina.com	10'	●	●	➤	➤	●	●	●	●	●	➤	➤	downtown Baltimore. Near everything
Henderson's Wharf Marina & Inn — Baltimore Inner Harbor — 410-732-1049 www.hendersonswharfmarina.com	15'	●	●	➤	➤	●	●		●	●	➤	●	private exclusive slips, 38-room inn, facilities for special events
Harbor East Marina — Baltimore Inner Harbor — 410-625-1700 www.harboreastmarina.com	10'	●	➤	➤	➤	●	●		●	●	➤	➤	Inner Harbor Location, 200+ slips, dining, nightlife
Baltimore Marine Center Inner Harbor — Baltimore Inner Harbor — 410-837-5339 www.baltimoreinnerharbormarinecenter.com	20'	●		●	●	●	●	●	●	●			
Baltimore Marine Center at HarborView — Baltimore Inner Harbor — 410-752-1122 www.harborviewmarinecenter.com	25'	●	●	➤	●	●	●	●	●	●	➤	➤	Full-service marina w/278 deep water slips
Tidewater Yacht Service at Port Covington — Patapsco River/Middle Branch — 410-625-4992 www.tysc.com	18'	●	●	➤	➤	●	●		➤	●	●	●	Large yacht repairs 77-ton lift, floating docks
Fairview Marina — Patapsco River — 410-437-3400 www.fairviewmarina.com	8'	●	➤	➤	●	●	●	●	●	●		●	Pool, beach, playground, gas, pump-out
Atlantic Marina Resort — Patapsco River — 410-437-6926 www.atlanticmarinaresort.com	4'	●	●	●	●	●	●	●	●	●		●	Pool, beach, playground, gas, pump-out
Pleasure Cove Marina — Bodkin Creek — 410-437-6600 www.pleasurecovemarina.com	6.5'	●	●	●	●	●	●	●	●	●	●	●	fully stocked marine store, boat rentals, heated dry storage
Atlantic Marina on the Magothy — Magothy River/Gray's Cr. — 410-360-2500 www.atlanticmarinaresort.com	6'	●	●	●	●	●	●		➤	●	●	●	Ship store, boatel, fuel, pump-out, 25-ton-lift
Magothy Marina — Magothy River — 410-647-2356 www.magothymarina.com	14'	●	●	●	●	●	●	●	●	●		➤	Ramp, pool, fuel, pump-out, Wi-Fi, picnic area
Podickory Point Yacht & Beach Club — Magothy River — 410-757-8000 www.podickorypoint.com	6'	●		●	●	●	●	●	●	●	➤	➤	Clubhouse, boatel, tennis, beach, lift slips
Chesapeake Harbour Marina — Severn River/outside Back Cr. — 410-268-1969 www.chesapeakeharbour.com	8'	●	➤	➤	●	●	●	●	●	●	➤	➤	Pvt beach, pools, tennis courts, 24-hour security
Horn Point Harbor Marina — Severn River/Back Creek — 410-263-0550 www.hornpointharbor.com	6.5'	●	➤	➤	●	●			●	➤	➤		
Annapolis Landing Marina — Severn River/Back Creek — 410-263-0090 www.annapolislandingmarina.com	9'	●	●	●	●	●	●	●	●	●	➤	➤	Cable TV, fuel, annual & transient slips, playground
Mears Marina Annapolis — Severn River/Back Creek — 410-268-8282 www.mearsannapolis.com	9'	●	➤	➤		●	●	●	●	●	➤	➤	Walk downtown; poolside cafe/tiki bar, tennis, grills
Port Annapolis Marina — Severn River/Back Creek — 410-269-1990 www.portannapolis.com	10'	●	➤	➤	●	●	●	●	●	●	●	●	50-ton lift, full/DIY repairs, bikes
Bert Jabin Yacht Yard — Severn River/Back Creek — 410-268-9667 www.bjyy.com	9'	●	●	➤	●	●	●	●	➤	●	●	●	Hi-Dry boatel, ship's store, full-service marina
J. Gordon & Company, Inc. — Severn River/Back Creek — 410-263-0054 www.jgordonco.com	6'		➤	➤	●	●		●	●	●	●	●	

	MLW	Transient Slips/Moorings	Floating docks	Gas	Diesel	Pumpout	Showers	Pool	Laundry	Wi-Fi	Haulout	Repairs	Other
Eastport Yacht Center Severn River/Back Creek · 410-280-9988 · www.eastportyachtcenter.com	12'	•		➤	➤	•	•		•	•	•	•		One minute from the Bay
Annapolis Harbor Boat Yard Severn River/Annapolis Harbor · 410-268-0092 · www.annapolisharbor.net	10'		•	➤	➤							•	•	full-service repairs
Pier 4 Marina Severn River/Spa Creek · 410-990-9515 · www.pier4annapolis.com	8'		•	➤	➤		•			•		➤	➤	Across Spa Creek from Annapolis YC. Floating docks
Annapolis City Marina Severn River/Annapolis Harbor · 410-268-0660 · www.annapoliscitymarina.com	12'	•			•	•	•	•		•	•		➤	Complete on-water dock shop and fuel dock
South Annapolis Yacht Centre Severn River/Spa Creek · 410-263-1643 · www.sa-yc.com	10'	•		➤	➤	➤	•				•	•	•	50-ton ultrawide lift, full-service yard, covered slips
The Yacht Basin Company Annapolis Harbor/Spa Creek · 410-263-3544 · www.yachtbasin.com	12'	•			•	•	•			•	•	➤	➤	Wi-Fi, cable; Vessels to 240' in heart of town
Annapolis City Dock Severn River/Spa Creek/Annapolis Harbor · 410-263-7973 · www.annapolis.gov	12'	•		➤	➤	•	•		•			➤	➤	moorings and slips for transients
Western Chesapeake—South River to Potomac River														
Selby Bay Marina South River/Selby Bay · 410-798-0232 · www.selbybaymarina.com	7'	•		•	•	•	•			•	•	•	•	picnic area
Liberty Yacht Club & Marina South River · 410-266-5633 · www.libertymarina.com	15'	•		•	•	•	•	•		•	•	•	•	Full-service, 25-ton lift; snack shop
Pier 7 Marina South River · 410-956-2288 · www.piersevenmarina.com	10'	•		➤	➤	•	•			•		•		
Casa Rio Marina South River/Rhode R./Cadle Cr. · 301-261-7111 · www.casariomarina.com	5'	•		➤	➤	•	•		➤		•	•		2 lifts, launch, dry storage, painter, DIY storage
Rhode River Marina Rhode River/Bear Neck Creek · 410-798-1658 · www.rhoderivermarina.com	6'	•		•	•	•	•			•		•	•	Boatel, slips, lift, engine repair, fuel, pump-out
Hartge Yacht Harbor West River/Lerch Cr. · 443-607-6306 · www.hartgeyachtharbor.com	8'	•		➤	➤	•	•			•	•	•	•	Protected slips, moorings, full-service marina.
Hartge Yacht Yard West River/Tenthouse Cr. · 410-867-2188 · www.hartgeyard.com	6'			➤	➤	•	•	•			•	•	•	full marine services with factory trained and certified techs
Pirate's Cove West River/Galesville · 410-867-2300 · www.piratescovemd.com	10'	•		➤	➤	•	•	•	•	•	•	➤	➤	Pirate's Cove Dock Bar
Shipwright Harbor Herring Bay/Rockhold Cr. · 410-867-7686 · www.shipwrightharbormarina.com	7'	•		➤	➤	•	•	•		•	•		•	Beautiful picnic area with gazebos, grills. Dog park
Harbour Cove Marina Herring Bay/Rockhold Cr. · 301-261-9500 · www.harbourcove.com	4'			•	➤	•	•	•	•		•		•	Full Service, mechanics, pool, laundry, storage
Herrington Harbour North Herring Bay/Rockhold Cr./Tracys Cr. · 410-867-4343 · www.herringtonharbour.com	7'	•		➤	➤	•	•	•	•	•	•		•	Marina resort, full service, DIY yard, West Marine, dock bar
Herrington Harbour South Herring Bay · 410-741-5100 · www.herringtonharbour.com	7'	•	•	➤	➤	•	•	•	•	•	•	➤	➤	Eco-lifestyle marina resort, beachfront lodging, dining
Rod N Reel Marina West Chesapeake Beach/Fishing Cr. · 301-855-3572 · www.cbresortspa.com	10'	•		➤	➤	•	•	•	➤	➤		•	•	2-ton lift; near water park, ballfields, beach
Rod N Reel Dock Chesapeake Beach/Fishing Cr. · 301-855-8450 · www.cbresortspa.com	6'	•		•	•	•	•	•	•	➤	•	➤	➤	Charter fishing, tackle shop, 72-room hotel & spa, restaurants
Breezy Point Marina Breezy Point · 410-414-9292 · www.breezypointmarina.com	4.5'	•		•	•	•	•			•	•	•		Immediate access to Bay, 5 miles S. of Ches. Beach
Flag Harbor Yacht Haven Chesapeake Bay · 410-586-1915 · www.flagharbor.com	7'			•	➤	•	•	•		•	•	•		condo marina with newly renovated docks, easy access to bay

	MLW	Transient Slips/Moorings	Floating docks	Gas	Diesel	Pumpout	Showers	Pool	Laundry	Wi-Fi	Haulout	Repairs	Other
Solomons Yachting Center Patuxent R./Back Creek 410-326-2401 www.solomonsyachtingcenter.net	12'	•	•	•	•	•	•	•	•	•	•	➤	Floating piers, pool, lounge area, DIY yard
Zahniser's Yachting Center Patuxent R./Back Creek 410-326-2166 option 4 www.zahnisers.com	12'	•		➤	➤	•	•	•	•	•	•	•	quantum sail loft, marine surveyor, sailing school & Charters
Comfort Inn Beacon Marina Patuxent R./Back Creek 410-326-6303 www.choicehotels.com	12'	•		➤	➤	•	•	•	•		➤	➤	
Spring Cove Marina Patuxent R./Back Creek 410-326-2161 www.springcovemarina.com	12'	•		•	•	•	•	•	•	•	•	•	park-like setting, pool bar and grill in-season
Solomons Harbor Marina/Holiday Inn Patuxent R./Back Creek 410-326-1052 www.solomonsharbormarina.com	8'	•		➤	➤	•	•	•	•	•	➤	➤	Transient dockage to 65 ft., cable
Calvert Marina Patuxent R./Back Creek 410-326-4251 www.calvertmarina.com	14'	•		•	•	•	•	•	•	•	•	•	Floating docks, covered slips, 2 restaurants, BoatU.S. discount
Washburn's Boat Yard Patuxent R./Back Creek 410-326-6701 www.washburnsboatyard.com	12'			➤	➤						•	•	
Boatel California Patuxent River 301-737-1400 www.boatelcalifornia.com	6'	•				•	•				•	•	New/used boats, sales/service/ parts; private marina
Point Lookout Marina Potomac R./Smith Creek 301-872-5000 www.pointlookoutmarina.com	9'	•	•	•	•	•	•		•	•	•	•	Sunset Cove Restaurant open thur-sun; courtesy car
Dennis Point Marina & Campground St. Mary's River/Carthagena Cr. 301-994-2288 www.dennispointcampground.com	10'	•	•	•	•	•	•		•	•	•	•	75-ton lift, dog park, boat ramp, cabins
Cedar Cove Marina Potomac R./Herring Creek 301-994-1155 www.cedarcovemarina.com	6'	•			➤		•		•	•	•	•	
Combs Creek Marina LLC Potomac R./Breton Bay/Combs Cr. 301-475-2017 www.combscreekmarina.com	6'	•		➤		•	•						Newtown Neck St. Park nearby, St. Clements Island nearby
Cather Marine Potomac R./St. Patrick Cr. 301-769-3335 www.cathermarine.com	5'	•		•	➤	•	•				•	•	
Coltons Point Marina Potomac R./St. Patrick Cr. 301-769-3121 www.coltonspointmarina.com	5'	•		•	•	•	•	•	•	•	•	•	30-ton lift, pavilion, lounge, big screen TV

Eastern Shore—Chesapeake City to Kent Narrows

	MLW	Transient Slips/Moorings	Floating docks	Gas	Diesel	Pumpout	Showers	Pool	Laundry	Wi-Fi	Haulout	Repairs	Other
Bohemia Bay Yacht Harbour Bohemia R. 410-885-2601 www.bbyh.com	5'	•	•	•	•	•	•	•	•	•	•	•	Full service yard; 50-ton lift, marine accessories, Wi-Fi
Harbour North Marina C&D Canal 410-885-5656 www.sunsetcafemd.com	3'	•		•	➤	•	•		•	•	•	•	waterfront bar & restaurant, marine supplies
Triton Marina Elk River 410-620-3060 www.tritonmarina.com	5'	•	•	•	•	•	•		➤	•	•	•	full-service marina in park-like setting. New/used boat sales
Two Rivers Yacht Basin Bohemia R. 410-885-2257 www.tworiversyachtbasin.com	4'	•		•	➤	•	•				•	•	dock store, ice, snacks, marine supplies
Hack's Point Marina Bohemia R. 410-275-9151 www.hackspointmarina.com	6'	•	•	➤	➤	•	•				•	•	Floating docks, full-service dept. public ramp
Georgetown Yacht Basin Sassafras R. 410-648-5112 www.gybinc.com	13'	•	•	•	•	•	•	•	•	•	•	•	moorings, 110-ton lift, full service, Kitty Knight House, beach
Skipjack Cove Yachting Resort Sassafras R. 410-275-2122 www.skipjackcove.com	12'	•		•	•	•	•	•	•	•	•	•	Pool, tennis, Wi-Fi, lounge, exercise room
Duffy Creek Marina Sassafras R. 410-275-2141 www.duffycreekmarina.com	6'	•		•	•	•	•	•	•	•	•	•	Secluded wake-free basin, beach, picnic areas
Sassafras Harbor Marina Sassafras R. 410-275-1144 www.sassafrasharbormarina.com	12'	•	•	➤	➤	•	•	•	•	•	•	•	Covered slips, floating docks, activities ctr, 70-ton lift, cable tv

	MLW	Transient Slips/Moorings	Floating docks	Gas	Diesel	Pumpout	Showers	Pool	Laundry	Wi-Fi	Haulout	Repairs	Other
Sailing Associates Marina Sassafras R. 410-275-8171 www.sailingassociates.com	12'	•	•	➤	➤	•	•	•	➤	•	•	•	park nearby, beaches nearby, family friendly, pet friendly
Granary Marina Sassafras R. 410-648-5112 www.gybinc.com	12'	•		•	•	•	•	➤	•	•	➤	➤	Slips to 140ft; 240v, 100amp. Sassafras Grill, Granary restaurants
Gregg Neck Boat Yard Sassafras R./Swantown Cr. 410-648-5360	10'	•			•	•		➤	•	•	•		Used boats, pile driving, crane
Wharf At Handy's Point Worton Creek 410-778-4363 www.thewharfathandyspoint.com	9'	•	➤	➤	•	•	•	•		•	•		full-service yard, 35-ton lift
Worton Creek Marina Worton Creek/Buoy #34 410-778-3282 www.wortoncreek.com	6'	•		•	•	•	•	•	•	•	•	•	60' slips, picnic area, 70-ton lift, restaurant
Great Oak Landing Marina Fairlee Creek 410-778-5007 www.mearsgreatoaklanding.com	8'	•		•	•	•	•	•	•	•	•		Tennis, hot tub, basketball, volleyball, pool
Tolchester Marina Chesapeake Bay/Buoy #21/Tolchester 410-778-1400 www.tolchestermarina.com	6'	•	•	•	•	•	•	•	•	•	•	•	restaurant, beach bar
Swan Creek Marina Swan Cr. 410-639-7813 www.swancreekmarina.com	7'	•	➤	➤	•	•		➤	•	•	•		Rigging, carpentry, electronics, welding, moorings
Gratitude Marina Swan Cr. 410-639-7011 www.gmarina.com	6.5'	•	•	•	•	•		➤	•	•	•		
Haven Harbour Marina Swan Cr. 410-778-6697 www.havenharbour.com	6'	•		•	•	•	•	•	•	•	•	•	Full-service resort; two pools, waterfront bar/grill
Moonlight Bay Marina & Inn Mouth of Swan Creek 410-639-2660 www.moonlightbayinn.com	7'	•	➤	➤	➤	•	➤	➤	•	➤	➤		firepit, bbqs, bikes
Osprey Point Marina Restaurant & Inn Swan Cr. 410-639-2194 www.ospreypoint.com	6'	•	➤	➤	•	•	•	•	•	•	➤	➤	Floating docks, pool, gourmet restaurant/bar
Rock Hall Landing Marina Rock Hall Harbor 410-639-2224 www.rockhalllanding.com	7'	•	•	➤	➤	•	•	•	•	•			closest marina to town
Sailing Emporium Rock Hall Harbor 410-778-1342 www.sailingemporium.com	7'	•		•	•	•	•	•	•		•	•	Free pump-out. Transport to dining, yacht sales
North Point Marina Rock Hall Harbor 410-639-2907 www.northpointmarina.net	8'	•		•	•	•	•	•	•	•	➤	➤	Picnic area, gas grills, covered slips, rental bikes
Lankford Bay Marina Chester River/Lankford Creek 410-778-1414 www.lankfordbaymarina.net	7'	•		•	•	•	•	•	•	•	•	•	Cable, bus to Rock Hall, Wi-Fi, pool, fuel, full service
Rolph's Wharf Chester River/Buoy #35 410-778-6389 www.rolphswharf.com	8'	•	•	•	•	•	•	•	-	•	•	•	Pet- and kid friendly, beach bar
Lippincott Marine Kent Narrows 410-827-9300 www.lippincottmarine.com	7'	•	➤	➤	•	•	•	•	•	•	•	•	Full-service, storage, new/brokerage boat sales
Mears Point Marina Kent Narrows 410-827-8888 www.mearspoint.com	8'	•		•	•	•	•	•	•	•	•	•	gym, pool bars, restaurants, kids club
Clarks Landing Marina Kent Island/Eastern Bay/Crab Alley Cr. 410-604-4300 www.clarkslanding.com	6'			•	•	•	•				•	•	Specializing in engine repairs; haulout, storage
Castle Harbor Marina Chester River/Kent Island 410-643-5599 www.castlemarina.com	6'	•		•	•	•	•	•	•	•	➤	➤	Cross-island bike trail nearby; large pool
Piney Narrows Yacht Haven Kent Narrows 410-643-6600 www.pineynarrowsmarina.com	7'	•		•	•	•	•	•	•	•	•	•	Brokerage, condo slips, sales & rentals
Bay Bridge Marina Kent Island 410-643-3162 www.baybridgemarina.com	6.5'	•	•	•	•	•	•	•	•	•	•	•	beach, floating docks, cable, gym, full-service yard

Eastern Shore—St. Michaels to Crisfield

	MLW	Transient Slips/Moorings	Floating docks	Gas	Diesel	Pumpout	Showers	Pool	Laundry	Wi-Fi	Haulout	Repairs	Other
St. Michaels Marina Eastern Bay/Miles R./St. Michaels 410-745-2400 www.stmichaelsmarina.com	10'	●		●	●	●	●	●	●	●	➤	➤	Bikes, cable TV, Wi-Fi
St. Michaels Harbour Inn, Marina & Spa Eastern Bay/Miles R./St. Michaels 410-745-9001 ext 160 www.harbourinn.com	8'	●	➤	➤	●	●	●	●	●		➤	➤	Exercise room, spa, pool, bikes, coffee, van
Lowes Wharf Marina Inn Tilghman Isl./Ferry Cove/E of Poplar Is 410-745-6684 www.loweswharf.com	5'	●		●	●	●	●		●	●			Guest Rooms, charters, kayak/bike rentals
Knapps Narrows Marina & Inn Knapps Narrows 410-886-2720 www.knappsnarrowsmarina.com	6'	●	●	●	●	●	●	●	●	●	●	●	Full repair facility
Tilghman Island Marina Knapps Narrows 410-886-2500 www.tilghmanmarina.com	6'	●	➤	➤	●	●	●		●			●	renting boats, kayaks, jetskis, sup's, bikes
Harrisons Chesapeake House Choptank R./Harris Cr. 410-886-2121 www.chesapeakehouse.com	6'	●		●	➤	●	●	●	●		●	➤	Gift/nautical shop, fishing charters, cruisers welcome
Campbell's Boatyard at Jack's Point Tred Avon R./Town Cr. 410-226-5105 www.campbellsboatyards.com	6'	●	●	●	●	●	●		➤	●	●	●	restoration, repairs, fuel, floating docks
Brewer Oxford Boat Yard & Marina Tred Avon R./Town Cr. 410-226-5101 www.byy.com	10'	●		●	●	●	●	●	●	●	●	●	Bike, car rentals; cable, 75-ton lift
Campbell's Bachelor Point Yacht Co. Tred Avon R./Town Cr. 410-226-5592 www.campbellsboatyards.com	9'	●	➤	➤	●	●	●		●	●	●	●	70-ton lift, dry storage, repairs
Hinckley Yacht Services Tred Avon R./Town Cr. 410-226-5113 www.hinckleyyachts.com	7'	●	➤	➤	●	●	●		●		●	●	full-service marina in Oxford
Campbell's Town Creek Boatyard Tred Avon R./Town Cr. 410-226-0213 www.campbellsboatyards.com	6'	●	➤	➤	●	●			●	●	➤	➤	custom boatbuilding, restoration
Cutts & Case Shipyard Tred Avon R./Town Cr. 410-226-5416 www.cuttsandcase.com	8'	●	➤	➤	➤	●			➤	●	●	●	Full repairs, railway, yacht design, boatbuilding
Oxford Yacht Agency Tred Avon R./Town Cr. 410-822-8556 www.oya.com	6'	●	➤	➤		●			●	●	●	●	Tennis, basketball, park
Oxford Yacht Agency At Dickerson Harbor Choptank R./LaTrappe Cr. 410-822-8556 www.oya.com	6'	●				●			●	●	●		Protected harbor; inside storage for large boats
Generation III Marina Choptank River 410-228-2520	8'	●	➤	●	●	●			➤	●	●	●	
Hyatt River Marsh Marina Choptank River/Cambridge/Green 27 410-901-6380 www.hyattrivermarshmarina.com	7'	●	●	●	●	●	●	●	●	●	➤	➤	Golf, spa, small boat rentals, mini golf, tennis
Somers Cove Marina Tangier Sound/Annemessex River 410-968-0925 www.somerscovemarina.com	8'	●	●	●	●	●	●	●	●	●	➤	➤	State park nearby, safe, protected harbor, events venue
Gootee's Marine Honga R./Wallace Cr. 410-397-3122 www.gootees.com	4'	●		●	●	●					●	●	New and used boat sales. Yamaha service

Worton Creek Marina

23145 Buck Neck Road, Chestertown, MD 21620
Ph: 410-778-3282 | Fax: 410-778-3395
Email: marina@wortoncreek.com
WortonCreek.com

description of facilities

Worton Creek Marina is a medium sized full service marina on Maryland's beautiful Eastern Shore. Family owned and operated since 1949, the marina is located just 1.5 miles off the Chesapeake Bay. Combining old fashioned charm in a friendly, laid back atmosphere, the marina offers both full amenities and an outstanding service department. Come visit Worton Creek Marina to enjoy a relaxing weekend in a beautiful and tranquil setting.

marina approach & docking

Follow the Chesapeake Bay Ship Channel to Marker #36, just south of Worton Point. Turn east and proceed past Marker #34A to red mark #2 at the entrance to Worton Creek. Keeping the two green day marks to port, follow the creek as it turns to starboard, passing between first two marinas on your port and a mooring field to starboard. Proceed upstream (south) keeping to center of the creek. Worton Creek Marina will be on your port just past Mill Creek and is the only marina on the creek with covered slips.

We monitor Channel 16.

at a glance

DOCKAGE RATE: $1.50/ft plus electric, $8.00 for 1-30; $15.00 for 2-30 or 1/50

PAYMENT: Major Credit Cards, cash, check

HOURS: Sun – Thurs 8-4:30; Fri 8-5, Sat 8-6

TRANSIENT SLIPS/TOTAL SLIPS: 20/110

VHF/WORKING: 16/10

MLW/LOA*: 6'/90'

ELECTRIC: 30/50A/single phase

PUMP-OUT: Yes

FUEL: Diesel, mid-grade gas

REPAIR: Yes

RESTAURANT/MILES: The Harbour House Restaurant on-site

POOL: Yes

HAUL-OUT: Yes, 25 & 70 ton lifts

HEAD/SHOWER: Yes/Yes

LAUNDRY: Yes

INTERNET ACCESS: Yes, free WiFi

CABLE: No

SHOPPING: The Creek Boutique Gift Shop on-site

STORAGE: Wet/Dry

AIRPORT/MILES: BWI/1.5 hrs, PHL/1.5 hrs

TRANSPORTATION: Enterprise Rent-a-Car nearby

SPECIAL: Outstanding service department, very protected "hurricane hole" harbor

LAT: 39° 16.5' N
LON: -76° 10 W

*MLW = Mean Low Water Depth
LOA = Longest vessel that can be accommodated

Resort-style Boating in the Heart of Canton

Baltimore Marine Centers at Lighthouse Point

2736 Lighthouse Point East,
Baltimore, MD 21224
Ph: 410-675-8888 | Fax: 410-675-3568
Email: Lighthouse@BMCMarinas.com
BMCMarinas.com

description of facilities

One of the largest and most amenities-rich marinas in the harbor, BMC Lighthouse Point is a boater's paradise. Located along the waterfront of Canton in Baltimore's renowned Inner Harbor, BMC's signature Lighthouse Point Marina is a popular, resort style destination offering a full service yachting facility with concrete floating piers, fuel and pump out service, state of the art health club, large swimming pool with separate kiddie area and hot tub and several on-site restaurants. Lighthouse Point has fine tuned the marina and its amenities to ensure that visitors always have a satisfying boating experience while on Maryland's Chesapeake Bay.

marina approach & docking

Patapsco River, pass under the Key Bridge, leave Ft. McHenry to port. BMC at Lighthouse Point will be on your starboard.

Coordinates Latitude: 39° 16.54´ N Longitude: 76° 36.84˝ W.

We monitor Channels 16 and 68.

LAT: 39° 16.54'N
LON: -76° 36.84"W

Baltimore's Premiere Yachting Center
Offering the Bay's Finest Facilities

Anchorage Marina

2501 Boston Street, Baltimore, MD 21224
Ph: 410-522-7200
Email: receptiondesk@anchoragemarina.com
AnchorageMarina.com

description of facilities

Anchorage Marina, Baltimore's premiere yachting center, furnishes the highest quality facilities and services available on the Chesapeake Bay.

Conveniently located in Baltimore City in the upscale Canton area, Anchorage Marina is just minutes from the Inner Harbor, I-95 and I-83 with fine restaurants, entertainment, groceries, marine supplies, and shopping within walking distance. Baltimore's largest marina features a floating pier system with full-length finger piers and a floating swimming pool. You can enjoy the pride and pleasure of slip ownership at Baltimore's Anchorage Marina. Slips of most sizes are available for purchase. Slips also can be leased on a monthly basis or rented for overnight, a weekend or a week. Come take a look at the Anchorage, you'll want to make it your home, too.

marina approach & docking

By water, the Anchorage is situated on the Northwest Harbor of the Patapsco River, just one mile inside of Fort McHenry, one of many historic sites in the area. From the Chesapeake Bay enter the Patapsco River. Proceed under Francis Scott Key Bridge (185' clearance). At Fort McHenry bear to starboard entering the Northwest Harbor. Follow East then West channel. Anchorage is to starboard, located at 39.16.77 / 076.34.96. Water depth into marina exceeds 10 feet.

LAT: 39° 16' 77"N
LON: -76° 34' 96"W

at a glance

DOCKAGE RATE: $2.00/ft

PAYMENT: MC/Visa/Discover

HOURS: M-Th, Sun 9am – 5pm; Fri & Sat 9am – 6pm

TRANSIENT SLIPS/TOTAL SLIPS: 50/565

VHF/WORKING: 16/67

MLW/LOA*: 10'/150'

ELECTRIC: Single/double 30/50 amp

PUMP-OUT: Stationary and portable

FUEL: Nearby

REPAIR: Nearby

RESTAURANT/MILES: Many within easy walk

POOL: Floating pool on the pier

HAUL-OUT: Nearby

HEAD/SHOWER: Yes/Yes

LAUNDRY: Yes

INTERNET ACCESS: In public areas

CABLE: Available

SHIP'S STORE: Nearby

NEAREST TOWN/MILES: Largest marina in the Baltimore Harbor

SHOPPING: Groceries, everything nearby

STORAGE: Wet winter

AIRPORT/MILES: 20 minutes to BWI

TRANSPORTATION: Water taxi, taxis

YACHT BROKERAGE: On-site

SPECIAL: Easy walk to Fells Point/Canton, water taxi to Inner Harbor, floating piers w/full-length finger piers, boaters lounge, On-site security

*MLW = Mean Low Water Depth
LOA = Longest vessel that can be accommodated

Stay and Play in the Heart of Downtown Baltimore

Harbor East Marina

40 International Drive, Baltimore, MD 21202
Ph: 410-625-1700 | Fax: 410-625-1724
Email: harboreastmarina@harboreast.com

description of facilities

Harbor East Marina is the prime location for boaters looking to stay and play in Baltimore. Located in the heart of the city, the Harbor East area of Baltimore boasts 12 square blocks of fine dining restaurants, boutique and luxury hotels, bars, clubs and fantastic retailers. The marina is also within walking distance of Little Italy and Fell's Point for boaters looking to get out and explore some of Baltimore's fine history.

In addition to nearby neighborhoods, guests can also walk to the National Aquarium, Harborplace, Maryland Science Center and the Historic Ships from the marina, while a quick cab will take sports fans to Camden Yards and the M&T Bank Stadium. Water taxis are available for those who prefer to explore the harbor by water. At the marina, boaters also have access to amenities directly on-site, including a bath/shower facilities, a lounge and party area and WiFi. Those looking for a pool and health club can purchase a $9 day pass at the Maryland Athletic Club just down the street.

marina approach & docking

Harbor East Marina is at the base of the new Legg Mason building. When you have the Domino Sugar sign off your port stern, the marina will be visible to your starboard bow. Fairway and slips are clearly marked. On windy days, pay particular attention to the direction and speed of the wind as it tends to change rapidly.

The docks are floating structures with a wood deck and rubber protection strips. Most slips are single loaded with a full-length finger pier on each side of your vessel. Reservations are accepted via phone and on Snag-A-Slip. Call on VHF channel 68 for slip assignment and docking.

Harboreastmarina.com

LAT: 39° 16' 58.6194"N
LON: -76° 36' 4.2114"W

at a glance

DOCKAGE RATE: Transients, seasonals and annuals. Dock and dine.

IN SEASON PRICING: Weekday, $2.50/ ft. Weekend, $3/ft. Pricing may vary for special events.

PAYMENT: All cards; Snag-A- Slip

HOURS: In-season, 7:30am – 10pm; winter, 9am – 4pm.

TRANSIENT SLIPS/TOTAL SLIPS: 100/200

VHF/WORKING: 9-16-68/68

MLW/LOA*: 6´-20´/125´ on perimeter pier

ELECTRIC: 50 amp, 125V/250V

PUMP-OUT: Nearby

REPAIR: 2 full-service boatyards nearby

RESTAURANT/MILES: More than 20 within 12 blocks.

HAUL-OUT: Up to 82 tons at nearby Port Covington Maritime Center

HEAD/SHOWER: Yes/Yes; clean, bright, tiled

LAUNDRY: 2 washers/dryers

CABLE: Yes

SHIP'S STORE: 1.5 miles

NEAREST TOWN/MILES: Harbor East at the dock, close to Little Italy, Fells Point, Canton.

SHOPPING: Everything within blocks from marina.

AIRPORT/MILES: BWI/20 minutes

TRANSPORTATION: Water shuttle, taxi

SPECIAL: Live music on Summer Saturdays

CANCELLATION: 48 hours

*MLW = Mean Low Water Depth
LOA = Longest vessel that can be accommodated

One of the Most Sought-after Destinatiions in the City

Baltimore Marine Centers at Inner Harbor

400 Key Highway, Baltimore, MD 21230
Ph: 410-837-5339 | Fax: 410-539-0722
Email: InnerHarbor@BMCMarinas.com
BMCMarinas.com

description of facilities

The premiere location and updated facilities of the BMC Inner Harbor Marina make it one of the most sought after destinations in the city. On the promenade at Baltimore's beautiful Inner Harbor and directly at the foot of Federal Hill, the city views are breathtaking. This marina was renovated in 2007 and offers 115 state-of-the-art concrete floating dock slips, a pump out station at each slip, fuel pier, an on-site award winning seafood restaurant and a short walk to Baltimore's downtown attractions, festivities and restaurants, including the Inner Harbor, historic Federal Hill, the Visitor's Center and stadiums. Enjoy city living at its best from your slip at BMC Inner Harbor Marina.

marina approach & docking

Chesapeake Bay to the Brewerton Channel (Patapsco River), follow the Patapsco River in until Fort McHenry.

Take Fort McHenry down your port side, follow the Harbor channel all the way into the city. Our facility is the last marina on your port side. Look for the Rusty Scupper Restaurant and Inner Harbor Marina fuel signs.

We monitor Channels 16, and 69.

LAT: 39° 16' 55"N
LON: -76° 36' 30"W

at a glance

DOCKAGE RATE: Mon-Thurs $2.50/ft, Fri-Sun and Holidays or events $3.00/ft

PAYMENT: MC/Visa/Disc/AmEx/checks

HOURS: Sun 9-4, Mon-Th 9-5, Fri & Sat 9-6

TRANSIENT SLIPS/TOTAL SLIPS: 90/130

VHF/WORKING: 16/69

MLW/LOA*: 20'/300'

ELECTRIC: 50/250, single/3-phase 100 amp, 480V/200 amp, 3-phase for mega yachts

PUMP-OUT: Yes, at fuel dock or in your slip

FUEL: Gas/Diesel, quantity discounts

REPAIR: Yes, Pier 7/Clinton St.

RESTAURANT/MILES: On-site

POOL: Yes, at hotel

HAUL-OUT: 85-ton lift, Pier 7/Clinton St.

HEAD/SHOWER: Yes/Yes

LAUNDRY: Yes

INTERNET ACCESS: Yes, WiFi

CABLE: Yes

NEAREST TOWN/MILES: In the heart of the city

SHOPPING: Everything w/in easy walk

STORAGE: At Pier 7 - wet or land

AIRPORT/MILES: BWI/20 minutes

TRANSPORTATION: Water taxi, taxis, easy walk, Heliport at Pier 7

SPECIAL: Boater's lounge, clean showers/laundry facilities, access to pool and health club

*MLW = Mean Low Water Depth
 LOA = Longest vessel that can be accommodated

A Casual Vibe with First-Class Amenities

Baltimore's Premier Marine
Service Facility Service - It's All We Do!

Tidewater Yacht Service

321 East Cromwell Street, Baltimore, MD 21230
Ph: 410-625-4992 | Fax: 410-539-3078
Email: bbrandon@tysc.com

description of facilities

Tidewater Yacht Service is the most modern boat repair facility on the Chesapeake. The service facility at Port Covington provides fast, convenient haulout and repair for larger vessels. For haul outs, there are 75- and 35-ton travel lifts installed on concrete runways with 18 feet MLW as well as a 20,000-pound forklift. Tidewater's discount marine store has a wide range of boat supplies and parts, great prices and a knowledgeable staff. A 6,000-square-foot office and retail building is connected to a 9,000-square-foot repair building with 30 foot high doors which can accommodate vessels up to 55 feet in length. The goal here is simple: to provide the highest level of service at the best possible price.

marina approach & docking

Port Covington is on the south side of Locust Point on the Middle Branch of the Patapsco. From the ICW follow the Brewerton Channel to the Fort McHenry Channel and proceed northwest to Fort McHenry. Leave Fort McHenry to starboard. Stay parallel to the shoreline. Tidewater's service facility at Port Covington Maritime Center is straight ahead.

www.tysc.com

LAT: 39° 15' 694" N
LON: -76° 36' 000" W

at a glance

DOCKAGE RATE: $1.50/ft

PAYMENT: MC/Visa/Discover/Checks/ Cash

HOURS: 6 days in season

TRANSIENT SLIPS/TOTAL SLIPS: 10/22

VHF/WORKING: 16/69

MLW/LOA*: 18´/200´+ at pier

ELECTRIC: Year-round

PUMP-OUT: Yes

REPAIR: Mobile service in the harbor. Power, sail, rigging, emergency repairs, engine, generator, A/C, refrigeration, woodwork, electrical, Awlgrip, canvas, upholstery, detailing

HAUL-OUT: 75/35-ton lifts; 20,000 lb. forklift. Priority given to short hauls

INTERNET ACCESS: Wireless available

SHIP'S STORE: Large, fully stocked store known for its extensive parts dept. and knowledgeable staff fluent in "boat talk"

NEAREST TOWN/MILES: In the city

SHOPPING: Everything close by

STORAGE: Rack storage for boats to 40´, plus 7.75 acres paved/lighted area with year-round water and electric for vessels to 80´

AIRPORT/MILES: 20 minutes to BWI

TRANSPORTATION: Water taxi, taxis

SPECIAL: Baltimore's best, most comprehensive repair facility, Discount marine store

*MLW = Mean Low Water Depth
 LOA = Longest vessel that can be accommodated

PLEASURE COVE
A Suntex Marina

Pleasure Cove Marina

1701 Poplar Ridge Rd., Pasadena, MD 21122
Ph: 410-437-6600
Email: PCM@SuntexMarinas.com
PleasureCoveMarina.com

description of facilities

Pleasure Cove marina is a full-service marina in Pasadena, Maryland, located just 15 minutes from Annapolis & Baltimore with competitive slip rates, ample storage in their heated and sprinkled buildings, and deep water slips. Pleasure Cove is more than your average marina. They pride themselves in offering more to their customers. Pleasure Cove's unparalleled amenities include a marine store, service center, boat and watersport rentals, pool, member's lounge, laundry facility, gym & much more! See our website at www.pleasurecovemarina.com or call 410-437-6600.

marina approach & docking

From Craighill Channel Marker # 21 turn West 325 Degrees (float free zone). Enter Bodkin Creek by Rounding Green Marker #3 and proceeding Southwest to Red Marker #12, turn to West entering Main Creek and proceed to Pleasure Cove Marina and the Cheshire Crab Restaurant.

LAT: 39° 7' 46.0596"N
LON: -76° 28' 28.2432"W

at a glance

DOCKAGE: Wet slips, outdoor covered dry storage, and indoor heated & sprinkled dry storage

PAYMENT: Cash/All major credit cards

HOURS: Summer- Mon. thru Thurs. 9am-6pm; Fri. thru Sun. 9am-8pm; Winter- 9am-5pm

TRANSIENT SLIPS/TOTAL SLIPS: 22

VHF/WORKING: 68

MLW/LOA*: 7'

ELECTRIC: 30/50 Amp metered electric

PUMP-OUT: Yes

FUEL: Yes

REPAIR: Yes

RESTAURANT/MILES: The Chesire Crab on-site

POOL: Yes

HAUL-OUT: Yes

HEAD/SHOWER: Yes/Yes

LAUNDRY: Yes

INTERNET ACCESS: WiFi

CABLE: No

SHIPS STORE: Yes

NEAREST TOWN/MILES: 3 mi

SHOPPING: 3 mi

STORAGE: Yes

AIRPORT/MILES: BWI airport

YACHT BROKERAGE: No

SPECIAL: Join the Suntex Captain's Club and SAVE on transient dockage, fuel and more! Limited time...complimentary club membership when you stay at one of our East Coast locations.

*MLW = Mean Low Water Depth
LOA = Longest vessel that can be accommodated

Join Us for the Weekend, or for the Season

Haven Harbour Marina

20880 Rock Hall Avenue, Rock Hall, MD 21661
Ph: 800-506-6697
Email: email@havenharbour.com
HavenHarbour.com

description of facilities

Haven Harbour Marina is a complete, full-service facility with over seven acres of beautifully manicured gardens, two pools and full recreational amenities (bike and kayak rentals, croquet, bocce, shuffleboard) and on-site lodging at the expanded Inn at Haven Harbour. The fully stocked marine store is the largest in the area, and repair and refit services are the most comprehensive on the upper Chesapeake with ABYC-certified specialists in all yacht repair disciplines. Come see why Haven Harbour was designated National Marina of the Year.

marina approach & docking

Located about 11 miles north of the bay bridge, Haven Harbour is on The Haven off of Swan Creek. Arriving from the upper bay, travel down the Tolchester Channel until you see the range lights for the Brewerton Channel extension. This range will allow you to cross the Swan Point Bar with a 5' draft at MLW. Look for the 52' tall yellow tower range light and you'll see the white light on land atop of a 110' tower. After crossing the bar, turn north leaving green can "5" to port. Once in Swan Creek stay in the middle of the waterway but honor the two red seasonal nun buoys by Deep Landing, then head east leaving the Swan Creek Marina mooring field just to starboard. Watch for two green cans as you approach R "14", and then turn 150° south and head down The Haven past Osprey Point Marina less than half nautical mile. We monitor VHF 16.

LAT: 39° 8' 34"N
LON: -76° 14' 57"W

at a glance

DOCKAGE RATE: $2.00/ft mid-week, $2.40/ft weekends

PAYMENT: MC/VISA/Discover/check/cash

HOURS: 8 am – 5 pm; 7 days/wk

TRANSIENT SLIPS/TOTAL SLIPS: Yes/200

VHF/WORKING: 16/68

MLW/LOA*: 6'/70'

ELECTRIC: 30 amp/125 volt & 50 amp/250 volt

PUMP-OUT: Yes, at fuel dock and slips

FUEL: Gas and Diesel on-site

REPAIR: Full-service and repair, all yachts, power & sail

PROPANE: Nearby, CNG on-site

RESTAURANT/MILES: Passages Bar & Grill/ on-site, open weekends

POOL: 2 pools on-site (adult & family)

HAUL-OUT: 55 tons, up to 110,000 lbs.

HEAD/SHOWER/LAUNDRY: Yes/Yes/Yes; additional separate heads with vanities

INTERNET ACCESS: Wireless

SHIP'S STORE: Fully stocked on-site. Gift shop on-site.

NEAREST TOWN/MILES: Rock Hall/.5

SHOPPING: Yes

STORAGE: Wet/Dry

AIRPORT/MILES: BWI/60

TRANSPORTATION: Shuttle on weekends

YACHT BROKERAGE: On-site

SPECIAL: Pools, fitness room, bikes, kayaks & paddleboards, croquet, bocce, shuffleboard. Waterman's Museum on-site. Inn at Haven Harbour with 4 buildings and 20 guest rooms.

*MLW = Mean Low Water Depth
LOA = Longest vessel that can be accommodated

ANNAPOLIS CITY MARINA

Annapolis City Marina
410 Severn Ave, Annapolis, MD 21403
Ph: 410-268-0660 | Fax: 410-268-1761
Email: dockmaster@annapoliscitymarina.com
www.annapoliscitymarina.com

description of facilities

Annapolis City Marina provides you with the liveliness of downtown Annapolis and the quiet tranquility of Eastport. Our friendly and knowledgeable staff will be glad to assist you wherever you may need a hand. Every slip contains a finger pier, water and electrical hook-ups, and free wireless internet for your convenience. Our marina offers a variety of services to set you sailing quickly including a full service fuel dock and a fully stocked store that includes beer, wine, block and cube ice, Starbucks coffee, snacks, ice cream, and boat supplies. As an added convenience we offer clean bathhouses, laundry facilities, a grill and picnic area, and gated parking.

marina approach & docking

The entrance to Annapolis is quite easy to navigate, although shoals do exist. As you round "Greenbury Point" you can follow the fairway marked by cans, bells, and nuns for about 3/4 mile. This will allow you to clear "Horn Point" shoal to port (FL. 6 sec. PA). The Severn River and the U.S. Naval Academy will be directly in front of you. Bearing to port you will enter Annapolis Harbor. At the split channel marker bear left leaving the mooring field to starboard. Approaching the Spa Creek Bridge, Annapolis City Marina is the large gray and red facility to port. Our fuel dock is a small red barn with black trim and a silver roof.

at a glance

DOCKAGE RATE: Seasonal daily rate $2.50/ft, including electricity & water ($75 min). Hourly rate for lunch or dinner $10/hr

PAYMENT: Cash, Visa, MC, AMEX, Discover

HOURS: Seasonal hours 8-8, 7 days

TRANSIENT SLIPS/TOTAL SLIPS: 86 fixed pier, in-water slips

VHF/WORKING: VHF channel 9

MLW/LOA*: 14'/ Can accommodate boats up to 100' on our fuel dock

ELECTRIC: 30/50 Amp

PUMP-OUT: Yes

FUEL: Gas and diesel w/ volumn discounts

RESTAURANT/MILES: Carrol's Creek on-site

HEAD/SHOWER: Yes/Yes

LAUNDRY: Yes

INTERNET ACCESS: WiFi

SHIP'S STORE: Fully stocked ship's store w/ beer, wine, ice, food

SHOPPING: Nearby

SPECIAL: Short walk or water taxi to downtown

LAT: 38° 58.349'N
LON: -76° 29.025'W

*MLW = Mean Low Water Depth
LOA = Longest vessel that can be accommodated

Port Annapolis Marina

7074 Bembe Beach Road,
Annapolis, MD 21403
Ph: 410-269-1990 | Fax: 410-269-5856
Email: info@portannapolis.com
PortAnnapolis.com

description of facilities

On an impeccably landscaped 16-acre site, Port Annapolis features over 245 deep-water slips in the shelter of Back Creek. The 75 and 55-ton Travelifts accommodate yachts 25'-70', and up to 26' beam including catamarans. Friendly, knowledgeable staff include experts in electrical, fiberglass, carpentry, engines & rigging. Well-maintained showers & restrooms are available and there is an Event Pavilion for club socials or meetings, and can be rented for land-based occasions. With all this, it's no wonder that Port Annapolis is the Bay's most popular destination for both sail and power boaters. Transients & cruising clubs welcome!

marina approach & docking

From the north: at can G "1", two miles south of the Chesapeake Bay Bridge's center span, steer a course of 280° to daymark G "1E" (approx. 2.5 miles), the entrance to Back Creek. After passing daymark G "7", proceed up Back Creek to Port Annapolis Marina on the port side (before the water tower).

From the South: at "1AH", northwest of Thomas Point, steer a course of 331° to daymark R "2E" (approx. 2.4 miles), the entrance to Back Creek. After passing daymark G "7", proceed up Back Creek to Port Annapolis Marina on the port side (before the water tower).

Once inside the creek you will see many facilities and usually a spread of anchored boats. Port Annapolis is located on your port side and can be contacted on VHF 16.

LAT: 38° 57' 56.16"N
LON: -76° 28' 42.8874"W

at a glance

DOCKAGE RATE: $2.75/ft including water and electric

PAYMENT: Major credit cards

HOURS: Mon-Fri 8am – 5pm

TRANSIENT SLIPS/TOTAL SLIPS: 20/250

VHF/WORKING: 16/71

MLW/LOA*: 10'/70'

ELECTRIC: 30/50 Amp

PUMP-OUT: Yes, dockside & mobile

FUEL: Next door

REPAIR: Full-service maintenance and repair facility

RESTAURANT/MILES: Wet Dog Café/ on-site, many others by water taxi

POOL: Shoreside Pool open 12-8pm daily

HAUL-OUT: 75T & 55T lifts hauling to 26' beam

HEAD/SHOWER: Yes/Yes; in 3 bath houses

LAUNDRY: Yes

INTERNET ACCESS: Wireless

CABLE: Yes

SHIP'S STORE: Fully stocked marine supply

NEAREST TOWN/MILES: Annapolis/3

SHOPPING: Nearby

STORAGE: Yes

AIRPORT/MILES: BWI/22

TRANSPORTATION: Shuttle van, bicycles and water taxi

YACHT BROKERAGE: Several on-site

SPECIAL: Event Pavillion & Club Room available for socials and meetings. 5 min. to Historic Annapolis, City Dock, shopping, exercise room

*MLW = Mean Low Water Depth
LOA = Longest vessel that can be accommodated

Hartge Yacht Harbor

4883 Church Lane, Galesville, MD 20765
Ph: 443-607-6306 | Fax: 443-607-6308
Email: info@HartgeYachtHarbor.com
www.hartgeyachtharbor.com

description of facilities

Hartge Yacht Harbor combines a friendly atmosphere with outstanding service. Located on the scenic West River just 4 miles from the Chesapeake Bay, we offer 270 protected slips and 60 moorings for annual and transient guests. The service department provides hauling and launching, painting, rigging, mechanical, carpentry, and fiberglass repair. Located in a quiet, picturesque setting, customer service is our priority.

marina approach & docking

From Thomas Point Light cruise southwest to Fl Red 2.5s lighted daymark #2 at the cross-road to the West & Rhode Rivers. Set a course for 263 degrees and follow this heading for 2 miles into entrance of the West River then make turn to port at Fl Red 4s lighted daymark #4. Pass Green daymark #5 and proceed one-half mile from this point, passing Fl Red 4s lighted daymark #6, pass the docks off to starboard and finally Green daymark #7. Make right turn into Lerch Creek. Once inside you will see the docks and moorings of Hartge Yacht Harbor. Contact the dockmaster on VHF 9 for slip assignment and directions for within the marina.

at a glance

DOCKAGE RATE: Annual dockage for boats 25-70 feet. Moorings available. Covered slips. Transients $2/foot per night

PAYMENT: MC/Visa/Amex/Discover

HOURS: 8:00 - 5:00 Monday through Friday, 8:00 - 12:00 Saturday

TRANSIENT SLIPS/TOTAL SLIPS: 20/280, also moorings available

VHF/WORKING: 9'/72'

MLW/LOA*: 8'/70'

ELECTRIC: 30/50 Amp

PUMP-OUT: Available

FUEL: Nearby

REPAIR: On-site

RESTAURANT/MILES: Pirates Cove and Thursdays are within short walking distance

HAUL-OUT: Yes

HEAD/SHOWER: Yes/Yes

INTERNET ACCESS: Wireless

SHIP'S STORE: Nearby

NEAREST TOWN/MILES: Located in Galesville

SHOPPING: Antique shops in town

STORAGE: Yes

AIRPORT/MILES: BWI/32

YACHT BROKERAGE: On-site

SPECIAL: Yacht Brokers, Yacht Charters, Nautical Museum, Carpentry, Rigging, and Mechanical shops. Grassy areas and large trees on the grounds make a perfect location for gatherings and picnics. Family owned since 1865 in quiet, picturesque Galesville

*MLW = Mean Low Water Depth
LOA = Longest vessel that can be accommodated

Family-owned

Herrington Harbour North Marina Resort & Yacht Yard

389 Deale Road, Tracey's Landing, MD 20779
Ph: 410-867-4343 | 1-800-297-1930
Fax: 410-867-2435
Email: hhn@herringtonharbour.com

description of facilities

Herrington Harbour North is a full-service yachting destination offering an award winning waterfront resort with 600 protected slips surrounded by a resort landscaping and a full-service yacht yard. Swimming pool, fitness room, customer lounges along with bikes and kayaks plus many landscaped water overlooks to cookout or just sit and relax. West Marine Store is located on the property. Contractors are available for service repairs and yacht detailing. Herrington Harbour North is consistently recognized as an innovative destination suppported by trained employees resulting in an award winning Marina Resort and Yacht Yard. We operate 4 travel lifts ranging from 35 to 70 tons which service our professionally maintained storage area allowing us to keep over 1,200 yachts securely stored for service. For the do-it-yourself yacht owners water and electricity are at your land site.

marina approach & docking

Herrington Harbour North is located on the western shore of the Chesapeake Bay, in the northwest corner of Herring Bay. From green can 83 A, proceed southwest for Herring Bay green #1 (four-legged). Proceed on a westerly course through a float-free channel to Herring Bay red #2 (four-legged). Pass #2 (leave to starboard) and passing green#3 to port, proceed on a northwesterly course towards Rockhold Creek channel green #1 (four-legged), leaving the rock jetty to both starboard and port. Approach depth of the marina and Rockhold Creek is 7 feet MLW. The docks are wooden structures with finger piers and tie-off pilings. The marina monitors VHF channel 9 & 16 upon your approach.

HerringtonHarbour.com

LAT: 38° 45' 86"N
LON: -76° 32' 80"W

at a glance

DOCKAGE RATE: $2.25/ft

PAYMENT: MC/Visa/Amex/Discover

HOURS: 9am – 5pm, 7 days

TRANSIENT SLIPS/TOTAL SLIPS: Call for availability/600

VHF/WORKING: 9/16

MLW/LOA*: 7´/120´

ELECTRIC: 30A/110V $6/night, 50A/240V $12/night

PUMP-OUT: Yes

FUEL: Gas & Diesel at Herrington South

REPAIR: Full-service, DIY

RESTAURANT/MILES: Poolside Bar, Dockside Restaurant on-site

POOL: Private & kiddie pools, spa

HAUL-OUT: Up to 70 tons

HEAD/SHOWER: Yes/Yes

LAUNDRY: 2 washers & dryers

INTERNET ACCESS: Complimentary WiFi

SHIP'S STORE: West Marine store/on-site

NEAREST TOWN/MILES: Deale/.5

SHOPPING: Antiques, gifts, grocery nearby

GOLF: Twin Shields, nearby

STORAGE: Wet/Dry

AIRPORT/MILES: Reagan National/35, BWI/30 (shuttle available)

YACHT BROKERAGE: Yes

SPECIAL: Shoreside swimming pool, kiddie pool, heated whirlpool spa, fitness center, customer lounges, nature walks, picnic areas with grills, playground, outdoor games, kayaks, bikes, seminars, security and slipholder parties including outdoor movies, catering.

*MLW = Mean Low Water Depth
 LOA = Longest vessel that can be accommodated

Family-owned

Herrington Harbour South Marina Resort

7149 Lake Shore Drive, North Beach, MD 20714
Ph: 410-741-5100 Fax: 301-855-6819
Email: hhs@herringtonharbour.com
HerringtonHarbour.com

description of facilities

Herrington Harbour South is complete with all the amenities of a fine exotic getaway. There are 600 protected boat slips with direct access to the Bay and exceptional facilities that cater to every boater's needs. The 1500' channel, maintained at 7' MLW, takes you from your berth to deep, open water boating with a multitude of exciting destinations within easy reach. South is also a favorite choice for weddings, catered events, beachfront lodging, dining in our restaurant, and relaxing days on the Chesapeake. Visit Herrington Harbour South...a Great Place for Boats, Nature and People.

marina approach & docking

Herrington Harbour South is located on the western shore of the Chesapeake Bay, about 18 miles south of Annapolis. From green can 81A, proceed NW. Find FL G 1 PA, then set a course of approximately 262 degrees and you should see QK FlG1, which marks the entrance by the jetties. Leave the green marker 1 to port and go between the jetties. Proceed into the channel and line up on the range markers. There is plenty of water in the channel approach and a reported seven feet of water in the channel and at the docks at mean low water. The well-kept docks are wooden structures with finger piers and tie-off pilings. Call on VHF channel 9 or 16 upon your approach. Proceed to the fuel dock where you will be assigned a slip. The staff hours are from 8:00 a.m. to 6:00 p.m. on weekdays and 8:00 a.m. to 8:00 p.m. on weekends.

LAT: 38° 44' 12"N
LON: -76° 32' 20"W

at a glance

DOCKAGE RATE: In Season Sun-Thurs $2.25/ft, Fri-Sat & Holidays $3.25.ft, Off Season $2.25/ft, Boat US Discount 25%

PAYMENT: MC/Visa/Amex/Discover

HOURS: 8am – 6pm, office 9am – 5pm

TRANSIENT SLIPS/TOTAL SLIPS: Call/600

VHF/WORKING: 9/16

MLW/LOA*: 7'/100'

ELECTRIC: 30/50 Amp, $6/$12

PUMP-OUT: Yes

FUEL: Gas/Diesel

REPAIR: Full-service, DIY at Herrington Harbour North (HHN)

RESTAURANT/MILES: Mango's Bar & Grill, Chesapeake Market & Deli/on-site

POOL: Olympic-size, kiddie pool, private beach

HAUL-OUT: At Herrington Harbour North

HEAD/SHOWER: Yes/Yes, excellent

LAUNDRY: 5 washers/dryers

INTERNET ACCESS: Complimentary WiFi

CABLE: Yes

NEAREST TOWN/MILES: North Beach & Chesapeake Beach/2

SHOPPING: Deli, grocery on-site

STORAGE: Wet

AIRPORT/MILES: Reagan National/35, BWI/35 (shuttle available)

SPECIAL: Pools. Outdoor movies. Private beaches. Sauna and fitness center. Playground, picnic areas, tennis, kayaks & paddleboards, volleyball, horseshoes, water aerobics. Small sailboat rentals and sailing camps. Slipholder parties. Catering. Hair Salon.

*MLW = Mean Low Water Depth
 LOA = Longest vessel that can be accommodated

Gateway to the Best of the Bay

Knapps Narrows Marina

6176 Tilghman Island Road, Tilghman, MD 21671
Ph: 410-886-2720 | Fax: 410-886-2716
Email: knappsnarrows@bluecrab.org
KnappsNarrowsMarina.com

description of facilities

With a central Chesapeake Bay location, this beautiful marina and inn at Tilghman Island is safely tucked inside Knapps Narrows. On-site amenities include a pool, restaurant, tiki bar, air-conditioned shower houses, barbeque grills, laundry, fuel dock, wifi, 20 room inn, courtesy cars and bikes. The floating dock has easy access for transients. It can accommodate groups and large boats (up to 150 feet). We serve our guests a complimentary continental breakfast every morning. The fuel dock is open April 1 through November with friendly dock hands to assist you. Knapp's Narrows Marina is a full-service facility specializing in Awlgrip painting, blister repair and fiberglass. Our slips are minutes to the best sailing and fishing on the Chesapeake.

marina approach & docking

Knapp's Narrows Marina is located at Tilghman Island in Knapp's Narrows. There are two entrances. Entering Knapp's Narrows from either entrance is considered returning.

From the Chesapeake Bay, daymark "1" will be left to port. After "5" you will see a long floating dock to port. Entrance to Knapp's Narrows Marina is immediately after the floating dock on the port side. *From the Choptank River,* keep daymark "5" to port. Pass through the Tilghman Island drawbridge and we are located to your immediate starboard side. You may pull into our fuel dock. Bridge opens on demand. Signal is one long, one short, or bridge tender monitors VHF channel 13. Bridge phone is 410-886-2588. Knapp's Narrows Marina monitors VHF channel 16.

LAT: 38° 43' 20.1"N
LON: -76° 19' 55.4154"W

at a glance

DOCKAGE RATE: $2.00/ft, 1000' floating dock

PAYMENT: MC/Visa/Discover

HOURS: 8am – 8pm

TRANSIENT SLIPS/TOTAL SLIPS: 30

VHF/WORKING: 16

MLW/LOA*: 6'/150'

ELECTRIC: 30/50 amp, 120 to 220 volts

PUMP-OUT: Yes

FUEL: 89 Octane Gas & Diesel

REPAIR: Full-service

RESTAURANT/MILES: Marker 5 Restaurant, 410-886-1122, Tu-Sun 11am-11pm, outdoor bar, fresh cuisine and local seafood. /on-site

POOL: Yes

HAUL-OUT: 35-ton travel lift

HEAD/SHOWER: Yes/Yes; clean & A/C

LAUNDRY: Yes

INTERNET ACCESS: Free WiFi

CABLE: No

SHIP'S STORE: No

NEAREST TOWN/MILES: <1 mi

SHOPPING: Ice, marine parts, groceries & tackle shop within walking distance

GOLF/TENNIS: Nearby/No

STORAGE: Plenty of dry storage

AIRPORT/MILES: 24

SPECIAL: Complimentary continental breakfast. Park & playground facilities, picnic benches and BBQ grills. Salon. A 20-room Inn located at the marina, with pet-friendly rooms & conference center

*MLW = Mean Low Water Depth
LOA = Longest vessel that can be accommodated

CAMPBELL'S
BOATYARDS ★ CUSTOM YACHTS ★ YACHT SALES

Town Creek · Jack's Point · Bachelor Point

CAMPBELL'S
★ BOATYARDS ★

Campbell's Boatyard at Jack's Point

106 Richardson Street, Oxford, MD 21654
Ph: 410-226-5105 | Fax: 410-226-5962
Email: info@campbellsboatyards.com
www.campbellsboatyards.com

description of facilities

Campbell's Boatyards has three facilities located in Oxford, Talbot County, MD. All three have transient dockage with picnic areas, laundry facilities, and a library onsite, as well as complimentary wifi and bicycles. Come relax and enjoy the view at Campbell's!

Campbell's Boatyard @ Jack's Pt. and Campbell's Town Creek Boatyard both are located on Town Creek in Oxford. In addition to transient dockage, both facilities offer annual dockage, boat repairs, maintenance, engine repowers, haulouts, winterization and dry storage. Our Jack's Pt. location has a 25 ton travel lift.

Campbell's Bachelor Pt. Yacht Co. is located on the Tred Avon River as you approach Oxford. This location offers transient dockage with a pool, picnic area, ice and laundry, in addition to complimentary wi-fi and bicycles for your use. The facilities offers full-service maintenance, repairs and repairs, in addition to Haul-out and launching services with a 70 metric ton travel lift, in addition to dry storage and Indoor dry storage. Certified Cummins mechanic on-site.

marina approach & docking

Campbell's Boatyard at Jack's Point is located on Town Creek in Oxford. The first marina on your port side as you enter the Creek (adjacent to daymark R "10), the marina features 6.5 feet of water depth and slips up to 100 feet. Contact our office for details on our other 2 facilities!

at a glance

DOCKAGE RATE: $2.00/ft/night + $5.00/night for electricity

PAYMENT: MC/Visa/Discover

HOURS: 8 am – 4:30 pm

TRANSIENT SLIPS/TOTAL SLIPS: 34 slips/20 floating dock slips

VHF/WORKING: 16

MLW/LOA*: 6'/65'

ELECTRIC: 30/50 amp

PUMP-OUT: Yes

REPAIR: Full-service

PROPANE: No

RESTAURANT/MILES: Walking distance to Oxford

POOL: Off premises

HAUL-OUT: Upgraded 25-ton Travel Lift

HEAD/SHOWER: Yes/Yes

LAUNDRY: Nearby

INTERNET ACCESS: Yes

CABLE: No

SHIP'S STORE: No

NEAREST TOWN/MILES: 1/2 mile

SHOPPING: Nearby

STORAGE: Yes

AIRPORT/MILES: 15

TRANSPORTATION: Bikes available

YACHT BROKERAGE: Located at Bachelor Point

*MLW = Mean Low Water Depth
LOA = Longest vessel that can be accommodated

LAT: 38° 41' 18.3732"N
LON: -76° 10' 3.9972"W

Solomons' Most Popular Full-Service Resort Marina

Spring Cove Marina

455 Lore Road, P.O. Box 160,
Solomons, MD 20688
Ph: 410-326-2161 | Fax: 410-326-4187
Email: info@springcovemarina.com
SpringCoveMarina.com

description of facilities

Spring Cove Marina is a 248-slip facility on close to 10 acres of property with an abundance of trees, lawns, gardens and natural vegetation, making this one of the most attractive marinas on the East Coast. It offers the services and amenities you would expect of a first class modern marina, but with the friendliness of a family run business. The large pool with The Wheelhouse Bar and Grill overlooks Back Creek and the 13 individual tiled bathrooms are always spotless. The marina offers a full service boatyard.

marina approach & docking

On entering Solomons Harbor, maintain a northwesterly heading, leaving the small island in the middle of the harbor to port. You will see the daymark R "4" (leave it on your starboard side) at the entrance to Back Creek after you have passed the island and then follow Back Creek for about ¾ mile. When you reach daymark "8", Spring Cove Marina will be directly ahead. Call on VHF channel 16 or phone from "8" for docking instructions. If you need fuel, you can proceed directly to the fuel dock which is about 300 yards north of "8". Once you have fueled, you will receive directions and have a dockhand standing by to help you into your slip.

LAT: 38° 20.1"N
LON: -76° 27.7"W

at a glance

DOCKAGE RATE: $2.00-$2.95/ft

PAYMENT: MC/Visa/AMEX/Discover

HOURS: 8am - 5pm. Later in the season

TRANSIENT SLIPS/TOTAL SLIPS: 20/248

VHF/WORKING: 16/68

MLW/LOA*: 12'/100'

ELECTRIC: 30/50 Amp

PUMP-OUT: From your slip

FUEL: Gas/Diesel

REPAIR: Yes

RESTAURANT/MILES: On-site is Wheelhouse Bar & Grill, other nearby within walking distance

POOL: Yes

HAUL-OUT: Yes

HEAD/SHOWER/LAUNDRY: Yes/Yes/Yes

INTERNET ACCESS: Yes

SHIP'S STORE: Yes; Groceries available

NEAREST TOWN/MILES: Solomons, 1/2 mile

SHOPPING: Yes

STORAGE: Winter dry storage and long-term dry storage

AIRPORT/MILES: St. Mary's Airport/7, DCA/64

TRANSPORTATION: Courtesy shuttle

YACHT BROKERAGE: Yes

SPECIAL: Picnic area and bikes. Our lovely solar-powered, electric courtesy shuttle is a great way to see the town and experience the charm of Solomons

*MLW = Mean Low Water Depth
 LOA = Longest vessel that can be accommodated

Point Lookout Marina

16244 Millers Wharf Road
Ridge, Maryland 20680
301-872-5000
www.pointlookoutmarina.com

description of facilities

Point Lookout Marina offers a beautifully landscaped setting on 24 acres, just 6 miles from the Bay. Marina guests can enjoy the pool, playground and picnic area. The marina has 160 slips and can accommodate vessels up 200' and pleasure cruises of 30-40 boats. Relax and enjoy........in Sunset Cove Restaurant with outdoor seating overlooking Smith Creek. Full service and emergency repairs for all major in-board and out-board engines. Electrical, awlgrip, brightwork, and shipwrights services. Mobile Dustless Blasting available for restoration of boats, cars, concrete, wood and more. Checkout our website for more details and our calendar of special events.

marina approach & docking

We are located in Smith Creek, about seven nautical miles from the peninsula of Point Lookout in the Chesapeake Bay and immediately east of St. Mary's River. When cruising Chesapeake Bay, turn into the Potomac River and then find Smith Creek to starboard. As you enter the creek, Point Lookout Marina is off to starboard. Contact the marina on channel 16 or give us a call on the phone.

at a glance

DOCKAGE RATE: 1.50/foot

PAYMENT: MC, Visa, Discover, Amex

HOURS: 8am - 8pm in season, 8am - 5pm off season

TRANSIENT SLIPS/TOTAL SLIPS: 35/160

VHF/WORKING: 16

MLW/LOA*: 9'/200'

ELECTRIC: 30/50 Amp

PUMP-OUT: Yes

FUEL: gas, diesel

REPAIR: full service and emergency repair

PROPANE: Yes

RESTAURANT/MILES: Sunset Cove on site and 1 other within 1/4 mile walk

POOL: Yes

HAUL-OUT: 35 ton travel lift and 80 ton rail lift

HEAD/SHOWER: sparkling clean, air-conditioned restrooms and showers

LAUNDRY: Yes

INTERNET ACCESS: free WiFi

SHIP'S STORE: well-stocked with marine supplies, also with drinks, snacks, ice, etc.

NEAREST TOWN/MILES: Historic St. Mary's City / 8 miles

SHOPPING: nearby grocery and hardware

STORAGE: acres of dry storage

TRASPORTATION: courtesy car & loaner bicycles

SPECIAL: 2 Furnished Cabin Rentals (call for reservations), Woodlawn B&B and Winery nearby

*MLW = Mean Low Water Depth
 LOA = Longest vessel that can be accommodated

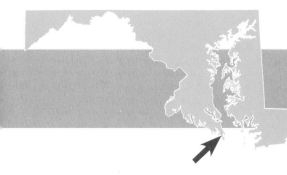

LAT: N 38° 06.933
LON: W 76° 24.033

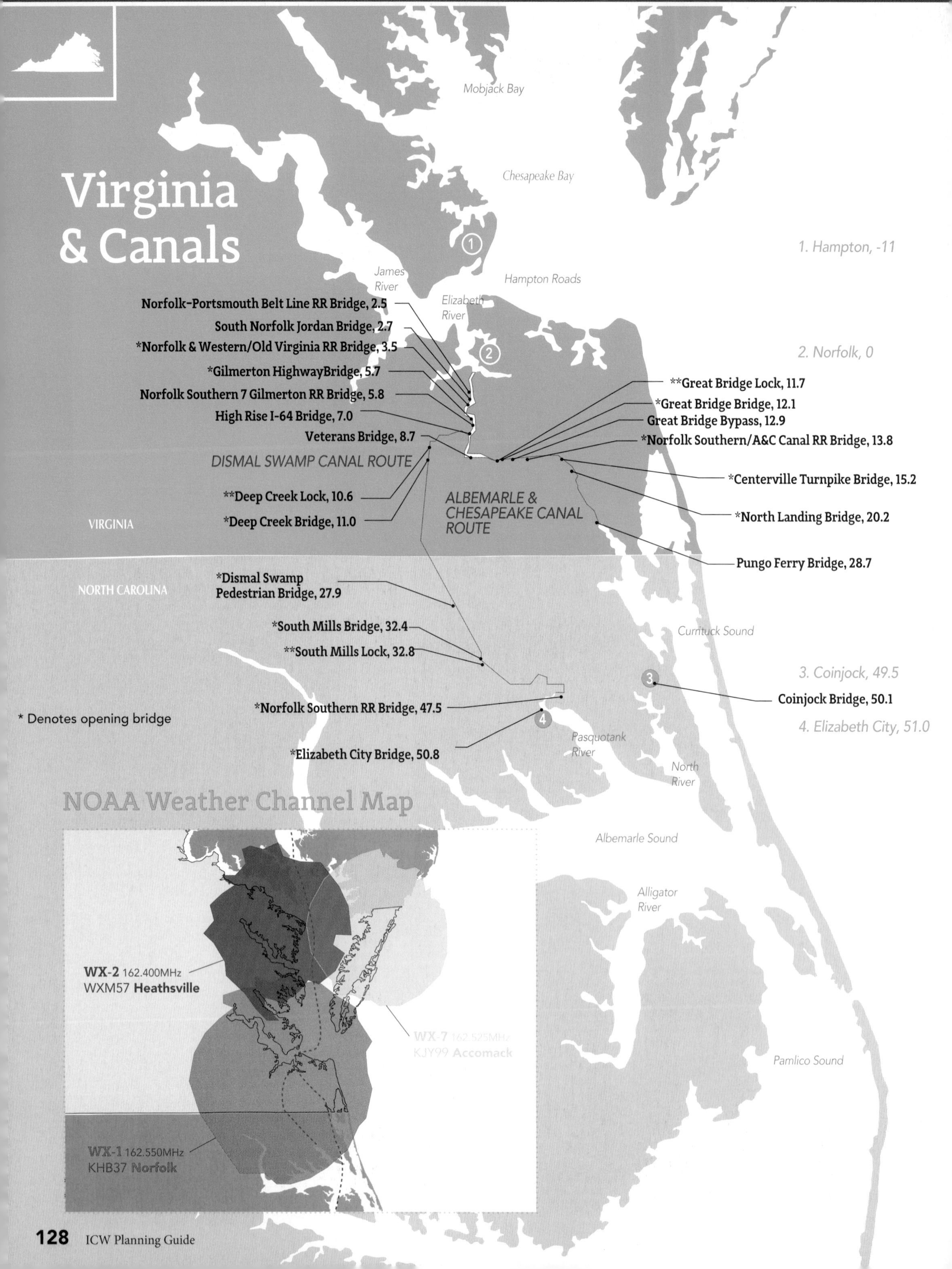

Virginia & Canals

Mobjack Bay

Chesapeake Bay

1. Hampton, -11

James River

Hampton Roads

Elizabeth River

2. Norfolk, 0

Norfolk–Portsmouth Belt Line RR Bridge, 2.5
South Norfolk Jordan Bridge, 2.7
*Norfolk & Western/Old Virginia RR Bridge, 3.5
*Gilmerton HighwayBridge, 5.7
Norfolk Southern 7 Gilmerton RR Bridge, 5.8
High Rise I-64 Bridge, 7.0
Veterans Bridge, 8.7

**Great Bridge Lock, 11.7
*Great Bridge Bridge, 12.1
Great Bridge Bypass, 12.9
*Norfolk Southern/A&C Canal RR Bridge, 13.8
*Centerville Turnpike Bridge, 15.2
*North Landing Bridge, 20.2
Pungo Ferry Bridge, 28.7

DISMAL SWAMP CANAL ROUTE

ALBEMARLE & CHESAPEAKE CANAL ROUTE

**Deep Creek Lock, 10.6
*Deep Creek Bridge, 11.0

VIRGINIA

NORTH CAROLINA

*Dismal Swamp Pedestrian Bridge, 27.9
*South Mills Bridge, 32.4
**South Mills Lock, 32.8

Currituck Sound

3. Coinjock, 49.5

Coinjock Bridge, 50.1

*Norfolk Southern RR Bridge, 47.5

4. Elizabeth City, 51.0

* Denotes opening bridge

*Elizabeth City Bridge, 50.8

Pasquotank River

North River

Albemarle Sound

Alligator River

NOAA Weather Channel Map

WX-2 162.400MHz
WXM57 **Heathsville**

WX-7 162.525MHz
KJY99 **Accomack**

WX-1 162.550MHz
KHB37 **Norfolk**

Pamlico Sound

ICW Mile 2.5
36°81.16'N 076°29.04'W

*Norfolk-Portsmouth Belt Line RR Bridge
Type: Lift
Closed Height: 6'
Schedule: Usually open except for passage of trains.
Contact: VHF 13
Comments: Closings are announced on VHF 13 at 30 minutes, 15 minutes and immediately before.

ICW Mile 2.7
36°80.84'N 076°29.00'W

South Norfolk Jordan Bridge
Type: Fixed
Height: 145'

ICW Mile 3.5
36°79.70'N 076°29.29'W

Norfolk and Western/ Old Virginia RR Bridge
Type: Lift
Closed Height: 10'
Schedule: Usually open, except for passage of trains.
Contact: VHF 13
Comments: Tender will respond to "Old Virginia Railroad Bridge."

ICW Mile 5.7
36°77.52'N 076°29.49'W

*Gilmerton Highway Bridge
Type: Lift
Closed Height: 35'
Schedule: Opens on demand from 8:30 a.m. to 3:30 p.m. Will not open weekdays from 6:30 to 8:30 p.m. and 3:30 to 5:30 p.m.
Contact: VHF 13 757-485-5488
Comments: Check schedule for changes during construction.

ICW Mile 5.8
36°77.49'N 076°29.48'W

*Norfolk Southern 7/ Gilmerton RR Bridge
Type: Bascule
Closed Height: 7'
Schedule: Usually open except for passage of trains.
Contact: VHF 13

ICW Mile 7.0
36°75.80′N 076°29.61′W

High Rise/I 64 Bridge
Type: Bascule
Closed Height: 65′

Albemarle & Chesapeake Canal

ICW Mile 8.7
26°83.15′ N 080°06.02′ W

Veterans Bridge
Type: Fixed
Height: 95′
Comments: Veterans Bridge
replaces the old Steel Bridge
(bascule).

ICW Mile 11.7
36°72.36′N 076°24.75′W

*Great Bridge Lock
Schedule: Coordinates with openings of Great Bridge Bridge, which
opens on the hour, 6 a.m. to 7 p.m.
Contact: VHF 13 757-547-3311
Comments: The lock's west side
is rubber and so easier to fend
off. The east side is steel and concrete, so fenders or fenderboards
are a must. You'll need your own
fore and aft docklines.

ICW Mile 12.1
36°72.10′N 076°23.98′W

*Great Bridge Bridge
Type: Bascule
Closed Height: 6′
Schedule: Opens on the hour
from 6 a.m. to 7 p.m. Otherwise
on request.
Contact: VHF 13 757-547-3311

ICW Mile 12.9
36°72.10'N 076°22.63'W

Great Bridge Bypass
Type: Fixed
Height: 65'

ICW Mile 13.8
36°72.20'N 076°21.01'W

***Norfolk Southern/
A&C Canal RR Bridge**
Type: Bascule
Closed: 7'
Schedule: Usually open, except
for passage of trains.

ICW Mile 15.2
36°72.37'N 076°18.64'W

***Centerville Turnpike
Bridge**
Type: Swing
Closed Height: 4'
Schedule: Opens on the hour
and half-hour from 8:30 a.m. to 4
p.m. weekdays. Does not open
weekdays from 6:30 to 8:30 a.m.
and 4 to 6 p.m. All other times,
opens on request.
Contact: VHF 13 757-547-3631

ICW Mile 20.2
36°71.78'N 076°10.02'W

*North Landing Bridge
Type: Swing
Closed Height: 3'
Schedule: Opens on the hour and
half-hour from 6 a.m. to 7 p.m.
All other times on request.
Contact: VHF 13 757-482-3081

ICW Mile 28.7
36°61.46'N 076°04.96'W

Pungo Ferry Bridge
Type: Fixed
Height: 65

ICW Mile 50.1
36°34.08'N 075°95.43'W

Coinjock Bridge
Type: Fixed
Height: 65

Photo by TR Colasanto

Dismal Swamp Canal

ICW Mile 10.6
36°74.64'N 076°33.97'W

**Deep Creek Lock
Schedule: Openings daily at 8:30 a.m., 11 a.m., 1:30 and 3:30 p.m.
Contact: VHF 13 757-487-0831
Comments: Schedule may change due to low water or mechanical difficulties. It is a good idea to confirm the schedule before starting out. Have lines for bow and stern ready and fenders in place.

ICW Mile 11.0
36°74.11'N 076°34.49'W

*Deep Creek Bridge
Type: Bascule
Closed Height: 4'
Schedule: Bridge operates in conjunction with the lock, and both are operated by the locktender. Opens at roughly 8:30 a.m., 11 a.m., 1:30 p.m. and 3:30 p.m.
Contact: VHF 13 757-487-0831

ICW Mile 27.9
36°50.57'N 076°35.56'W

*Dismal Swamp Pedestrian Bridge
Type: Pontoon
Closed Height: 0'
Schedule: Usually open for boats traveling on the canal. This bridge, which allows pedestrians to visit the Dismal Swamp Park exhibit, is generally closed at night.
Contact: VHF 16 252-771-6593

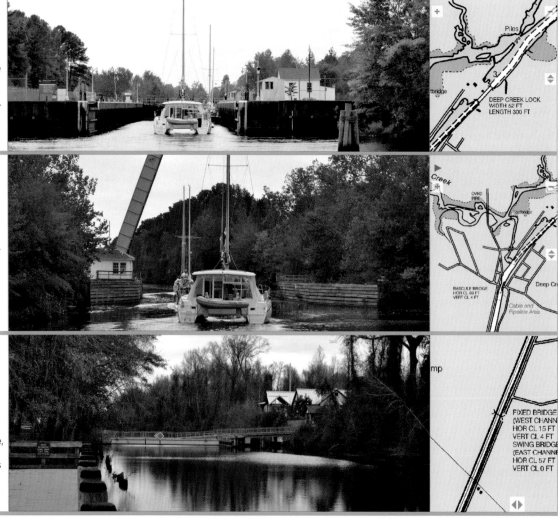

ICW Mile 31.5
36°45.77′N 076°33.28′W

Highway 17 Bypass Bridge
Type: Fixed
Height: 65′

ICW Mile 32.4
36°44.59′N 076°32.71′W

***South Mills Bridge**
Type: Bascule
Closed Height: 4′
Schedule: Opens in conjunction with South Mills Lock, so operates on the same schedule: 8:30 a.m., 11 a.m., 1:30 p.m. and 3:30 p.m.
Contact: VHF 13 252-771-5906

ICW Mile 32.8
36°43.95′N 076°32.42′

***South Mills Lock**
Schedule: Daily openings at 8:30 a.m., 11 a.m., 1:30 p.m. and 3:30 p.m.
Contact: VHF 13 252-771-5906
Comments: Schedule may change due to low water or mechanical difficulties. It is a good idea to confirm the schedule before starting out. (Use number above.) Have lines ready and fenders in place.

ICW Mile 47.5
36°32.05′N 076°18.12′W

***A&C/Norfolk RR Bridge**
Type: Swing Closed Height: 3′
Schedule: Usually open.
Comments: Be aware that the opening for this bridge is narrow and the current can run strong.

ICW Mile 50.8
36°30.12′N 076°21.71′W

***Elizabeth City Bridge**
Type: Bascule
Height: 2′
Schedule: Opens on request, except on weekdays, when it closes from 7 to 9 a.m. and 4 to 6 p.m., except for openings at 7:30 and 8:30 a.m. and 4:30 and 5:30 p.m.
Contact: VHF 13 252-331-4772

Virginia

Potomac River to Deltaville

	MLW	Transient Slips/Moorings	Floating docks	Gas	Diesel	Pumpout	Showers	Pool	Laundry	Wi-Fi	Haulout	Repairs	Other
Cole's Point Marina Resort Potomac River/Coles Point 804-472-4011 www.colespointmarina.com	7'	●		●	●	●	●	●	●	●	●	●	Beach, store, cottages, pavilion, campsites, trails
Colonial Beach Yacht Center Potomac R./Colonial Beach 804-224-7230 www.cbycmarina.com	4'	●		●	●	●		➤	●	●	●		Trolley, protected harbor, beach, golf carts
Port Kinsale Marina Potomac River/Yeocomico River 804-472-2044 www.portkinsale.com	8'	●		●	●	●	●	●	●	●		●	Screened pavilion, picnic area, B&B, gas grills
Olverson's Lodge Creek Marina, Inc. Potomac R./Yeocomico R./Lodge Cr. 800-529-5071 www.olversonsmarina.com		●		●	●	●	●	●	●	●	➤	➤	Covered land boat & RV storage. Rental house
Smith Point Marina Little Wicomico River/Sloop Creek 804-453-4077 www.smithpointmarina.com	4.5'	●	●	●	●	●	●		●	●	●	●	
Reedville Marina Great Wicomico R./Cockrell Cr. 804-453-6789 www.reedvillemarina.com	14'	●		●	●	●	●		●				Ship's store; Boat U.S. marina; Crazy Crab
Tiffany Yachts Great Wicomico River 804-453-3464 www.tiffanyyachtsinc.com	10'	●		●	●	●	●			●	●	●	full-service marine facility with 88-ton lift and 2 railways
Ingram Bay Marina Great Wicomico R./Towles Cr. 804-580-7292 www.ingrambaymarina.com	7'	●		●	●	●	●	●	●	●		●	Courtesy car, picnic area, lounge, pet friendly
Chesapeake Boat Basin Northern Neck/Indian Cr. 804-435-3110 www.chesapeakeboatbasin.com	14'	●	●	●	●	●	●		➤	●		●	Floating docks, close to town, clean restrooms
Windmill Point Marina Rappahannock R./Windmill Point 804-436-1818 www.windmillptmarina.com	5.5'	●	●	●	●	●	●	●		●			Floating docks, pool bar with food service
The Tides Inn Rappahannock R./Carter Cr. 804-438-5000 www.tidesinn.com	7'	●	●	●	●	●	●	●	●	●		➤	Tennis, spa, golf, bicycles, full resort amenities
Yankee Point Marina Rappahannock R./Corrotoman R. 804-462-7018 www.yankeepointmarina.com	8'	●		●	●	●	●	●	●	●	●	●	Restaurant, ships store, picnic areas, dinghy dock, boat ramp
Greenvale Creek Marina Rappahannock R./Greenvale Cr. 804-761-7813 www.greenvalemarina.com	5'	●		●	●	●	●		●	●		●	Covered slips to 45', non-ethanol fuel; repairs
Urbanna Town Marina at Upton's Point Rappahannock R./Urbanna Cr. 804-758-5440 www.urbanna.com	10'	●	➤	➤	●	●	➤	●	●	●	➤	➤	Free dinghy landing, free Wi-Fi
Dozier's Port Urbanna Marine Center Rappahannock R./Urbanna Cr. 804-758-0000 www.doziermarinegroup.com	9'	●	➤	➤	●	●			●	●	●		40-ton lift; In Town
Norton Yachts Rappahannock R./Broad Cr. 804-776-9211 www.nortonyachts.com	6'	●		●	●	●	●		●	●	●	●	Sailing sch., charters, full-service yard, boat sales, courtesy car
Deltaville Yachting Center Rappahannock R./Broad Creek 804-776-9898 www.dycboat.com	6'	●		●	➤	●	●	●			●	●	Full-service ABYC yard, 50-ton lift, boatel, sales
Dozier's Regatta Point Yachting Center Rappahannock R./Broad Cr. 804-776-8400 www.doziermarinegroup.com	7.5'	●	●	➤	➤	●	●	●	●	●	➤	●	Wi-Fi, floating docks, courtesy car
Norview Marina Rappahannock R./Broad Cr. 804-776-6463 www.norviewmarina.com	6.5'	●	●	●	●	●	●	●	●	●	●	●	boathouse, 82-ton lift, boatel, Zimmerman marine onsite
Deltaville Marina Piankatank R./Jackson Cr. 804-776-9812 www.deltavillemarina.com	9'	●		●	●	●	●	●	●	●	●	●	Full-service marina/yard with amenities, ABYC techs
Fishing Bay Harbor Marina Piankatank R./Fishing Bay 804-776-6800 www.fishingbay.com	15'	●		●	●	●	●	●	●	●	➤	➤	Deepwater dockage, lounge, Wi-Fi, cable
Chesapeake Boat Works Piankatank R./Fishing Bay 804-776-8833 www.chesapeakeboatworks.com	15'	●	➤	➤	➤	●	●	➤		●	●	●	Boatyard, all repairs, dry storage

	MLW	Transient Slips/Moorings	Floating docks	Gas	Diesel	Pumpout	Showers	Pool	Laundry	Wi-Fi	Haulout	Repairs	Other
Stingray Point Boat Works Rappahannock R./Broad Cr. 804-776-7070 www.stingraypointboatworks.com	6'	➤		➤	➤	●	➤	●	●	●		➤	Full-service boatyard
Stingray Point Marina Rappahannock R./Broad Cr. 804-776-7272 www.stingraypointmarina.com	6.5'		➤	➤	●	●	●	●	●	➤		➤	Replica of the 1858 Stingray Pt Lighthouse; annual slips only
Gwynn's Island to James River													
Morningstar Marina Gwynn's Island Milford Haven 804-384-9698 www.morningstarmarinas.com	6'	●		●	➤	●	●			●	●		
Zimmerman Marine Mobjack Bay/East R. 804-725-3440 www.zimmermanmarine.com	6'	●			●	●			●	●	●		Boatyard, all repairs, custom boatbuilders
Severn Yachting Center Mobjack Bay/Severn R./Willets Creek 804-642-6969 www.severnyachtingcenter.com	7'	●	●	●	●	●	●		●	●	●		Large yacht capacity, fixed; floating slips, 75-ton lift
Crown Pointe Marina York R./Perrin R. 804-642-6177 www.crownpointemarina.com	7'	●		●	●	●	●	●	●	●			Non-Ethanol fuel, gas grills, picnic porch
York River Yacht Haven York R./Sarah Cr. 804-642-2156 www.yorkriveryachthaven.com	8'	●		●	●	●	●	●	●	●	●		Courtesy car; repairs, transport to Yorktown
Wormley Creek Marina York R./Wormley Cr. 757-898-5060 www.wormleycreekmarina.com	6'	●		●	●	●	●		➤	●	●		Crane, 37.5 ton lift, wood & F/G repairs
Dare Marina York R./Poquoson R./Chisman Cr. 757-898-3000 www.daremarina.com	5.5'	●	●	●	●	●				●	●		New and used boat sales, paddleboard rentals, sales
Salt Ponds Marina Resort Thimble Shoals Light/Chesapeake Bay 757-850-4300 www.saltpondsmarinaresort.com	10'	●	●	●	●	●	●	●	●	●	➤	●	On the Bay, 2 pools, private beach, VHF 16
Bell Isle Marina Back R./Wallace Cr. 757-850-0466 www.bellislemarina.com	6'	●	➤	➤	●	●			➤	●	●		Dry storage, 55-ton lift, forklift, repairs, rigging
Southall Landings Marina Salt Ponds/south of Back R. 757-850-9929 www.southallmarina.com	6'	●	➤	➤	●	●	●	●	●	●	➤	➤	Pool, laundry, no boat tax, fixed docks
Bluewater Yachting Center Hampton River 757-723-6774 www.bluewateryachtsales.com	12'	●	●	●	●	●	●	●	●	●		●	Shuttle to downtown, bts to 200'; floating docks
Old Point Comfort Marina Hampton R./Mill Cr./Fort Monroe 757-788-4308 www.oldpointcomfortmarina.com	15'	●		●	●	●	●	➤	●	●	●	●	Open to the public; restaurant on-site; adjacent to Ft. Monroe
Downtown Hampton Public Piers Hampton R. 757-727-1276 www.hamptonpublicpiers.com	12'	●	➤	➤	●	●	●	●	●	●	➤	➤	Shops, restaurants summer bus & rental car near
Sunset Boating Center Hampton R./Sunset Cr. 757-722-3325 www.sunsetboatingcenter.com	10'	●		●	●	●	●		●		●	●	Boat U.S. marina, fuel & transient discounts
Deep Creek Landing James R./Deep Cr./Newport News 757-877-9555 www.deepcreeklanding.com	5'	●		●	●	●	●		●	●	●	●	Floating docks, banquet facility, full-service marina
Kingsmill Resort James R. 757-253-3919 www.kingsmill.com	7'	●		●	●	●	●	●					Golf, tennis, spa, gym, pools; near Busch Gardens
Smithfield Station James R./Pagan River 757-357-7700 www.smithfieldstation.com	7'	●	●	➤	➤	●	●	●	➤	●		➤	➤	Shopping, restaurant, hotel, pool, bathhouse, bar
Willoughby Bay to Virginia Beach													
Bay Point Marina Little Cr./Fisherman's Cove 757-362-8432 www.littlecreekmarina.com	6'	●	➤	➤	●	●	●	●	●	●	➤	➤	Wi-Fi, customer lounge, Lagoon restaurant
Cobb's Marina Little Creek Inlet 757-588-5401 www.cobbsmarina.com	10'	●	●	➤	➤	●	●		➤	●	●	●	All new floating docks, 50-ton and 75-ton hoist

	MLW	Transient Slips/Moorings	Floating docks	Gas	Diesel	Pumpout	Showers	Pool	Laundry	Wi-Fi	Haulout	Repairs	Other
Fisherman's Wharf Marina Rudee Inlet/Virginia Beach 757-428-2111 www.fishermanswharfmarina.com	8'	•		➤	➤	•	•		➤	•		•	Walk to beach, inshore/off-shore fishing
Little Creek Marina Little Cr./Fisherman's Cove 757-362-3600 www.littlecreekmarina.com	15'	•		•	•	•	•	•	•	•	•	•	Wi-Fi, lounge
Long Bay Pointe Boating Resort Lynnhaven Inlet/Long Cr. 757-321-4550 www.longbaypointemarina.com	6'	•		•	•	•	•		➤		➤	➤	Hair Salon, fitness center, 2 restaurants
Marina Shores Lynnhaven Inlet/Long Cr. 757-496-7000 www.marinashoresmarina.com	8'	•		•	•	•	•	•	•		•	•	
Rebel Marine Service Willoughby Bay 757-580-6022 www.rebelmarina.com	8'	•	•	➤	➤	•	•		•	•	➤	➤	Free Wi-Fi, courtesy cars, boater lounge, courtesy car
Rudee's Inlet Station Marina Rudee Inlet 757-422-2999 www.rudeesmarina.com	8'	•		•	•	•	•		➤	•		•	Near beach/boardwalk; 2 restaurants, outdoor bar
Virginia Beach Fishing Center Rudee Inlet/Virginia Beach 757-491-8000 www.virginiafishing.com	6'	•		•	•	•	•		➤	•		•	Closest entrance to the Atlantic Ocean
Willoughby Harbor Marina Willoughby Bay 757-583-4150	6'	•		➤	➤	•	•		•	•	➤	➤	Boat U.S. marina, floating docks, cable, cat. pier
Elizabeth River to Great Bridge													
Waterside Marina Elizabeth R./Norfolk/Mile Marker 0 757-625-3625 www.watersidemarina.com	20'	•		➤	➤	•	•		•	•	➤	•	Near Nauticus, USS Wisconsin, theaters & mall
Tidewater Yacht Marina Elizabeth R./Mile Marker Zero 757-393-2525 www.tyamarina.com	10'	•		•	•	•	•	•	•	•	•	•	500' Megayacht dock, fast fueling, 100amp 1/3 phase
Ocean Marine Yacht Center Elizabeth R./1/2 mile S of MM 0 757-399-2920 www.oceanmarinellc.com	25'	•	•	•	•	•	•	•	•	•	•	•	Full parts, service depts, certified techs on staff
Portsmouth Boating Center Elizabeth River 757-397-2092	8'	•		•	•	•	•		•	•	•	•	70 ton lift, dry & land storage, Boat U.S. discount
Scott's Creek Marina Elizabeth R./Scott's Cr. 757-399-2628 www.scottscreekmarina.com	12'	•		➤	➤	•	•		•	•	➤	➤	Lending library, free laundro-mat & pump-out ($5)
Top Rack Marina Chesapeake, Va./MM 8 757-227-3041 www.toprackmarina.com		•	•	•	•		•		•	•	•		Full-service; marine supplies; Restaurant on-site
Atlantic Yacht Basin Great Bridge/MM 9 757-482-2141 www.atlanticyachtbasin.com	12'	•		•	•	•	•		•	•	•	•	Full-service, freshwater covered storage
Eastern Shore Virginia													
Parks Marina Tangier Island 757-891-2567	6'	•		➤	➤		•			•	•		
Deep Creek Marina and Boatyard Deep Creek/Above Onancock, Va. 757-787-4565	4.5'	•								•	•		Dry storage, 25-ton lift; wood, engine repair
The Wharf at Onancock Onancock 757-787-7911 www.onancock.com	8'	•	•	•	•	•	•		➤	•		➤	walk to restaurants, galleries, shops, historic sites
The Oyster Farm at Kings Creek Kings Cr./Cape Charles 757-331-8640 www.theoysterfarmatkingscreek.com	6.5'	•	•	•	•	•	•	•	•	•	➤	•	Fuel pier, floating docks, boats to 150'
Cape Charles Town Harbor Cape Charles Harbor 757-331-2357 www.capecharlesbythebay.com	7'	•	•	•	•	•	•		➤			➤	beach, museum & shops nearby
Cape Charles Yacht Center Cape Charles Harbor 757-331-3100 www.ccayachtcenter.com	18'	•	•	➤	➤	•	•		➤	•	•	•	75-ton lift, power to 3-phase, 480, 1,000 feet of face dockage
Island House Restaurant & Marina Bradford Bay 757-789-3222 www.theislandhouserestaurant.com	10'			•	•	•	•		•				

Coles Point Marina

190 Plantation Drive
Hague, VA 22469
Ph: 804-472-4011
Email: info@colespointmarina.com
colespointmarina.com

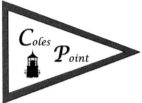

Coles Point Marina & Camp Ground

description of facilities

Coles Point Marina can be Your Private Hideaway perfectly located on the lower Potomac River. No time will be wasted getting to the fishing or sailing grounds as access to the river is instantaneous. Our marina has the largest protected harbor with the closest proximity to the lower Potomac River than any other marina!

marina approach & docking

Coles Point Marina is conveniently located on the Virginia shore of the lower Potomac River, just downriver of Ragged Point Light. Coming into the mouth of the Potomac from the Chesapeake Bay we're located just over 17 miles upriver from Point Lookout MD and approximately 26 miles from Smith Point, VA.

at a glance

DOCKAGE RATE: Daily Rates: $1.50/ft. Uncovered $1.75/ft. Covered Weekly Rates (7 days) $ 6.00 /ft . Uncovered $7.00 /ft . Covered Monthly Rate (30 days) $10.50/ft . Uncovered $12.15/ft . Covered

PAYMENT: Cash, checks, and major credit/debit cards (except AMEX)

HOURS: May 31 - Sept 5 M-Thurs, 9 - 5 Fri & Sat, 8 - 7 Sun, 8 - 5 Sept 6 - May 30 Tues-Sun, 9 - 5 Closed on Mondays

TRANSIENT SLIPS/TOTAL SLIPS: 138

MLW/LOA*: 7´/Up to 70'

ELECTRIC: Yes

PUMP-OUT: Yes

FUEL: Gas & Diesel

REPAIR: Yes

PROPANE: Yes

RESTAURANT/MILES: On site, Tim's at Cole's Point

POOL: Yes

HAUL-OUT: Yes

HEAD/SHOWER: Yes/Yes

LAUNDRY: Yes

INTERNET ACCESS: WiFi

CABLE: No

SHIP'S STORE: Drinks, snacks and ice

NEAREST TOWN/MILES: 20 miles

STORAGE: Yes

AIRPORT/MILES: 75 miles

TRANSPORTATION: No

SPECIAL: Cottage rentals, beach, campsites, trails

*MLW = Mean Low Water Depth
LOA = Longest vessel that can be accommodated

Smith Point Marina

989 Smith Point Road, Reedville, VA 22539
Ph: 804-453-4077 | Fax: 804-453-4077
Email: dan1@smithpointmarina.com
SmithPointMarina.com

description of facilities

For 60 years, Smith Point Marina has provided a picturesque, friendly and safe harbor, fuel and reliable repairs to boats transiting the Middle Bay. Our local service includes winterization, shrink wrap and storage and our 10T Travellift and 3T Forklift allow us to service and repair many long range cruisers. At our conveniently located gas dock, we provide 87 no-ethanol gas and diesel fuels, pump-out and dockage for boats to 60′. Our floating ship store is stocked with snacks, sodas, ice and ice cream. Our Marina Store has boat parts, oil, fuel additives and clothing, along with bait and tackle. We have the Bay's best bath house facilities, a laundromat, library, and free WIFI. Our ramp accommodates boats to 35′ and our camping area includes a rental camper for 6.

marina approach & docking

Smith Point Marina is only 3/4 mile off the bay. Entrance to the Little Wicomico River is from Smith Point Light. Contrary to NOAA chart markings, the sand bottom carries 6 feet MLW. The Jetties are dredged often, but to avoid any sandbars, enter on the North side and a few boat lengths in, shift to the South side. Once inside, follow the markers to Green 9, turn left and pass Green 1S (Slough Creek) to port. Pass Red 2 to starboard and then glide serenely around Green markers 3, 5, and 7 to line up for the gas dock. Note: you should be passing between the three Green markers and the shore. That is where God placed the deep water! We (Jeanne and Dan) look forward to your visit.

LAT: 37° 53.02′N
LON: -76° 15.03′W

at a glance

DOCKAGE RATE: Transient docking $2.00-$2.25 per foot and $.25 BOAT/US discount

PAYMENT: Visa, MC, Discover, cash

HOURS: 7:30am – 5pm

TRANSIENT SLIPS/TOTAL SLIPS: 10/99

VHF/WORKING: 16/68

MLW/LOA*: 4′6″/60′

ELECTRIC: 30/50 Amp

PUMP-OUT: Yes

FUEL: No-ethanol 87 gas, diesel

REPAIR: Engine, running gear, hull, electrical, winterization and storage

RESTAURANT/MILES: 6 miles

POOL: No

HAUL-OUT: Hauling (10T travel lift, 3T forklift)

HEAD/SHOWER/LAUNDRY: Yes/Yes/Yes

INTERNET ACCESS: Yes

SHIP'S STORE: Yes

NEAREST TOWN/MILES: Nearby/6

SHOPPING: Limited

STORAGE: Boats up to 36′

AIRPORT/MILES: 90 miles

TRANSPORTATION: Car rental

YACHT BROKERAGE: No

SPECIAL: Great Fishing, Quiet Hideaway

*MLW = Mean Low Water Depth
LOA = Longest vessel that can be accommodated

We're the closest marina to the Chesapeake Bay!

* Pet Friendly *

INGRAM BAY MARINA

Ingram Bay Marina
545 Harveys Neck Rd
Heathsville, VA 22473
Ph: 804-580-7292
ingrambaymarina.com

description of facilities

Between the place where the Potomac and Rappahannock Rivers empty into the Chesapeake Bay is a peninsula called the Northern Neck of Virginia. It may seem to be the end of the earth but when you arrive you find a lovely destination ….. the perfect getaway. This is a family owned and operated marina, with a charter fishing service and rental cabins. We have been blessed to live here since 1985. It's quite simply, our life. And a good life it is, that we are privileged to share with you. We love our little corner of the world and our business allows us to live and work and play on our beloved Chesapeake Bay.

Whether it's your home away from home…. …..Or your vacation getaway …..
This is the perfect place for the action packed vacation. Situated near Reedville, right on the Chesapeake Bay and the Inter-Coastal Waterway puts you right on top of the very best fishing and sailing in the region. It's the closest marina to the bay. Open & Covered Slips – Every one has a view of the Bay.

marina approach & docking

We are on Towles Creek located at the mouth of the Great Wicomico River.
From the Great Wicomico Light take a 255 degree heading to the Red #2 MC Dayshape Then turn to the North and follow to the next Red #2 day shape. Continue each 1/4 mile to the next markers (#3 and #4). Then turn to port and follow the #5 marker into the jetties. Now you are in the Ingram Bay Marina Oasis!

at a glance

DOCKAGE RATE: Call for rates

PAYMENT: Cash/Check/CC (discounts available)

HOURS: 7 days/wk

TRANSIENT SLIPS/TOTAL SLIPS: 55

VHF/WORKING: 16/6

MLW: 6.5' MLW/10 ft entrance channel

LOA: 65'

ELECTRIC: 30/50 amp

PUMP-OUT: Yes

FUEL: NON-ETHANOL Gas and Diesel Fuel

REPAIR: Some repairs

PROPANE: No

RESTAURANT/MILES: 6 miles

POOL: Coming soon

HAUL-OUT: No

HEAD/SHOWER: Yes

LAUNDRY: Yes

INTERNET ACCESS: WiFi

CABLE: No

SHIP'S STORE: Snacks, ice, bait and tackle

NEAREST TOWN/MILES: 12 miles

SHOPPING: Nearby

GOLF/TENNIS: Nearby

STORAGE: Yes

AIRPORT/MILES: Topping/15 miles

TRANSPORTATION: Courtesy Vehicle

YACHT BROKERAGE: No

SPECIAL: Home of Capt. Billy's Charters / CABIN RENTALS, BOAT/CANOE/KAYAK rentals

*MLW = Mean Low Water Depth
LOA = Longest vessel that can be accommodated

Windmill Point Marina

40 Windjammer Lane, White Stone, VA 22578
Ph: 804-436-1818 | Fax: 804-436-9009
Email: info@windmillptmarina.com
windmillptmarina.com

description of facilities

They say that nature smiled on Windmill Point and you can see the result: white sand beach, a well protected harbor and a view that rivals the Florida Keys and the Caribbean. Ninety-six new slips include both traditonal wood docks and aluminum and vinyl docks by Poralu of Canada. There are floating and fixed docks for boats of all sizes. Have accommodated several hundred footers.

The Tiki Bar and Grill, overlooking the patio and pool, is open 7 days a week (during the season) including great seafood at KC's at Windmill Point complimenting their Kilmarnock location. Music is provided weekends. Historic towns of Lancaster County offer casual and gourmat restaurants, groceries, shopping, historic sites and PGA gold courses.

marina approach & docking

From the river or from the Chesapeake Bay, approach the marina over an old sandbar; if your vessel draws 5 feet or more call ahead (804-436-1818) or VHF channel 16/72) refer to Tide Table and approach at high tide only. Lighted navigation markers number 5 and 6 are about one-half mile from the jetty entrance. A prominent line of rocks on top of the jeffy are to starboard and extend another 100 feet, then become submerged. Channel depth is 5 feet MLW while the harbor depth is 7 feet MLW. Completed basins are presented; to port are docks A through E; to starboard are docks J and K. Future docks are planned straight ahead.

All open slips are for rent annually or seasonally and for transient guests. Please stop in or call 804-436-1818. Online, use site info@windmillptmarina.com.

LAT: 37° 36.900' N
LON: 076° 17.400' W

at a glance

DOCKAGE RATE: $8.00/ft/month, Annual: $11.00/ft/month, Seasonal: $1.50/ft Transients

PAYMENT: MC/Visa/AMEX/cash/check

HOURS: 9-6 Sun - Thurs / 8-8 Fri & Sat

TRANSIENT SLIPS/TOTAL SLIPS: 35/96

VHF/WORKING: 16/72

MLW/LOA*: 5'/90' depending upon craft

ELECTRIC: 30 amp - 125 Volt / 50 amp - 250 Volt

PUMP-OUT: $15.00

FUEL: Gas & Diesel

REPAIR: No

PROPANE: No

RESTAURANT/MILES: 2 Onsite

POOL: 1 Riverfront pool

HEAD/SHOWER: Yes/Yes

LAUNDRY: Yes

INTERNET ACCESS: Yes

CABLE: Yes

SHIP'S STORE: Yes

NEAREST TOWN/MILES: 8 miles

SHOPPING: White Stone, Kilmarnock, Irvington

GOLF/TENNIS: Tartan & Golden Eagle Courses

AIRPORT/MILES: Richmond, Va./75, Norfolk, Va.60

YACHT BROKERAGE: No

SPECIAL: White Sand Beaches, Courtesy Vehicle Available

*MLW = Mean Low Water Depth
 LOA = Longest vessel that can be accommodated

STINGRAY POINT BOAT WORKS

Stingray Point Boat Works

19047 General Puller Hwy, Deltaville, VA 23043
Ph: 804-776-7070 | Fax: 804-776-0003
Email: info@stingraypointboatworks.com
StingrayPointBoatworks.com

LAT: 37° 33' 70"N
LON: -76° 18' 570"W

Stingray Point Marina

Stingray Point Marina

19167 General Puller Hwy, Deltaville, VA 23043
Ph: 804-776-7272
Email: info@stingraypointmarina.com
StingrayPointMarina.com

LAT: 37° 33' 63"N
LON: -76° 18' 429"W

Classic Integrity. Quality Service.

Deltaville Yachting Center & Chesapeake Yacht Sales

18355 General Puller Highway, Deltaville, VA 23043
Ph: 804-776-9898 | Fax: 804-776-6998
Email: info@dycboat.com
DYCBoat.com

description of facilities

Deltaville Yachting Center, home of Chesapeake Yacht Sales (dealer for Catalina Yachts) was named Middlesex County's first Virginia Clean Marina in 2002. Located on Broad Creek, DYC is just one mile from the Chesapeake Bay in a peaceful, protected setting with a friendly, professional atmosphere. DYC has 76 covered and uncovered slips, 150 boat Hi-Dri boatel and a 4 acre boatyard. Full service repair yard with excellent customer service rating. ABYC and factory trained techs. Mainship, Albin, Catalina & Carolina Classic specialists. Chosen Best of Bay 2010-2016, Best Marina for Natural Environment, Best Boatyard, Best General Repairs, Best Engine Work, Best Electronics. For both power & sail, DYC provides quality service and classic integrity to the boat you love. We help with all boats from 10 foot run abouts to 60 foot cruisers, so you can have fun boating.

marina approach & docking

Enter Broad Creek from Rappahannock River at G "1". Proceed into creek and follow the red and green markers. After passing R "2S" stay close to the red roofed marina's C Dock (Norview Marina). Ahead you will see DYC's C and D Docks. To starboard will be covered A & B Docks as well as DYC's travel lift.

LAT: 37° 33' 34.0"N
LON: -76°18' 45.0"W

at a glance

Dockage Rate: $1.33/ft without BoatUS card, $1.00/ft with a BoatUS card

Payment: MC/Visa/Discover/cash

Hours: 8am – 4:30pm M-F, 9am – 4:30pm Sat, Sunday by appointment

Transient Slips/Total Slips: 4/76

VHF/Working: 16/72

MLW/LOA*: 6'/60'

Electric: 30/50 Amp

Pump-out: 2 stations on-site

Fuel: Non-ethanol gas

Repair: Repowers, rigging, gelcoat/fiberglass, paint, interiors, A/C, gensets – Cummins, Onan, Yanmar

Restaurant/Miles: Most restaurants/1.3

Haul-out: 50 ton travel lift & 2 forklifts

Head/Shower: 10 heads/7 showers; clean

Internet Access: Free WiFi

Ship's Store: Boutique, parts, snacks

Nearest Town/Miles: Deltaville/.5

Shopping: DYC Ship's Store, snacks, convenience items, parts, boutique

Storage: Boatyard (full-service & DIY), Enclosed Boatel, Covered & Open Slips

Transportation: Courtesy car, Enterprise Rental discount

Yacht Brokerage: Catalina Yachts dealer. Carolina Classic, Mainship & Albin Specialists.

*MLW = Mean Low Water Depth
LOA = Longest vessel that can be accommodated

Deltaville's Destination of Choice!

Fishing Bay Marina
DELTAVILLE, VIRGINIA

CHESAPEAKE BOAT WORKS
DELTAVILLE, VIRGINIA

Fishing Bay Marina

519 Deagles Road, Deltaville, VA 23043
Ph: 804-776-6800 | Fax: 804-884-3851
Email: info@fishingbay.com
FishingBay.com

description of facilities

Fishing Bay Marina is a state-of-the-art facility with a laid-back charm. We are located in a protected haven just minutes from the Chesapeake Bay. The marina is composed of fixed as well as floating concrete docks. Amenities include ValvTect Marine Fuels (gas and diesel, includes highspeed), free pump-out to tenants and transients, large pool with fountain, Wi-fi, well-stocked ship's store, digital cable TV, Captain's lounge, clean air conditioned bathhouses, laundry, picnic area with grills. A friendly and knowledgeable staff are ready to assist you with your boating needs.

marina approach & docking

Fishing Bay Marina is located at the mouth of the Piankatank River and the Chesapeake Bay. Follow the channel into the Piankatank River and make sure to leave R 8 and R 8A to starboard. Then head west leaving Stove Point and R 10 and R 10A to starboard and head north onto Fishing Bay. The marina is located in the Northwest corner of Fishing Bay. Marina staff monitor VHF channel 16. When approaching the marina, call for a slip assignment and docking assistance.

LAT: 37° 32' 27.8304" N
LON: 76° 20' 25.6920" W

at a glance

DOCKAGE RATE: Transient $1.65 per foot LOA; Annual Slips $1800 to $6000

PAYMENT: MC/Visa/check/cash

HOURS: 8am – 5pm, 7 days a week

TRANSIENT SLIPS/TOTAL SLIPS: 15 transient/126 annual

VHF/WORKING: 16/72

MLW/LOA*: 15'18'/200'+

ELECTRIC: 30/50 Amp

PUMP-OUT: Yes

FUEL: Valvtect Marine Fuels, Gas/Diesel

REPAIR: Chesapeake Boat Works next to marina

PROPANE: 5 miles

RESTAURANT/MILES: 1 mile

POOL: Yes

HAUL-OUT: Chesapeake Boat Works next to marina

HEAD/SHOWER: Yes/Yes

LAUNDRY: Yes

INTERNET ACCESS: Yes, free

SHIP'S STORE: Yes

NEAREST TOWN/MILES: 1 mile

SHOPPING: 1 mile

TRANSPORTATION: Courtesy Car/ Bicycles

YACHT BROKERAGE: Nearby

*MLW = Mean Low Water Depth
LOA = Longest vessel that can be accommodated

A Chesapeake Bay Landmark—
Full of History, Amenities, Luxury, and Class

A **Suntex** *Marina*

York River Yacht Haven

8109 Yacht Haven Road,
Gloucester Point, VA 23062
Ph: 804-642-2156 | Fax: 804-642-4766
Email: yryh@suntexmarinas.com
YorkRiverYachtHaven.com

description of facilities

Only 20 minutes away from Colonial Williamsburg, York River Yacht Haven is where friends and family gather together. We are a family-oriented, full-service marina, which is dedicated to providing the finest facilities and service to our fellow yachtsmen. Whether you are from the local boating area or are headed North or South bound, our marina is ideal for accommodating you. Our transients are offered a safe and secure protected facility with a variety of local services and entertainment. Our YRYH Team continually monitor VHF channel 16 and are always available for docking and fueling assistance. Next time you are in the area, stop in for a visit!

marina approach & docking

York River Yacht Haven is a full-service marina in Gloucester Point, VA, located at the mouth of Sarah Creek, opposite Yorktown. Our 14 acre rural site is in a natural "hurricane hole", storm protected from every quadrant.

LAT: 37° 15.394′N
LON: -76° 28.765′W

at a glance

DOCKAGE RATE: Please call

PAYMENT: Visa/MC/Discover/Amex

HOURS: 9am – 5pm

TRANSIENT SLIPS/TOTAL SLIPS: 20/288

VHF/WORKING: 16/9

MLW/LOA*: 9′/160′

ELECTRIC: 30/50/100

PUMP-OUT: Yes

FUEL: Gas/Diesel

REPAIR: Full-service boatyard

RESTAURANT/MILES: York River Oyster Co./on-site

POOL: Yes

HAUL-OUT: Yes/60T

HEAD/SHOWER: Yes/Yes

LAUNDRY: Yes

INTERNET ACCESS: Yes

SHIP'S STORE: Marine store renovated in 2014

NEAREST TOWN/MILES: Yorktown/3, Williamsburg/17

SHOPPING: Grocery 2 miles, Premium Outlets 19 miles

GOLF/TENNIS: 12 mi

STORAGE: Wet/Dry storage on-site

AIRPORT/MILES: Norfolk/37, Newport News/12

AMENITIES: Boat and watersport rentals, event space and banquet room, and laundry

YACHT BROKERAGE: Bluewater Yacht Sales/on-site

SPECIAL: Join the Suntex Captain's Club and SAVE on transient dockage, fuel and more! Limited time...complimentary club membership when you stay at one of our East Coast locations.

*MLW = Mean Low Water Depth
LOA = Longest vessel that can be accommodated

CHRIS GLENNON
PHOTOGRAPHER

Cape Charles Town Harbor and Marina

11 Marina Rd, Cape Charles, VA 23310
Ph: 757-331-2357
Email: townharbor@capecharles.org
capecharles.org

description of facilities

Welcome to Cape Charles Town Harbor and Marina! Transient vessels both motor and sail appreciate the harbor for its ease of navigation, its deep water marina and facilities. A short distance from the Atlantic Ocean, the deep draft channel makes the Chesapeake Bay easy access. The new breakwaters shield the harbor from swells and help protect the marina during storms. Designated a Virginia Clean Marina, this full-service facility is just a short walk to the historic town of Cape Charles. Many amenities are just steps away - golf, restaurants, museums. Transportation arrangements available.

marina approach & docking

Cape Charles Harbor, 9 miles northward of Wise Point, is a dredged basin on the south side of the town of Cape Charles. A well-marked dredged channel leads to the harbor between sand flats on the south and a stone jetty on the north. Two small dredged basins are eastward of the main harbor basin. The northerly basin is known as the Harbor of Refuge, and the southerly basin as Mud Creek Basin. (See Notice to Mariners and latest edition of charts for controlling depths.) The current velocity is about 1.3 knots 0.5 mile southwest of the Cape Charles City Entrance Light 1. Cape Charles Coast Guard Station is on the spit between Mud Creek and the Harbor of Refuge 1.

LAT: - 37-16.00 N
LON: - 076-01.000 W

at a glance

DOCKAGE RATE: $1.75/ft

PAYMENT: MC/VISA/Disc/Amex/ck/cash

HOURS: In season: 7 days/wk Apr 15 thru Oct / Off season: M-F 8-5

TRANSIENT SLIPS/TOTAL SLIPS: 96/148

VHF/WORKING: Monitor 16 Talk 06

MLW/LOA*: Up to 20ft/170'

ELECTRIC: 30/50/100 amp

PUMPOUT: Yes

FUEL: Diesel, Reg Gas & Non Ethanol Gas

REPAIR: In harbor

PROPANE: Nearby

RESTAURANT/MILES: On site, The Shanty

POOL: No

HAUL-OUT: In harbor

HEAD/SHOWER/LAUNDRY: Yes/Yes/Walking Distance

INTERNET ACCESS: WiFi

CABLE: No

SHIP'S STORE: Snacks, drinks and ice, necessity marine supplies

NEAREST TOWN/MILES: Cape Charles

SHOPPING: Walking distance

GOLF/TENNIS: Nearby

STORAGE: On site

AIRPORT/MILES: Norfolk Int'l / 40

YACHT BROKERAGE: Nearby

SPECIAL: Beach, golf cart rentals, Bed & Breakfasts nearby

*MLW = Mean Low Water Depth
LOA = Longest vessel that can be accommodated

Cape Charles Yacht Center

1011 Bayshore Road, Cape Charles, VA 23310
Ph: 757-331-3100
Email: info@ccyachtcenter.com
CCYachtCenter.com

description of facilities

Located on the mouth of the Chesapeake Bay and buffered from the elements, our facility is the ideal place to shelter any boat, large or small. We are a full-service ship/boatyard with the hauling capacity of up to 75 tons. Whether you are looking for an overnight haven, service or storage for your vessel, we can accommodate you. Our deep water marina is within walking or biking distance to golf, tennis, swimming, shopping, restaurants and all the activities Cape Charles has to offer.

marina approach & docking

Cape Charles Yacht Center is located in the town of Cape Charles, on the Eastern Shore of Virginia. Vessels will enter the Cherrystone Inlet Channel, just northwest of the Old Plantation Flats. CCYC is located within the Basin of the Cape Charles Harbor. Contact Dockmaster, Steve Smith.

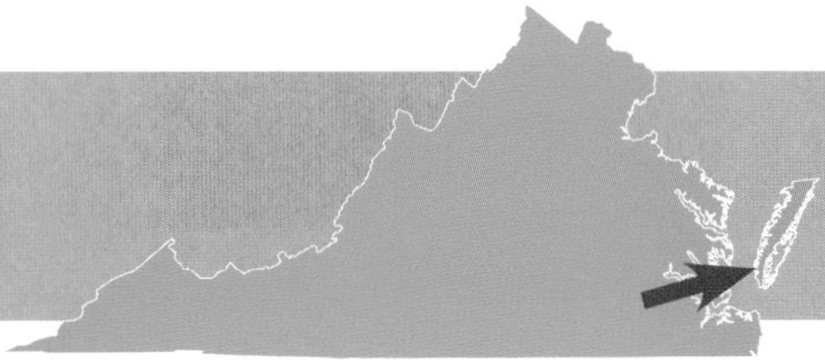

at a glance

DOCKAGE RATE: $2.00/ft daily $6.00/ft weekly

PAYMENT: Cash, check, all major credit cards

HOURS: 8:00 am - 5:00pm

TRANSIENT SLIPS/TOTAL SLIPS: 20

VHF/WORKING: 16/65

MLW/LOA*: 12'/220'

ELECTRIC: 30 Amp single-phase, up to 100 Amp 3-phase, 480 volts

PUMP-OUT: Yes

FUEL: Yes

REPAIR: Full-service facility

PROPANE: Yes

RESTAURANT/MILES: .5 mi

POOL: .5 mi

HAUL-OUT: 75-ton Marine Travelift

HEAD/SHOWER: Yes/Yes

LAUNDRY: Nearby

INTERNET ACCESS: WiFi

SHIP'S STORE: Yes

NEAREST TOWN/MILES: .5 mi

SHOPPING: .5 mi

GOLF/TENNIS: .5 mi

STORAGE: Free winter storage on the hard

AIRPORT/MILES: 38 mi

TRANSPORTATION: Yes

YACHT BROKERAGE: Yes

*MLW = Mean Low Water Depth
LOA = Longest vessel that can be accommodated

LAT: 37° 15' 47.2716"N
LON: -76° 0' 54.3384"W

THE OYSTER FARM
AT KINGS CREEK
CAPE CHARLES, VA

The Oyster Farm at Kings Creek

500 Marina Village Cir
Cape Charles, VA 23310
Ph: 757-331-8640
TheOysterFarmatKingsCreek.com

description of facilities

The Oyster Farm complex on the Chesapeake Bay in Cape Charles spans 39 acres. It operates a full service Marina with 124 floating slips, an elegant but casual waterfront Seafood Eatery, multiple Event Venue and Catering facilities, and a variety of on-site villas that are available as event or vacation rentals. In addition, recreational and sporting equipment rentals are available on the premises. The owner of this complex is making significant investments in the lower Eastern Shore of Virginia to increase local employment opportunities, stimulate travel to the region, and to share the wonderful resources of the Chesapeake with the world.

marina approach & docking

Cape Charles is located just 10 miles north of the Chesapeake Bay Bridge tunnel on Virginia's Eastern Shore. The marina is located north of Cape Charles Harbor in Kings Creek. Our controlling depth is approx. 7' MLW. To enter Kings Creek proceed north from Cape Charles #1CB to Kings Creek #2, #3 and #4. Turn hard right to approx. 093M and follow the Aids to Navigation around the point to The Oyster Farm at Kings Creek. All slips are floating with finger piers on both sides running the full length of the slip. On approach A-dock is the first pier on the right which can handle boats up to 80' in length. The arm of A-dock will handle vessels up to 150'. C-dock is the main pier with the fuel dock located at the T-head. Proceed along the fuel pier to D-dock and F-dock. We have a full description of the channel. The Marina monitors VHF-FM Channels 16/68 or call us at 757-331-8640.

Best of the Bay 2016 Chesapeake Bay Magazine

LAT: 37° 16' 41.3394"N
LON: -76° 0' 43.1634"W

at a glance

DOCKAGE RATE: In Season: Annual $7.00/mo, Annual $72.00/yr, Semi Annual $8.00/mo, Semi Annual $42.00/yr, Quarterly $27.00/ft/pd, Monthly $10.00/ft/pd, Nightly $2.00/ft/pd, Hourly $5.00 Min. 2, Oyster Docks $6.00/ft/pd

PAYMENT: Visa, MC, AMEX, DISC, Cash, check

HOURS: In Season Hours: Sunday - Thursday 8:00am - 6:00pm, Friday 8:00am - 7:00pm, Saturday 7:00am - 7:00pm, Off Season Hours: March 16th - May 3rd: 8:00am - 5:00pm Daily

TRANSIENT SLIPS/TOTAL SLIPS: 60/124

VHF/WORKING: 16/9

MLW/LOA*: 7'/150'

ELECTRIC: 30/50/100 Amp

PUMP-OUT: Yes

FUEL: Gas/Diesel

REPAIR: Nearby

RESTAURANT/MILES: Onsite, Seafood Eatery/C-Pier

HAUL-OUT: Nearby

HEAD/SHOWER: Yes/Yes

LAUNDRY: Yes

SHIP'S STORE: Yes

NEAREST TOWN/MILES: Cape Charles/1 mile

SHOPPING: Cape Charles/1 mile

GOLF/TENNIS: Bay Creek 2 miles/Central Park ½ mile

AIRPORT/MILES: NOR/28 miles

TRANSPORTATION: Bikes and Golf Carts

SPECIAL: Beautifully designed restrooms with 7 showers, Laundry facilities, Event planning and banquets

*MLW = Mean Low Water Depth
 LOA = Longest vessel that can be accommodated

Salt Ponds Marina Resort

11 Ivory Gull Crescent, Hampton, VA 23664
Ph: 888-881-0897 | 757-850-4300
Email: office@saltpondsmarinaresort.com

description of facilities

Salt Ponds Marina Resort is conveniently located in Hampton, Virginia (VA), right off the Chesapeake Bay, making it a perfect stopping point whether you are traveling south through the Intracoastal Waterway or heading for points north of the Bay. The Marina has 254 floating docks with wide full-length fingers & rubber rub rails. We welcome both transient and long-term tenants, accommodating vessels up to 110 feet.

Enjoy a great view and delicious food on the deck of our waterfront restaurant or relax at the poolside cabana bar. Soak up the sun, swim some laps, or just take a refreshing dip in either of our two swimming pools. Spend the day at Salt Ponds Beach or nearby Buckroe Beach. Host your family gathering, power squadron, or boat group rendezvous at our banquet room, boater's lounge, or poolside deck. Take advantage of year-round sportfishing in the Bay and the Atlantic. Process your catch at our official weigh station and two fish cleaning stations. It's only 53 miles to the Norfolk Canyon or 3.5 hours to the Gulf Stream, and there's no boat tax in Hampton.

marina approach & docking

Salt Ponds Marina Resort lies in a protected basin directly off the Chesapeake Bay, with no bridges or locks, midway between Back River and the Hampton Roads Bridge Tunnel (Old Point Comfort), or 3.5 miles northwest of Thimble Shoals Light. The Inlet into Salt Ponds is city owned/maintained and is dredged to 8ft MLLW every other year to remove encroaching sand. Four very tall radio towers may be spotted behind the inlet, visible by day, and at night their red lights flash high in the sky. Keep them on the starboard bow as you approach. A rock jetty marks the north side of the channel. Soft mud bottom and easy navigation once inside the basin. We are located just ahead on the left side and our fuel dock is just beyond marker R"16". We monitor VHF channel 16 and switch to 9 to assist you.

at a glance

DOCKAGE RATE: Transient $1.50/ft/night, annual $7.50/ft/month

PAYMENT: MC/Visa/Amex/check/cash

HOURS: In-season 7:30am – 7pm, Winter 7:30am – 5:30pm

TRANSIENT SLIPS/TOTAL SLIPS: Varies/254

VHF/WORKING: 16/9

MLW/LOA*: 8'-12'/110'

ELECTRIC: 30/50 and dual 30 Amp

PUMP-OUT: Yes

FUEL: Mid-grade gas and diesel

REPAIR: Mobile available

PROPANE: Nearby

RESTAURANT/MILES: Full service restaurant overlooking the water on-site

POOL: Two pools

HAUL-OUT: Nearby

HEAD/SHOWER: Yes/Yes

LAUNDRY: Two

INTERNET ACCESS: Free wireless

SHIP'S STORE: Yes

NEAREST TOWN/MILES: Hampton/5

SHOPPING: Nearby

GOLF/TENNIS: Nearby/Nearby

AIRPORT/MILES: Newport News-Williamsburg Int'l and Norfolk Int'l

TRANSPORTATION: Cab and rental car

SPECIAL: Year-round facilities, Salt Ponds Beach, Buckroe Beach, Colonial Williamsburg, Busch Gardens

Scan this code to visit us!

*MLW = Mean Low Water Depth
LOA = Longest vessel that can be accommodated

SaltPondsMarinaResort.com

LAT: 37° 3' 26.172"N
LON: -76° 17' 3.804"W

COME FACE-TO-FACE WITH ADVENTURE.

THIS IS

Hampton

VIRGINIA

Hampton has been home to unique characters and an adventurous spirit for over 400 years. Discover the attractions, the history and the flavorful culture that make Hampton a city you will want to visit again and again.
800.800.2202 VisitHampton.com

Old Point Comfort Marina

100 McNair Drive, Bldg 207,
Fort Monroe, VA 23651
Ph: 757-788-4308 | Fax: 757-788-4354
OldPointComfortMarina.com

description of facilities

Old Point Comfort Marina offers a multitude of services, good protection and quiet charm, coupled with a rich historic flavor. SLIPS/TRANSIENT DOCKAGE: Available to the public. ANNUAL SLIP LEASE: $6.50/ft per month (includes shore power, water and WiFi). MONTHLY LEASE: $8.50/ft per month (includes shore power, water and WiFi). SEASONAL SLIP LEASE: $7.50/ft per month (includes shore power, water and WiFi). TRANSIENT DOCKAGE: $2.00/ft per night, weekly rate of $5.50/ft. After 3 months, no longer considered transient and must sign lease. Liveaboards are not authorized at Old Point Comfort Marina. Twenty-four hour security provided. BOAT US AND MARINA LIFE MEMBERS: $1.50/ ft per night.

Vessels up to 50 feet can be accommodated. Old Point Comfort Marina, a Virginia Clean Marina, includes a ship's store, fuel dock, boat ramp, indoor maintenance facility, and a restaurant topside. The ship's store, gas pumps, sewage pump outs, and boat ramp are open to the public.

marina approach & docking

From the Thimble Shoal Tower on the lower Bay, it is about three nautical miles to the tip of Old Point Comfort. A series of shipping channel markers will direct you southwest to deep water. You will see Chamberlin Hotel as you approach the point. Follow the point's south end. At the point's southwest corner, turn north, leaving port flashing green #1 and the entrance for the Hampton Roads Tunnel. Old Point Comfort Marina is opposite flashing green #3. Enter at the north end of the wave screen. When docking vessel, be aware that OPCM has a swift current.

facebook.com/oldpointcomfortmarina

LAT: 37° 0' 10.3674"N
LON: -76° 18' 49.8234"W

at a glance

DOCKAGE RATE: Varies; see Description of Facilities for details

PAYMENT: MC/Visa/AMX/Discover/Cash

HOURS: Varies seasonally, call ahead

TRANSIENT SLIPS/TOTAL SLIPS: 10/314

VHF/WORKING: 16/68

MLW/LOA*: 15'/50'

ELECTRIC: 30/50 Amp

PUMP-OUT: 2 & 1 dump station

FUEL: Gas/Diesel

REPAIR: On-site & nearby

RESTAURANT/MILES: 2nd floor

HAUL-OUT: On-site for vessels up to 27'

HEAD/SHOWER: Yes/Yes

LAUNDRY: Yes

SHIP'S STORE: Yes

NEAREST TOWN/MILES: 1.5 mi

SHOPPING: Groceries/2 miles

GOLF/TENNIS: Yes, 2 miles/Yes, 1 mile

AIRPORT/MILES: Norfolk Int'l & Patrick Henry Int'l

TRANSPORTATION: Taxi, bus service

SPECIAL: Located on historic landmark, Virginia Air & Space Museum, Busch Gardens, Water Country USA, Virginia Beach, Casemate Museum, Colonial Williamsburg, Jamestown, Yorktown.VA Official Weigh Station, Small Boat Launch

*MLW = Mean Low Water Depth
LOA = Longest vessel that can be accommodated

It All Begins at Mile Zero!

Tidewater Yacht Marina

10 Crawford Pkwy, Portsmouth, VA 23704
Ph: 757-393-2525 | Fax: 757-393-7845
Email: tidewater@suntexmarinas.com
TidewaterYachtMarina.com

description of facilities

Tidewater Yacht Marina is in the center for all waterfront festivals. We offer a world-class marina with fixed and floating docks, in-slip fast-fueling, the area's only floating pool, mega yacht docking, transient and long term docking in an ice-free, protected harbor, newly renovated marine store and service center, restaurant and many other amenities. Make sure to stop in and experience Tidewater Yacht Marina at Mile Marker Zero!

marina approach & docking

Located just south of Red Buoy 36, MM 0 ICW on the west side of the Elizabeth River. Our entrance is marked by our Valvtect sign. Fixed and floating docks with in-slip fueling available. Protected, ice-free harbor.

at a glance

DOCKAGE RATE: Please call
PAYMENT: Visa/MC/Discover/Amex
HOURS: 8am – 6pm
TRANSIENT SLIPS/TOTAL SLIPS: 100/300
VHF/WORKING: 16/68
MLW/LOA*: 12'/300'
ELECTRIC: 110/220v, 20/50/100S, single 100 and 3-phase
PUMP-OUT: Yes
FUEL: Gas/Diesel, Fast-fueling
REPAIR: Complete Service Center
RESTAURANT/MILES: On-site, short walk to many others
POOL: Yes
HEAD/SHOWER: Yes/Yes
LAUNDRY: Yes
INTERNET ACCESS: Yes
SHIP'S STORE: Marine store renovated in 2014
NEAREST TOWN/MILES: Downtown/0.5, Norfolk/ferry ride
SHOPPING: Grocery 1 mile
GOLF/TENNIS: 5 mi/8 mi
STORAGE: Wet
AIRPORT/MILES: Norfolk (ORF)/9
TRANSPORTATION: Yes, land & sea
YACHT BROKERAGE: North Point Yacht Sales
SPECIAL: Join the Suntex Captain's Club and SAVE on transient dockage, fuel and more! Limited time...complimentary club membership when you stay at one of our East Coast locations.

*MLW = Mean Low Water Depth
LOA = Longest vessel that can be accommodated

LAT: 36° 50.483′N
LON: -76° 17.883′W

A Suntex Marina

Ocean Yacht Marina

1 Crawford Court
Portsmouth, VA 23704
Ph: 757-321-7432
Email: ocean@suntexmarinas.com
oceanyachtmarina.com

description of facilities

Ocean Yacht Marina is located just 1/2-mile south of mile marker zero on the Intracoastal Waterway in Portsmouth, Virginia. The marina features all of the amenities that a boater could ask for including an indoor dry storage building, a complete parts department, two newly renovated marine stores, fuel dock and for boats of all sizes, a service and repair facility second to none-Ocean Marine Yacht Center. Ocean Yacht Marina is a first-class destination with an emphasis oncustomer service! In 2015, Suntex Marinas acquired the marina and gave it a new name: Ocean Yacht Marina! It will continue to serve the same boats and guests with the utmost care and attention to detail.

marina approach & docking

Located just .5 mile south of mile marker zero on the Intracoastal Waterway, N 36° 49.900' / W 076° 17.760', and minutes away from the Norfolk International Airport.

at a glance

HOURS: Summer 8-6 Winter 8-5

TRANSIENT SLIPS/TOTAL SLIPS: 122 deep water, all floating up to 65', 1500' of alongside dockage

VHF/WORKING: 16/68

ELECTRIC: 30/50/100 amps, 3-Phase and 480v available

FUEL: 2 high volume fuel stations for vessels up to 105'

REPAIR: Home of Ocean Yacht Marine Center - one of the largest mega-yacht facilities in the US featuring a 1250T Syncrolift

RESTAURANT/MILES: Several are a short walk or ferry ride away

HEAD/SHOWER: Yes

LAUNDRY: Yes

INTERNET ACCESS: Yes

CABLE: Yes

SHIP'S STORE: 2 fully stocked marine stores supported by West Marine

SHOPPING: Nearby

GOLF/TENNIS: Nearby

STORAGE: Indoor dry storage for boats up to 40'

AIRPORT/MILES: 15 minutes from the Norfolk/Virginia Beach International Airport

TRANSPORTATION: Rental vehicles and taxi

SPECIAL: Join the Suntex Captain's Club and SAVE on transient dockage, fuel and more! Limited time...complimentary club membership when you stay at one of our East Coast locations.

*MLW = Mean Low Water Depth
 LOA = Longest vessel that can be accommodated

North Carolina

NOAA Weather Channel Map

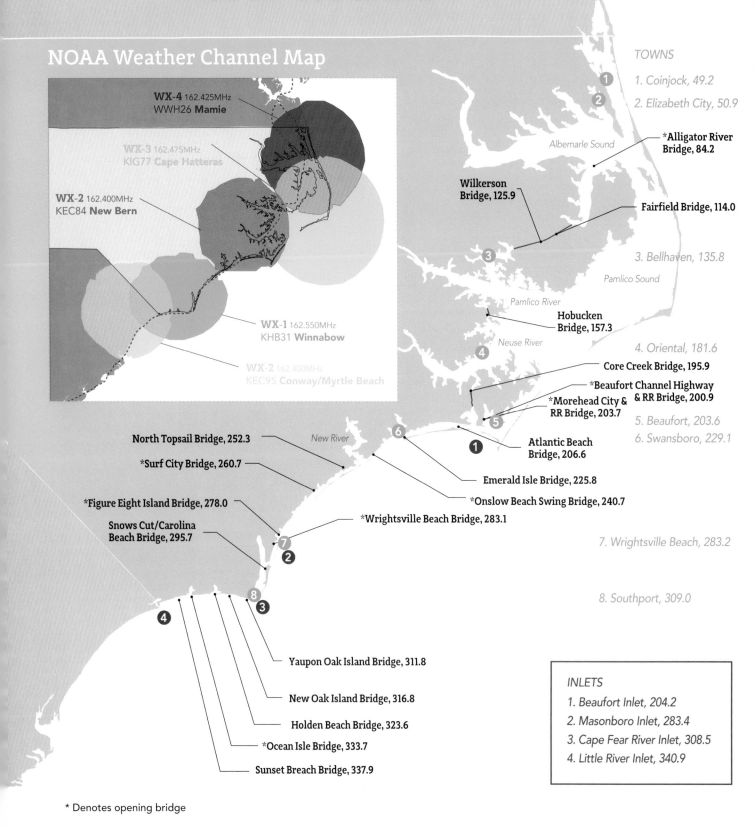

WX-4 162.425MHz
WWH26 **Mamie**

WX-3 162.475MHz
KIG77 **Cape Hatteras**

WX-2 162.400MHz
KEC84 **New Bern**

WX-1 162.550MHz
KHB31 **Winnabow**

WX-2 162.400MHz
KEC95 **Conway/Myrtle Beach**

TOWNS

1. Coinjock, 49.2

2. Elizabeth City, 50.9

Albemarle Sound

*Alligator River Bridge, 84.2

Wilkerson Bridge, 125.9

Fairfield Bridge, 114.0

3. Bellhaven, 135.8

Pamlico Sound

Pamlico River

Hobucken Bridge, 157.3

Neuse River

4. Oriental, 181.6

Core Creek Bridge, 195.9

*Beaufort Channel Highway & RR Bridge, 200.9

*Morehead City & RR Bridge, 203.7

5. Beaufort, 203.6

Atlantic Beach Bridge, 206.6

6. Swansboro, 229.1

North Topsail Bridge, 252.3

New River

Emerald Isle Bridge, 225.8

*Surf City Bridge, 260.7

*Onslow Beach Swing Bridge, 240.7

*Figure Eight Island Bridge, 278.0

*Wrightsville Beach Bridge, 283.1

Snows Cut/Carolina Beach Bridge, 295.7

7. Wrightsville Beach, 283.2

8. Southport, 309.0

Yaupon Oak Island Bridge, 311.8

New Oak Island Bridge, 316.8

Holden Beach Bridge, 323.6

*Ocean Isle Bridge, 333.7

Sunset Breach Bridge, 337.9

INLETS

1. Beaufort Inlet, 204.2

2. Masonboro Inlet, 283.4

3. Cape Fear River Inlet, 308.5

4. Little River Inlet, 340.9

* Denotes opening bridge

ICW Mile 84.2
35°90.03'N 76°0.87'

*Alligator River Bridge
Type: Swing
Height: 14'
Schedule: Will open on demand 24 hrs.; will not open in high winds (35 mph or higher).
Contact: VHF 13 252-796-7261

ICW Mile 114.0
35°35.6'N 76° 13.99'W

Fairfield Bridge
Type: Fixed
Height: 65'
Comments: If tide boards are missing, check water marks on pilings to determine water levels.

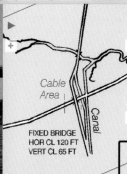

ICW Mile 125.9
35°33.32'N 76°26.32'W

Wilkerson Bridge
Type: Fixed
Height: 64'
Comments: Note the 64' clearance rather than typical 65. Check height boards first.

ICW Mile 157.3
35°14.78'N 76°35.49'W

Hobucken Bridge
Type: Fixed
Height: 65'

ICW Mile 195.9
34°49.54'N 76°41.47'W

Core Creek Bridge
Type: Fixed
Height: 65'

ICW Mile 201.0
34°42.43'N 76°39.79'W
***Beaufort Channel Bridge**
Type: Bascule *Closed Height:* 13'
Schedule: No openings Mon-Fri
6:30-8 a.m. and 4:30-6 p.m. Other
times and weekends on the hour
and half-hour 6 a.m.-11 p.m.
Contact: VHF 13 252-728-3279
Comments: For boats bound for
Beaufort, not Morehead City.

ICW Mile 203.8
34°43.25'N 76°41.61'

Morehead City Bridge
Type: Fixed
Height: 65'

ICW Mile 203.8
34°43.25'W 76°41.34'W

***Morehead City
RR Bridge**
Type: Bascule
Closed Height: 4'
Schedule: Usually open; closes for
RR traffic.

ICW Mile 206.6
34°13.19'W 76°44.1W

Atlantic Beach Bridge
Type: Fixed
Height: 65'
Comments: Check height boards
before going through; high tides
can make height closer to 63'.

ICW Mile 225.8
34°40.5'N 77°03.93'W

Emerald Isle Bridge
Type: Fixed
Height: 65'

ICW Mile 240.7
34°34.39'N 77°16.27'W

*Onslow Beach Bridge
Type: Swing
Closed Height: 12'
Schedule: Will open on hour and half-hour daily. Use northwest draw. May be closed during Camp Lejeune exercises.
Contact: VHF 13 910-450-7376

ICW Mile 252.3
34°29.99'N 77°25.78'W

N Topsail Beach Bridge
Type: Fixed
Height: 65'

ICW Mile 260.7
34°25.89'N 77°32.98'W

*Surf City Bridge
Type: Swing
Closed Height: 12'
Schedule: Will open on the hour 7 a.m to 7 p.m. Won't open in high winds.
Contact: VHF 13 910-328-4291
Comments: Water shallows near the fishing pier.

ICW Mile 278.0
34°16.5'N 77°45.65'W

*Figure Eight Island Bridge
Type: Swing
Closed Height: 20'
Schedule: Will open on the hour and half-hour. Won't open in high winds.
Contact: VHF 13, 910-686-2018

ICW Mile 283.1
34°13.1'N 77°48.76'W

*Wrightsville Beach Bridge
Type: Bascule
Closed Height: 20'
Schedule: Will open on the hour from 7 a.m. to 7 p.m.
Contact: VHF 13, 910-256-2886
Comments: On the 3rd and 4th Saturday of September, closes for triathlon.

ICW Mile 295.7
34°03.33'N 77°53.99'W

Carolina Beach Bridge
Type: Fixed
Height: 65'

ICW Mile 311.8
33°55.3'N 78°04.34'W

Yaupon Beach Bridge
Type: Fixed
Height: 65'

ICW Mile 323.6
33°54.97'N 78°16.09'W

Holden Beach Bridge
Type: Fixed
Height: 65'

ICW Mile 335.6
33°53.75'N 78°26.31'W

Ocean Isle Bridge
Type: Fixed
Height: 65'

ICW Mile 337.9
33°52.99'N 78°30.64'W

Sunset Beach Bridge
Type: Fixed
Height: 65'

North Carolina

Va. Border to New Bern

Marina	MLW	Transient Slips/Moorings	Floating docks	Gas	Diesel	Pumpout	Showers	Pool	Laundry	Wi-Fi	Haulout	Repairs	Other
Midway Marina & Motel Currituck Sound/MM 49.5 252-453-3625 www.midwaymarinamotel.com	10'	•		•	•	•	•	•	•			➤	protected basin, pet friendly; Crabbie's Restaurant
Coinjock Marina Coinjock/ICW Mile 50 252-453-3271 www.coinjockmarina.com	10'	•		•	•	•	•		•	•			Dockside restaurant, ship's store, cable tv
The Pelican Marina Pasquotank R./Elizabeth City 252-335-5108	7'	•	➤	➤	•	•		•			➤	➤	short walk to town
Albemarle Plantation Albemarle Sound/Yeopim Creek 252-426-4037 www.albemarleplantation.com	7'	•		•	•	•	•	•	•			•	full-service, deep-water marina
Edenton Marina Albemarle Sound/Pembroke Cr. 252-482-7421 www.edentonmarina.com	6'	•		•	•		•		•				Short walk to Historic Edenton
Alligator River Marina/Shell Gas Station Alligator River/Columbia/MM 84 252-796-0333	8'	•		•	•	•	•		•	•		•	
Everett Marine Scuppernong River/Columbia 252-796-0435 www.cypresscovenc.com	5.5'		•	•	•	•		•	•	•	•		
Manteo Waterfront Marina Roanoke Sound/Manteo 252-473-2133 www.townofmanteo.com/marina	8'	•	➤	➤	•	•		•	•	➤	➤		Dining, shopping, supplies within walking distance
Shallowbag Bay Marina Roanoke Sound/Manteo 252-202-8505 www.shallowbagbaymarina.com	8'	•	•	•	•	•	•	•	•			➤	ship's store, restaurant, fitness center
Pirate's Cove Marina Roanoke Sound/Manteo 252-473-3906 www.fishpiratescove.com	8'	•		•	•	➤	•	•	➤	•	➤	➤	charter fishing, ship's store, tiki hut
Belhaven Waterway Marina Pungo River /Belhaven MM 136 252-944-0066 www.belhavenmarina.com	7'	•	➤	➤	•	•		•			•	•	restaurant, drug store, grocery, marine supply nearby
River Forest Marina Pungo River/BelhavenMM 136 252-943-0030 www.riverforestmarina.com	9'	•		•	•	•	•		•	•		•	Complimentary golf carts for guests
Carolina Wind Yachting Center Pamlico River/Washington 252-946-4653 www.carolinawind.com	20'	•	➤	➤	•	•	➤	•			➤	➤	at historic Haven's Wharf
Washington Waterfront Docks Pamlico River/Washington 252-252-9367 www.washingtonnc.gov/boating-information	6'	•	➤	➤	•	•		•					free dockage for up to 48 hrs.; dinghy dock
Bath Harbor Marina Pamlico River/Bath Creek 252-923-5711 www.bathharbor.com	8'	•	➤	➤	•	•		•				•	restaurant, picnic area, courtesy car
Hurricane Boatyard & Marina Bay R./between marks 18 and 20 252-745-3369 www.hurricaneboatyard.com	8'	•	•			•		•	•	•	•		Safe harbor; storage on the hard. Power and water hookups
Whittaker Creek Yacht Harbor Neuse River/Whittaker Creek/MM 181 252-670-3759	8'	•		•	•	•	•	•	•				pet friendly
Deaton Yacht Service Neuse River/Whittaker Creek/MM 181 252-249-1180 www.deatonyachts.com	5'	•	➤	➤	•	•		•		•	•	•	
Oriental Harbor Marina Pamlico Sound/Neuse River/MM 182 252-671-9692 www.orientalharbor.com	7'		➤	➤	•	•		•					
Oriental Marina & Inn Pamlico Sound/Neuse R./MM 182 252-249-1818 www.orientalmarina.com	6.5'	•		•	•		•	•	•			•	
River Dunes Harbour Club & Marina Neuse R./Broad Creek/MM 173 252-249-4908 www.riverdunes.com	8'	•	•	•	•	•	•	•	•	•	➤	➤	Courtesy car, provisioning company on-site; hot tub, tennis
Bridge Pointe Marina Neuse River/Trent River/New Bern 252-637-7372 www.bridgepointe.com	6'	•	•	➤	➤	•	•	•	•	•	➤	➤	ice, marine supplies nearby, lounge, cable tv, picnic area

Pamlico Sound

	MLW	Transient Slips/Moorings	Floating docks	Gas	Diesel	Pumpout	Showers	Pool	Laundry	Wi-Fi	Haulout	Repairs	Other
Hatteras Harbor Marina Pamlico Sound/Hatteras 800-676-4939 www.hatterasharbor.com	8'	●		➤	●			●		●	●		➤	groceries, food, restaurants, supplies, laundry nearby
Hatteras Landing Marina Pamlico Sound/Hatteras 252-986-2077 www.hatteraslanding.com	9'	●		●	●	●	●			●				marine store, beer, wine, fish cleaning
Village Marina Pamlico Sound/Hatteras 252-986-2522 www.villagemarinahatteras.com	7'	●		●	●					●				
The Anchorage Inn & Marina Pamlico Sound/Silver Lake/Ocracoke Is 252-928-6661 www.theanchorageinn.com	9'	●		●	●	●	●	●	●					bike, scooter rentals; dockage to 100 ft

Adams Creek to Swansboro

	MLW	Transient Slips/Moorings	Floating docks	Gas	Diesel	Pumpout	Showers	Pool	Laundry	Wi-Fi	Haulout	Repairs	Other
Sea Gate Marina Adams Cut/MM 193.3 252-728-4126 www.seagatenews.com	6'	●		●	●	●	●	●	●	●	●			lounge, TV, Wi-Fi; ship's store
Bock Marine Core Creek/MM 196.5 252-728-6855 www.bockmarine.com	8'	●		➤	➤			●		●	●	●	●	ship's store, courtesy car, new boater's lounge
Jarrett Bay Boatworks Core Creek/Beaufort/MM 198 252-728-2690 www.jarrettbay.com	10'				●	●	●	●				●	●	
Beaufort Docks Beaufort/MM 200.9 252-728-2503	20'	●	●	●	●	●	●			●	●		●	diesel delivered in slip; courtesy cars; nearby beach, marine store
Town Creek Marina Beaufort/1.3 south of MM 202 252-728-6111 www.towncreekmarina.com	12'	●		●	●	●	●			●	●	●	●	full-service boatyard w/50-ton lift, courtesy van, restaurant
Morehead City Yacht Basin Calico Creek/Morehead City/MM 203.5 252-726-6862 www.moreheadcityyachtbasin.com	10'	●		●	●	●	●				●		●	restaurants nearby
Portside Marina Morehead City/MM 205 252-726-7678 www.portsidemarina.com	89'	●		●	●	●	●			●	●	●	●	ship's store, certified mechanics, tackle, bait
Morehead City Docks Bogue Sound/Morehead City/MM 205 252-726-2457 www.moreheadcity.nc.gov	10'	●	●	➤	➤			●		➤				
Morehead Gulf Docks- Geer Oil Company Bogue Sound/Morehead City/MM 205 252-726-5461 www.moreheadgulfdocks.com	13'	●	●	●	●									high speed pumps, ship's store
Taylor Boat Works Peletier Creek/MM 209 252-726-6374	6'	●		➤	●			●				●	●	
Dudley's Marina MM 228 252-393-2204 www.dudleysmarinanc.com	8'	●		●	●	➤		●		➤	●	●	●	Marine store, beach nearby
Casper's Marina White Oak River/MM 229.3 ICW 46-C 910-326-4462 www.caspersmarina.com	10'	●		●	●	●	●			➤	●		➤	

Sneads Ferry to S.C. Line

	MLW	Transient Slips/Moorings	Floating docks	Gas	Diesel	Pumpout	Showers	Pool	Laundry	Wi-Fi	Haulout	Repairs	Other
Swan Point Marina Sneads Ferry/MM 247 910-327-1081 www.swanpointmarina.com	5'	●	●	➤	➤			●		●	●	●	●	
Anchors Away Boatyard Day marker 90/ICW MM 264 910-270-4741 www.anchorsawayboatyard.com	5'	●		➤	➤							●	●	full-service and DIY boatyard
Seapath Yacht Club & Transient Dock Wrightsville/MM 283 910-256-3747 www.seapathyachtclub.com	8'	●	●	●	●	●	●			●	●		➤	courtesy van, non-ethanol gas
Dockside Marina/Restaurant and Bar Wrightsville/MM 283 910-256-3579 www.thedockside.com	6'	●		➤	➤	●					●			restaurant on site, weigh station, ice
Masonboro Yacht Club & Marina Wilmington/MM 288 910-791-1893 www.masonboro.com	6'	●	●	➤	➤			●		●	●		➤	

	MLW	Transient Slips/Moorings	Floating docks	Gas	Diesel	Pumpout	Showers	Pool	Laundry	Wi-Fi	Haulout	Repairs	Other
Wilmington Marine Center Cape Fear River/MM 297 910-395-5055 www.wilmingtonmarine.com	6'	•	•	•	•	•	•		►	•	•	•	safe, secure, protected basin
Cape Fear Marina/Bennett Bros. Yachts Cape Fear River/14 mi. N of MM 297 910-772-9277 www.bbyachts.com	10'	•	•	►	►	•	•		•	•	•	•	Full-service yard, 70-ton extra wide lift; protected location
Wilmington City Docks Cape Fear River/15 mi. N of MM 297 910-520-6875 www.wilmingtonrecreation.com	16'	•	•	►	►	•			►				Heart of the historic district. Walk to downtown, dining, nightlife
Deep Point Marina c/o Bald Head Island Ltd Cape Fear River/Southport/MM 307 910-269-2380 www.baldheadisland.com	10'	•		•	•	•	•		•	•			
Bald Head Island Marina Cape Fear River/Green Buoy 13A 910-457-7380 www.baldheadisland.com	7'	•		•	•	•	•		•	•			
Joyner Marina Carolina Beach/MM 295 910-458-5053 www.joynermarina.com	6'	•		•	•	•	•		•			•	restaurants nearby, ship's store
Southport Marina Southport/MM 309 910-457-9900 www.southport-marina.com	8'	•		•	•	•	•		•	•		•	In heart of Southport; amenities, walk to restaurants
South Harbour Village Transient Dock ICW marker #9/MM 311 910-454-7486 www.southharbourvillagemarina.com	10'	•		•	•	•	•		•	•	►	•	diver on staff; cable tv, direct ICW access; restaurants on-site
St. James Marina MM 315 910-253-0463 www.stjamesplantation.com	8'	•		•	•	•	•		•		•		Grille and Tiki Bar
Holden Beach Marina Holden B/E. of MM 51/MM 322 910-842-5447	6'	•	•	•	•		•					•	
Ocean Isle Marina & Yacht Club Marker 98/MM 335 910-579-6440 www.oceanislemarina.com	6'	•	•	•	•	•	•		•	•		•	

At the Heart of Historic Manteo

Manteo Waterfront Marina

P.O. Box 1328, 207 Queen Elizabeth Avenue,
Manteo, NC 27954-1328
Ph: 252-473-3320 | 252-305-4800

description of facilities

Situated in a picturesque and tranquil village setting less than a mile from Roanoke Sound, the Manteo Waterfront Marina offers excellent protection from the weather for vessels up to 150 feet. Quaint tree-lined streets, over 40,000 square feet of specialty retail shops on the waterfront, and several excellent restaurants and inns make staying at the Manteo Waterfront Marina an experience you will want to repeat year after year. The Waterfront Marina is at the center of Old Town Manteo.

This part of the Outer Banks is steeped in history. Manteo is the principal town on Roanoke Island, the place where in 1587 Sir Walter Raleigh established the first English colony in the New World - the settlement now known as the Lost Colony. For more than 400 years the disappearance of these original pioneers has remained a mystery and a cause of speculation for countless visitors and historians.

marina approach & docking

From Roanoke Sound Channel marker "30A" turn to the West-Southwest between Manteo Channel entrance markers R "2M" and G "3". Continue past the G "5", and then sequentially past the R "6", "8" and "10". Turn onto a course of around 340° magnetic and you will be pointed at our facilities, a few hundred yards ahead. Controlling depth in Roanoke Channel and in the Manteo Channel is greater than 7 feet.

Take the alternate ICW from Coinjock, to Manteo and through the Pamlico Sound to Oriental and save 17 miles of driving the ditch! Because there is virtually no tide here, our docks are stationary with finger piers and tie-off pilings. Our facilities are available year round, and though reservations are recommended, they are not required. We monitor Ch 16 VHF and Ch 9 VHF. and you can call us from your cell phone at 252-473-3320. Please call for more information or to make reservations, and make a point to visit us on your way North or South. Discover this magical place.

at a glance

DOCKAGE RATE: $1.65/ft May-Oct, $1.40/ft Nov-Apr

PAYMENT: MC/Visa/personal checks/cash/Traveler's checks

HOURS: In-season, FT manager on-site

TRANSIENT SLIPS/TOTAL SLIPS: 25/53

VHF/WORKING: 16/9

MLW/LOA*: 8′ or more/150′

ELECTRIC: $3.50 -30 Amp, $7.00 - 50 Amp, 30 Amp/no AC free, 100 Amp at transient dock

PUMP-OUT: Available

FUEL: Nearby

REPAIR: Available locally

PROPANE: Nearby

RESTAURANT/MILES: Six/on-site

HAUL-OUT: Available locally

HEAD/SHOWER: Yes/Yes; modern, clean

LAUNDRY: 2 washer/2 dryers

INTERNET ACCESS: Wireless

CABLE: Yes

SHIP'S STORE: Less than a mile

NEAREST TOWN/MILES: In Manteo

SHOPPING: On-site

AIRPORT/MILES: Less than three miles

TRANSPORTATION: Rental cars

SPECIAL: Bagged ice on-site, children's playground

LAT: 35° 54′ 43.3434″N
LON: -75° 40′ 5.88″W

*MLW = Mean Low Water Depth
LOA = Longest vessel that can be accommodated

MonteoWaterfront.com

Transients Welcome, Short and Long-Term

The Friendly Marina Located on Historic Roanoke Island

Shallowbag Bay Marina

1100-B S Bay Club Drive, Manteo, NC 27954
Ph: 252-305-8726 | Fax: 252-305-8463
Email: info@ShallowbagBayMarina.com
ShallowbagBayMarina.com

description of facilities

This friendly 72-slip marina is nestled on Roanoke Island in the town of Manteo with easy access to stores, restaurants, and beaches. The services and hospitality will make you want to return and return. Open year round, you get in-slip fueling, a fully stocked ship's store, electric service, water and Internet – plus Stripers, a full service restaurant overlooking the marina. Diesel, ethanol-free gas and pump-out station are available. Boats up to 65′ in length can be accommodated. Take advantage of our clubhouse with TV, exercise facility, pocket-billiards or ping-pong table and in-season our swimming pool and hot tub. Showers, laundry facilities, grill and bicycles are available. We can arrange for car rentals or even some grocery shopping.

marina approach & docking

By Sea: Enter Roanoke Sound via Oregon Inlet. Turn north toward Manteo, and clear the high bridge to R "30A" then turn west-southwest.

By Waterway: Take southeast channel at tip of Roanoke Island East to "36" and proceed south to "29C" then turn west between Manteo channel markers R "2M" and G "3". From there continue past G "5", then sequentially past R "6" and "8" to "10". Turn 90 degrees and head approximately 250 degrees magnetic to our orange-and-white informational marker. Here pick up our channel markers. Stay to the right of the green markers to the entrance to the marina. They mark the edge of a shoal.

It is critical to remain within the channels. Be careful not to cut the northwest corner when entering the Manteo channel from the north. Although there is no measurable tide in our location, a strong wind from the northeast may lower normal depths by a foot or so.

LAT: 35° 54′ 43.0914″N
LON: -75° 40′ 25.6074″W

at a glance

DOCKAGE RATE: $1.75/ft daily - $7.35/ft weekly - $15/ft monthly

PAYMENT: MC/Visa/Discover/Amex/cash

HOURS: Open year round. Full time manager on-site

TRANSIENT SLIPS/TOTAL SLIPS: 30/72

VHF/WORKING: 16/69

MLW/LOA*: 6′- 8′/65′

ELECTRIC: 30/50 AMP

PUMP-OUT: Yes

FUEL: 93 ethanol-free premium

REPAIR: Mechanics on call

RESTAURANT/MILES: Stripers Bar & Grille, overlooks marina, many others nearby

POOL: Yes

HAUL-OUT: Nearby

HEAD/SHOWER: Yes/Yes; 6 showers

LAUNDRY: Yes

INTERNET ACCESS: Yes

SHIP'S STORE: Yes

NEAREST TOWN/MILES: Manteo/Downtown walking distance

SHOPPING: Grocery, clothing, unique gifts

GOLF/TENNIS: Nearby/Nearby

STORAGE: Short term trailer parking

AIRPORT/MILES: Dare/5, Norfolk/65

TRANSPORTATION: Rental cars, taxis, bicycles

SPECIAL: Fishing Charters, Parasailing, Fish Cleaning Station, Bagged Ice, Many Local Attractions

*MLW = Mean Low Water Depth
LOA = Longest vessel that can be accommodated

Pirate's Cove Yacht Club & Marina

2000 Sailfish Drive, Manteo, NC 27954
Ph: 252-473-3906 | 1-800-367-4728
Fax: 252-473-2807
FishPiratesCove.com

description of facilities

Pirate's Cove Yacht Club & Marina offers 195 slips for boats from the smallest to 90 feet in length with 30- to 200-amp hook-ups. The marina has very little tide effect. Pirate's Cove Yacht Club & Marina features an excellent ship's store with fuel, marine items, bait, tackle and one of the best displays of sports and resort clothing in the area. Visitors have the use of our restrooms and showers. For those who stay awhile, the swimming pool and clubhouse are available for a small charge. A restaurant with an unequaled view is on the second floor of the marina. The staff is dedicated to offering the most personal service available anywhere.

marina approach & docking

Pirate's Cove Yacht Club & Marina is located on the west side of Roanoke Sound in a sheltered basin just north of the Roanoke Sound High Bridge (Washington Baum). Heading south, bear southeast after leaving statute mile 65 at the entrance to Albemarle Sound. The marina is approximately 23 statute miles from the Sound. If you continue from Roanoke Sound into Pamlico Sound, it is approximately 90 miles to Oriental. There is reported to be 13 feet of water in the channels and 10 feet at the docks. The docks are stationary with fingerpiers and tie-off pilings. Call on VHF channel 78 and 16 for slip assignment and docking assistance seven days a week. The marina is open year-round.

at a glance

DOCKAGE RATE: $2.00/ft/daily/weekly, $25.00/ft/monthly, call for annual

PAYMENT: MC/Visa/Amex/cash/check

HOURS: In-season 5am – 7pm, Off-season 8am – 5pm

TRANSIENT SLIPS/TOTAL SLIPS: 195 total slips

VHF/WORKING: 16/78

MLW/LOA*: 8'/90'

ELECTRIC: 30/200 Amp, with dockage

FUEL: Gas/Diesel, in-slip fueling

REPAIR: Upon request

PROPANE: Available upon request

RESTAURANT/MILES: On-site

HAUL-OUT: Nearby at Industrial Park

HEAD/SHOWER: Yes/Yes; modern & clean

INTERNET ACCESS: Wifi available

CABLE: With dockage, phone on request

SHIP'S STORE: On-site, large, well-stocked, full line of offshore tackle, groceries, ice, supplies & resort wear

NEAREST TOWN/MILES: Nags Head/across bridge, Manteo/2, beach/0.5

SHOPPING: On-site, Outlet malls/0.5

GOLF/TENNIS: Nearby/0.5; discount at local links/Yes; fitness center on-site

AIRPORT/MILES: Manteo Regional/3

TRANSPORTATION: Cab, limo

YACHT BROKERAGE: Yes, on-site

*MLW = Mean Low Water Depth
LOA = Longest vessel that can be accommodated

LAT: 35° 53' 38.9754"N
LON: -75° 38' 25.5834"W

Morehead City Yacht Basin

Morehead City Yacht Basin
208 Arendell Street, Morehead City, NC 28557
Ph: 252-726-6862 | Fax: 252-726-1939
Email: dockmaster@moreheadcityyachtbasin.com
MoreheadCityYachtBasin.com

description of facilities

The newly-renovated Morehead City Yacht Basin is a favorite mid-Atlantic stopping point for those cruising north/south, fishing the Pamlico Sound and Outer Banks' waters, or beginning the ocean voyage to the Caribbean and beyond. This sheltered, deepwater basin has 10-12 foot minimum depths at dockside, little or no current to contend with, and easy access to the Intracoastal Waterway and Beaufort Inlet. MCYB now offers 88 slips (45 ft. to 65 ft. long with widths to 24 ft.) as well as 1250 feet of linear, sidetie dockage (accommodates vessels over 200'). Floating docks (fashioned of Brazilian cumuru wood and washed river gravel) assure easy refueling and passenger access to docked vessels regardless of tide conditions. Amenities include: Dual hookups (30/50/100 Amp); clean laundry and bathing facilities; clubhouse/lounge (complete with library); yacht brokerage services; and a courtesy vehicle. Conveniently located near downtown Morehead City and within walking distance to banks, shops, dry cleaners, bus station, the Post Office, churches, and many fine restaurants.

marina approach & docking

Just North of the Morehead City (Highway 70) High Rise Bridge at ICW Mile 203.5 and just South of ICW Marker "38", turn West into Calico Creek (a federally maintained deep-water channel) leaving redmarkers to starboard and you will see the Morehead City Yacht Basin. The Fuel Dock is on the West side of "B" dock. Hail the MCYB dockmaster on VHF Channel 16 for further directions.

at a glance

DOCKAGE RATE: Competitive

PAYMENT: MC/Visa/Amex/Discover

HOURS: 8:30 - sunset

TRANSIENT SLIPS/TOTAL SLIPS: 1250' side-to-side space, + slips 45'-65' long/88

VHF/WORKING: 16/71

MLW/LOA*: 8'-10'/200'

ELECTRIC: 30/50/100 Amp

PUMP-OUT: Yes

FUEL: High-speed gas/diesel

REPAIR: On-call

PROPANE: Available nearby

RESTAURANT/MILES: Many within easy walking distance

HEAD/SHOWER/LAUNDRY: Yes/Yes/Yes

INTERNET ACCESS: WiFi

CABLE: Only available in clubhouse

SHIP'S STORE: Yes

NEAREST TOWN/MILES: Morehead City

SHOPPING: Yes

STORAGE: Daily/weekly/monthly

AIRPORT/MILES: Private/2, commercial/40

TRANSPORTATION: Taxi, courtesy car for short periods

SPECIAL: Proximity to charter fleet, antique shops and tours of historic Beaufort, Fort Macon State Park, popular beaches, local hospital, churches, shopping, restaurants

*MLW = Mean Low Water Depth
LOA = Longest vessel that can be accommodated

LAT: 34° 43' 21.1794"N
LON: -76° 42' 17.3154"W

On the Historic Beaufort Waterfront

Beaufort Docks Marina
500 Front Street, Beaufort, NC 28516
Ph: 252-728-2503

description of facilities

This is one of the most popular stops for yachtsmen on the waterway. This historic town has been carefully restored and reflects the best features of an early American seaport. There are many attractions, such as historic homes dating to the early 1700s, quaint shops, museums, many good restaurants and delightful scenery. This is an all-transient facility with 98 berths, all of which are floating docks. Fuel is available in each slip. Yachts up to 250' can be accommodated. Beaufort is a strategic stop for boats cruising to the islands, as the Gulf Stream is usually within 30 miles of Beaufort. One of the unusual aspects of this facility is that all vessels can be fueled in their berths without having to go to a separate fuel dock.

marina approach & docking

The preferred entrance to Beaufort is through Beaufort Harbor Channel (sometimes referred to as Bulkhead Channel) at the southern tip of Radio Island. At Ships Channel "22", enter Beaufort Harbor Channel heading north to Channel Marker "1BH" and "2". Leave "1BH" to port as it marks the end of a rock jetty and "2" to starboard and proceed up the channel to the marina.

The alternate channel if you are coming from the north and choose not to use Beaufort Harbor Channel is to enter Russell's Slough at ICW "29" leaving it to port and pick up marker "RS" leaving it to starboard. Heading south, leave G "29" at statute mile 200.9 to port and pick up flashing G "RS" across from ICW "30" that marks the entrance to the Russell Slough Channel. Leave "RS" to starboard and G "3" to port and proceed south. Follow the channel leaving Gallants Pt. to port and head to the red-over-green, leaving it to starboard. Go between markers G "7" and "RG". Follow the Gallants Channel markers through the Beaufort Bascule Bridge to RG "TC" which marks the entrance to Taylors Creek and the Beaufort Docks.

DOCKAGE RATE: Competitive, accomodate yachts up to 250'

PAYMENT: MC/Visa/Amex

HOURS: 8am – sunset

TRANSIENT SLIPS/TOTAL SLIPS: 98/98

VHF/WORKING: 16/9

MLW/LOA*: 16'/300'

ELECTRIC: 30/50/100 AMP, both single & 3-phase

PUMP-OUT: Yes

FUEL: Competitive pricing, in-slip fueling

REPAIR: Electrical, engine, prop, sail

PROPANE: Nearby

RESTAURANT/MILES: 19/walking distance

HEAD/SHOWER: Yes/Yes

LAUNDRY: Nearby; closed Sundays

INTERNET ACCESS: Free wireless internet

SHIP'S STORE: Yes

NEAREST TOWN/MILES: In center of town

SHOPPING: Grocery, supply shops

GOLF/TENNIS: Nearby/Nearby

STORAGE: Wet

AIRPORT/MILES: County/1.5, Commercial/40

TRANSPORTATION: Courtesy cars, taxi, airport shuttle

YACHT BROKERAGE: Nearby

*MLW = Mean Low Water Depth
LOA = Longest vessel that can be accommodated

LAT: 34° 43' 3.648"N
LON: -76° 39' 55.4754"W

Deep Water Access—at End of Shipping Channel—Easy Nighttime Access

Portside Marina

209 Arendell Street, Morehead City, NC 28557
Ph: 252-728-2503 | Fax: 252-726-6923
Email: portsidemarina@aol.com

description of facilities

Portside Marina is the closest marina to the Beaufort Inlet. Deep-water access is provided via the Morehead shipping channel for both day and night travelers. Fuel after hours by appointment.

Great restaurants are within easy walking distance. A large marine hardware store is also within easy walking distance. After hours service is available via reservations. Special motel rates are provided by a local motel. Major chain grocery stores, West Marine, Walmart and others are just a short cab ride away.

marina approach & docking

From the ocean, follow the shipping channel to the end.

From the north, the city is easily approached by "rounding" the south side of the state port bulkhead for a final approach on the west side. Stay close to the state port for deeper water. At the southwest corner of the state port, turn north for a short ride to the Morehead City Channel. (Usually big red cranes work the west side). Portside Marina is well marked on a large dry-stack building.

From the south, stay in the ICW (mile marker 205) to the southwest corner of the state port. Then turn north in the shipping channel for the final approach to Portside Marina.

at a glance

DOCKAGE RATE: Varies w/season -Base rate $1.50/ft w/ Boat US discount

PAYMENT: MC/Visa/cash

HOURS: 8am – 5pm - After-hours by appointment

TRANSIENT SLIPS/TOTAL SLIPS: 8/30

VHF/WORKING: 16/10

MLW/LOA*: 8´-9´/120´

ELECTRIC: 20/30/50 AMP

PUMP-OUT: Yes

FUEL: Gas/Diesel, fuel after hours by appt.

REPAIR: Yes

RESTAURANT/MILES:
10 within walking distance

HAUL-OUT: Power only, under 30´

HEAD/SHOWER: Yes/Yes

LAUNDRY: Yes

INTERNET ACCESS: WiFi access

SHIP'S STORE: Yes

NEAREST TOWN/MILES:
Morehead City/3 blocks

SHOPPING: Nearby/Cab ride

GOLF/TENNIS: Yes/Yes; Cab ride

AIRPORT/MILES: Beaufort - local 3 miles/ Regional - USAir - New Bern/40 miles

TRANSPORTATION:
Cab, Limo & Rental cars

YACHT BROKERAGE: Yes

SPECIAL: Located at end of ship channel, Deep water all the way to docks

*MLW = Mean Low Water Depth
LOA = Longest vessel that can be accommodated

LAT: 34° 43' 158"N
LON: -76° 42' 299"W

Transient Sail and Powerboats Welcome

Dudley's Marina

P.O. Box 1148, Swansboro, NC 28584
Ph: 252-393-2204 | Fax: 252-393-2380
Email: dudleys@dudleysmarinanc.com
DudleysMarinaNC.com

description of facilities

Dudley's Marina is a full-service marina that can accommodate vessels to 125 feet. The marina is located on the west side of the waterway, just south of Bogue Sound. It is strategically located just north of Camp Lejeune and makes an excellent layover point when the ICW is closed by the military.

Ashore, the marina building houses the dock offices, ship's store and showers. Transient sail and power yachts are always welcome.

The boatyard at the marina has a 100-ton railway that can accommodate vessels to 65 feet. Dry-stack storage is available for vessels to 26 feet. The full-service boatyard specializes in gas and diesel engine repairs, prop and shaft service, wooden and fiberglass hull repairs and awlgrip painting. Historic Swansboro is the "Friendly City by the Sea."

marina approach & docking

Dudley's Marina is located at marker "46A" and White Oak River at ICW statute mile 227. The marina is located seven miles north of Camp Lejeune. There is reported to be an eight-foot approach depth and eight feet of water at the docks at MLW. The marina has both floating and stationary docks and can accommodate vessels to 125 feet. Docking is alongside and in slips. The staff monitors VHF channel 16. Summer hours are from sunrise to sunset daily, and winter hours are from 7 a.m. to 7 p.m. daily.

LAT: 34° 40' 54.8394"N
LON: -77° 6' 43.812"W

at a glance

DOCKAGE RATE: $.75/ft

PAYMENT: MC/Visa/Amex/Discover/ BP Visa

HOURS: Sunrise – sunset in summer, 7am – 7pm in winter

TRANSIENT SLIPS/TOTAL SLIPS: 14/26

VHF/WORKING: 16/68

MLW/LOA*: 8'/125'

ELECTRIC: 30/50 amp included in dockage

PUMP-OUT: Nearby

FUEL: High-speed fueling, BP gas, diesel

REPAIR: Full-service boatyard

PROPANE: Nearby

RESTAURANT/MILES: Nearby– Yanamama's Restaurant, Riverside, The Icehouse, Saltwater Grill, and Swansboro Food & Beverage Co.

POOL: Ocean swimming, 4 miles

HAUL-OUT: 100-ton railway

HEAD/SHOWER: Yes/Yes; clean, tiled

INTERNET ACCESS: FWireless

SHIP'S STORE: Marine supplies, hardware, accessories, bait, ice, etc.

NEAREST TOWN/MILES: Swansboro/.25

SHOPPING: Walking distance, courtesy car

STORAGE: Yes

AIRPORT/MILES: Jacksonville/30

TRANSPORTATION: Courtesy car, taxi

SPECIAL: Tackle Shop at ship's store

*MLW = Mean Low Water Depth
LOA = Longest vessel that can be accommodated

NOAA Weather Channel Map

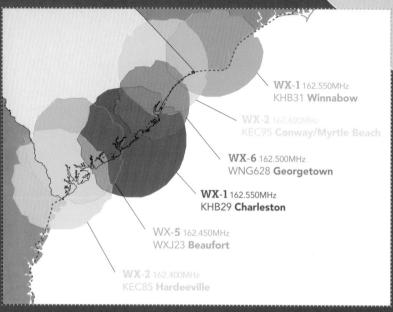

WX-1 162.550MHz
KHB31 **Winnabow**

WX-2 162.400MHz
KEC95 **Conway/Myrtle Beach**

WX-6 162.500MHz
WNG628 **Georgetown**

WX-1 162.550MHz
KHB29 **Charleston**

WX-5 162.450MHz
WXJ23 **Beaufort**

WX-2 162.400MHz
KEC85 **Hardeeville**

South Carolina

Grand Dunes Bridge, 358.0

Conway Bypass Twin Bridge, 355.4

*Barefoot Landing Bridge, 353.3

N. Myrtle Beach Connection Bridge, 349.3

*Little River Swing Bridge, 347.3

Cherry Grove/Nixon Crossroads Bridge, 347.1

1 1. Little River Inlet, 341.8

1. Myrtle Beach, 358.5

Grissom Parkway Bridge, 360.6

*Seaboard Coast Line RR Bridge, 365.4

Highway 501 Bridge, 365.5

Fantasy Harbor Bridge, 366.4

*Socastee Swing Bridge, 371.0

Route 544 Bridge, 371.1

Lafayette/Ocean Highway Bridge, 402.1

2. Georgetown, 403.0

2. Winyah Bay Inlet, 406.2

3. McClellanville, 430.0

Bull Bay

Isle of Palms Bridge, 458.9

*Ben Sawyer Memorial Bridge, 462.2

4. Charleston, 469.3

3. Charleston Harbor Entrance, 464.5

Mark Clark/Wappoo Creek Hwy 30 Bypass Bridge, 469.9

*Wappoo Creek Hwy 171 Bridge, 470.8

John F. Limehouse Bridge, 479.3

McKinley Washington Jr. Bridge, 501.3

4. N Edisto River Inlet, 496.7

5. Beaufort, 536.3

St. Helena Sound

*Ladies Island Bridge, 536.0

McTeer Bridge, 539.7

5. Port Royal Sound Inlet, 549.0

Wilton J. Graves Twin Bridges, 557.6

6. Hilton Head, 563.7

6. Tybee Roads Inlet, 575.8

* Denotes opening bridge

33°85.327' N 78°65.415' W

Cherry Grove/Nixon Cross-roads Bridge
Type: Fixed
Height: 65'

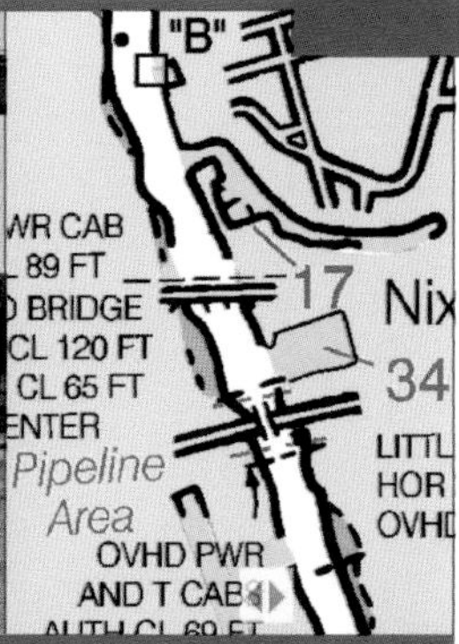

33°85.180' N 78°65.625' W

*Little River Swing Bridge
Type: Swing
Closed Height: 7'
Schedule: Opens on request.
Contact: VHF 09 843-280-5919
Comments: Current can be strong around bridge

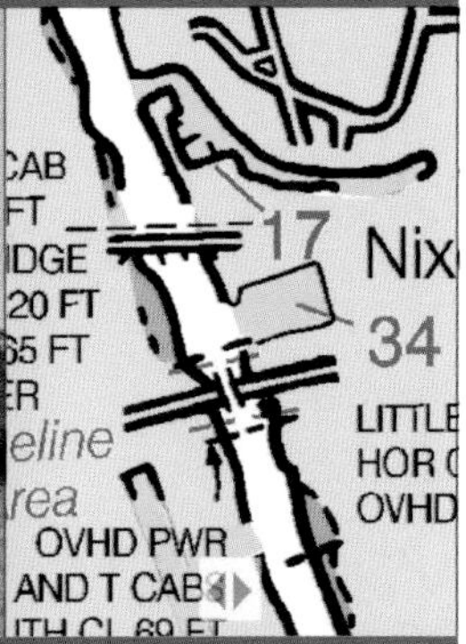

33°83.400' N
78°68.420' W

Robert Edge Parkway Bridge/N. Myrtle Beach Connection Bridge
Type: Fixed
Height: 65'

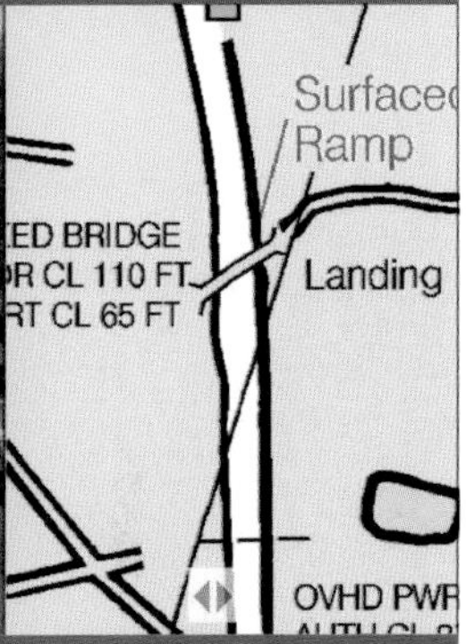

33°80.305' N
78°74.157' W

*Barefoot Landing Bridge
Type: Swing
Closed Height: 29'
Schedule: Opens on request.
Contact: VHF 09 843-3291
Comments: Will not open in high winds (30-35 kts). Tide board is missing on the south side of bridge.

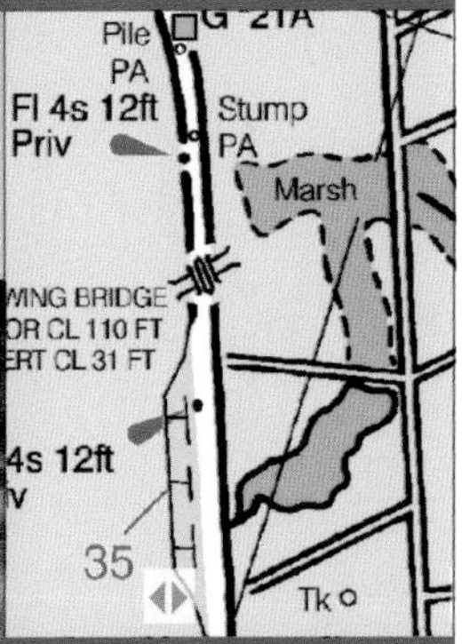

33°78.993' N
78°77.707' W

Conway Bypass Twin Bridges
Type: Fixed
Height: 65'
Comments: Active Captain reports tideboards missing for northbound boats.

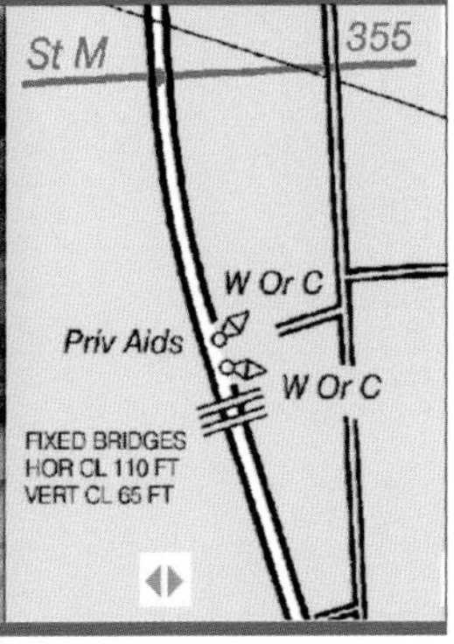

33°76.683' N
78°81.495' W

Grande Dunes Bridge
Type: Fixed
Height: 65'

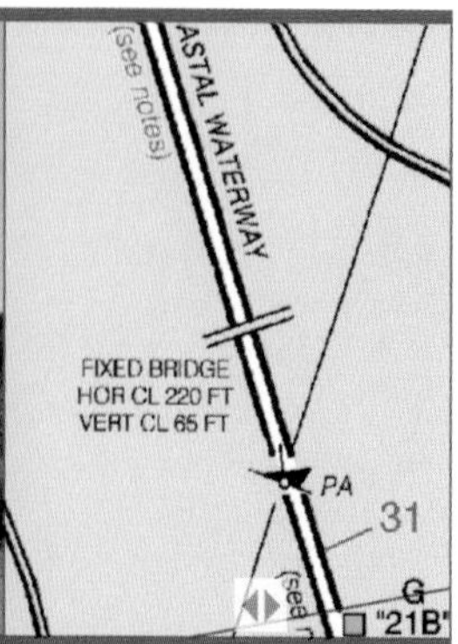

33°74.969 N 78°94.911' W

Grissom Parkway Bridge
Type: Fixed
Height: 65'

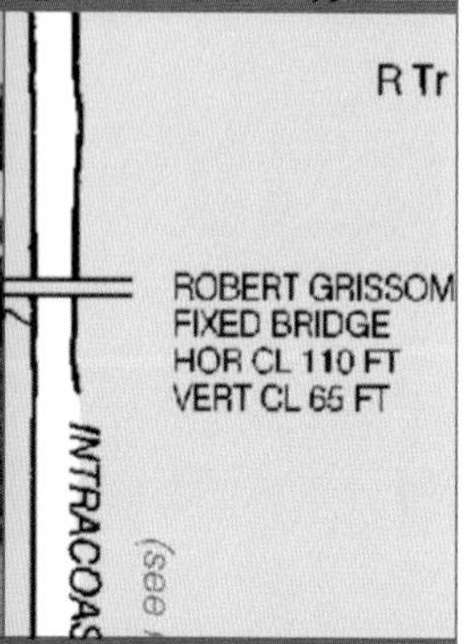

33°71.462' N
78°92.163' W

***Myrtle Beach/
Seaboard Coast Line RR
Bridge**
Type: Bascule
Closed Height: 16'
Schedule: Usually open
Contact: VHF 09

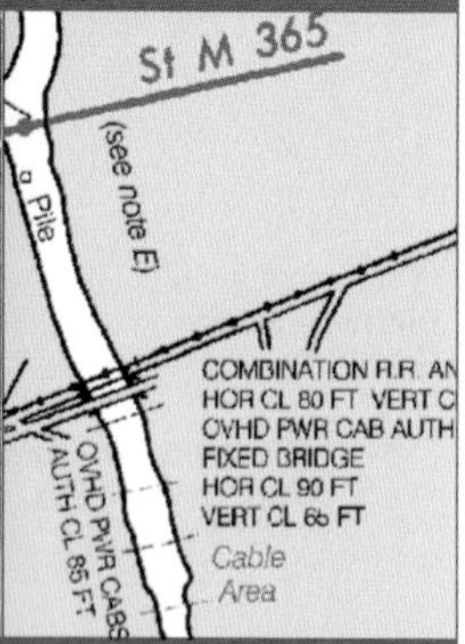

33°71.423' N
78°92.193' W

Highway 501 Bridge
Type: Fixed
Height: 65'

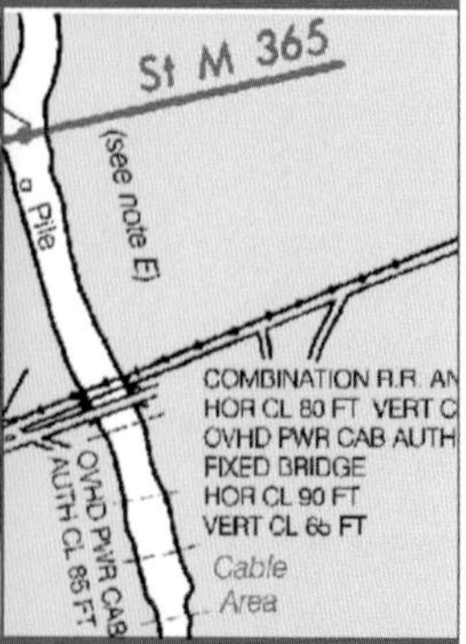

33°70.527' N
78°93.410' W

**Fantasy Harbor
Bridge**
Type: Fixed
Height: 65'

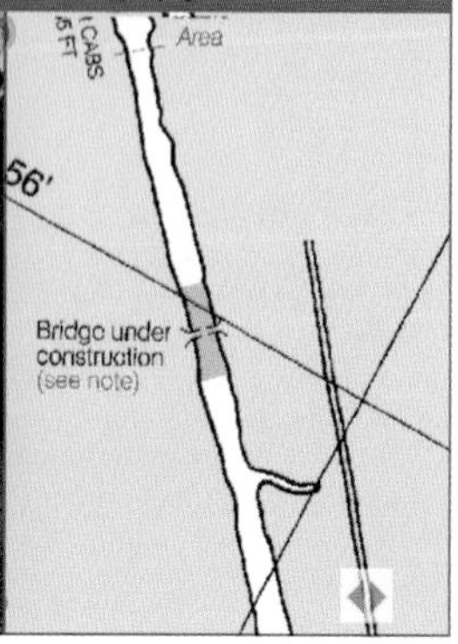

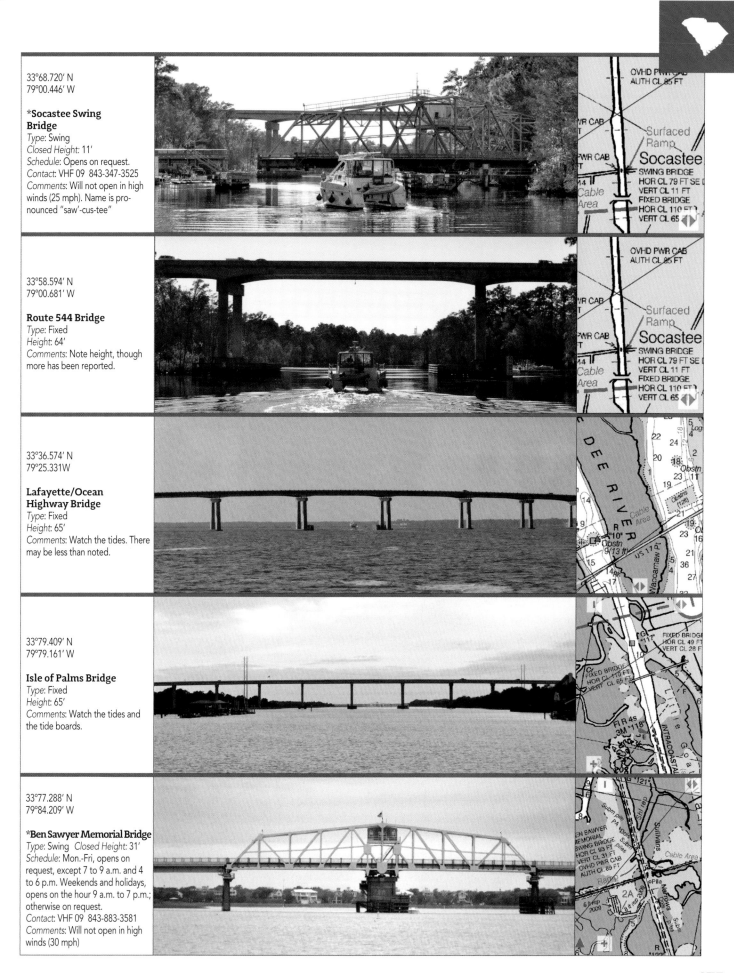

33°68.720' N
79°00.446' W

***Socastee Swing
Bridge**
Type: Swing
Closed Height: 11'
Schedule: Opens on request.
Contact: VHF 09 843-347-3525
Comments: Will not open in high
winds (25 mph). Name is pro-
nounced "saw'-cus-tee"

33°58.594' N
79°00.681' W

Route 544 Bridge
Type: Fixed
Height: 64'
Comments: Note height, though
more has been reported.

33°36.574' N
79°25.331W

**Lafayette/Ocean
Highway Bridge**
Type: Fixed
Height: 65'
Comments: Watch the tides. There
may be less than noted.

33°79.409' N
79°79.161' W

Isle of Palms Bridge
Type: Fixed
Height: 65'
Comments: Watch the tides and
the tide boards.

33°77.288' N
79°84.209' W

*Ben Sawyer Memorial Bridge
Type: Swing *Closed Height:* 31'
Schedule: Mon.-Fri, opens on
request, except 7 to 9 a.m. and 4
to 6 p.m. Weekends and holidays,
opens on the hour 9 a.m. to 7 p.m.;
otherwise on request.
Contact: VHF 09 843-883-3581
Comments: Will not open in high
winds (30 mph)

32°77.052′ N
79°95.797′ W

Mark Clark/Wappoo Creek Hwy 30 Bypass Bridge
Type: Fixed
Height: 67′

32°76.670′ N
79°97.412′ W
Wappoo Creek Hwy 171 Bridge
Type: Bascule *Closed Height:* 33′
Schedule: April 1 to Nov. 30, Mon.-Fri. 9 a.m. to 3:30 p.m. and Sat.-Sun. 9 a.m. to 7 p.m., opens on the hour and half-hour. Dec. 1 to March 30, 9 am to 4 pm, opens on request, with last opening at 3:50. April 1 to May 31 and Oct. 1 to Nov. 30, Mon.-Fri., except holidays, closed 6 to 9 a.m. and 4 to 6:30 p.m. June 1 to Sept. 30 and Dec. 1 to March 30, Mon.-Fri., except holidays, closed 6:30 to 9 a.m. and 4 to 6:30 p.m.
Contact: VHF 09 or 843-4157
Comment: Check in with bridge tender to confirm opening time.

32°78.568′ N
80°10.748′ W

John F. Limehouse Bridge
Type: Fixed
Height: 65′

32°63.712′ N
80°34.018′ W

McKinley Washington Jr. Bridge
Type: Fixed
Height: 65′

32°42.738' N
80°66.900' W

*Ladys Island Bridge
Type: Swing   *Closed Height:* 30'
Schedule: Mon.-Fri., except
holidays, closed from 6:30 to 9 a.m.
and 3 to 6 p.m.; opens on hour
from 9 a.m. to 3 p.m. Otherwise,
including weekends and holidays,
opens on request.
Contact: VHF 09   843-521-2111
Comments: Note that this is a
new and much more restrictive
schedule.

32°39.402' N
80°67.698' W

McTeer Bridge (Beaufort)
Type: Fixed
Height: 65'
Comments: Tide boards have been
removed during construction work;
call Port Royal Landing Marina for
local knowledge at 843-525-6664.

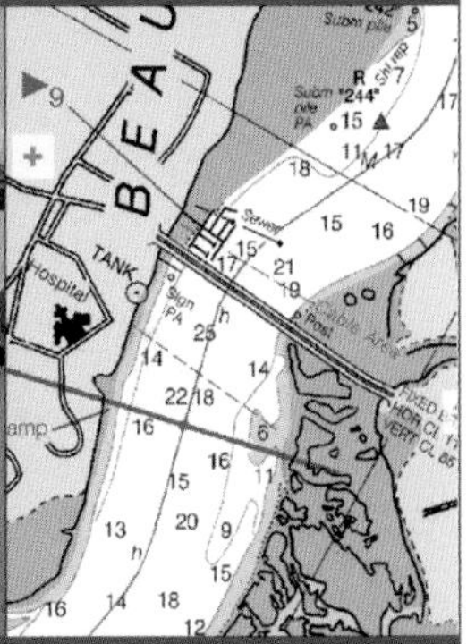

32°22.475' N 80°78.170' W

**Wilton J. Graves
Twin Bridge**
Type: Fixed
Height: 65'

South Carolina

Little River to McClellanville

	MLW	Transient Slips/Moorings	Floating docks	Gas	Diesel	Pumpout	Showers	Pool	Laundry	Wi-Fi	Haulout	Repairs	Other
Cricket Cove Marina Little River/MM 345 843-249-7169 www.cricketcovemarina.com	8'	●	●	●	●	●	●		●		●	➤	ship's store, lounge, restaurant on-site
Coquina Yacht Club Little River/Coquina Harbor/MM 346 843-249-9333 www.coquinayachtclub.com	8'	●	●	➤	➤	●	●		●		➤	➤	groceries, drug store, restaurants, marine supplies nearby
Myrtle Beach Yacht Club MM 346 843-249-5376 www.myrtlebeachyachtclub.com	12'	●	●	●	●	●	●	●	●			➤	Picnic shelter, ship's store, cable TV
Grande Harbour Marina Little River/MM 346.5 843-427-7934 www.grandeharbourhome.net	4'		●	●	➤		●		●	●	●		full-service boatyard, non-ethanol fuel, Ship's store, dry storage
Anchor Marina N. Myrtle Beach/MM 347 843-249-7899 www.anchormarina.wix.com/anchor-marina	4'	●		●	●	●	●			●	●		Ian's Waterway Bar & Grill
Harbourgate Resort & Marina N. Myrtle Beach/MM 347.5 843-249-8888 www.harbourgatemarina.com	10'	●			●	●	●	●	●	●		●	sushi restaurant, tiki bar, charter fishing, ship's store
The Marina at Dock Holidays N. Myrtle Beach/MM 348.2 843-280-6354 fuel dock: 843-249-4925	7'	●	●	●	●	●	●					●	Restaurant on-site, ethanol-free gas, fishing charters, cable tv
Grande Dunes Marina Myrtle Beach/MM 357.5 843-315-7777 www.grandedunes.com/marina	8'	●	●	●	●	●	●	●	●	●			courtesy van, fitness center, golf courses, hotel, bar/restaurant
Osprey Marina Myrtle Beach/MM 373 843-215-5353 www.ospreymarina.com	9'	●		●	●	●	●		●				
Bucksport Plantation Marina Waccamaw R./MM 377 843-397-5566 www.bucksportplantation.com	20'	●					●		●	●		➤	cable tv, ship's store, restaurant
Wacca Wache Marina Murrells Inlet/MM 383 843-651-2994 www.waccawachemarina.com	8'	●	●	●	●	●	●		●	●	●		restaurant, tour boats, intl. airport, major shopping, restaurants
Reserve Harbor Pawleys Island/MM 389 843-314-5133 www.reserveharbor.com	5'			●	●	●	●	●	●	●			non-ethanol gas; concierge service, ship's store
Heritage Plantation Marina Pawleys Island/MM 394 843-237-3650 www.heritageplantation.com	32'	●	●			●	●	●		●			
Georgetown Landing Marina Pee Dee River/Georgetown/MM 403 843-546-1776 www.georgetownlandingmarina.com	17'	●		●	●	●	●		●	●			ethanol-fre gas, ship's store, restaurant nearby
Harborwalk Marina Sampit River/Winyah Bay/N of MM 403 843-546-4250 www.harborwalkmarina.com	10'	●	●	●	●	●	●		●	●	➤	➤	Cable, lounge; pharmacy nearby; in heart of Georgetown
Leland Oil Company Jeremy Cr./McClellanville/MM 430 843-887-3641	5.5'	●	●	●	●		●		●	●		●	walk to restaurants, town

Isle of Palms to Hilton Head

	MLW	Transient Slips/Moorings	Floating docks	Gas	Diesel	Pumpout	Showers	Pool	Laundry	Wi-Fi	Haulout	Repairs	Other
Isle of Palms Marina Isle of Palms/MM 456.5 843-886-0209 www.iopmarina.com	12'	●	●	●	●	●	●	●	➤	●	●		double-wide boat ramp, cable TV, golf, shopping nearby
Charleston Harbor Resort & Marina Charleston Harbor/Patriots Pt. 843-297-2949 www.charlestonharbormarina.com	14'	●	●	●	●	●	●	●	●	●			water taxi to historic district; restaurant on-site; concierge
Pierside Boatworks Cooper R./R. Marker 52 843-554-7775 www.piersideboatworks.com	5'				●						●	●	full-service yard
Toler's Cove Marina Ben Sawyer Bridge/MM 462.3 843-881-0325 www.tolerscovemarina.com	8'	●		●	●	●	●	●	●				
Cooper River Marina Cooper River/Red 4s 843-406-6966 www.CharlestonCountyParks.com	20'	●	●	➤	➤	●	●		●	●		➤	Ships store, lounge, laundry, dockside assistance
Charleston Maritime Center Cooper River/N. of Charleston Harbor 843-853-3625 www.cmcevents.com	10'	●	●	●	●	●	●		●	●	➤	➤	free laundry, located downtown, walk to 24-hour grocery

	MLW	Transient Slips/Moorings	Floating docks	Gas	Diesel	Pumpout	Showers	Pool	Laundry	Wi-Fi	Haulout	Repairs	Other
Charleston City Marina Ashley River/MM 469.5 843-723-5098 www.megadock.us	20'	•	•	➤	•	•	•		•	•		•	mobile service, high-speed fueling, 3,000 ft transient dock
Rivers Edge Marina Ashley River/N.W. of Charleston Harbor 843-554-8901 www.riversedgemarina.com	3.5'	•	•	•		•	•				•	•	Ship's store, lounge, remodeled docks, launch ramp
The Harborage at Ashley Marina Ashley River/MM 470 843-722-1996 www.theharborageatashleymarina.com	17'	•		•	•	•	•		•	•			courtesty van to downtown, cable, lounge
Ripley Light Yacht Club Ashley R./Ripley CoveMM 471 877-747-5391/843-766-0908 www.ripleylightyc.com	7'	•		➤	➤	•	•						restaurants, hotels nearby
St. Johns Yacht Harbor Stono River/Johns Island/MM 472.5 843-557-1027 www.stjohnsyachtharbor.com	13'	•	•	•	•	•	•	•	•	•			Ethanol-free fuel, courtesy car
Ross Marine Stono River/Johns Island/MM 476 843-559-0379 www.rossmarine.com	12'		➤	•				➤		•	•		master yacht repair center & supply
Bohicket Marina and Market Bohicket Cr./North Edisto Int/MM 497 843-768-1280 www.bohicket.com	20'	•		•	•	•	•		•	•	➤	➤	Lounge, restaurants, shopping nearby
Dataw Island Marina Morgan R./Parrott Ck./MM 521 843-838-8410 www.datawmarina.com	20'	•	•	•	•	•	•		•	•			ship's store, playground, cable tv, 24-hr security
Marsh Harbor Boatworks Beaufort R..Ladys Island/MM 534 843-521-1500 www.marshharborboatworks.com/	4'					•					•	•	full-service boatyard
Lady's Island Marina Beaufort R./Factory Cr./MM 536 843-522-0430 www.ladysislandmarina.com	10'	•	•	➤	➤	•	•	•	•	•			restaurant on-site, walk to grocery, marine store, pet-friendly
Downtown Marina of Beaufort Beaufort River/MM 536 843-524-4422 www.downtownmarinabeaufort.com	15'	•	•	•	•	•	•		•	•		➤	moorings, cable tv, ship's store, courtesy transportation
Port Royal Landing Marina Beaufort R./MM 539 843-525-6664 www.portroyallandingmarina.com	15'	•	•	•	•	•	•	➤	•	•	➤	•	Courtesy car for overnight boaters during business hours
Skull Creek Marina Skull Cr./Hilton Head/MM 555 843-681-8436 www.theskullcreekmarina.com	9'	•	•	•	•	•	•		•	•	•	➤	
Hilton Head Harbor Marina Hilton Head/MM 557 843-681-3256 www.hiltonheadharbor.com	20'	•	•	•	•		•	•	•	•		➤	ethanol-free, mid-grade gas
Palmetto Bay Marina Broad Creek/Hilton Head/MM 563.8 843-785-3910 www.Palmettobaymarinahhi.com	20'	•	•	•	•	•	•		•	•	•	•	restaurants, charters, shopping, bars; trailer parking
Shelter Cove Marina Hilton Head/E. of MM 563.8 843-842-7001 www.sheltercovehiltonhead.com	8'	•	•	•	•	•	•	•	•	•		•	dining, shopping, ship's store, watersport rentals
Harbour Town Yacht Basin Calibogue Sound/MM 564 843-363-8335 www.seapinesresort.com	7'	•	•	•	•	•	•	•	•	•	➤	➤	Valvtech fuel

Amenities, Service, Convenience...Isle of Palms Marina

Isle of Palms Marina

P.O. Box 550, 50 41st Avenue,
Isle of Palms, SC 29451
Ph: 843-886-0209 | Fax: 843-886-0058
IOPMarina.com

description of facilities

From the moment you enter our channel, it's our job to meet your smallest need and your greatest expectations, from lending a hand with dock lines to acquainting you with the Isle of Palms land-side amenities. Our slips are fully equipped to make your stay enjoyable and comfortable. In addition, the marina has a three-lane public boat ramp, well-lit and secure floating docks, city water, complimentary wireless internet, cable TV and modern, private showers. Our full-service, 75-slip marina is the most convenient stopover to enjoy South Carolina's coast, only minutes from beautiful beaches, luxury oceanfront accommodations, award-winning golf courses, excellent shopping and Charleston's historic district. The Isle of Palms Marina is the perfect place to tie up and wind down.

marina approach & docking

Isle of Palms Marina is located on the east side of the Intracoastal Waterway, north of Charleston at mile 456.5 and south of ICW marker "116". The minimum depth of water in the channel is reported to be 12 feet.

The marina has floating docks with rubber protection guards. In addition, the marina has 20 slips reserved for transients as well as 300 feet of face dock alongside the restaurant that can accommodate larger vessels. Reservations are accepted. Call VHF 16, and dock personnel will assign you a slip and assist with docking. The staff is on duty during daylight hours with extended hours during the summer months.

at a glance

DOCKAGE RATE: Up to $2.00/ft ($50 min), includes water with slip rental

PAYMENT: MC/Visa/Amex

HOURS: Staff is on duty during daylight hours with extended hours during summer

TRANSIENT SLIPS/TOTAL SLIPS: 20/75

VHF/WORKING: 16/71

MLW/LOA*: 12'/200'

ELECTRIC: $7.00/30 amp, $10.00/50 amp

PUMP-OUT: $5.00/tank

FUEL: Gas and diesel w/volume discounts

REPAIR: Marine services on call

PROPANE: Yes

RESTAURANT/MILES: One on-site, several nearby

HEAD/SHOWER/LAUNDRY: Yes/Yes/Yes

INTERNET ACCESS: Complimentary wireless

SHIP'S STORE: Well-stocked on premises

NEAREST TOWN/MILES: Mt. Pleasant and Charleston

SHOPPING: On-site, Nearby

STORAGE: Dry

AIRPORT/MILES: Charleston Int'l/30 mins

TRANSPORTATION: Island-wide courtesy shuttle and rental cars nearby. Limo service available

SPECIAL: Boat and Wave Runner rentals, parasailing and kayaking on premises, inshore/offshore fishing charters

*MLW = Mean Low Water Depth
 LOA = Longest vessel that can be accommodated

LAT: 32° 48' 19.6554"N
LON: -79° 45' 35.784"W

Experience the Lowcountry Charm

Port Royal Landing Marina

1 Landing Drive, Port Royal, SC 29935
Ph: 843-525-6664 | Fax: 843-525-9166
Email: information@portroyallandingmarina.com
PortRoyalLandingMarina.com

description of facilities

Port Royal Landing Marina is the gateway into the historical Beaufort/Port Royal area of South Carolina and all that goes with it. The ambiance is more serene, the access easier, and the service will exceed your expectations. To experience the ultimate in Southern hospitality, slip in or out of Beaufort/Port Royal with ease at the Port Royal Landing Marina.

THE ROYAL TREATMENT: Excellent service is our nature. The friendly attitude, the special attention to details, and the way we treat each and every boater will make Port Royal Landing Marina a favorite stop along the Waterway. We intend to exceed your expectations.

marina approach & docking

Port Royal Landing Marina is located on the Intracoastal Waterway at mile 539. There is plenty of water for docking and over 600 feet of easy in/easy out transient face dock. Please call ahead for reservations. Our dock hands carry handheld VHF radios to assist with docking communications. We are open 7 days a week from 8:00 a.m. until 6:00 p.m. (December through March, 8:00 a.m. until 5:00 p.m.). All our docks are floating concrete. We monitor VHF channel 16 or call (843) 525-6664 for reservations.

at a glance

DOCKAGE RATE: $2.00/ft ($0.15/ft discount for BoatUS, MTOA, Active Captain & repeat customers

PAYMENT: MC/Visa/Amex/Discover/debit/cash

HOURS: 8am – 6pm, Winter: 8am – 5pm

TRANSIENT SLIPS/TOTAL SLIPS: 20/145

VHF/WORKING: 16/12

MLW/LOA*: 18'/130'

ELECTRIC: 30/50 Amp

PUMP-OUT: Yes/Fuel dock & slip

FUEL: Gas/Diesel (ValvTect)

REPAIR: Service on-call

PROPANE: Exchange on-site

RESTAURANT/MILES: Full bar/grill on-site

HEAD/SHOWER: Yes/Yes; A/C, very clean, coded entry

LAUNDRY: Yes, 24 hours

INTERNET ACCESS/CABLE: Free w/overnight dockage

SHIP'S STORE: Yes, including Nautical charts, clothing, 1 lb. fuel cylinders for grills, fishing tackle & bait. Weekday overnight free delivery on special orders

NEAREST TOWN/MILES: Port Royal/2, Beaufort/2

SHOPPING: Yes

TRANSPORTATION: Courtesy car available during business hours

SPECIAL: Free Access to nearby indoor and outdoor pools, spa, sauna, steam room, & fitness center

*MLW = Mean Low Water Depth
 LOA = Longest vessel that can be accommodated

LAT: 32° 24' 25.416"N
LON: -80° 40' 36.2634"W

Shop. Dine. Play.
Hilton Head's Happening Harbour

Shelter Cove Marina

1 Shelter Cove Lane,
Hilton Head Island, SC 29928
Ph: 844-391-7550 | Fax: 843-842-8645
Email: sheltercovemarina@palmettodunes.com
palmettodunes.com/marina

description of facilities

Shelter Cove Harbour and Marina, on mile marker 8 Hwy 278, is an oasis for waterfront shopping, dining and spectacular water views. Shelter Cove offers six restaurants and a variety of fine shopping. Located across from Palmetto Dunes Oceanfront Resort, Shelter Cove Harbour and Marina is the place to unwind from a day of championship golf, tennis and other activities. Be sure to bring the whole family because Shelter Cove offers entertainment seven nights a week during the summer, with special activities just for kids! Featured events continue during the fall, holiday season and spring. Don't miss Hilton Head's happening harbour!

marina approach & docking

Approach Broad Creek from Calibogue Sound by leaving Broad Creek's channel marker #"1" to port. Proceed up Broad Creek, following the well-marked, deep-water channel (12 feet at mean low water) to "18" and "19". Go between the markers and proceed up the channel to "22", which is located at the beginning of the marina. We monitor VHF channel 16. Please call for information 843-842-7001 (toll-free 866.400.7894) or e-mail us at shelter-covemarina@palmettodunes.com.

at a glance

DOCKAGE RATE: Per/ft varies with length

PAYMENT: MC/Visa/Amex/Discover

HOURS: 7:00 am – 9:00 pm & seasonal

TRANSIENT SLIPS/TOTAL SLIPS: 20/175

VHF/WORKING: 16/71

MLW/LOA*: 7'/140'

ELECTRIC: 30/50/100 Amps, monthly

PUMP-OUT: Yes

FUEL: Gas/Diesel, 89 octane non-ethanol

REPAIR: Yes

PROPANE: No

RESTAURANT/MILES: 6 restaurants on-site

POOL: Yes

HEAD/SHOWER/LAUNDRY: Yes/Yes/Yes

INTERNET ACCESS: WiFi

CABLE: Yes

SHIP'S STORE: Yes

NEAREST TOWN/MILES: Centrally located on Hilton Head Island

SHOPPING: Yes

GOLF/TENNIS: Yes/Yes

STORAGE: Wet

AIRPORT/MILES: 5 mi

TRANSPORTATION: Yes (seasonal)

YACHT BROKERAGE: Yes

*MLW = Mean Low Water Depth
LOA = Longest vessel that can be accommodated

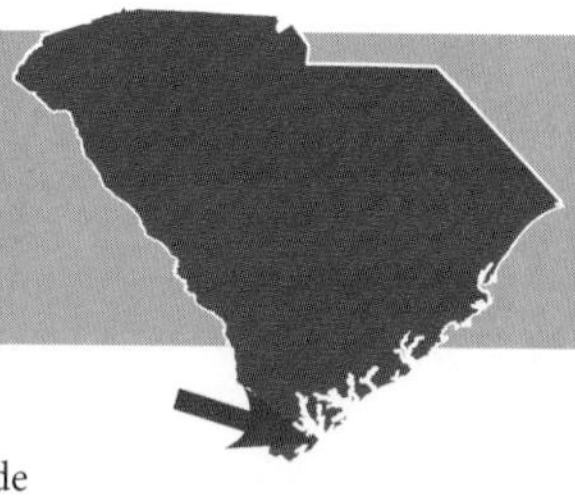

LAT: 32° 10' 92"N
LON: -80° 43' 56"W

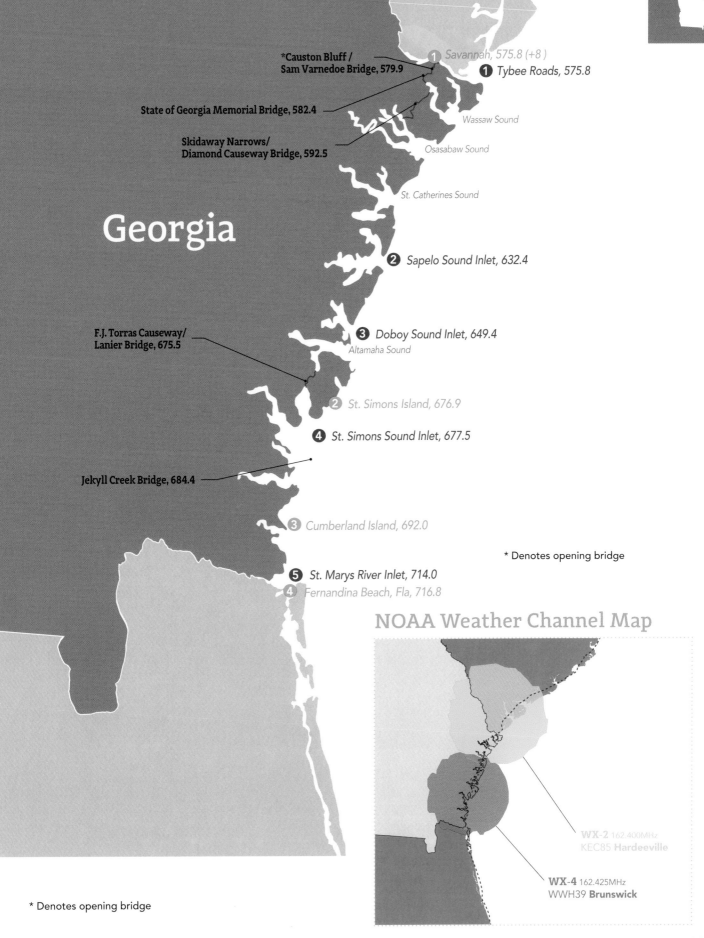

*Causton Bluff /
Sam Varnedoe Bridge, 579.9

State of Georgia Memorial Bridge, 582.4

Skidaway Narrows/
Diamond Causeway Bridge, 592.5

1 Savannah, 575.8 (+8)

1 Tybee Roads, 575.8

Wassaw Sound

Osasabaw Sound

St. Catherines Sound

Georgia

2 Sapelo Sound Inlet, 632.4

3 Doboy Sound Inlet, 649.4

Altamaha Sound

F.J. Torras Causeway/
Lanier Bridge, 675.5

2 St. Simons Island, 676.9

4 St. Simons Sound Inlet, 677.5

Jekyll Creek Bridge, 684.4

3 Cumberland Island, 692.0

* Denotes opening bridge

5 St. Marys River Inlet, 714.0

4 Fernandina Beach, Fla, 716.8

NOAA Weather Channel Map

WX-2 162.400MHz
KEC85 **Hardeeville**

WX-4 162.425MHz
WWH39 **Brunswick**

* Denotes opening bridge

ICW Mile 579.9
32°06.218' N
81°02.952' W

*Causton Bluff/Sam
Varnedoe Bridge
Type: Twin Bascule
Closed Height: 21'
Schedule: Mon.-Fri., from 6:30 to
9 a.m. and from 4:30 to 6:30 p.m.,
will open only at 7 a.m., 8 a.m.
and 5:30 p.m. All other times, will
open on request.
Contact: VHF 09 912-897-2511

ICW Mile 582.4
32°03.402' N
81°04.588' W

State of Georgia
Memorial Bridge
(Thunderbolt)
Type: Fixed
Height: 65'

ICW Mile 592.5
32°94.742' N
81°06.588' W

Skidaway Narrows/Dia-
mond Causeway Bridge
Type: Fixed
Height: 65'
Comments: Old bascule bridge
has been removed.

ICW Mile 674.2
32°17.142' N
81°42.497' W

F.J. Torras Causeway/
Lanier Bridge
Type: Fixed
Height: 65'

ICW Mile 684.3
32°17.142' N
81°42.497' W

Jekyll Creek Bridge
Type: Fixed
Height: 65'
Comments: Normal tide runs
7.5' here, so if you have a tall
mast, watch the clearance during
especially high water.

Georgia

	MLW	Transient Slips/Moorings	Floating docks	Gas	Diesel	Pumpout	Showers	Pool	Laundry	Wi-Fi	Haulout	Repairs	Other
Westin Savannah Harbor Golf Resort & Spa Savannah Harbor/8 mi W of MM 576 912-201-2021 www.westinsavannah.com/marina	20'	●		➤	➤			●	●		●			Golf, tennis, bicycles, gym, beautician services, restaurants
Hyatt Regency Savannah Savannah River/8 miles west of MM 576 912-238-1234 www.hyattdockssavannah.com	27'	●	●					●	●		●			Overnight accommodations, 30, 50, 100 amp power incl.
Bull River Marina Bull River/4 miles northeast of MM 586 912-897-7300 www.bullrivermarina.com	20'	●	●	●	●	●	●			●			Fishing charters, kayak rentals, fossil hunts, nature tours, store
Morningstar Marinas/Bahia Bleu Wilmington R./Thunderbolt/MM 582 912-354-2283 www.morningstarmarinas.com	15'			●	●	●	●	●		●		●		ship's store, non-ethanol gas, complimentary docking lessons
Hinckley Yacht Service Wilmington R./Thunderbolt/MM 582.3 912-629-2400 www.hinckleyyachts.com/service/savannah	12'	●	●	➤	➤	●	●		➤	●	●	●	courtesy car, 20 min. to downtown Savannah & Tybee islands
Thunderbolt Marine Wilmington R./Thunderbolt/MM 583 912-352-4931 www.thunderboltmarine.us	20'	●		●	●	●	●		●	●		●	ship's store, 24-7 security
Sail Harbor Marina & Boatyard Turner Creek/SE of MM 585.4 912-897-2896 www.sailharbormarina.com	7'	●	●	➤	➤	●	●		●	●	●	●	Site of the 1996 Olympic Sailing events! 50-ton lift
Hogan's Marina Turner Cr./1 mi. E of 585.4 912-897-3474 www.hogansmarina.com	21'	●		●	➤	●	●				●	●	marine store, ice, beer, bait, kayak rentals
Isle of Hope Marina Skidway R./MM 590/Marker 46A 912-354-8187 www.iohmarina.com	15'	●	●	●	●	●	●	●	●	●			historic district
Delegal Creek Marina Little Ogeechee R./Skidway Is/MM 601 912-224-3885	9'	●		●	●	●	●		●			●	ice, golf cart, access to club facilities
Ft. McAllister Marina Ogeechee R./MM 605 912-727-2632 www.fortmcallistermarina.net	19'	●	●	●	●	●	●		●	●	●		Ft. McAllister State Park 1/4 mi away. "Fish Tales" restaurant
Kilkenny Marina Kilkenny Cr./2 mi. W of MM 614 912-727-2215	13'	●	●	●	●		●		●	●			live bait, beer, restaurant next door
Halfmoon Marina North Newport R./6 mi. W of MM 622 912-884-5819	15'	●		●	●		●						non-ethanol fuel, ship's store
Hampton River Marina Hampton R./St Simons Is/E of MM 664 912-638-1210 www.hrmarina.com	14'	●	●	●	●		●					●	ship's store
Morningstar Marinas at Golden Isles Frederica R./MM 675 912-480-0266 www.morningstarmarinas.com	10'	●		●	●	●	●	●	●		➤	●	
Brunswick Landing Marina Brunswick R./East R./NW of MM 680 912-265-9264 www.brunswicklandingmarina.com	28'	●	●	●	●	●	●		●	●	●	●	walking distance to downtown Brunswick
Jekyll Harbor Marina Jekyll Cr./MM 685 912-635-3137 www.jekyllharbor.com	10'	●		●	●	●	●	●	●	●	●	●	
Lang's Marina St. Marys R./2 mi W of MM 712 912-882-4452 www.cumberlandislandferry.com	12'			●	●	●	●				➤		

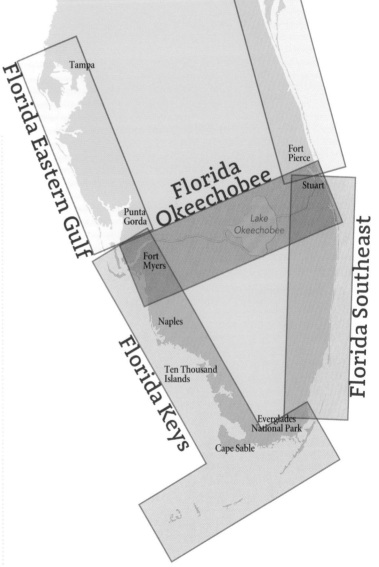

Florida

Jacksonville

Cedar Key

New Smyrna Beach

Homosassa Springs

Tampa

Florida North

Florida Eastern Gulf

Fort Pierce

Florida Okeechobee

Stuart

Punta Gorda

Lake Okeechobee

Florida Southeast

Fort Myers

Naples

Ten Thousand Islands

Florida Keys

Everglades National Park

Cape Sable

NOAA Weather Channel Map

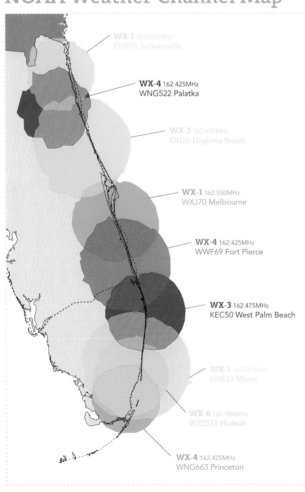

WX-1 162.550MHz KHB39 Jacksonville

WX-4 162.425MHz WNG522 Palatka

WX-2 162.400MHz KIH26 Daytona Beach

WX-1 162.550MHz WXJ70 Melbourne

WX-4 162.425MHz WWF69 Fort Pierce

WX-3 162.475MHz KEC50 West Palm Beach

WX-1 162.550MHz KHB34 Miami

WX-6 162.500MHz WZ2531 Hialeah

WX-4 162.425MHz WNG663 Princeton

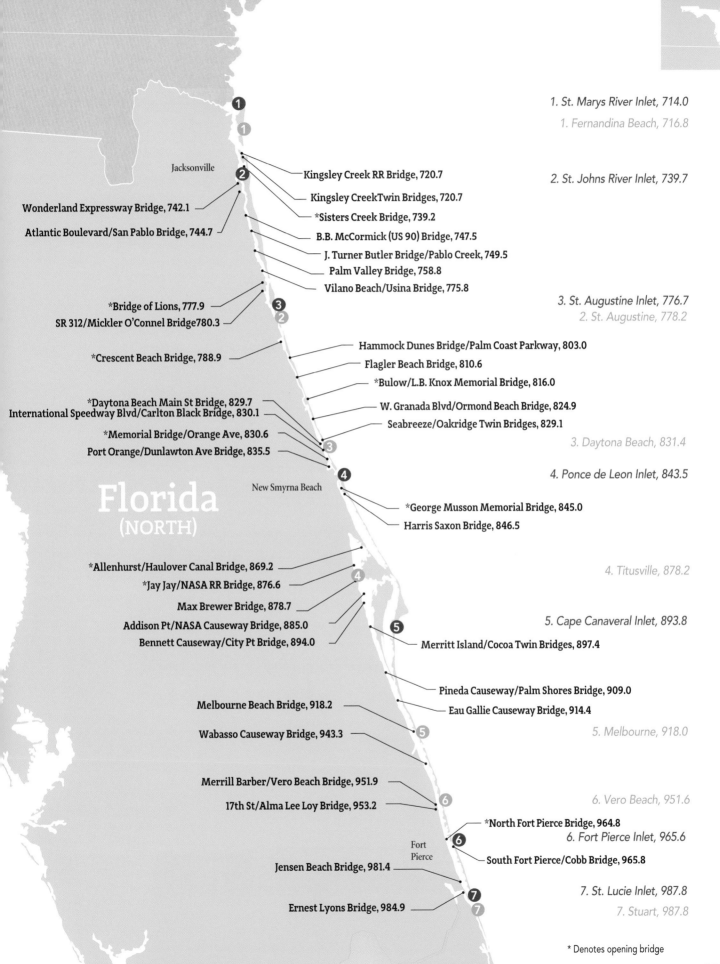

1. St. Marys River Inlet, 714.0

1. Fernandina Beach, 716.8

Jacksonville

Kingsley Creek RR Bridge, 720.7

2. St. Johns River Inlet, 739.7

Kingsley CreekTwin Bridges, 720.7

Wonderland Expressway Bridge, 742.1

*Sisters Creek Bridge, 739.2

Atlantic Boulevard/San Pablo Bridge, 744.7

B.B. McCormick (US 90) Bridge, 747.5

J. Turner Butler Bridge/Pablo Creek, 749.5

Palm Valley Bridge, 758.8

Vilano Beach/Usina Bridge, 775.8

*Bridge of Lions, 777.9

3. St. Augustine Inlet, 776.7

SR 312/Mickler O'Connel Bridge780.3

2. St. Augustine, 778.2

Hammock Dunes Bridge/Palm Coast Parkway, 803.0

*Crescent Beach Bridge, 788.9

Flagler Beach Bridge, 810.6

*Bulow/L.B. Knox Memorial Bridge, 816.0

W. Granada Blvd/Ormond Beach Bridge, 824.9

*Daytona Beach Main St Bridge, 829.7

Seabreeze/Oakridge Twin Bridges, 829.1

International Speedway Blvd/Carlton Black Bridge, 830.1

*Memorial Bridge/Orange Ave, 830.6

3. Daytona Beach, 831.4

Port Orange/Dunlawton Ave Bridge, 835.5

4. Ponce de Leon Inlet, 843.5

Florida
(NORTH)

New Smyrna Beach

*George Musson Memorial Bridge, 845.0

Harris Saxon Bridge, 846.5

*Allenhurst/Haulover Canal Bridge, 869.2

4. Titusville, 878.2

*Jay Jay/NASA RR Bridge, 876.6

Max Brewer Bridge, 878.7

Addison Pt/NASA Causeway Bridge, 885.0

5. Cape Canaveral Inlet, 893.8

Bennett Causeway/City Pt Bridge, 894.0

Merritt Island/Cocoa Twin Bridges, 897.4

Pineda Causeway/Palm Shores Bridge, 909.0

Melbourne Beach Bridge, 918.2

Eau Gallie Causeway Bridge, 914.4

Wabasso Causeway Bridge, 943.3

5. Melbourne, 918.0

Merrill Barber/Vero Beach Bridge, 951.9

6. Vero Beach, 951.6

17th St/Alma Lee Loy Bridge, 953.2

*North Fort Pierce Bridge, 964.8

6. Fort Pierce Inlet, 965.6

Fort Pierce

South Fort Pierce/Cobb Bridge, 965.8

Jensen Beach Bridge, 981.4

7. St. Lucie Inlet, 987.8

Ernest Lyons Bridge, 984.9

7. Stuart, 987.8

* Denotes opening bridge

ICW Mile 720.7
30°62.799 N 81°48.386 W

*Kingsley Creek
Twin Bridges*
Type: Fixed
Closed Height: 65'
Comments: Height will be less
than 65' when tide exceeds its
normal high of 6.2'.

ICW Mile 720.7
30°62.88' N 81°48.45' W

**Kinglsey Creek
RR Bridge*
Type: Swing
Closed Height: 5'
Schedule: Open unless a train is
coming
Comments: Watch for strong cur-
rent through these bridges.

ICW Mile 739.2
30°39.39' N 81°45.98' W

**Sisters Creek
Bridge*
Type: Bascule
Closed Height: 24'
Schedule: Opens on demand.
Contact: VHF 09   800-865-5794
Comments: Watch for cross cur-
rents. A new high-rise bridge is
under construction.

ICW Mile 742.1
30°36.08' N 81°44.29' W

*Wonderland
Expressway Bridge*
Type: Fixed
Closed Height: 65'

ICW Mile 744.7
30°32.34' N 81°43.85' W

*Atlantic Boulevard/
San Pablo Bridge*
Type: Fixed
Closed Height: 65'

ICW Mile 747.5
30°28.81' N 81°42.12' W

*B.B. McCormick
Bridge*
Type: Fixed
Height: 65'

ICW Mile 749.5
30°25.73' N 81°42.81' W

*J. Turner Butler Bridge/
Pablo Creek*
Type: Fixed
Height: 65'

ICW Mile 758.8
20°13.28' N 81°38.55' W

Palm Valley Bridge
Type: Fixed
Height: 65'

ICW Mile 775.8
29°91.77' N 81°30.13' W

*Vilano Beach/
Usina Bridge*
Type: Fixed
Height: 65'

ICW Mile 777.9
29°89.23' N 81°30.74' W

*Bridge of Lions
Type: Bascule Closed Height: 23'
Schedule: 7 a.m. to 6 p.m. on request (you must ask) on hour and
half-hour, except Monday-Friday,
no openings at 8 a.m., noon and 5
p.m. Other times on request.
Contact: VHF 09 800-865-5794
Comments: Watch the tide board;
the closed height may be up to 4
feet lower than 23'.

ICW Mile 780.3
29°86.72' N 81°30.69' W

*SR 312/Mickler
O'Connel Bridge*
Type: Fixed
Height: 65'

ICW Mile 788.9
29°76.87' N 81°25.81' W

**Crescent Beach
Bridge*
Type: Bascule
Closed Height: 25'
Schedule: Opens on demand.
Contact: VHF 09   800-865-5794

ICW Mile 803.0
29°57.37' N 81°18.91' W

*Hammock Dunes Bridge/
Palm Coast Parkway*
Type: Fixed
Height: 65'

ICW Mile 810.6
29°47.76' N 81°13.65' W

Flagler Beach Bridge
Type: Fixed
Height: 65'

ICW Mile 816.0
29° 24.51' N 81° 06.05' W

**Bulow/L.B. Knox
Memorial Bridge*
Type: Bascule
Closed Height: 15'
Schedule: Opens on demand.
Contact: VHF 09 386-441-0777

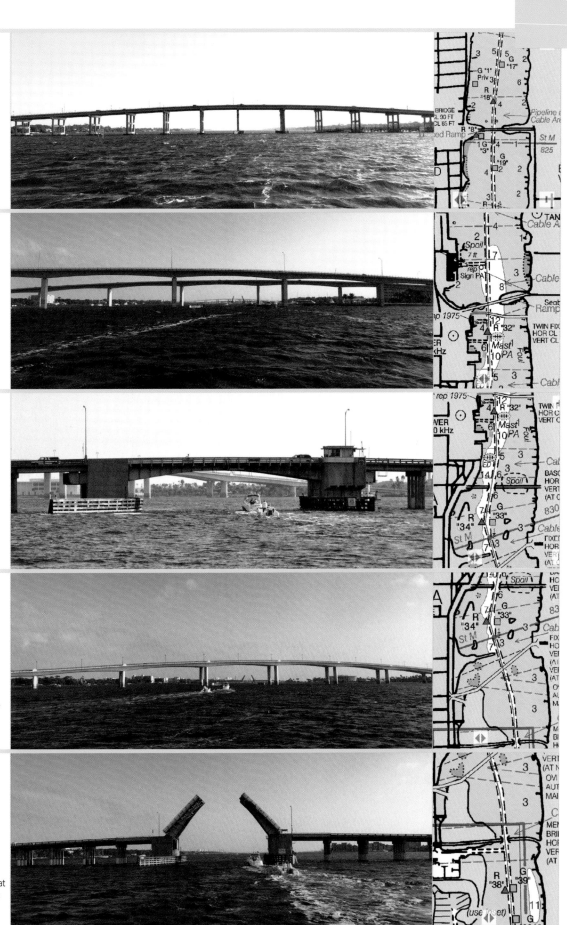

ICW Mile 824.9
29°28.71' N 81°05.22' W

*W. Granada
Boulevard/
Ormond Beach Bridge*
Type: Fixed
Height: 65'

ICW Mile 829.1
29°23.11' N 81°02.27' W

*Seabreeze/Oakridge
Bridge*
Type: Fixed
Height: 65'

ICW Mile 829.7
29°22.26' N 81°01.90' W

**Daytona Beach
Main Street Bridge*
Type: Bascule
Closed Height: 22'
Schedule: Opens on demand.
Contact: VHF 09 386-239-6477

ICW Mile 830.1
29°21.64' N 81°01.52 W

*International
Speedway Boulevard/Carl-
ton Black Bridge*
Type: Fixed
Height: 65'
Comment: Although tide board
reads 63', bridge is 67' in middle,
according to Coast Guard.

ICW Mile 830.6
29°21.11' N 81°01.10' W

**Memorial Bridge/
Orange Avenue*
ICW Mile: 830.6
Type: Bascule
Closed Height: 21'
Schedule: Opens on demand,
except Monday-Friday, 7:45 to
8:45 a.m., when it will open only at
8:15, and 4:45-5:45 p.m., when it
will open only at 5:15.
Contact: VHF 09 386-239-6540

ICW Mile 835.5
29°14.83' N 81°97.53' W

*Port Orange/
Dunlawton Avenue Bridge*
Type: Fixed
Height: 65'

ICW Mile 845.0
29°03.90' N 80°90.50' W

**George Musson
Memorial Bridge*
Type: Bascule   Closed Height: 23'
Schedule: From 7 a.m. to 7 p.m.,
opens on the hour, 20 minutes
past and 40 minutes past. At other
times, opens on request.
Contact: VHF 09 386-424-2024
Comments: You must alert the
bridgetender ahead of time that
you want to pass through.

ICW Mile 829.7
29°023.55' N 80°91.80' W

Harris Saxon Bridge
Type: Fixed
Height: 65'

ICW Mile 869.2
28°73.65' N 80°75.45' W

**Allenhurst/Haulover
Canal Bridge*
Type: Bascule
Closed Height: 27'
Schedule: Opens on demand.
Contact: VHF 09 321-867-4859

ICW Mile 876.6
28°65.07' N 80°80.68' W

**Jay Jay/NASA
RR Bridge*
Type: Bascule
Closed Height: 7'
Schedule: Open except for passage of trains. Bridge will close
8 minutes after red lights begin
flashing and open about 5 minutes
after train passes.
Contact: The bridge is unat-
tended.

ICW Mile 878.9

*Max Brewer
Bridge*
28°62.18' N 80°79.80 W
Type: Fixed
Height: 65'

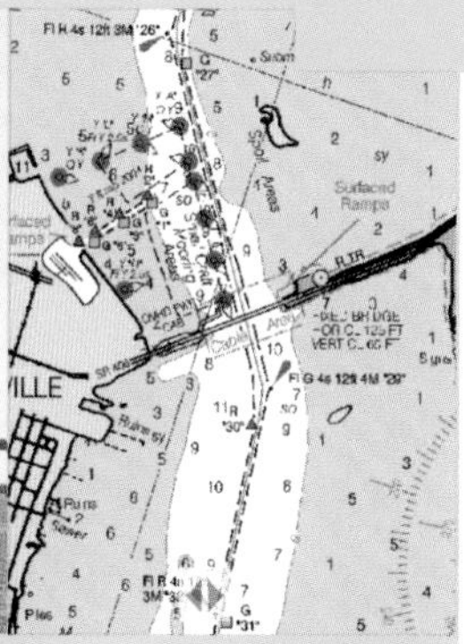

ICW Mile 885.0
28°52.73' N 80°76.55' W

**Addison Point/
NASA Causeway Bridge*
Type: Bascule
Closed Height: 27'
Schedule: Opens on request,
except Monday-Friday, from 6:30
to 8 a.m. and 3:30 to 5 p.m., when
it will not open, holidays excluded.

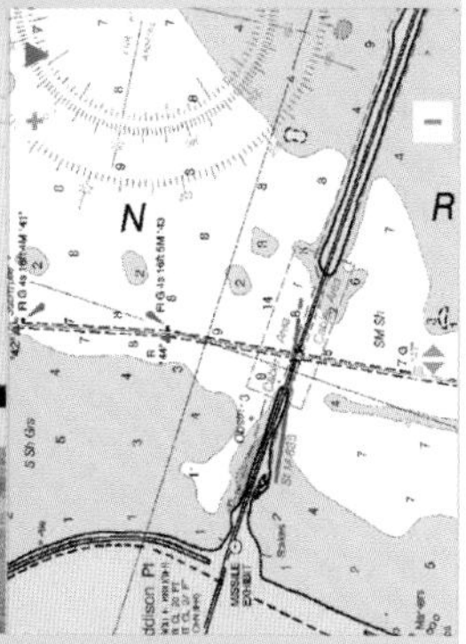

ICW Mile 894.0
28°40.27' N 80°73.46' W

*Bennett Causeway/
City Point Bridge*
Type: Fixed
Height: 65'

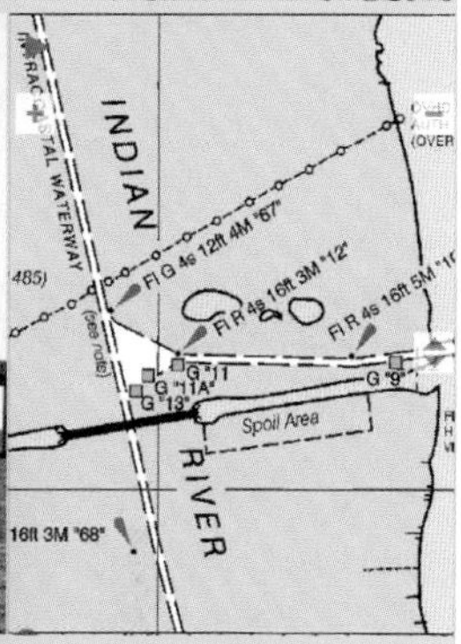

ICW Mile 897.4
28°35.65' N 80°71.81' W

*Merritt Island/Cocoa
Twin Bridges*
Type: Fixed
Height: 65'

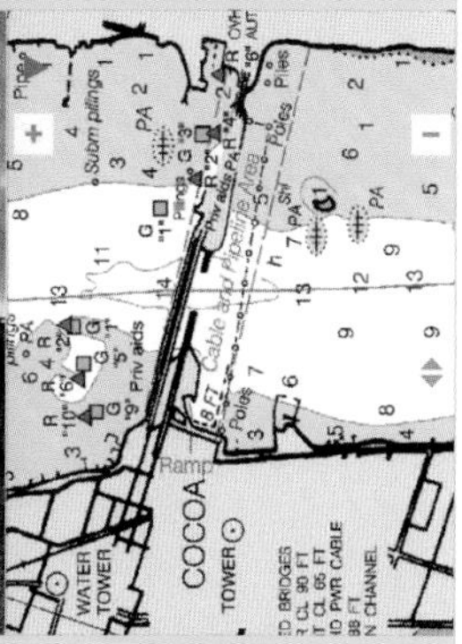

ICW Mile 909.0
28°20.63' N 80°65.01' W

*Pineda Causeway/
Palm Shores Bridge*
Type: Fixed
Height: 65'

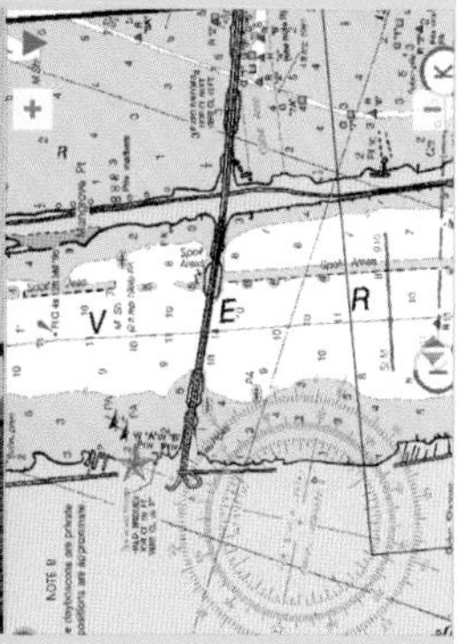

ICW Mile 914.4
28°13.25' N 80°61.77' W

Eau Gallie
Causeway Bridge
Type: Fixed
Height: 65'

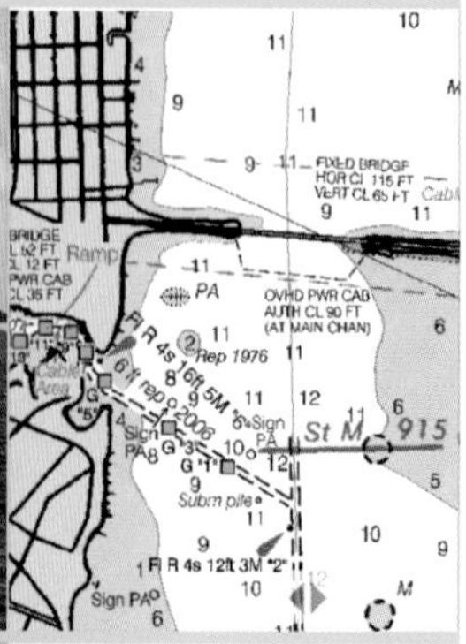

ICW Mile 918.2
28°08.40' N 80°59.15' W

Melbourne Beach
Bridge
Type: Fixed
Height: 65'

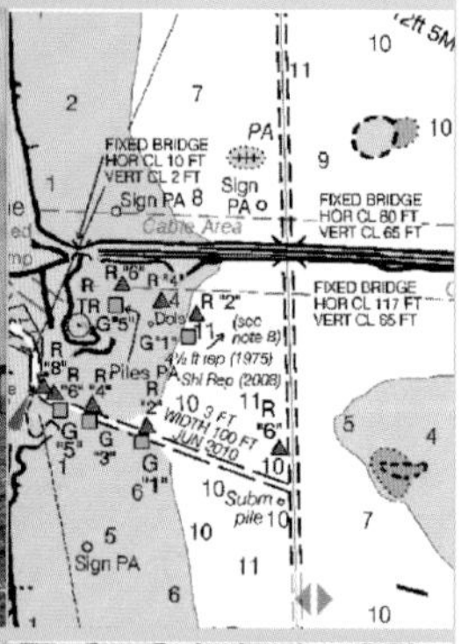

ICW Mile 943.3
27°76.11' N 80°41.61' W

Wabasso Causeway
Bridge
Type: Fixed
Height: 65'
Comments: Strong north wind will
keep tide up, so watch tide board.

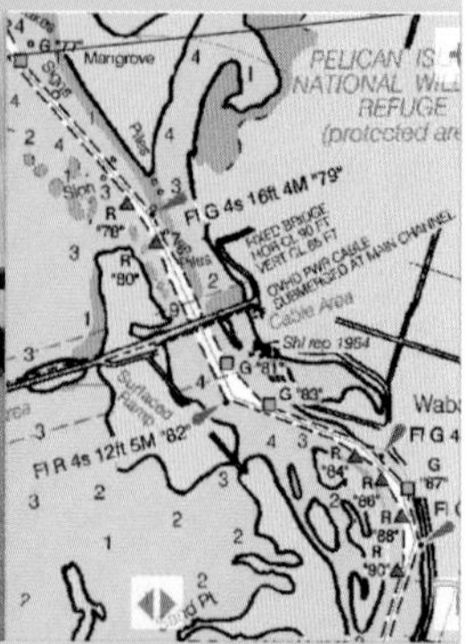

ICW Mile 951.9
27°65.27' N 80°37.41' W

Merrill Barber/
Vero Beach Bridge
Type: Fixed
Height: 65'

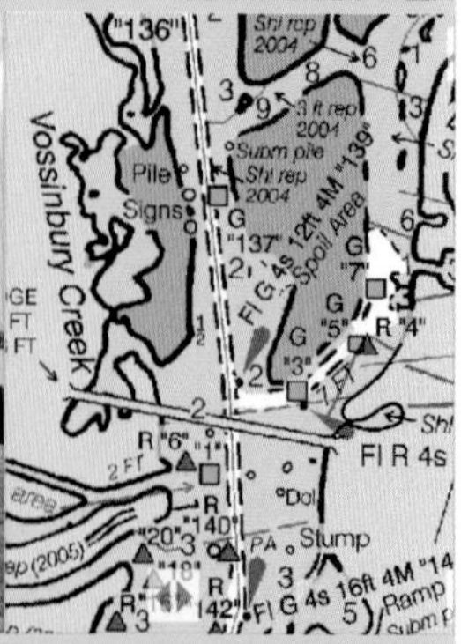

ICW Mile 953.2
27°63.24' N 80°37.10' W

17th Street/
Alma Lee Loy Bridge
Type: Fixed
Height: 65'

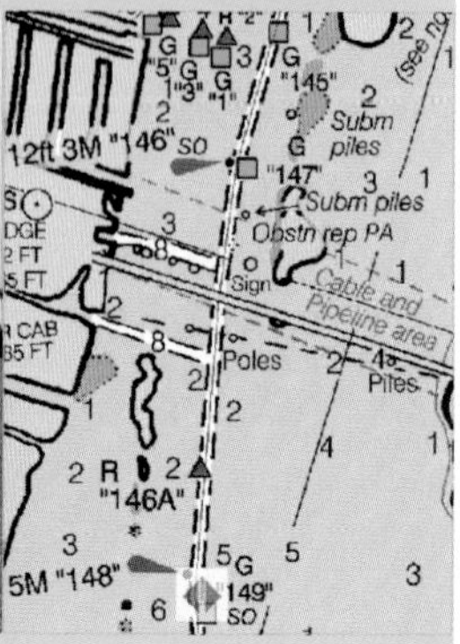

ICW Mile 964.8
27°47.19' N 80°32.44' W

**North Fort
Pierce Bridge*
Type: Bascule
Closed Height: 23'
Schedule: Opens on request.
Contact: VHF 09 772-468-3993

ICW Mile 965.8
27°45.81' N 80°31.82' W

*South Fort Pierce/
Cobb Bridge*
Type: Fixed
Height: 65'

ICW Mile 981.4
27°25.33' N 80°21.87' W

Jensen Beach Bridge
Type: Fixed
Height: 65'

ICW Mile 984.9
27°20.68' N 80°19.18' W

Ernest Lyons Bridge
Type: Fixed
Height: 65'

Florida North

Other

Fernandina Beach to Stuart

	MLW	Transient Slips/Moorings	Floating docks	Gas	Diesel	Pumpout	Showers	Pool	Laundry	Wi-Fi	Haulout	Repairs	Other
Amelia Island Yacht Basin Amelia Island/Day Marker 13 904-277-4615 www.ameliaislandyachtbasin.com	5.5'	•		•	•	•	•		•	•	•	•	restaurant on-site, marine store
Fernandina Harbor Marina Fernandina/MM 716 904-310-3300 www.fhmarina.com	6'	•	•	•	•	•	•	➤	•	•		➤	
The Marina at Ortega Landing Ortega River/St. Johns R. 904-387-5538 www.ortegalanding.com	6'	•	•	➤	➤	•	•	•	•	•	➤	•	jacuzzi, ice, clubhouse, free loaner bikes, pets welcome
River City Marina St. Johns R./Southbank Riverwalk 904-398-7918 www.rivercitybrew.com	10'	•		•	•		•		•				River City Brewing Company. free dockage for diners
Palm Cove Marina Jacksonville Beach/MM 747 904-223-4757 www.palmcovemarina.com	6'	•	•	•	•	•	•		•	•	•	•	
Beach Marine Jacksonville Beach/MM 747.6 904-249-8200 www.jaxbeachmarine.com	6'	•	•	•	•	•	•		•	•	•	•	Yanmar, crusader, Mercruiser, Volvo certified
Camachee Cove Yacht Harbor St. Augustine/775.7 904-829-5676 www.camacheeisland.com	6'	•		•	•	•	•	•	•	•	•	•	restaurants, shopping nearby,
Conch House Marina Resort Salt run/St. Augustine Inlet/MM 776.8 904-824-4347 www.conch-house.com	8'	•	•	•	•	•	•	•	•	•		•	
St. Augustine Municipal Marina Matanzas R./St. Augustine/MM 777.7 904-825-1026 www.staugustinemarina.com	15'	•	•	•	•	•	•		•	•		➤	located in downtown St. Augustine historic district
St. Augustine Marine Center San Sebastian R./MM 780 904-824-4394 www.staugustinemarine.com	12'	•		•	➤	•	•			•	•	•	ethanol-free gas, minutes from historic downtown
Rivers Edge Marina San Sebastian R./Marker 29 904-827-0520 www.29riversedgemarina.com	8'	•	•	•	•	•	•		•	•			Fuel for slip customers only. Restaurant, hotel next door
Palm Coast Marina MM 803 386-446-6370 www.palmcoastmarina.net	8'	•		•	•	•	•		•	•		•	Marine store, European village/ restaurants, Captain's courtyard
Loggerhead Marina Daytona Beach Halifax R./South of R Mark 32MM 829.4 386-523-3100 www.loggerheaddaytonabeach.com	7'	•		➤	➤	•	•	•	•	•			restaurant on-site
Halifax Harbor Marina MM 830.5 386-671-3601 www.halifaxharbormarina.com	8'	•	•	•	•	•	•		•	•	➤		
Adventure Yacht Harbor Halifax R./MM 836 386-756-2180 www.adventureyachtharbor.com	6'	•		•	•	•			•	•		•	3 blocks from ocean
Inlet Harbor Marina Halifax R./839.6 386-767-3266 www.inletharbor.com	10'	•	•	•	•	•	•		•	•	➤	•	ValvTec, clean marina
Titusville Municipal Marina Indian R./Indian R. Lagoon/MM 878.9 321-383-5600 www.titusvillemarina.com	8'	•		•	•	•	•		•	•			dog park, boat ramp, outside contractors
Kennedy Point Yacht Club & Marina Indian R./MM 883 321-383-0280 www.kennedypointyachtclub.com	6'	•		➤	➤	•	•	•	•	•			
Cape Marina Banana R./Cape Canaveral Canal/C-11 321-783-8410 www.capemarina.com	12'		•	•	•	•	•	•	•	•	•	•	•	ethanol-free gas, ship's store
Harbortown Marina Port Canaveral Marina Indian R./Merrit Island/Barge Canal 321-453-0160 www.harbortownmarina.com	6'	•		•	•	•	•		•	•	•	•	grocery, restaurant, drug store nearby
Cocoa Village Marina Indian River/MM 897.3 321-632-5445 www.cocoavillagemarina.com	7'	•			•	•		•			➤		

	MLW	Transient Slips/Mooring	Floating docks	Gas	Diesel	Pumpout	Showers	Pool	Laundry	Wi-Fi	Haulout	Repairs	Other
Telemar Bay Marina Banana R./1 mi. N of MM 914 321-773-2468	8'	●	●	●	●	●			●	●	●		ship's store; close to restaurants, shopping, beach
Eau Gallie Yacht Basin Indian R./MM 914.2 321-242-6577 www.eaugallieyachtbasin.com	8'	●			●	●			●	●	●	●	ice, marine supplies, canvas shop
Waterline Marina Eau Gallie Basin/MM 914.7 321-254-0452 www.waterlinemarina.com	7'		➤	➤	●	●			●	●		●	
Melbourne Harbor Marina MM 918.5 321-725-9054 www.melbourneharbor.com	8'	●		●	●	●	●		●	●		●	
Treasure Coast Marina Indian R./Marker #35 321-733-3390 www.treasurecoastmarina.com	3.5'	●		●			●					➤	restaurant/bar on-site
Capt. Hiram's Sebastian Inlet Marina Sebastian Inlet/MM 937 772-589-4345 www.hirams.com	5'	●			●	●	●	●	●	●			grocery, marine supplies nearby
Vero Beach City Marina ICW Day Marker #139/ MM 951 772-231-2819 www.covb.org	8'	●		●	●	●			●	●		●	
Loggerhead Marina Vero Beach Indian R. Lagoon/Vero Beach/MM 949 772-770-4470 www.loggerheadverobeach.com	6'	●		●	●	●	●		●	●			Ship's store, grocery one mile away. Loaner bikes on-site
Harbortown Marina - Fort Pierce West of Red daymarker #184/MM 965 772-466-7300 www.harbortownmarina-fortpierce.com	6'	●		●	●	●	●	●	●	●	●	●	lounge, gated marina, concierge, shopping, dining nearby
Taylor Creek Marina Indian R./Taylor Cr./Marker 184 772-465-2663 www.anchorsaweighmarine.net	3'		●	➤						●	●		ethanol-free gas, marine store
Fort Pierce City Marina Indian River/Marker 188 772-461-0880 www.fortpiercecitymarina.com	6.5'	●	●	●	●	●	●		●	●			Downtown marina, restaurants, shopping, museums nearby
Nettles Island Marina Indian R./MM 979/Jensen Beach Bridge 772-229-2811 www.nettlesislandmarina.com	8'	●		●	●	●	●		●	●			propane refill; pet-friendly; restaurant, walk to beach
Four Fish Marina Indian R./Jensen Beach/ICW 222 772-334-0936 www.fourfishmarina.com	6'	●		●	●	●		➤		●	●		
Sailfish Marina of Stuart St. Lucie R./Manatee Pocket/Stuart 772-283-1122 www.sailfishmarinastuart.com	8'	●		●	●	●			●	●	●	●	Fish Heads Bait & Tackle; Yamaha repair
Hutchinson Island Marriott Resort St. Lucia R./MM 985 772-225-6989	6'	●		●	●	●	●	●	●	●			hotel and restaurant on-site
Pirate's Cove Resort & Marina Stuart/Manatee Pocket/MM 987.8 772-287-2500 www.piratescoveresort.net	6'			●	●	●	●	●	●				bait, tackle shop, ice, beer
Sunset Bay Marina & Anchorage St. Lucie R./Stuart 772-283-9225 www.sunsetbaymarinaandanchorage.com	8'	●	●	●	●	●	●		●	●			restaurant on-site. In Downtown Stuart
Loggerhead Marina Stuart St. Lucie R./Stuart 772-692-4000 www.loggerheadstuart.com	8'	●		●	●	●	●	●	●	●	●	➤	ship's store, bar & Grille on-site, catamaran slips

Camachee Island Marina Village

3070 Harbor Drive, St. Augustine, FL 32084
Ph: 904-829-5676 | 800-345-9269
Email: camacheecove@comcast.net
CamacheeIsland.com

description of facilities

This 260-slip, state-of-the-art marina is located just north of the Vilano Bridge at ICW statute mile 775.7 and ICW marker "57". Camachee Cove Yacht Harbor, with its floating concrete docks, is well maintained and is strategically located approximately one mile from historic St. Augustine, the oldest city in the nation. Restaurants and shopping in the historic district of St. Augustine are within walking distance or a short bike ride away.

This fully protected marina offers docks with water, cable, and 110/220 and 100 amp electric service. Showers, laundry facilities, courtesy cars, cookout and barbecue areas, and a customer lounge with internet access make a stay at this marina a delight.

Also located in the marina complex are a canvas shop, restaurant, hotel, yacht yard, yacht brokerage, marine supply and service store, and more. Bags of ice, 10lb blocks and crushed, and 201b crushed, are available at the ship's store and harbor office.

marina approach & docking

Camachee Cove Yacht Harbor is off the Intracoastal Waterway and has jetties on the north and south side of the channel designed to prevent shoaling. Marina personnel suggest that you exercise caution when entering the jetties, as there may be a swift current on an outgoing tide. There is little or no current in this well protected basin. Set your fenders low before docking. Reservations are accepted. The marina personnel monitor VHF channels 16 and 68. Call as you enter the harbor for docking instructions. Winter hours are from 7 a.m. to 6 p.m., and spring, summer and fall hours are 7 a.m. to 7 p.m., seven days a week. The ship's store is closed on Sundays. The yacht yard is closed on the weekends.

LAT: 29° 54' 53.784"N
LON: -81° 18' 27.612"W

at a glance

DOCKAGE RATE: Less than 50'/$1.95/ft, 51'+ $2.25/ft, Boat U.S. discount

PAYMENT: MC/Visa/Amex/Discover

HOURS: 7am–7pm, daylight savings time; 7am–6pm, standard time

TRANSIENT SLIPS/TOTAL SLIPS: 25/260

VHF/WORKING: 16/68

MLW/LOA*: 6'/120'

ELECTRIC: 30/50 amp, 100 amp slips

PUMP-OUT: No charge

FUEL: Valvtect diesel fuel & Gas

REPAIR: Full-service, on-site

RESTAURANTS: Kingfish Grille and Vinnie's Pizza

POOL: Yes

HAUL-OUT: 50-ton lift with widened haul-out well, monitors channel 16

HEAD/SHOWER/LAUNDRY: Yes/Yes/Yes

CABLE/INTERNET ACCESS: Yes, wireless Phone long-term customers only

SHIP'S STORE: Yes

NEAREST TOWN/MILES: St. Augustine/1

SHOPPING: First Mate Yacht Services; Publix and Liquor 1 mile

STORAGE: Short-term

AIRPORT/MILES: JAX Int'l/1 hour; NE Regional 15 minutes

TRANSPORTATION: Courtesy cars

YACHT BROKERAGE: Admiral Yacht Sales

SPECIAL: Boater's lounge, book exchange, weather computer, Tow Boat U.S., Free Wifi

*MLW = Mean Low Water Depth
 LOA = Longest vessel that can be accommodated

Where the Tropics Begin

Vero Beach City Marina

3611 Rio Vista Blvd., Vero Beach, FL 32963
Ph: 772-231-2819 | 772-978-4960
Fax: 772-231-6893 | Email: marina@covb.org

description of facilities

Vero Beach City Marina, a Florida Clean Marina, prides itself on being a center for maritime information and hospitality for over 3,000 visiting boats each year. The marina has an expansive mooring field with 57 moorings available to the boating public as well as 30 transient slips available on a daily or monthly basis. We also have dry storage for vessels up to 22 feet. Very popular, the moorings may be reserved in advance. However, vessels may be rafted together during the busy winter season. The marina has a dinghy dock, lounge and laundry as well as a park and picnic area. Showers are included in the mooring fee. Fueling, waste disposal and pump-out facilities are also available. Free bus service is provided throughout the community. The Vero Beach Yacht Club adjoins the marina and is available to members of the Florida Yacht Council. Our friendly staff is available 9 hours per day to assist the boating community. There is a 3-acre off-leash dog exercise area adjacent to the marina.

marina approach & docking

Vero Beach City Marina is located at marker "139" (mile 952) just north of the Merrill Barber Bridge (65-foot clearance). When approaching from the south, make a hard turn to the east keeping "139" well off your port side and favoring the bridge on your starboard side. Slowly turn to the northeast and follow the channel markers into the turning basin. When approaching from the north, turn before you reach the bridge with "139" well off to your port side.

The approach depth is 8 to 10 feet. There is shoaling on the point of the island just north of the bridge, so favor the bridge side in your approach. The approach from the north is a manatee-protection-zone from "137" and should be negotiated at slow speeds.

The mooring basin in Vero Beach is a no-anchoring zone. For information or approach directions, hail the Vero Beach Harbormaster on VHF channel 16 from 8:00 a.m to 5:00 p.m.

at a glance

DOCKAGE RATE: Call for pricing

PAYMENT: All major credit cards

HOURS: 8:00 am – 5:00 pm

TRANSIENT SLIPS/TOTAL SLIPS: 30/108, Moorings/57, dry storage

VHF/WORKING: 16/66.A, 68

MLW/LOA*: 8'/150'

ELECTRIC: 30 Amp $5.00, 50 amp $8.75

PUMP-OUT: $5.00, free with $50.00 fuel, Pump-out boat

FUEL: Valvtect Diesel/non-ethanol Valvtect Gasoline, pumps 8am – 5pm

REPAIR: Yes

RESTAURANT/MILES: Renowned fresh seafood market and restaurant/0.5 mi

POOL: No

HAUL-OUT: No

HEAD/SHOWER: Yes/Yes

LAUNDRY: Yes

CABLE: Yes, cable TV hookups

SHIP'S STORE: Yes

NEAREST TOWN/MILES: One mile to beach, two miles to town

SHOPPING: Numerous shops and stores

STORAGE: Yes

AIRPORT/MILES: Melbourne Int'l Airport/1 hr; Orlando Int'l/1 hr 45min.

TRANSPORTATION: Yes, free bus service Monday – Saturday

YACHT BROKERAGE: Yes

*MLW = Mean Low Water Depth
LOA = Longest vessel that can be accommodated

COVB.org

LAT: 27° 39' 27.18"N
LON: -80° 22' 8.6772"W

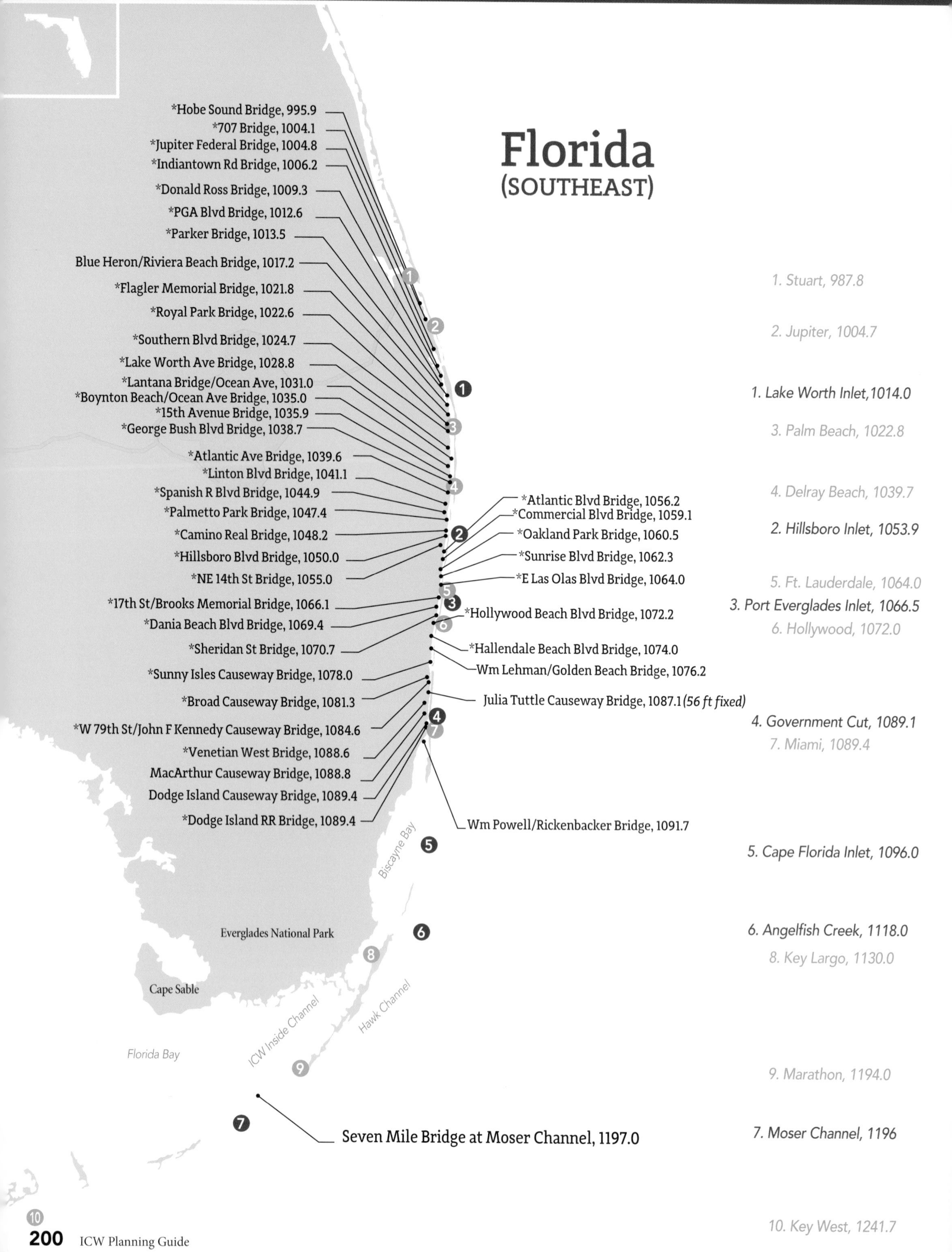

Florida
(SOUTHEAST)

*Hobe Sound Bridge, 995.9
*707 Bridge, 1004.1
*Jupiter Federal Bridge, 1004.8
*Indiantown Rd Bridge, 1006.2
*Donald Ross Bridge, 1009.3
*PGA Blvd Bridge, 1012.6
*Parker Bridge, 1013.5
Blue Heron/Riviera Beach Bridge, 1017.2
*Flagler Memorial Bridge, 1021.8
*Royal Park Bridge, 1022.6
*Southern Blvd Bridge, 1024.7
*Lake Worth Ave Bridge, 1028.8
*Lantana Bridge/Ocean Ave, 1031.0
*Boynton Beach/Ocean Ave Bridge, 1035.0
*15th Avenue Bridge, 1035.9
*George Bush Blvd Bridge, 1038.7
*Atlantic Ave Bridge, 1039.6
*Linton Blvd Bridge, 1041.1
*Spanish R Blvd Bridge, 1044.9
*Palmetto Park Bridge, 1047.4
*Camino Real Bridge, 1048.2
*Hillsboro Blvd Bridge, 1050.0
*NE 14th St Bridge, 1055.0
*17th St/Brooks Memorial Bridge, 1066.1
*Dania Beach Blvd Bridge, 1069.4
*Sheridan St Bridge, 1070.7
Sunny Isles Causeway Bridge, 1078.0
*Broad Causeway Bridge, 1081.3
*W 79th St/John F Kennedy Causeway Bridge, 1084.6
*Venetian West Bridge, 1088.6
MacArthur Causeway Bridge, 1088.8
Dodge Island Causeway Bridge, 1089.4
*Dodge Island RR Bridge, 1089.4

*Atlantic Blvd Bridge, 1056.2
*Commercial Blvd Bridge, 1059.1
*Oakland Park Bridge, 1060.5
*Sunrise Blvd Bridge, 1062.3
*E Las Olas Blvd Bridge, 1064.0
*Hollywood Beach Blvd Bridge, 1072.2
*Hallendale Beach Blvd Bridge, 1074.0
Wm Lehman/Golden Beach Bridge, 1076.2
Julia Tuttle Causeway Bridge, 1087.1 *(56 ft fixed)*
Wm Powell/Rickenbacker Bridge, 1091.7

1. Stuart, 987.8
2. Jupiter, 1004.7
1. Lake Worth Inlet, 1014.0
3. Palm Beach, 1022.8
4. Delray Beach, 1039.7
2. Hillsboro Inlet, 1053.9
5. Ft. Lauderdale, 1064.0
3. Port Everglades Inlet, 1066.5
6. Hollywood, 1072.0
4. Government Cut, 1089.1
7. Miami, 1089.4
5. Cape Florida Inlet, 1096.0
6. Angelfish Creek, 1118.0
8. Key Largo, 1130.0
9. Marathon, 1194.0
7. Moser Channel, 1196
10. Key West, 1241.7

Biscayne Bay
Everglades National Park
Cape Sable
ICW Inside Channel
Hawk Channel
Florida Bay

Seven Mile Bridge at Moser Channel, 1197.0

ICW Mile 995.9
27°06.46' N 081°12.23' W

*Hobe Sound Bridge
Type: Bascule
Closed Height: 21'
Schedule: Opens on request.
Contact: VHF 09 772-546-5234
Comments: Tide board says to add 4' at center. (North board was missing January 2015)

ICW Mile 1004.1
26°95.25' N 080°07.88' W

*707 Bridge
Type: Bascule
Closed Height: 25'
Schedule: Opens on request.
Contact: VHF 09 561-746-4261
Comments: This tide board, too, says add 4' at center.

ICW Mile 1004.8
26°94.75' N 080°08.49' W

*Jupiter Federal Bridge
Type: Bascule
Closed Height: 26'
Schedule: Opens on request.
Contact: VHF 09 561-746-4907
Comments: Tide board says add 4' at center.

ICW Mile 1006.2
26°93.39' N 080°08.40' W

*Indiantown Rd Bridge
Type: Bascule
Closed Height: 35'
Schedule: Opens on the hour and half-hour.
Contact: VHF 09 561-746-7114
Comments: Active Captain notes that a boat needs to do 6 knots to make the opening of the Donald Ross Bridge.

ICW Mile 1009.3
26°88.19' N 080°06.93' W

*Donald Ross Bridge
Type: Bascule
Closed Height: 35'
Schedule: Opens on the hour and half-hour.
Contact: VHF 09 561-626-3030

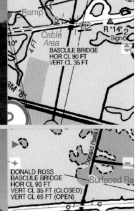

ICW Mile 1012.6
26°84.45' N 80°06.65' W

*PGA Boulevard Bridge
Type: Bascule
Closed Height: 24'
Schedule: Opens on the hour and
half-hour.
Contact: VHF 09 561-624-3684

ICW Mile 1013.7
26°83.15' N 080°06.02' W

*Parker Bridge
Type: Bascule
Closed Height: 25'
Schedule: Opens on the quarter
hour and three-quarter hour.
Contact: VHF 09 561-624-4175

ICW Mile 1017.2
26°78.30' N 080°04.53' W

Blue Heron Bridge
Type: Fixed
Closed Height: 65'

ICW Mile 1021.8
26°71.82' N 080°04.70' W

***Flagler Memorial
Bridge**
Type: Bascule
Closed Height: 17'
Schedule: Please note that due to
construction, Flagler was opening
only at quarter past the hour until
further notice. Otherwise, opens
at quarter past the hour, except at
8:15 a.m. and 4:15 p.m. weekdays.
Contact: VHF 09 561-833-7339

ICW Mile 1022.6
26°70.59' N 080°04.64' W

*Royal Park Bridge
Type: Bascule
Closed Height: 22'
Schedule: Opens on the hour and
half-hour.
Contact: VHF 09 561-655-5617

ICW Mile 1024.7
26°67.54' N 080°04.68' W

***Southern Boulevard
Bridge**
Type: Bascule
Closed Height: 14'
Schedule: Opens on the quarter
hour and three-quarter hour.
Contact: VHF 09 561-833-8852

ICW Mile 1028.8
26°61.54' N 080°04.37' W

***Lake Worth
Avenue Bridge**
Type: Bascule
Closed Height: 35'
Schedule: Opens on demand
(as of May 1, 2015).
Contact: VHF 09 561-540-2516
Comments: This schedule is
subject to change.

ICW Mile 1031.0
26°58.42' N 080°04.55' W

***Lantana Bridge/
Ocean Avenue**
Type: Bascule
Closed Height: 20'
Schedule: Opens on the hour and
half-hour.
Contact: VHF 09 561-233-3977

ICW Mile 1035.0
26°52.71' N 080°05.37' W

***Ocean Avenue Bridge
(Boynton Beach)**
Type: Bascule
Closed Height: 21'
Schedule: Opens on the hour and
half-hour.
Contact: VHF 09 561-733-0214

ICW Mile 1035.8
26°51.45' N 080°05.56' W

*15th Avenue Bridge
Type: Bascule
Closed Height: 21'
Schedule: Opens on request.
Contact: VHF 09 561-732-6461

ICW Mile 1038.7
26°47.40′ N 080°06.21′ W

***George Bush
Boulevard Bridge**
Type: Bascule
Closed Height: 9′
Schedule: Opens on request.
Contact: VHF 09 561-276-5948

ICW Mile 1039.6
26°46.16′N 080°06.39′W

*Atlantic Avenue Bridge
Type: Bascule
Closed Height: 12′
Schedule: Opens on the quarter
hour and three-quarter hour.
Contact: VHF 09 561-276-5435

ICW Mile 1041.1
26°43.98′N 080°06.52′W

***Linton Boulevard
Bridge**
Type: Bascule
Closed Height: 30′
Schedule: Opens on the hour and
half-hour.
Contact: VHF 09 561-278-1980

ICW Mile 1044.9
26°38.63′N 080°07.08′W

***Spanish River
Boulevard Bridge**
Type: Bascule
Closed Height: 25′
Schedule: Opens on the hour and
half-hour.
Contact: VHF 09

ICW Mile 1047.5
26°35.06′N 080°07.56′ W

*Palmetto Park Bridge
Type: Bascule
Closed Height: 15′
Schedule: Opens on the hour and
half-hour.
Contact: VHF 09 561-392-5903

ICW Mile 1048.2
26°33.94'N 080°07.72'W

*Camino Real Bridge
Type: Bascule
Closed Height: 9'
Schedule: Opens on the hour,
20 minutes past the hour and 40
minutes past the hour.
Contact: VHF 09 561-395-7132

ICW Mile 1050.0
26°31.44'N 080°08.09'W

***Hillsboro Boulevard
Bridge**
Type: Bascule
Closed Height: 16'
Schedule: Opens on the hour and
half-hour.
Contact: VFH 09 954-428-1090

ICW Mile 1055.0
26°25.026'N 080°09.003'W

***NE 14th Street
Bridge**
Type: Bascule
Closed Height: 12'
Schedule: Opens on the quarter
hour and three-quarter hour.
Contact: VHF 09 954-942-6909

ICW Mile 1056.0
26°23.18'N 080°09.38'W

***Atlantic Boulevard
Bridge**
Type: Bascule
Closed Height: 15'
Schedule: Opens on the hour and
half-hour.
Contact: VHF 09 954-941-7119

ICW Mile 1059.0
26°18.98'N 080°10.28'W

***Commercial
Boulevard Bridge**
Type: Bascule
Closed Height: 15'
Schedule: Opens on the hour and
half-hour.
Contact: VHF 09 954-772-3987

ICW Mile 1060.5
26°16.74'N 080°10.42'W

*Oakland Park Bridge
Type: Bascule
Closed Height: 22'
Schedule: Opens on the quarter
hour and three-quarter hour.
Contact: VHF 09 954-566-3711

ICW Mile 1062.6
26°13.80'N 080°10.83'W

*Sunrise Blvd Bridge
Type: Bascule
Closed Height: 25'
Schedule: Opens on the hour and
half-hour.
Contact: VHF 09 954-564-6986
Comments: On the first weekend
in May, the bridge is closed from
4 to 6 p.m. and on Saturday from
9:45 to 10:45 p.m.

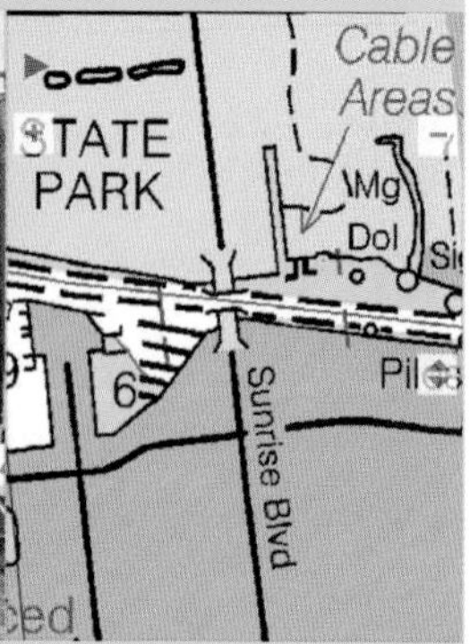

ICW Mile 1064.0
26°11.97'N 080°19.89'W

*E Las Olas
Boulevard Bridge
Type: Bascule
Closed Height: 24'
Schedule: Opens on the quarter-
hour and three-quarter hour.
Contact: VHF 09 954-463-0842
Comments: On the first weekend
in May, the bridge is closed 4 to 6
p.m. and on Saturday from 9:45 to
10:45 p.m.

ICW Mile 1065.9
26°10.06'N 080°11.85'W

*17th Street/Brooks
Memorial Bridge
Type: Bascule
Closed Height: 55'
Schedule: Opens on request on
the hour and half-hour.
Contact: VHF 09 954-524-7783

ICW Mile 1069.4
26°05.31'N 080°11.50'W

*Dania Beach
Boulevard Bridge
Type: Bascule
Closed Height: 22'
Schedule: Opens on the hour and
half-hour.
Contact: VHF 09 954-922-7833

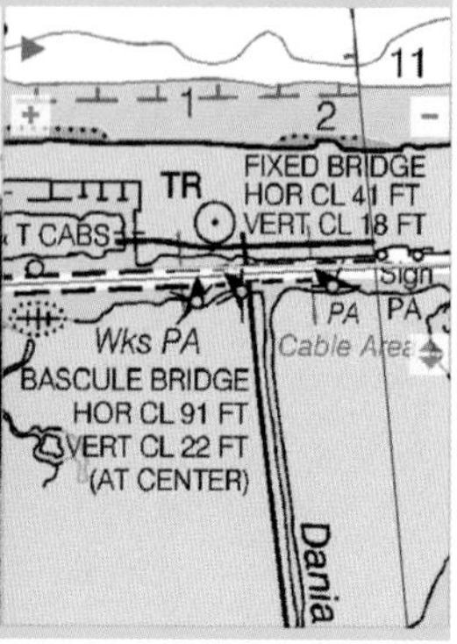

ICW Mile 1070.5
26°03.42'N 080°11.74'W

*Sheridan Street Bridge
Type: Bascule
Closed Height: 22'
Schedule: Opens on the quarter-hour and three-quarter hour.
Contact: VHF 09 954-923-2597

ICW Mile 1072.2
26°01.21'N 080°11.82'W

*Hollywood Beach
Boulevard Bridge
Type: Bascule
Closed Height: 25'
Schedule: Opens on the hour and half-hour.
Contact: VHF 09 954-922-3366

ICW Mile 1074.0
25°98.64'N 080°12.14'W

*Hallandale Beach
Boulevard Bridge
Type: Bascule
Closed Height: 22'
Schedule: Opens on the quarter-hour and three-quarter hour from 7:15 a.m. to 6:15 p.m.
Contact: VHF 09 954-456-6630

ICW Mile 1076.3
25°95.40'N 080°12.57'W

William Lehman/
Golden Beach Bridge
Type: Fixed
Height: 65'

ICW Mile 1078.0
25°92.97'N 080°92.97'W

*Sunny Isles
Causeway Bridge
Type: Bascule
Closed Height: 30'
Schedule: Weekdays, opens on the quarter-hour and three-quarter hour, 7 a.m. to 6 p.m., and on weekends and federal holidays, 10 a.m. to 6 p.m. Other hours, opens on request.
Contact: VHF 09 305-673-7625

ICW Mile 1081.4
25°88.74'N 080°14.24'W

*Broad Causeway Bridge
Type: Bascule
Closed Height: 16'
Schedule: Opens on the quarter-hour and three-quarter hour from 8 a.m. to 6 p.m. Otherwise on request.
Contact: VHF 09 305-866-4633

ICW Mile 1084.6
25°84.79'N 080°17.13'W

*W 79th Street/John F. Kennedy Causeway Bridge
Type: Bascule
Closed Height: 25'
Schedule: Opens on request.
Contact: VHF 09 305-758-1834

ICW Mile 1087.1
25°81.07'N 080°17.65'W

**Julia Tuttle
Causeway Bridge
Type: Fixed
Closed Height: 55'
Comments: Note that this is the lowest fixed bridge on the ICW, 10' below the standard height of 65'.

ICW Mile 1088.6
25°78.98'N 080°18.12'W

*Venetian West Bridge
Type: Bascule
Closed Height: 12'
Schedule: Weekdays from 7 a.m. to 7 p.m., from November 1 to April 30, opens on request on the hour and half-hour. Other times, opens on request.

ICW Mile 1088.8
25°78.73'N 080°18.11'W

MacArthur
Causeway Bridge
Type: Fixed
Height: 65'

ICW Mile

**Dodge Island
Causeway Bridge**
Lat/Lon: 25°77.91'N 080°18.21'W
ICW Mile: 1089.3
Type: Fixed
Height: 65'

ICW Mile

***Dodge Island
RR Bridge**
Lat/Lon: 25°77.91'N 080°18.21'W
ICW Mile: 1072.2
Type: Bascule
Closed Height: 22'
Schedule: Usually open except for
passage of trains.

ICW Mile 1091.6
25°74.64'N 080°18.38'W

**William Powell/
Rickenbacker Bridge**
Type: Fixed   Height: 78
Comments: This is the final bridge
on the official Atlantic ICW.

ICW Mile 1197.0
24°69.96'N 081°16.97'W

**Seven Mile Bridge at
Moser Channel**
Type: Fixed
Height: 63'
Comments: This is the main pas-
sage between the inside route
and Hawk Channel in the Keys. It
is also the main route from Hawk
Channel to the Gulf Coast.

Florida Southeast

Jupiter to Miami	MLW	Transient Slips/Moorings	Floating docks	Gas	Diesel	Pumpout	Showers	Pool	Laundry	Wi-Fi	Haulout	Repairs	Other
Loggerhead Marina Jupiter MM 1006.8 561-747-8980 www.loggerheadjupiter.com	10'		•		•	•	•		•			➤	store, restaurant, canoe/kayak rentals, full-service, concierge
Blowing Rocks Marina Jupiter Sound 561-746-3312 www.blowingrocksmarina.com	4'	•	•	•	•	•			•		•		ship's store, restaurant/tiki bar; non-ethanol gas
Jib Yacht Club and Marina Jupiter Inlet 561-746-3312 www.jibmarinajupiter.com	7.5'		•	•	•	•	•	•				➤	non-ethanol gas
Loggerhead Palm Beach Gardens MM 1009.4 561-627-6358 www.loggerheadpbg.com	8'	•	•	•	•	•			•	•			lounge; cable tv; ship's store
Soverel Harbour Marina MM 1013 561-691-9554 www.soverelmarina.com	7'	•	➤	•	•	•			•		•		walk to restaurants, shops, groceries
Old Port Cove Marina MM 1014/channel mark 27 561-626-1760 www.opch.com	15'	•	•	➤	•	•	•	➤	•	•			On-site restaurant, gym, two bars. Comp. shuttle
North Palm Beach Marina MM 1014 561-626-4919 www.opch.com	8'	•		•	•	•			•		•		restaurant nearby, concierge, cable, marine store, beer
Loggerhead Marina Riviera Beach Lake Worth Inlet 561-840-6868 www.loggerheadrivierabeach.com	6'		•	•	•	•					•	•	ship's store; near Peanut Island Park, beaches
New Port Cove Marine Center MM 1014 561-844-2504 www.opch.com	7'	•	•	•	•	•	•		•	•	•	•	Located across from Lake Worth Inlet and Peanut Island.
Rybovich Marinas & Shipyards MM 1020 561-840-8190 www.rybovich.com	14'	•	•	•	•	•	•		•	•	•	•	superyacht slips, crew campus, concierge service, in-slip fueling
Sailfish Marina Resort Palm Beach Inlet 561-844-1724 www.sailfishmarina.com	8'	•		•	•			•	•	•			closest marina to Lake Worth Inlet; restaurant on-site
Loggerhead Marina Lantana MM 1030 561-582-4422 www.loggerheadlantana.com	6'	•		•	•			•			•	•	ship's store, full-service repairs
Loggerhead Marina South Lantana Boynton Beach Inlet/MM 1031 561-721-3888 www.loggerheadslantana.com	6'	•		•	•			•	•		•	•	ship's store, health club
Palm Beach Yacht Center Between markers 44 and 42 561-588-9911 www.palmbeachyacht.com	5'		•	•	•	•			•	•	•		
Delray Harbor Club Marina Palm Beach/MM 1040 561-276-0376 www.delrayharborclub.com	8'	•		•	•		•	•	•	•		➤	walk to restaurants, shops, car rental, grocery
Boca Raton Resort & Marina MM 1045 561-447-3474 www.lxrluxurymarinas.com	10'	•			•	•	•	•					Cafe on-site, fine dining nearby, small boat rentals, tennis, beach
Lighthouse Point Marina Lake Placid marker 69/MM 1053 954-941-0227 www.lhpmarina.com	7'	•	•	•	•	•	•	•	•	•			closest marina to Hillsboro Inlet; restaurant on-site
Sands Harbor Marina MM 1056 954-942-9100 www.sandsharbor.com	10'	•		•	•	•	•	•	•	•			full-service; fishing supplies, hotel on-site
Hall of Fame Marina Daymarker #11/MM 1063 954-764-3975 www.halloffamemarina.net	59'	•	➤	➤	•	•	•	•	•	•		➤	clean marina, close to restaurants, shopping, beach
Bahia Mar Yachting Center MM 1064/between markers 11 & 13 954-627-6309 www.bahiamaryachtingcenter.com	13'	•		•	•	•	•	•	•	•		•	Concierge, high-speed fuel, restaurants, shop, in-slip pumpout
Las Olas Marina MM 1063 954-828-7200 www.fortlauderdale.gov	12'	•	➤	➤	•	•		•	•				cable TV, gated security, close to attractions and beach
Cooley's Landing New River 954-828-4626 www.fortlauderdale.gov	6'	•	➤	➤	•	•		•	•	•	➤	➤	in the middle of downtown Fort Lauderdale
New River/Downtown Docking New R./MM 1064 954-828-5423 www.fortlauderdale.gov	10'	•	➤	➤	•							➤	walk to grocery, shops, restaurants, cable TV

	MTW	Transient Slips/Moorings	Floating docks	Gas	Diesel	Pumpout	Showers	Pool	Laundry	Wi-Fi	Haulout	Repairs	Other
Marina Bay Marina Resort South New R. 954-791-7600 www.marinabay-fl.com	17'	●	●	●	●	●	●	●	●	●		➤	Pet friendly;tennis, fitness center, restaurant, business center
Lauderdale Marina Ft. Lauderdale/Marker #27 954-523-8507 www.lauderdalemarina.com	8.5'	●		●	●	●	●		➤			●	ethanol-free gas, premium diesel, ship's store
Pier 66 Marina MM 1065 954-728-3578 www.lxrluxurymarinas.com	17'	●	●	●	●	●	●	●	●	●			Newly renovated luxury marina; adjacent to Port Everglades
Hilton Fort Lauderdale Marina Port Everglades/ICW Marker 27 954-728-3578 www.lxrluxurymarinas.com		●	➤	➤		●	●	●	●				Water taxi stop, concierge, fitness center, fine dining
Yacht Haven Park & Marina Southfork/8 mi. from MM 1065 954-583-2322 www.yachthavenpark.com	10'	●	➤	➤	●	●	●	●	●				security gate, shuffleboard, Jungle Queen cruises
Banyan Bay Marina Dania Canal 954-893-0004 www.banyanbaymarina.net	5'	●	➤	➤		●						●	full-service repairs
Harbour Towne Marina Dania Canal 954-926-0300 www.harbourtownemarina.net	6'	●		●	●	●	●		●	●	●	●	5 minutes to Ft. Lauderdale airport
Royale Palm Yacht Basin Dania Canal/MM 1066 954-923-5900 www.royalepalm.com/marina/	6'		➤	➤	●	●		●			●	●	
Loggerhead Marina Hollywood MM 1073 954-457-8557 www.loggerheadhollywood.com	8'	●	➤	➤	●	●	●	●	●			➤	ship's store, sauna, fitness center, concierge service
Loggerhead Marina Aventura MM 1075.2 305-935-4295 www.loggerheadaventura.com	6'	●	➤	➤	●	●	●		●				valet shuttle service; restaurants and shops, groceries adjacent
Turnberry Isle Marina Yacht Club MM 1075.5 305-933-6934 www.turnberryislemarina.com	8'	●	➤	●	●	●	●	●					restaurants, resort on site; 1,600-foot lazy river
Loggerhead Marina South Miami Biscayne Bay/MM 1109 305-258-3500 www.loggerheadmiami.com	7'		●	●	●	●		●			●	●	restaurant, concierge, ship's store, lounge, kayak rentals
Bill Bird Marina at Haulover Park ICW #5/Bakers Haulover Cut 305-947-3525 www.miamidade.gov/parks/bill-bird.asp	8.5'	●		●	●	●	●		●				in Haulover Beach Park; restaurant
Pelican Harbor Marina Biscayne Bay/1084.5 305-754-9330 www.miamidade.gov	6'	●		●	●	●	●						freshwater hookup, sailboat mooring field; dinghy dock
Sea Isle Marina & Yachting Center Biscayne Bay/Miamia/MM 1088 305-377-3625 www.seaislemarina.com	11'	●		●	●	●	●		●	●		➤	convenience & supply store on-site
Crandon Marina Biscayne Bay/MM 1094 305-361-1281 www.miamidade.gov	6'	●		●	●	●	●		●				Crandon Park Beach, sailboat moorings, dive shop,
Sunset Harbour Yacht Club Biscayne Bay/MM 1088.6 305-398-6800 www.sunsetharbouryc.com	8'	●			●	●	●	●	●	●			fitness ctr; groceries, restaurants nearby
Miamarina at Bayside Marker 53/MM 1090 305-960-5180 www.miami-marinas.com	10'	●	➤	➤	●	●			●	●			Bayside Shopping Mall nearby
Miami Beach Marina Miami Beach/Government Cut 305-673-6000 www.miamibeachmarina.com	14'		●	●	●	●	●	●	●	●			Waterfront restaurant, marine store, deli, hair salon, brokerage
Dinner Key Marina Biscayne Bay/MM 1095 305-329-4755 www.miamigov.com/marinas	7'	●	➤	➤	●	●			●	●		➤	24-hr staff/security, US Customs clearing, 2 mi to beach
Matheson Hammock Marina Biscayne Bay 305-665-5475 www.miamidade.gov	5'			●	●	●							Red Fish Grill on-site
Black Point Marina Biscayne Bay/Featherbeds 305-258-4092 www.miamidade.gov	5.5'			●	●	●							dockside restaurant/bar; picnic pavilion
Homestead Bayfront Park & Marina Biscayne Bay/6 mi. S of Featherbeds 305-230-3034 www.miamidade.gov/parks	3.5'	●		●	●	●	●	●				➤	marine store, outdoor storage

Old Port Cove Marina

Old Port Cove Marina

116 Lakeshore Drive,
North Palm Beach, FL 33408
Ph: 561-626-1760 | Fax: 561-626-1249
marinas@opch.com | mmlave@aol.com
OPCH.com

description of facilities

Old Port Cove Marina has been proudly berthing yachts since 1973 in its two on-site basins. Considered a premium 5 star boater rated facility, the marinas feature state-of-the-art floating docks, in-slip pump-out, Wi-Fi and Cable TV. Old Port Cove is a 24-hour gated community that features a resort style marina accommodating vessels to 200'. Located off the ICW at Coast Guard Channel Marker 27; the marina is just minutes north of the Lake Worth Inlet and is a very popular "jumping-off" layover for cruisers headed to the Bahamas. Conversely, this property can easily become the annual or seasonal boater's homeport! A full range of amenities on-site include concierge service, Sandpiper's Cove Restaurant & Bar, a nicely equipped gym, boater's lounge, indoor laundry and complimentary shuttle to West Marine, Doris' Market and Publix Grocery Store. Complimentary use of the Olympic size pool at North Palm Beach Country Club is a treat boaters will enjoy. Make cruising plans today to enjoy all this beautiful facility has to offer.

marina approach & docking

Old Port Cove Marina has two on-site marinas, so please radio the marina office on VHF channel 16/8 for slip assignment. The marina is conveniently located at ICW marker "27", north of the Lake Worth Inlet. Our professional and friendly dock hands will gladly assist you with tying up.

Boat US members will receive a discount on both transient dockage as well as diesel fuel. Contact Mark Lavery, Marina Director or Vincent Frega, Marina Manager. 561-626-1760

LAT: 26° 49' 55.9914"N
LON: -80° 3' 25.236"W

at a glance

DOCKAGE RATE: Daily, Monthly, Seasonal and Annual Rates Available; Please Call for Details

PAYMENT: MC/Visa/Amex/check/cash

HOURS: 8am – 5:30pm Mon-Sat, 9am – 5pm Sunday

TRANSIENT SLIPS/TOTAL SLIPS: 20/200

VHF/WORKING: 16/8

MLW/LOA*: 8'/200'

ELECTRIC: 30/50/100 Amp

PUMP-OUT: At each slip

FUEL: Diesel

REPAIR: Some on-site

PROPANE: Nearby

RESTAURANT/MILES: On-site

POOL: At NPB Country Club

HEAD/SHOWER/LAUNDRY: Yes/Yes/Yes

CABLE: Yes

SHIP'S STORE: Nearby

NEAREST TOWN/MILES: .5 mi

SHOPPING: Nearby

GOLF/TENNIS: .5 mi

STORAGE: Available

AIRPORT/MILES: Palm Beach Int'l/10

TRANSPORTATION: Rental cars available

YACHT BROKERAGE: On-site

SPECIAL: Take the complimentary shuttle to area markets and shops. Designated as a Clean Marina, this facility recycles nearly everything in their commitment to protecting water quality and conserving aquatic ecosystems in the Lake Worth Lagoon.

*MLW = Mean Low Water Depth
LOA = Longest vessel that can be accommodated

North Palm Beach Marina

North Palm Beach Marina

1037 Marina Drive, North Palm Beach, FL 33408
Ph: 561-626-4919 | Fax: 561-626-8857
marinas@opch.com | Jim.Nester@opch.com
OPCH.com

description of facilities

North Palm Beach Marina features beautiful floating docks inset into a quiet, sheltered harbor just off the Intracoastal. No storm evacuations make this marina a very popular home port. Amenities include Cable TV, Wi-Fi, modern electric and pump-outs at each slip. Open seven days a week, the marina has a ships store which sells craft beer, wine, supplies, souvenirs and more. Gas and diesel fuel is pumped alongside the bulkhead or from the floating dock. Marina clients are welcome to enjoy all the amenities at their sister facility, Old Port Cove Marina, which includes casual waterfront dining in Sandpiper's Cove Restaurant & Bar and includes many great fast food options on the go. There is also a nicely equipped gym on site. Located across the highway, marina patrons have complimentary access to the Olympic size swimming pool at North Palm Beach Country Club. There is also a complimentary shuttle which takes boaters to West Marine, the new Doris Market and Publix grocery store. Whether staying long or short term, boaters will love this beautiful marina with quiet floating docks, friendly service and welcoming staff. Welcome Aboard!

marina approach & docking

Located between the north end of Lake Worth and the U.S. Route 1 Parker Bridge, the harbor entrance is on the ICW and is marked with a distinctive A-frame dock office which is open 7 days a week. Our responsible dock agents will cheerfully assist you into one of the 107 slips available for 25′ to 150′ vessels.

From the south: ICW turns westward after ICW marker "27". Marina is located on your left hand side just south of the Parker Bridge. From the north: Pass through the Parker Bridge. Marina is located on your immediate right. Please call Jim Nester and staff for dockage information. (561) 626-4919.

at a glance

DOCKAGE RATE: Daily, Monthly, Seasonal and Annual Rates Available; Please Call for Details

PAYMENT: MC/Visa/Amex

HOURS: Monday – Friday 8:30 -5:30, Sat – Sun 7:30 -5:30

TRANSIENT SLIPS/TOTAL SLIPS: 10/107

VHF/WORKING: 16/8

MLW/LOA*: 8′/150′

ELECTRIC: 30/50/100 Amp

PUMP-OUT: In-slip, sanitary

FUEL: Gas/Diesel

REPAIR: Professional yacht maintenance

POOL: Nearby at North Palm Beach CC

HEAD/SHOWER/LAUNDRY: Yes/With dressing rooms

CABLE/INTERNET: At each slip/WiFi

SHIP'S STORE: Cleaning supplies, mail service, fax, UPS, Fedex agent

NEAREST TOWN/MILES: North Palm Beach

SHOPPING: Within walking distance

GOLF/TENNIS: 18-hole course, driving range/North Palm Beach Country Club

STORAGE: In/out at Palm Beach Inlet

AIRPORT/MILES: Palm Beach Int'l/10

TRANSPORTATION: Rental cars nearby

SPECIAL: Our complimentary shuttle van will take boaters to area markets, West Marine and their company owned restaurant, Sandpiper's Cove R&B, located nearby.

*MLW = Mean Low Water Depth
LOA = Longest vessel that can be accommodated

LAT: 26° 49′ 43.287″N
LON: -80° 3′ 34.6134″W

New Port Cove Marine Center

255 E 22nd Court, Riviera Beach, FL 33403
Ph: 561-844-2504 | 561-863-5086
marinas@opch.com | bruce.grout@oph.com
OPCH.com

description of facilities

New Port Cove Marine Center features a beautiful state-of-the-art dry-stack storage system accommodating 300 vessels to 40′ in length. The facility is further enhanced by a wet-slip marina, comprised of 43 slips for vessels to 70′. A fully stocked marine store is open for your convenience seven days a week with concierge services, laundry and shower facilities. Complimentary morning coffee will help make your stay a pleasant one.

State-of-the-art gas and diesel floating docks, on-site repairs and detailing, make New Port Cove Marine Center, your one-stop boating facility. Located adjacent to the Lake Worth Inlet, world-renowned fishing grounds are literally minutes from the marina via the Lake Worth Inlet. Designated as a Clean Marina, the facility is commited to protecting water quality and conserving aquatic ecosystems in the Lake Worth Lagoon.

New Port's long-term staff are dedicated to providing friendly, exceptional service you can count on with each visit, seven days a week. Open to the public on a first come, first serve basis. Please contact Bruce H. Grout, General Manager, (561) 844-2504 for information.

marina approach & docking

Location, location, location! Located just minutes from Lake Worth Inlet, five blocks south of Blue Heron Bridge on the Intracoastal Waterway. Marked entry channel northwest of famous Peanut Island. Boat U.S. for our transient clients.

at a glance

DOCKAGE RATE: Daily, Monthly, Seasonal and Annual Rates Available; Please Call for Details

PAYMENT: MC/Visa/Amex

HOURS: 7am – 5pm in Season, 8am–6pm in Summer

TRANSIENT SLIPS/TOTAL SLIPS: 43 wet/300+ dry

VHF/WORKING: 16/8

MLW/LOA*: 6.5′/70′

ELECTRIC: 30/50 Amp

PUMP-OUT: Yes

FUEL: Easy access, gas & diesel via state-of-the-art floating docks

REPAIR: Gas/Diesel/Outboard & I/O w/ Mercury, Mercruiser, Yamaha Sales and Service, Honda

POOL: No. Beautiful beaches nearby

HAUL-OUT: Two Wiggins Fork Lifts 22k lb

HEAD/SHOWER/LAUNDRY: Yes/Yes/ Yes

CABLE: Included in most slips, Wifi

SHIP'S STORE: Full marine store, bait, tackle, ice, beer, soda, open 7 days a week, many stores within 1 mile

NEAREST TOWN/MILES: In Riviera Beach

SHOPPING: Within 1 mile

STORAGE: State-of-the-art storage

AIRPORT/MILES: Palm Beach Int'l/10

SPECIAL: BoatUS & MarinaLife members receive transient dockage discount w/ ID card

*MLW = Mean Low Water Depth
LOA = Longest vessel that can be accommodated

LAT: 26° 7782'N
LON: -80° 0514"W

Bring Your Family to Play in the Sport Fishing Capitol of the World

Plantation Yacht Harbor Marina

87000 Overseas Highway,
Islamorada, FL 33036
Ph: 305-852-2381 | Fax: 305-852-5817
Email: marinainfo@islamorada.fl.us
CapeParks.com

description of facilities

Located in the "Sport Fishing Capitol of the World", this 83 slip marina is half-way between Miami Airport and Key West. Within the 48 acres there are 35 acres of open space available for a serene nature walk. The public beach offers water sports galore. Included on site are sports fields, tennis courts, an olympic-size pool and dive complex, a skate park, playground and dog park.

The sheltered harbor offers every amenity. Just offshore of the complex you can enjoy flyfishing the flats of the remarkable Florida Bay or challenge the opposite shore with big game fishing for blue marlin. Dive enthusiasts will be in awe diving the coral reef of one of the seven worldwide wonders of nature.

Enjoy the many restaurants and attractions in the area providing a multitude of alternate entertainment, arts and crafts, boutiques and virtually all the shopping you could want.

marina approach & docking

The marina is located on the Intracoastal Waterway between marker "78" and "78A" with quick and easy access to the Atlantic Ocean or Florida Bay thru Snake Creek. The marina staff will assist with your lines and docking. Advance reservations are recommended. The marina monitors VHF channel 16.

at a glance

DOCKAGE RATE: Transient dockage rate $3.00/ft includes electric, water and pump-out

PAYMENT: MC/Visa/Amex/Discover

HOURS: 8am – 6pm

TRANSIENT SLIPS/TOTAL SLIPS: Call for availability/83

VHF/WORKING: 16

MLW/LOA*: 5'/75'

ELECTRIC: 30/50/100 Amp

PUMP-OUT: At every slip

FUEL: Gas/Diesel

REPAIR: Local mobile mechanics

RESTAURANT/MILES: Nearby

POOL: Yes

HAUL-OUT: No

HEAD/SHOWER: Yes/Yes; all new

LAUNDRY: Yes

INTERNET ACCESS: Free WiFi

CABLE: Yes

SHIP'S STORE: No

NEAREST TOWN/MILES: Islamorada/1

SHOPPING: Nearby

GOLF/TENNIS: Driving range/Yes

AIRPORT/MILES: Neaby

TRANSPORTATION: Available

YACHT BROKERAGE: Nearby

SPECIAL: Sandy beach, boat ramp, city park, acres of open area, five tennis courts, all new docks

*MLW = Mean Low Water Depth
LOA = Longest vessel that can be accommodated

LAT: 24° 57' 37.389"N
LON: -80° 34' 4.9398"W

Florida
(KEYS)

Naples

Ten Thousand Islands

Everglades National Park

Cape Sable

Florida Bay

Biscayne Bay

1 Miami, 1089.4

1 Cape Florida Inlet, 1096.0

2 Angelfish Creek, 1118.0

2 Key Largo, 1130.0

3 Marathon, 1194.0

3 Moser Channel, 1196

Seven Mile Bridge at Moser Channel, 1197.0

ICW Inside Channel

Hawk Channel

4 Key West, 1241.7

ICW Mile 995.9
27°06.46' N 081°12.23' W

*Hobe Sound Bridge
Type: Bascule
Closed Height: 21'
Schedule: Opens on request.
Contact: VHF 09 772-546-5234
Comments: Tide board says to
add 4' at center. (North board was
missing January 2015)

* Denotes opening bridge
** Denotes 55' fixed bridge

Florida Keys

Marina	MLW	Transient Slips/Moorings	Floating docks	Gas	Diesel	Pumpout	Showers	Pool	Laundry	Wi-Fi	Haulout	Repairs	Other
Gilbert's Resort Marina Jewfish Creek Bridge/MM 1134 305-451-1133 www.gilbertsresort.com	10'	●		●	●		●	●	●	●			motel, tiki bar on site
Anchorage Resort & Yacht Club Key Largo/MM 1134 305-451-0500 www.floridakeys.net/anchorageresort	8'	●					●	●	●	●			snorkeling, diving, resort hotel on-site; condo apts for rent
Marina Del Mar Resort and Marina Key Largo 305-453-7171 www.keylargomarina.com	4.5'	●	➤	➤			●	●	●	●		➤	4 pools, jacuzzi, fitness ctr, tennis
Pilot House Marina Hawks Channel/MM 1144 305-451-3142 www.pilothousemarina.com	4.5'	●		●	●	●	●	●	●	●			Pilot House Restaurant on-site
Boatman's Mangrove Marina Gulf Side/marker 91.7/MM 1149 305-852-8380 www.mangrovemarina.com	4'	●		●	●			●	●	●	●	●	full-service marina, ship's store, sheltered cove
Plantation Yacht Harbor Marina Islamorada/Btwn 78/78A/MM 1155/ 305-852-2381 www.pyh.com	5'	●		●	●	●	●	●	●	●		➤	located in 42-acre park; cable tv, tennis, beach, playground
Smugglers Cove Resort and Marina Islamorada/ICW 78A/MM 1156 305-664-3636 www.smugglerscoveislamorada.com	5'	●		●	●		●					●	Ship's store; pet-friendly; resort hotel; restaurant/tiki bar
Hawks Cay Resort & Marina Duck Key/MM 1180 305-743-9000, option 2 www.hawkscay.com	5'	●		●	●	●	●	●	●	●		➤	restaurants, attractions on-site; fishing, diving trips
Key Colony Beach Marina Key Colony Beach/marker 53 305-289-1310	6'	●		●	●	●		➤		●		➤	➤	Restaurant, marine supplies
Pancho's Marina and Fuel Dock Marathon/Boot Key Harbor 305-743-2281	8'	●		●	●	●	●						groceries, ice, tackle; restaurant, motel nearby
Burdines Waterfront Boot Key Harbor 305-743-5317 www.burdineswaterfront.com	8'	●		●	●	●			●				Restaurant, bait, beer, boating accessories
Sombrero Marina & Dockside Marathon/Boot Key Harbor/MM 1192 305-743-5663 www.sombreromarina.com	6'	●	➤	➤	●	●	➤	●	●			➤	groceries, restaurant nearby
Sombrero Resort & Marina Marathon/Marker 50/Gulf Side 305-289-7662 www.sombreroresortmarina.com	4'	●			●	●	●	●	●	●			resort amenities, restaurants, tiki bar, cable tv
Boot Key Harbor City Marina Marathon Harbor/MM 1194 305-289-8877 www.ci.marathon.fl.us	20'	●	➤	➤	●	●			●				226 moorings, restaurants, groceries marine supplies nearby
Marathon Marina and RV Resort Boot Key Harbor/MM 1195 305-743-6575 www.marathonmarinaandresort.com	9'	●		●	●	●	●	●	●	●	●	●	lounge, cable, in-slip pumpout, ship's store
Bahia Honda State Park & Marina S. of 7 mile bridge/MM 1204.9 305-872-3210 www.bahiahondapark.com	3.5'	●				●	●						diving charters, ice, snacks, state park
Little Palm Island Resort Newfound Harbor 305-872-2524 www.littlepalmisland.com	6'	●	➤	➤			●	●	●				
Oceanside Marina Stock Island/MM 1237 305-294-4676 www.oceansidekeywest.com	12'	●		●	●	●	●		●	●		●	restaurant on-site, cable TV,
Safe Harbour Marina Stock Island 305-294-9797 www.safeharbourmarinakw.com	10'	●	➤	➤	●	●	●	●	●	●			Hogfish Restaurant; fish market
Stock Island Marina Village Stock Island/MM 1237 305-294-2288	20'	●	●	●	●		●			●	●		ship's store, courtesy car, restaurant, pet-friendly
Sunset Marina Stock Island/MM 1239 305-296-7101 www.sunsetmarinakw.com	9'	●	●	●	●	●	●		●	●	●		entrance to Key West/Atlantic Ocean; Ship's store
Garrison Bight Marina Key West/MM1243 304-294-3093 www.garrisonbightmarina.net	6'	●			●							●	●	dry storage, repairs; restaurant on-site
Key West Bight Marina Key West/MM 1243 305-809-3984 www.cityofkeywest-fl.gov	12'	●		●	●	●	●		●	●			Historic Seaport, ferries to Fort Jefferson

Marina	MLW	Transient Slips/Moorings	Floating docks	Gas	Diesel	Pumpout	Showers	Pool	Laundry	Wi-Fi	Haulout	Repairs	Other
Conch Harbor Marina Key West/MM 1243.5 305-294-2933 www.conchharbormarina.com	12'	•		•	•	•	•	•	•	•			Walk to Duvall St. Non-ethanol gas, in-slip pump-out
A & B Marina Key West/MM 1245 305-294-2535 www.aandbmarina.com	10'	•	➤	•	•	•			•	•			water, cable tv, heart of Key West
City Marina at Garrison Bight Key West Bight/MM 1245 305-809-3981 www.keywestcity.com	12'	•	•	•	•	•	•	•			➤		
The Galleon Marina Key West/Gulf side 305-292-1292 www.galleonmarinakeywest.com	9'	•	➤	➤	•	•	•	•	•	•			24-hr. security, fresh water at slip, tiki bar, private beach
Westin Key West Resort and Marina Key West 305-292-4313 www.westin.com/keywest	14'	•	•	➤	➤	•	•	•	•	•			restaurants, groceries, fitness room, hotel

Marco Island to Captiva Island

Marina	MLW	Transient Slips/Moorings	Floating docks	Gas	Diesel	Pumpout	Showers	Pool	Laundry	Wi-Fi	Haulout	Repairs	Other
Marco Island Marina Capri Pass 239-642-2531 www.marcoislandmarina.com	7'	•	➤	➤	•	•	•	•	•	•			Close to town, taxi service avail.; Cable TV
Pelican Pier Marina Marco Isl./Big Marco Pass 239-389-2628	12'			•	➤								
Pelican Bend Marina Johnson Bay 239-394-3452 www.pelicanbendinc.com	5'	•		•	•								restaurant
Naples City Dock Gordon River/Naples City Bay 239-213-3070 www.craytoncove.com/marina.htm	7'	•		•	•	•	•			•		➤	
Marina at Naples Bay Resort East Naples/Gordon R. 239-530-5134 www.naplesbayresort.com/marina	5.5'	•	➤	➤	•	•	•	•	•	•			Resort Hotel wtih restaurant, concierge, shuttle service
Naples Boat Club Marina Gordon River Red Marker #40 239-263-2774 www.naplesboatclub.com	8'	•	•	•	•	•	•	•	•	•	•	•	groceries, restaurants nearby
Snook Bight Marina Estero Bay/Fort Myers Beach 239-765-4371 www.snookbightmarina.com	7'	•	•	•	•	•	•	•				•	restaurant, ship's store
Chokoloskee Island Park Chokoloskee Bay 239-695-2414 www.chokoloskee.com/marina.htm	3.5'	•	➤	➤			•		•				
Salty Sams Marina San Carlos Bay 239-463-7333 www.saltysamsmarina.com	6'	•		•	•	•	•		•	•	•	•	2 restaurants, full repair shop, minutes to beaches, shopping
Sanibel Marina Sanibel Island 239-472-2723 www.sanibelmarina.com	6'	•		•	•	•	•		•	•	•	•	restaurant, newly dredged inlet, sightseeing trips
York Road Marine San Carlos Bay/Pine Isl. Snd/marker 13 239-283-1149 www.yorkroadmarine.com	3.5'	•								•	•	•	full service repairs, power, sail, diesel, inboard, outboard
South Seas Island Resort Marina Captiva Isl./Gr marker 39/Redfish Pass 888-777-3625 www.southseas.com/marinas-en.html	5.5'	•		•	•	•	•	•	•				resort marina, restaurants, ethanol-free gas, ship's store
Tween Waters Inn & Marina Captiva Island 800-223-5865 www.tween-waters.com	5'	•		•	•	•	•	•	•				resort hotel, restaurants, shopping, beach
Pineland Marina Pine Island Sound/Marker 2 239-283-3593 www.pinelandmarina.com	3'			•	•								ship's store, ferry services, water taxi; launch ramp
Jug Creek Marina Pine Island 239-283-3331	3'	•		•	•			•				•	groceries, restaurants, shops nearby

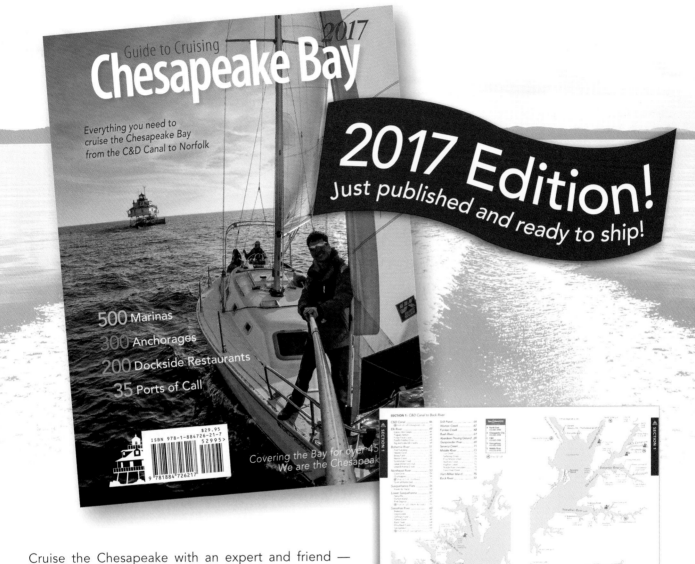
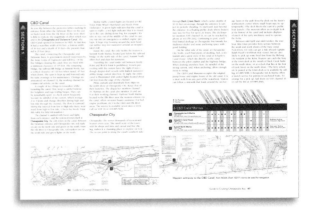

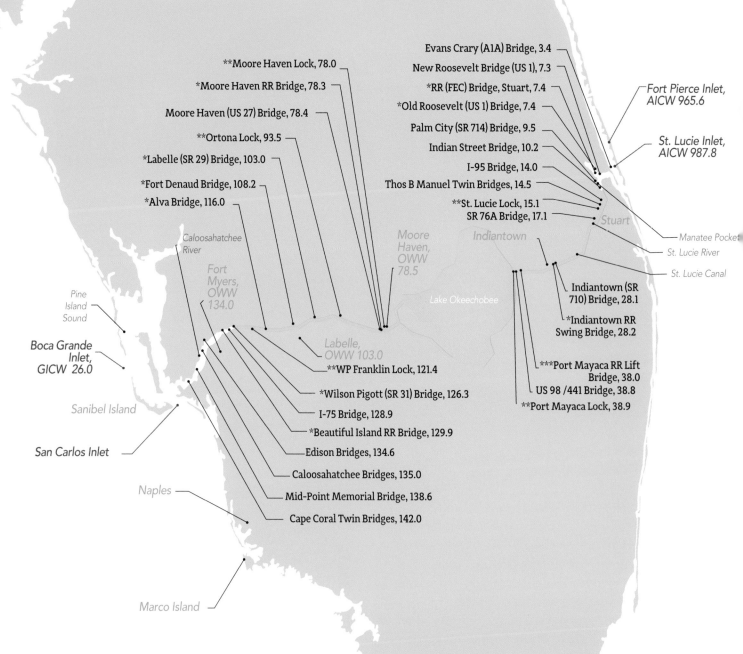

Florida
(OKEECHOBEE WATERWAY)

**Moore Haven Lock, 78.0
*Moore Haven RR Bridge, 78.3
Moore Haven (US 27) Bridge, 78.4
**Ortona Lock, 93.5
*Labelle (SR 29) Bridge, 103.0
*Fort Denaud Bridge, 108.2
*Alva Bridge, 116.0

Evans Crary (A1A) Bridge, 3.4
New Roosevelt Bridge (US 1), 7.3
*RR (FEC) Bridge, Stuart, 7.4
*Old Roosevelt (US 1) Bridge, 7.4
Palm City (SR 714) Bridge, 9.5
Indian Street Bridge, 10.2
I-95 Bridge, 14.0
Thos B Manuel Twin Bridges, 14.5
**St. Lucie Lock, 15.1
SR 76A Bridge, 17.1

Fort Pierce Inlet,
AICW 965.6

St. Lucie Inlet,
AICW 987.8

Caloosahatchee
River

Fort
Myers,
OWW
134.0

Moore
Haven,
OWW
78.5

Indiantown

Stuart

Manatee Pocket

St. Lucie River

St. Lucie Canal

Pine
Island
Sound

Lake Okeechobee

Indiantown (SR
710) Bridge, 28.1

*Indiantown RR
Swing Bridge, 28.2

Boca Grande
Inlet,
GICW 26.0

Labelle,
OWW 103.0

**WP Franklin Lock, 121.4

Sanibel Island

*Wilson Pigott (SR 31) Bridge, 126.3

***Port Mayaca RR Lift
Bridge, 38.0
US 98 /441 Bridge, 38.8
**Port Mayaca Lock, 38.9

I-75 Bridge, 128.9

San Carlos Inlet

*Beautiful Island RR Bridge, 129.9

Edison Bridges, 134.6

Caloosahatchee Bridges, 135.0

Naples

Mid-Point Memorial Bridge, 138.6

Cape Coral Twin Bridges, 142.0

Marco Island

* Denotes opening bridge
** Denotes lock

OWW Mile 3.4
27°19.892′ N 080°20.773′ W

Evans Crary Bridge
Type: Fixed
Height: 65′

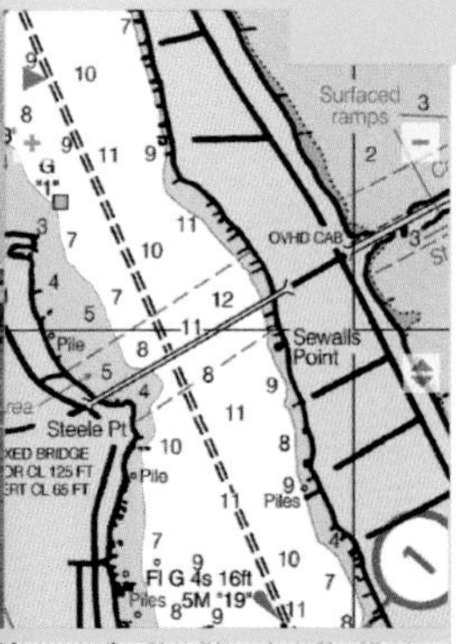

OWW Mile 7.3
27° 12.311′ N 080° 15.521′ W

New Roosevelt Bridge
Type: Fixed
Height: 65′

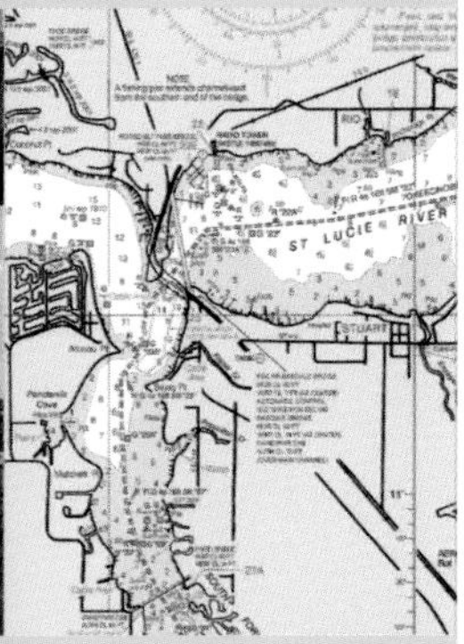

OWW Mile 7.4
27°12.220′ N 80° 15.607′ W

*Florida East Coast RR Bridge
Type: Bascule
Closed Height: 7′
Schedule: Open except for trains. Signal will change from green to red and horn will sound four blasts, pause, then repeat. Eight minutes later, bridge will lower.

OWW Mile 7.4
27°25.33′ N 80°21.87′ W

*Old Roosevelt Bridge
Type: Bascule *Closed Height:* 14′
Schedule: Monday-Friday, 7 a.m. to 6 p.m., opens on the hour and half hour, except from 7:30 to 9 a.m. and 4 to 5:30 p.m., when it opens at 8:15 a.m. and 4:45 p.m. Other times on demand. On weekends and holidays, from 8 a.m. to 6 p.m., opens on the hour and 20 and 40 minutes after. Bridge won't open on schedule when train is passing, but will open directly afterward.

Contact: VHF 09 772-692-0321

OWW Mile 9.5
27° 10.452' N 080° 15.653' W

Palm City (S.R. 714)
Type: Fixed
Height: 54'

OWW Mile 10.2
27°15.916' N 080°25.182' W

Indian Street Bridge
Type: Fixed
Height: 55'

OWW Mile 14.0
27°15.995' N 080°27.017' W

I 95 Twin Bridges
Type: Fixed
Height: 56'

OWW Mile 14,5
27°11.767' N 080°27.476' W

Florida Tpke Bridges
Type: Fixed
Height: 55'

OWW Mile 15.1
27°11.168' N 080°28.442' W

**St. Lucie Lock
Schedule: On request from 7 a.m.
to 5 p.m. During periods of low
water, however, openings may be
restricted only a few times a day
Contact: VHF 13 772-287-2665

OWW Mile 17.1
27°08.795' N 080°30.205' W

S.R. 76A Bridge
Type: Fixed
Height: 56'

OWW 28.1
27°01.231' N 080°45.490' W

Indiantown/S.R. 710 Bridge
Type: Fixed
Height: 55'

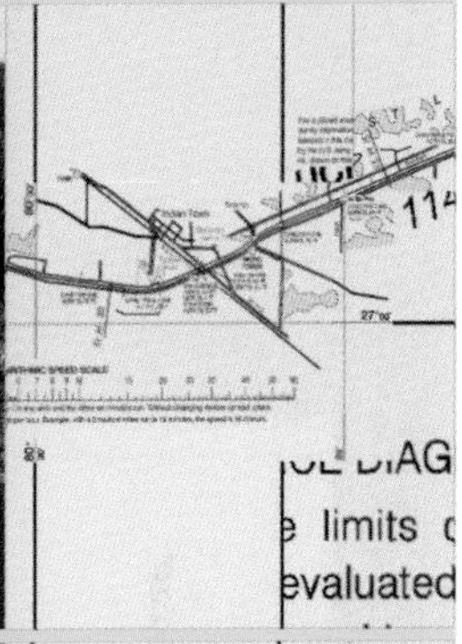

OWW 28.2
27°01.189' N 080°45.611' W

*Indiantown RR Bridge
Type: Swing
Closed Height: 7'
Schedule: Open except for passage of trains. Or will open on signal, except from 10 p.m. to 6 a.m., when it requires three hours notice.
Contact: VHF 09

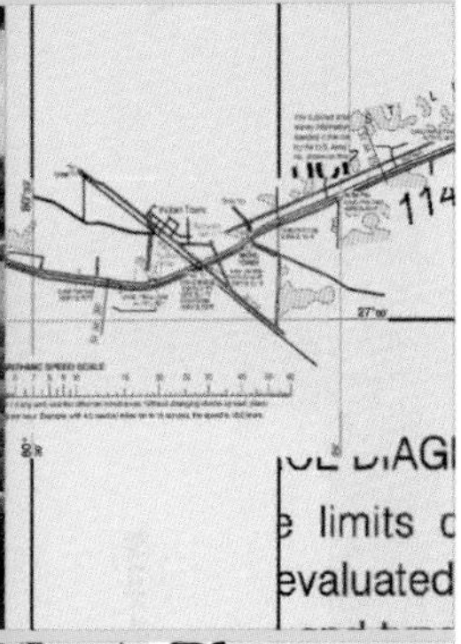

OWW 38
27°98.738' N 080°60.423' W

*****Port Mayaca RR
Lift Bridge**
Type: Lift
Closed Height: 49'
Schedule: Open except for passage of trains.
Contact: VFH 09
Comments: Note that this bridge has only 49' clearance and establishes the controlling height for the Okeechobee Waterway.

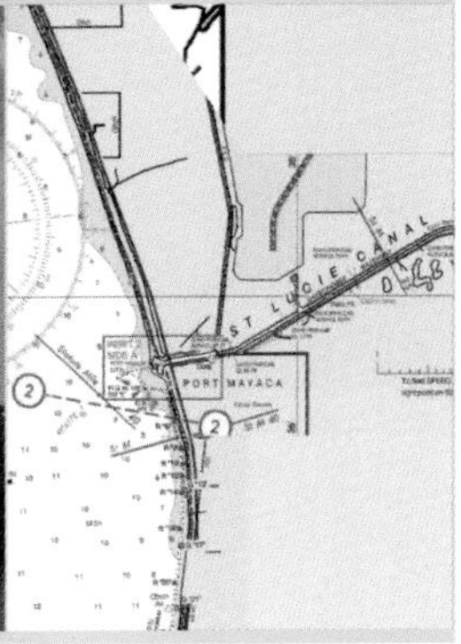

OWW Mile 38.8
26°98.532' N 080°61.703' W

Highway 98 Bridge
Type: Fixed
Height: 55'

OWW 38.9
26°98.451' N 080°62.027' W

**Port Mayaca Lock
Schedule: On request from 7 a.m. to 5 p.m. During high water this lock often remains open; during low water the openings may be reduced.
Contact: VHF 13 561-924-2858
Comments: Check the Lake Okeechobee water levels at *w3.saj.usace.army.mil/h2o/currentLL.shtml.*

OWW 78.0
26°83.938' N 081°08.723' W

Moore Haven Lock
Schedule: Opens on request 7 a.m. to 5 p.m.
Contact: VHF 13 896-946-0414
Comments: High winds can make locking difficult since there is no protection, especially for westbound boats. Tie up on the downwind wall, if possible.

OWW 78.3
26°83.500' N 081°08.842' W

*Seaboard RR Bridge
Type: Swing
Closed Height: 5'
Schedule: Open except for passage of trains, except from 10 p.m. to 6 a.m., when it doesn't have to open for boats. If closed, opens (by hand) on signal.
Contact: VHF 09

OWW 78.4
26°83.303' N 081°08.870' W

U.S. 27/Moore Haven Twin Bridges
Type: Fixed
Height: 55'

OWW 93.5
26°78.922' N 081°30.487'

**Ortona Lock
Schedule: Opens on request, 7 a.m. to 5 p.m.
Contact: VHF 13 863-675-0616
Comments: Watch for bad turbulence in the lock.

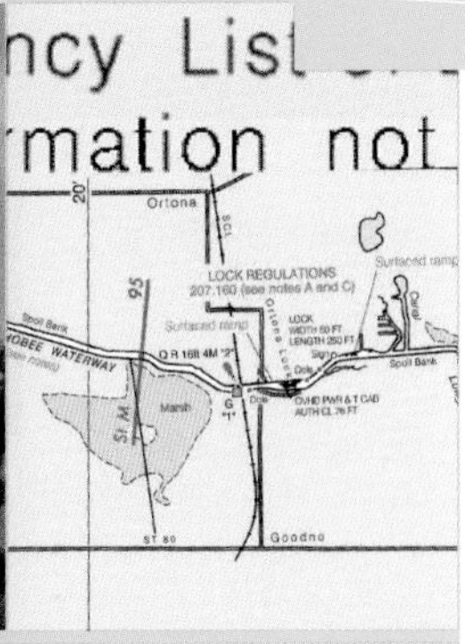

OWW 103
26°76.919' N 081°43.742' W

*LaBelle Highway Bridge
Type: Bascule
Closed Height: 28'
Schedule: Opens on request, except Monday-Friday from 7 to 9 a.m. and 4 to 6 p.m., when it need not open. From 10 p.m. to 6 a.m. requires 3 hours notice.
Contact: VHF 09 866-335-9696

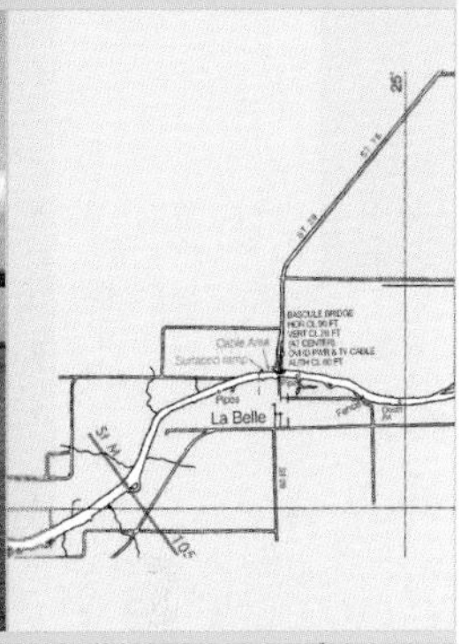

OWW 108.2
26°74.477' N 081°51.037' W

***Fort Denaud/
S.R. 78AW**
Type: Swing
Closed Height: 9'
Schedule: On request from 6 a.m. to 10 p.m. Later openings require 3 hour notice.
Contact: VHF 09 863-675-2055
Comments: Bridgetender must walk out to controls located at bridge's pivot point.

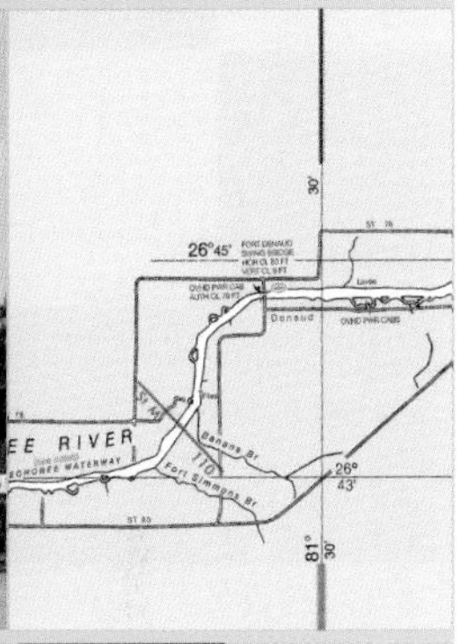

OWW 116
26°71.345' N 081°60.998' W

*Alva/Broadway Bridge
Type: Bascule
Closed Height: 23'
Schedule: Opens on request from 6 a.m. to 10 p.m. Later openings require 3 hour notice.
Contact: VHF 09

OWW 121.4
26°72.168' N 081°69.355' W

**W.P. Franklin Lock
Schedule: On request from 7 a.m. to 5 p.m. Fewer openings (usually ever 2 hours) during low water.
Contact: VHF 13 239-694-5451

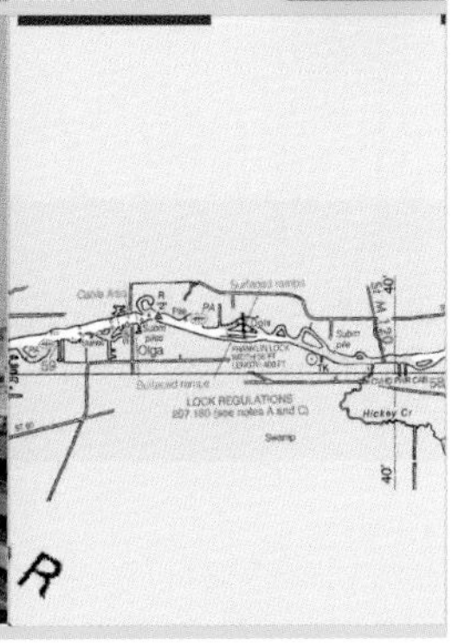

OWW 126.3
26°71.628' N 081°76.058' W

*Wilson Pigott Bridge
Type: Bascule
Closed Height: 27'
Schedule: On request from 6 a.m. to 10 p.m. Otherwise 3 hours notice required.
Contact: VHF 09 239-656-7800

OWW 128.9
26°69.737' N 081°79.927' W

I-75 Twin Bridges
Type: Fixed
Height: 55'

OWW 129.9
26°69.503' N 081°81.500' W

*SCL RR Bridge
Type: Lift
Closed Height: 5'
Schedule: Open except for trains.

OWW 134.6
26°65.162' N 081°86.800 W

Edison Bridges
Type: Fixed
Height: 55'

OWW 135
26°64.602' N 081°87.495' W

Caloosahatchee Bridge
Type: Fixed
Height: 55'

OWW 138.6
26°60.091' N 081°90.078' W

Veterans Memorial/Mid-Point Bridge
Type: Fixed
Height: 55'

OWW 142
26°56.043' N 081°92.715' W

Cape Coral Bridge
Type: Fixed
Height: 53'

Florida Okeechobee Waterway

Okeechobee Waterway	MLW	Transient Slips/Moorings	Floating docks	Gas	Diesel	Pumpout	Showers	Pool	Laundry	Wi-Fi	Haulout	Repairs	Other
Roland and Mary Ann Martins Marina Lake Okeechobee Waterway 863-983-3151 www.rolandmartinmarina.com	8'		●	●	●	●	●	●	●				courtesy car to nearby shops; restaurant on-site
Marinatown Yacht Harbour Caloosahatchee R./Marker 52 239-997-2767 www.marinatown.net	5'	●	➤	➤	●	●	●	●	●			●	restaurants nearby
Prosperity Pointe Marina Caloosahatchee R./red 40 239-995-2155 www.prosperitypointemarina.com	4.5'	●	●	➤	➤	●	●	➤	●	●		➤	storage area for RVs, trailers
Fort Myers Yacht Basin Caloosahatchee R./Okeech. MM 135 239-321-7080 www.cityftmyers.com	6'	●		●	●	●	●		●	●		●	restaurants nearby, next to Centennial Park
Legacy Harbour Marina Okeechobee Waterway/Marker 49 239-461-0775 www.legacyharbourmarina.com	7'	●	●	➤	➤	●	●	●	●	●			near downtown River District w/shops, restaurants, grocery
The Marina at Edison Ford Okeechobee WW/Marker 54 239-245-7320 www.marinaedisonford.com	7'	●			●	●	●		➤	●			walk to grocery, shopping and downtown Ft. Myers
City of Cape Coral Yacht Basin Caloosahatchee R./marker78A 239-574-0809 www.capecoral.net	5'	●		●	●	●	●	●	●			●	beach, fishing pier, boat ramp, restaurant nearby
Gulf Harbour Marina Caloosahatchee R./btw marks 73 & 74 239-437-0881 www.gulfharbourmarina.net	6'	●	●	●	●	●	●		●			●	
Tarpon Point Marina Caloosahatchee River/MM 92 239-549-4900 www.tarponpointmarina.com	8'	●	●	●	●	●	●	●	●	➤	●		

Cedar Key

Homosassa Springs

1. *Anclote Keys, 150.0*

*Honeymoon Island Bridge, 141.9

2. *Dunedin, 140.5*

Clearwater Memorial Causeway, 136.0

3. *Clearwater, 135.5*

1. *Clearwater Pass, 135.5*

*Welch Causeway, 122.8

*Treasure Island Causeway Bridge 119.0

*Corey Causeway Bridge, 117.7

4. *St. Petersburg, 115.0*

2. *Tampa Bay Inlet, 95.0*

Pinellas Bayway "C" Bridge, 114.0

*Pinellas Bayway "E" Bridge, 113.0

5. *Anna Marina Island, 88.7*

Dick Misener Bridge, 110.5

*Cortez Bridge, 87.4

6. *Sarasota, 73.0*

*Albee Road/Casey Key Bridge, 59.3

3. *Venice Inlet, 60.5*

*Hatchett Creek Bridge, 57.0

*Venice Avenue Bridge, 56.5

7. *Venice, 56.0*

*Circus/Tamiami Bridge, 55.0

*Manasota Bridge, 50.0

*Tom Adams Key Bridge, 43.5

*Boca Grande Swing Bridge, 34.3

8. *Boca Grande, 28.0*

4. *Boca Grande Pass, 26.0*

9. *Sanibel Island, 5.0*

5. *San Carlos Bay Inlet*

Belleair Beach Causeway Bridge, 131.8

*Indian Rocks Beach Bridge, 129.3

*Park Boulevard Bridge, 126.0

Tampa

Sunshine Skyway Bridge, 99.0

*Anna Maria Island Bridge, 89.2

Ringling Causeway, 73.6

*Siesta Key Bridge, 71.6

*Stickney Point Bridge, 68.6

*Blackburn Point Swing Bridge, 63.0

Sarasota Bay

Punta Gorda

Charlotte Harbor

Gasparilla Sound

Pine Island Sound

Fort Myers

Naples

Marco Island

* Denotes opening bridge

GICW Mile 34.3
26°82.697'N 82°27.012'W

*Boca Grande Causeway Bridge
Type: Swing
Closed Height: 22'
Schedule: Weekdays, hour and half-hour, 7 a.m. -6 p.m.; weekends opens every 15 minutes.
Contact: VHF 9; 941-697-2271
Comments: Construction equipment may still be in place.

GICW Mile 43.5
26°93.443'N 82°35.305'W

*Tom Adams Key Bridge
Type: Bascule
Closed Height: 24'
Schedule: On request
Contact: VHF 9

GICW Mile 50.0
27°01.163'N 82°41.000'W

*Mansota Bridge
Type: Bascule
Closed Height: 23'
Schedule: On request.
Contact: VHF 9

GICW Mile 55.0
27°07.865'N 82°43.015'W

*Circus Bridge
Type: Bascule
Closed Height: 25'
Schedule: On request.
Contact: VHF 9
Comments: Watch tide board for actual closed clearance.

GICW Mile 56.6
27°09.983'N 82°44.072'W

***Venice Avenue Bridge**
Type: Bascule
Closed Height: 30'
Schedule: Weekdays at 10, 30 and 50 minutes after the hour; no openings 4:35-5:35 p.m.
Contact: VHF 9

GICW Mile 56.9
27°10.330'N 82°44.412'W

***Hatchett Creek Bridge**
Type: Bascule
Closed Height: 30'
Schedule: Weekdays, 7 a.m.-4:20 p.m., opens on hour then every 20 minutes; no openings 4:25-5:25 p.m. Weekends, 7:30 a.m.-6 p.m., opens on hour and every 15 minutes.
Contact: VHF 9

GICW Mile 59.3
27°12.450'N 82°46.915'w

***Albee Road Bridge**
Type: Bascule
Closed Height: 12'
Schedule: On request.
Contact: VHF 9

GICW Mile 63.0
27°17.990'N 82°49.430'W

***Blackburn Point Bridge**
Type: Swing
Closed Height: 9'
Schedule: On demand.
Contact: VHF 9
Comments: Slow to open.

GICW Mile 68.6
27°25.437'N 82°53.137'W

Stickney Point Bridge
Type: Bascule
Closed Height: 18'
Schedule: Weekdays on hour then every 20 minutes. Weekdays on request.
Contact: VHF 9
Comments: 3' more at center.

GICW Mile 71.6
27°30.268'N 82°54.548'W

*Siesta Key Bridge
Type: Bascule
Closed Height: 22'
Schedule: Openings 7 a.m.-6 p.m., on the hour then every 20 minutes
Contact: VHF 9
Comments: 4' more at center.

GICW Mile 73.6
27°33.162'N 82°55.665'W

Ringling Causeway Bridge
Type: Fixed
Height: 65'

GICW Mile 87.4
27°46.890'N 82°69.222'W

*Cortez Bridge
Type: Bascule
Closed Height: 22'
Schedule: Jan. 15-May 15, 7 a.m.-6 p.m., on the hour and half-hour. May 16-Jan. 14, 6 a.m.-7 p.m., on the hour then every 20 minutes.
Contact: VHF 9

GICW Mile 89.2
27°49.675'N 82°69.467'W

*Anna Maria Island Bridge
Type: Bascule
Closed Height: 23'
Schedule: Jan. 15-May 15, 7 a.m.-6 p.m., on the hour and half-hour. May 16-Jan. 14, 6 a.m.-7 p.m., on the hour then every 20 minutes.
Contact: VHF 9

GICW Mile 99.0
27°61.897'N 82°65.435'W

Sunshine Skyway Bridge
Type: Fixed
Height: 175'

GICW Mile 110.5
27°41.563'N 82°40.737'W

Dick Misener (Maximo Pt) Bridge
Type: Fixed
Height: 65'

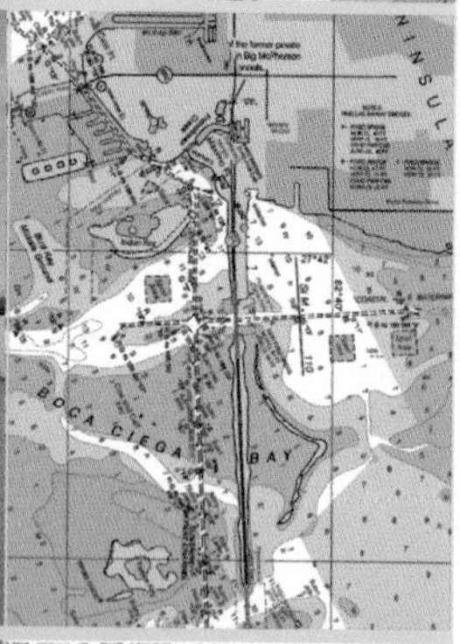

GICW Mile 113
27°41.610'N 82°43.075'W

***Pinellas Bayway Southern E Span**
Type: Bascule
Closed Height: 25'
Schedule: Weekdays opens on hour and half-hour except 2-6 p.m. Friday. Weekends on hour and half-hour. Otherwise on demand.
Contact: VHF 9

GICW Mile 114.0
27°42.575'N 82°43.505'W

Pinellas Bayway Northern C Span
Type: Fixed
Height: 64'

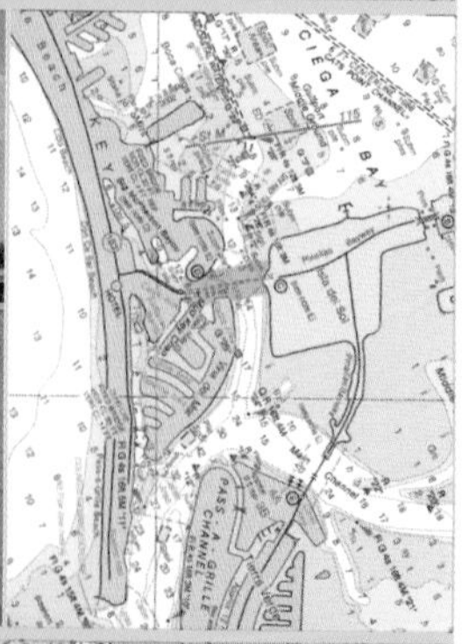

GICW Mile 117.7
27°44.766'N 82°44.774'W

***Corey Causeway Bridge**
Type: Bascule
Closed Height: 23'
Schedule: Weekdays 8 a.m.-7 p.m., and weekends 10 a.m.-7 p.m., opens on hour then every 20 minutes.
Contact: VHF 9

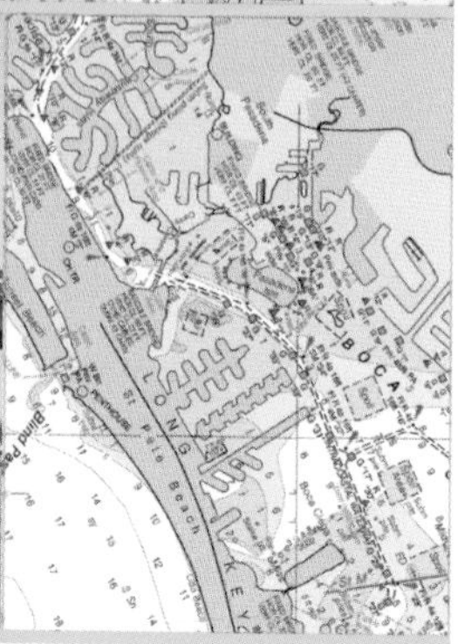

GICW Mile 119
27°46.239'N 82°45.202'W

*Treasure Island Bridge
Type: Bascule
Closed Height: 23'
Schedule: Weekdays 7 a.m.-7 p.m., opens on the hour then every 20 minutes. Weekends on the hour then every 15 minutes.
Contact: VHF 9

GICW Mile 122.8
27°48.422'N 82°47.694'W

*Welch Causeway Bridge
Type: Bascule
Closed Height: 25'
Schedule: On request
Contact: VHF 9

GICW Mile 126.0
27°50.636'N 82°50.292'W

*Park Avenue Bridge
Type: Bascule
Closed Height: 20'
Schedule: On request.

GICW Mile 129.3
27°53.009'N 82°50.720'

*Indian Rocks Beach Bridge
Type: Bascule
Closed Height: 25'
Schedule: On request.
Contact: VHF 9

GICW Mile 131.8
27°55.016'N 82°49.844'

Bellair Beach Causeway Bridge
Type: Fixed
Height: 74'

GICW Mile 136.0
27°57.977'N 82°48.335'W

Clearwater Causeway Bridge
Type: Fixed
Height: 74'

GICW Mile 141.9
28°03.067'N 82°47.722'W

*Honeymoon Island Bridge
Type: Bascule
Closed Height: 24'
Schedule: On request.
Contact: VHF 9; 727-738-2939

Florida Eastern Gulf

Punta Gorda to Tarpon Springs

	MLW	Transient Slips/Moorings	Floating docks	Gas	Diesel	Pumpout	Showers	Pool	Laundry	Wi-Fi	Haulout	Repairs	Other
Burnt Store Marina — Charlotte Harbor — 941-637-0083 www.burntstoremarina.com	6'	●		●	●	●	●	●	●			●	
Fisherman's Village Marina — Charlotte Harbor — 941-575-3000 www.fishville.com	7.5'	●		●	●	●	●	●	●			➤	West Marine, Publix, Downtown shops
DeSoto Marina — Peace River — 941-627-3474 www.nav-a-gator.com	4.5'	●		●							➤	➤	Nav-a-Gator restaurant on-site; ship's store
Uncle Henry's Marina Resort — Charlotte Harbor/ICW between 20 & 22 — 941-964-0154 www.unclehenrysmarina.com	6'	●		●	●	●	●		●	●		●	groceries, hotel adjacent
Palm Island Marina — Gasparilla Sound — 941-697-4356 www.palmislandmarina.com	7'	●		●	●	●	●	●	●	●	●	●	restaurant on-site; ferry to beaches; poolside grills, picnic
Royal Palm Marina — Lemon Bay/ICW marker 30 — 941-475-6882 www.royalpalmmarina.com	7'	●		●	●					●	●	●	Ship's store; restaurant; Yamaha, Suzuki certified
Crow's Nest Marina & Restaurant — Venice Inlet — 941-484-7661 www.crowsnest-venice.com	12'	●		●	●	●			●	●		➤	florida clean marina, ship's store, cable TV, courtesy bikes
Marina Jack — Sarasota Bay — 941-955-9488 www.marinajacks.com	10'	●		●	●	●			●	●		●	concierge shuttle, ship's store, moorings
Sara Bay Marina — Sarasota Bay — 941-359-0390 www.sarabaymarina.com	4.5'	●		●	●	●	●		●			●	tiki bar
Longboat Key Club Moorings — Sarasota Bay/ICW# 15 — 941-383-8383 www.longboatkeymarina.com	20'	●		●	●	●	●	●	●			●	Full resort amenities
Holiday Inn Harbourside Marina — ICW marker 34/35 — 727-517-3652 www.hiharbourside.com	6'	●	➤		➤		●	●	●			➤	hotel, restaurant on-site
Cove Sound Moorings — Anna Maria Sound/East of Marker 50 — 941-795-4852 www.cove-sound-moorings.com	5.5'	●	➤	➤			●			●	●	●	short walk to restaurants, Cortez Village, beach; protected basin
Bradenton Beach Marina — Anna Maria Island Snd/ICW marker #49 — 941-778-2288 www.bradentonbeachmarina.com	6'	●		●	●	●	●		●	●	●	●	nighttime security
Galati Yacht Sales — Bimini Bay M#1 — 941-778-0755 www.galatiyachts.com	6.5'	●		●	●	●	●			●	●	●	ship's store, restaurant, full-service shop, fishing charters
Blenker Boatworks & Marina — Mouth of Manatee R./markers 7-8 — 941-794-5500 www.blenkerboatworks.com	5'	●		●	➤						●	●	Near DeSoto National Park
Twin Dolphin Marina — Manatee River — 941-747-8300 www.twindolphinmarina.com	8'	●	●	●	●	●	●	●	●			●	restaurant on-site; ship's store; in downtown Bradenton
Riviera Dunes Marina Resort — Manatee R./marker 24A — 941-981-5330 www.rdmarina.com	15'	●	●	●	●	●	●	●	●	●			on-site restaurant; surveillance; adjacent to Downtown Ctr.
Regatta Pointe Marina — Tampa Bay/Manatee River — 941-729-6021 www.regattapointemarina.com	10'	●		●	●	●	●	●	●			➤	ship's store, restaurants, day spa on-site, non-ethanol gas
Tierra Verde Marina Resort — Gulf of Mexico/Tierra Verde Grand Ch — 727-867-0400 www.tierraverdemarinaresort.com	12'	●		●	●	●	●		●				
Little Harbor Marina — East Side of Tampa Bay — 813-645-2288 www.thelittleharbormarina.com	5'	●	●	●	●	●	●	●	●	●	●	●	
The Resort & Club at Little Harbor — East Tampa Bay/N. of Little Manatee R. — 813-645-3291 www.staylittleharbor.com	6'	●		●	●	●	●	●	●				
Maximo Marina — Boca Ciega Bay — 727-867-1102 www.maximomarina.com	10'	●		●	●	●			●		●	●	covered slips, protected harbor, restaurants nearby

	MLW	Transient Slips/Moorings	Floating docks	Gas	Diesel	Pumpout	Showers	Pool	Laundry	Wi-Fi	Haulout	Repairs	Other
Loggerhead Marina St. Petersburg Tampa Bay/S. St. Petersburg 727-867-2600 www.loggerheadstpete.com	4'	•		•	•	•	•	•		•			Ship's store; restaurants, shopping nearby
St. Petersburg Municipal Marina West Side Tampa Bay/Demers Landing 727-893-7329 www.stpete.org/marina.htm	10'	•		•	•	•	•		•			➤	mooring field, lounge w/ internet access
Harborage Marina at Bayboro Tampa Bay/St. Petersburg 727-821-6347 www.harboragemarina.com	12'	•	•	•	•	•	•	•	•	•			Waterside dining, groceries, shops nearby
Renaissance Vinoy Resort Marina Tampa Bay/St. Petersburg 727-824-8022 www.vinoymarina.com	12'	•		➤	➤	•	•			•			18-hole championship golf, fine dining, spa; close to shops
Clearwater Harbor Marina Clearwater/St Mile 135 727-224-7156 www.myclearwatermarina.com	7'	•	•	➤	➤	•	•		•	•			designated clean and resilient marina
Marker 1 Marina Clearwater Harbor/Honeymoon Isl. 727-733-9324 www.marker1marina.com	6'	•		•	•	•	•	•	•	•	•	•	
Turtle Cove Marina Anclote R./Tarpon Springs 727-934-2202 www.turtlecove-marina.com	6'	•	•	•	•	•	•	•	•	•	•	•	Tiki Bar, ship's store, lounge, playground
Anclote Harbors Marina Anclote R./Tarpon Springs 727-934-7616 www.ancloteharbors.com	6'	•	•	•	•	•			•	•	•	•	full-service, protected harbor, playground, BBOs
Belle Harbour Marina Anclote R./Tarpon Springs 727-243-8489 www.belleharbourmarina.com		•	•	•		•	•		•	•	•	•	
Port Tarpon Marina Anclote R./MM 39 727-937-2200 www.porttarponmarina.com	9'	•		•	•					•	•		lounge, gift shop, snacks
Anclote Village Marina Anclote R./Tarpon Springs 727-937-9737 www.anclotevillagemarina.com	7'	•	•	•	•				•	•	➤		

Big Bend to Pensacola

	MLW	Transient Slips/Moorings	Floating docks	Gas	Diesel	Pumpout	Showers	Pool	Laundry	Wi-Fi	Haulout	Repairs	Other
Sunset Landing Marina Pithlachascotte R. 727-849-5092 www.sunsetlandingmarinas.com	5'		•						•	•	•		
Port Hudson Marina Gulf of Mexico/Bayonet Point/Hudson 727-869-1840 www.porthudsonmarina.net	5'	•	•	•	•	•	•		➤	•	•		ship's store, night watchman, designated Clean Marina
Hernando Beach Marina Gulf of Mexico/Hernando Beach 352-596-2952 www.hernandobeachmarinas.com	13'	•	•	•		•				•	•		ship's store; groceries, restaurants nearby
Twin Rivers Marina Gulf of Mexico/Crystal R. 352-795-3552 www.twinriversmarina.com	8'		•	•	•		•			•	•		ship's store, bait,
River Haven Marina & Motel Gulf of Mexico/Steinhatchee R. 352-498-0709 www.riverhavenmarine.com	4'	•		•	•	•	•		•		•	➤	motel, ship's store
Sea Hag Marina Gulf of Mexico/Steinhatchee R. 352-498-3008 www.seahag.com	6'	•		•	•		•	•		•		•	full-service marina, new pool,
Water Street Hotel & Marina Apalachicola Bay 850-653-3700 www.waterstreethotel.com	6'	•	•	➤	➤		•	•					groceries, restaurant, drug store w/in walking dist.
Port St. Joe Marina St. Joseph Bay/Mkr 4/MM 328/ 850-227-9393 www.psjmarina.com	6.5'	•		•	•	•	•		•	•		➤	Gift shop, Charters, Dockside Seafood & Raw Bar
Panama City Marina St Andrews Bay/Gr. Flash 17/MM 290 850-872-7272 www.pcmarina.com	9'	•		•	•	•	•		•			➤	ship's store, walking distance to restaurants, shops
St. Andrews Marina St. Andrews Bay/Panama City 850-872-7240 www.pcgov.org	8'	•	•	•	•	•			•				
Treasure Island Marina St Andrews Bay/Grand Lagoon 850-234-6533 www.treasureislandmarina.net	6'	•		•	•	•	•				•	•	

	MLW	Transient Slips/Moorings	Floating docks	Gas	Diesel	Pumpout	Showers	Pool	Laundry	Wi-Fi	Haulout	Repairs	Other
Bay Point Marina St Andrews Bay/Grand Lagoon 850-235-6911 www.baypointmarina.net	6'	●		●	●	●	●	●	●	●	➤	●	launch ramp, outside contractors; pontoon rental; restaurant
Legendary Marina Moreno Point/Destin 850-337-8200 www.legendarymarina.com	6'			●	●	●	●				●	●	ethanol free gas; ship's store; dry storage
Harborwalk Marina Choctawatchee Bay/Destin 850-337-8250 www.harborwalk-destin.com	4'	●		●	●	●		●					convenience store, gift shop, charter fishing
Legendary Marina at Ft. Walton Beach Choctawatchee Bay/Ft. Walton Beach 850-243-7861 www.legendarymarine.com	8'			●	●	●	●						
Bluewater Bay Marina Choctawhatchee Bay/Rocky Bayou 850-897-2821 www.bluewaterbaymarina.com	6'	●	●	●	●	●	●	●	●	●	●	●	state park nearby, seafood restaurant onsite
Shalimar Yacht Basin & Marina Choctawatchee Bay/Fort Walton 850-651-0510 www.shalimaryachtbasin.com	8'	●		●	●	●	●		●	●	●	●	Courtesy car upon arrival
Pelican's Perch Marina and Boatyard Pensacola Bay/Bayou Chico 850-453-3471 www.pelicansperchmarina.com	6'		●	➤	➤					●	●		
Palm Harbor Marina Pensacola Bay/Bayou Chico 850-455-4552 www.pensacolamarinas.com	6.5'	●	●			●			●				protected moorings, cable tv, security gate, dinghy docks
Island Cove Marina Pensacola Bay/Bayou Chico 850-455-4552 www.pensacolamarinas.com	6'	●	●			●			●	●			cable tv, security gate, moorings
Yacht Harbor Marina Pensacola Bay/Bayou Chico 850-455-4552 www.pensacolamarinas.com	6.5'	●	●			●			●				security gate, covered picnic area, dinghy rack
Pensacola Shipyard Marina and Boatyard Pensacola Bay/Bayou Chico 850-439-1451 www.pensacolamarina.com	7'	●	●			●	●		●	●	●	●	launch ramp, ship's store, full-service repairs
Palafox Pier & Yacht Harbour Marina Pensacola Bay/downtown Pensacola 850-432-9620 www.marinamgmt.com/page/PalafoxPier	15'	●	●	●		●	●			●	●		ship's store, cable, non-ethanol gas, walk to shops, restaurants
Bahia Mar Marina Pensacola Bay/Bayou Chico 850-432-9620 www.bahiamarmarine.com	4'	●	●	●	●	●	●		●	●	●	●	non-ethanol fuel, full-service yard

The Friendly Yacht Basin with Country-Club Amenities

CITY OF CAPE CORAL
Yacht Basin

City of Cape Coral Yacht Basin

5815 Driftwood Parkway,
Cape Coral, FL 33904
Ph: 239-574-0809 | Fax: 239-542-5329
CapeParks.com

description of facilities

Cape Coral Yacht Basin is a well-maintained marina located in a landscaped resort setting. There are a host of on-site recreational activities such as tennis, racquetball, swimming at the pool or beach, a picnic area with BBQ, bike-riding, hiking and fishing at the 620-foot fishing pier. A municipal yacht club complex is located adjacent to the yacht basin. There is a new fuel dock on-site with a store that features bait and tackle and hot-food service.

The marina is located a short distance from golf, shopping centers, a 10-plex theater and many restaurants. Fort Myers, with its many attractions such as the Thomas Edison and Henry Ford Estates, is just across the Cape Coral Fixed Bridge.

You will be impressed with the friendliness of the competent marina staff.

marina approach & docking

Cape Coral Yacht Basin is located at statute mile 144 on the Okeechobee Waterway. Go west to ICW marker R "78" and head north running parallel with the fishing pier. Daymarks are located near the pier to guide you into the marina. The depth of water in the channel is five feet, and there is 5 feet of water in the basin. The normal tide is one and a half feet.

The docks in the well-protected marina basin are stationary with finger piers and tie-off pilings. Reservations are accepted, so call on land line if possible. Call on VHF channel 16 for assistance and docking instructions. Marina personnel are on duty from 7:30 a.m. to 5 p.m., seven days a week.

at a glance

DOCKAGE RATE: Transient, Daily at $1.75/ft, Electric $3.50; Monthly at $12.00/ft, Electric $35.00

PAYMENT: MC/Visa

HOURS: 7:30am – 5pm

TRANSIENT SLIPS/TOTAL SLIPS: 10/89

VHF/WORKING: 16/68

MLW/LOA*: 5´/50´

ELECTRIC: Transient, $3.50 daily

PUMP-OUT: Yes

FUEL: Gas/Diesel

REPAIR: Mechanics, divers on call

RESTAURANT/MILES: On-site

POOL: Junior Olympic-sized, municipal beach

HAUL-OUT: Boat ramp

HEAD/SHOWER: Clean, tiled

LAUNDRY: One washer/dryer

SHIP'S STORE: Oil, beer, soda

NEAREST TOWN/MILES: Cape Coral, Fort Myers/1

SHOPPING: Nearby in town

GOLF/TENNIS: In region/On-site

AIRPORT/MILES: Southwest Int'l/30 mins.

TRANSPORTATION: Taxi, rental cars, bikes

YACHT BROKERAGE: Nearby

SPECIAL: Picnic area w/grills, playground, Thomas Edison and Henry Ford estates in Fort Myers across Cape Coral Bridge

YachtHavenPark.com

LAT: 26° 32' 42.2154"N
LON: -81° 57' 2.3754"W

Legacy Harbour Marina

2044 West First Street, Fort Myers, FL 33901
Ph: 239-461-0775 | Fax: 239-461-0776
Email: info@legacyharbourmarina.com
LegacyHarbourMarina.com

description of facilities

Legacy Harbour Marina is located two blocks from historic downtown Fort Myers and three blocks from the Edison-Ford Winter Estates. The marina's 131 slips range from 40 to 80 feet and can accommodate transient boats of 100 feet plus. Large fairways make our slips easily accessible and our floating docks are state-of-the-art featuring the latest in utilities. Our slips are surrounded by one of the largest "floating breakwaters" on the Gulf of Mexico.

Legacy Harbour Marina is a full-featured facility with all the modern conveniences. Amenities include a pump-out at every slip; full electric, metered at the slip; cable TV; laundry; air conditioned restrooms/showers; heated pool and WI-FI. The boater's lounge is available for relaxing after a cruise or for private parties. The view from the lounge is spectacular.

marina approach & docking

Legacy Harbour Marina is located on the Okeechobee Waterway, 17 miles from the Gulf of Mexico. If you are heading east, pass marker "49", turn at the white flag on the piling. Leave the flag to starboard and proceed to the end of the breakwater, taking a 130 degree course. Turn right into the marina.

If you are heading west, after passing the Caloosahatchee Bridge, turn left before the marina flag on the piling, leave the white flag to starboard and proceed on a 130 degree course to the end of the breakwater. Turn right into the marina.

The Okeechobee River depths to the marina run 8½ feet at MLW*. The bottom is composed of "soft mud". Vessels up to 120 feet can maneuver within the marina and can be accommodated with side-tie moorage. Call us for more details.

LAT: 26° 38' 28.4994"N
LON: -81° 52' 30.36"W

at a glance

DOCKAGE RATE: $3.45/ft (Nov 1-Apr 30), $2.80/ft (May 1-Oct 31)

PAYMENT: MC/VISA/AmEx/Disc

HOURS: 8am – 7pm

TRANSIENT SLIPS/TOTAL SLIPS: 10/131

VHF/WORKING: 16/12

MLW/LOA*: 7'/100'+

ELECTRIC: 30/50/100 Amp, metered at slip

PUMP-OUT: At every slip

FUEL: Available upon request

REPAIR: Approved vendors

RESTAURANT/MILES: On-site

POOL: Yes

HEAD/SHOWER: Yes/Yes; with A/C

LAUNDRY: Yes

INTERNET ACCESS: WiFi

CABLE: 20 channels including local

SHIP'S STORE: Ice and vending

NEAREST TOWN/MILES: Fort Myers/ walking distance

SHOPPING: Grocery and shopping within walking distance

GOLF/TENNIS: Nearby/Nearby

AIRPORT/MILES: SW FL Int'l (RSW)/16

TRANSPORTATION: Taxi, rental cars

SPECIAL: Enjoy the view from the deck overlooking the Caloosahatchee River. Close to Edison-Ford Winter Estates and downtown Fort Myers. Picnic facility, mail and office service available

*MLW = Mean Low Water Depth
LOA = Longest vessel that can be accommodated

Advertiser's Index